WILD guide

West of Ireland

Hidden Places, Great Adventures and the Good Life

Candida Frith-Macdonald & Daniel Start

Tower Waterfall, p256

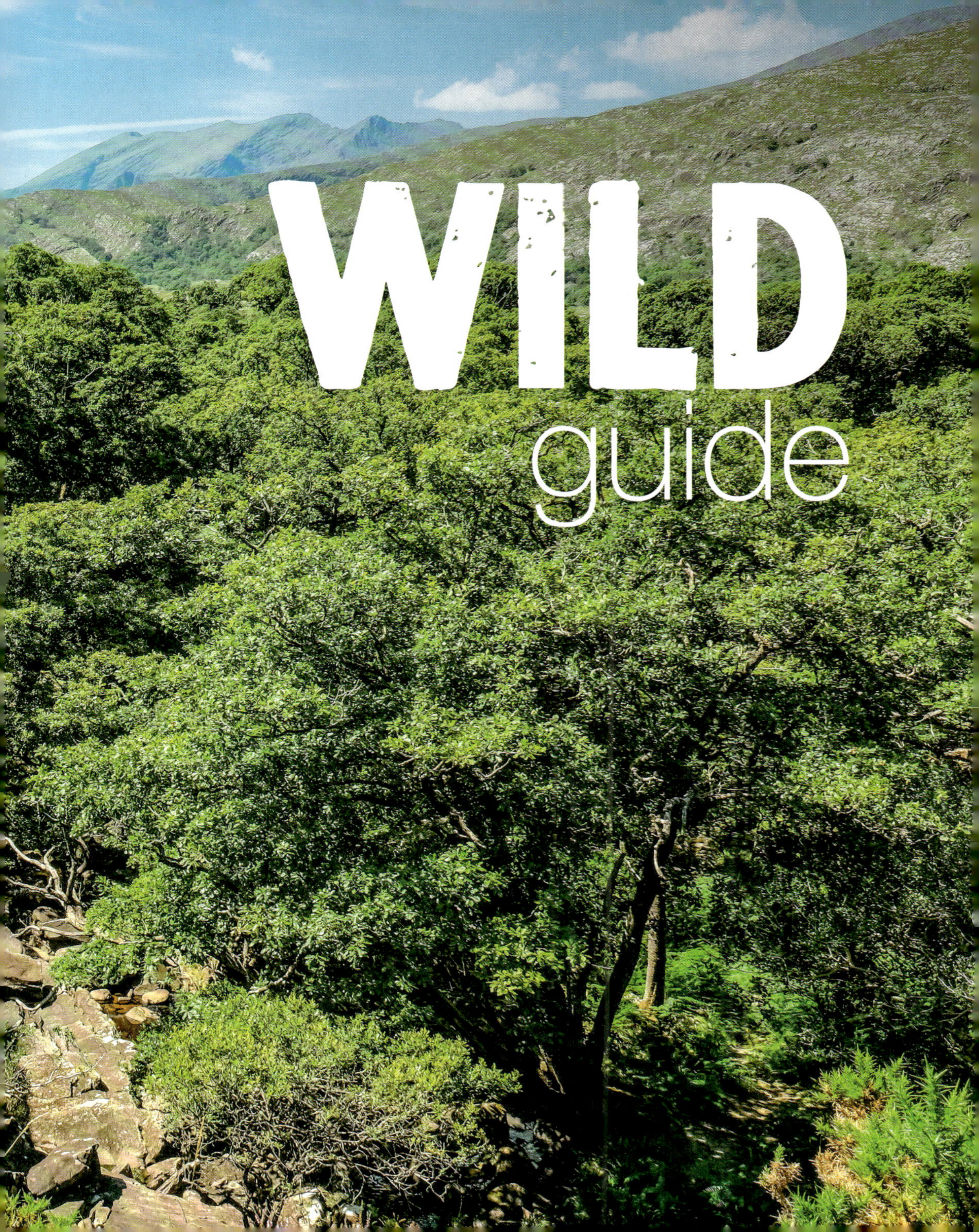
WILD
guide

Rabach's Glen, p277

Contents

Regions

Donegal & Borders

Mayo & Roscommon

Galway

Clare & Limerick

Kerry

Cork

Boat Strand, p49

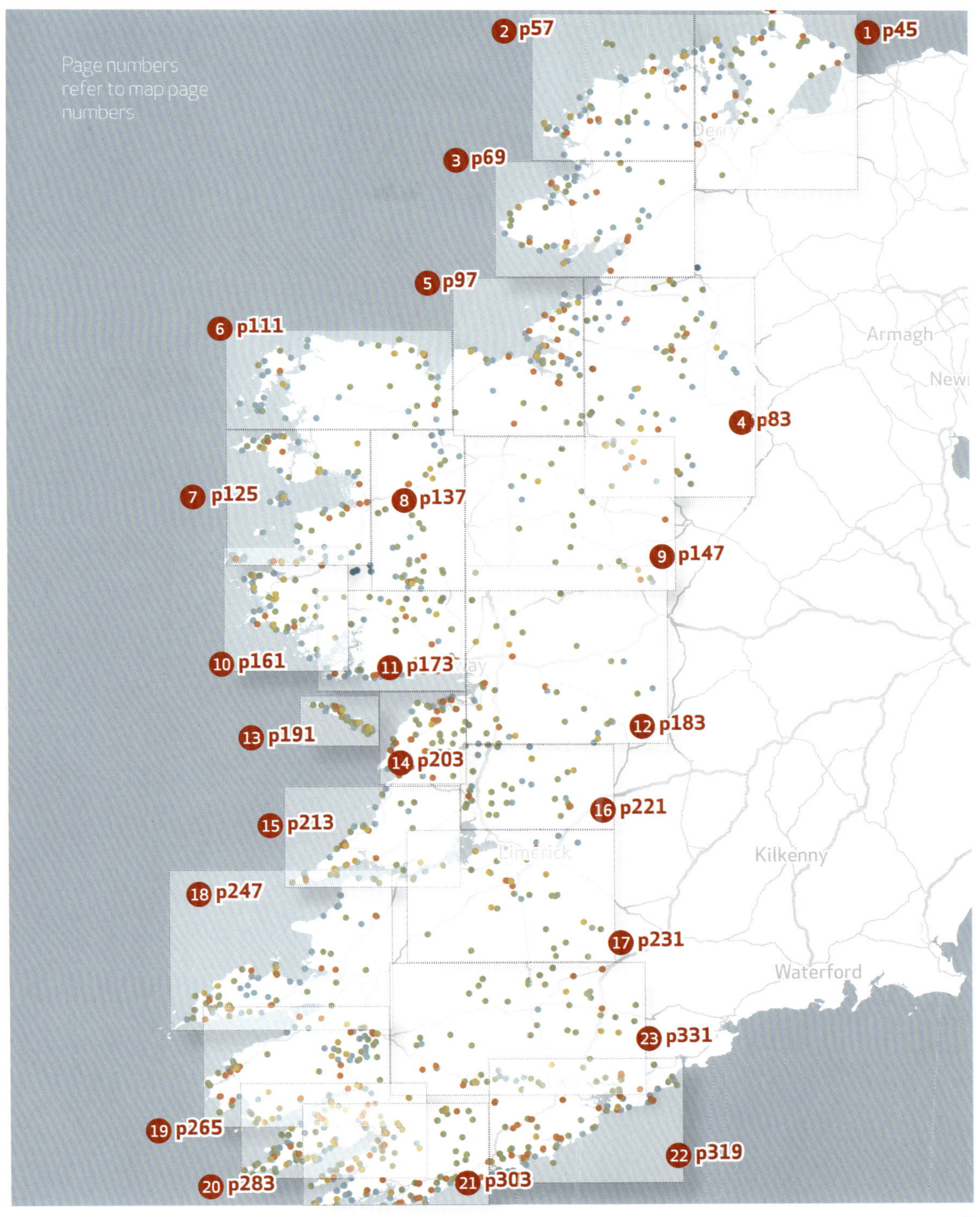
Page numbers refer to map page numbers
1 p45
2 p57
3 p69
4 p83
5 p97
6 p111
7 p125
8 p137
9 p147
10 p161
11 p173
12 p183
13 p191
14 p203
15 p213
16 p221
17 p231
18 p247
19 p265
20 p283
21 p303
22 p319
23 p331
Derry
Armagh
Limerick
Kilkenny
Waterford

Cuas Caves, p269

Introduction

The west of Ireland is so packed with dramatic sites and beautiful beaches that it feels as if it's been a classic 'riviera' forever, but early visitors wrote more often about the gentler south coast. Today we have a greater appreciation of this region's wild beauty, and five of Ireland's six national parks are here: Glenveagh, Wild Nephin, Connemara, Burren, Killarney, and Páirc Náisiúnta na Mara. Skellig Michael (or Sceilg Mhichíl) has been a UNESCO World Heritage site since 1996, and the distinctive blue zig-zag signs of the Wild Atlantic Way have been leading visitors along the west coast for over a decade.

Ancient Land

Ireland's oldest rocks, formed over 500 million years ago, are found from Donegal to Mayo. Cork and Kerry's mountains of Old Red Sandstone and Galway's granite peaks are from 350 million years ago, while Clare's famous Burren limestone pavement and fossil-packed Flaggy Shore formed under tropical seas over 300 million years ago. Until about 13,000 years ago most of the landscape was scoured by repeated ice ages, in which glaciers carved beautiful valleys like the fjord of Killary Harbour, sculpted the distinctive slopes of Ben Bulbin, and formed the drumlin islands of Clew Bay. At the coast itself, relentless Atlantic waves have driven deep to form caves and blowholes in some places, while in others they have ground corals and shells into white beaches and stunning machair dunes that are home to rare flowers and birds.

Ireland's topology is sometimes likened to a great saucer with the highest peaks near the coast, from Errigal in Donegal to Carrauntoohil in Kerry. Inland, smaller summits punctuate a lower, rolling landscape and flat blanket bogs that stretch for miles. These are one of Europe's most important carbon sinks and rich in both wildlife and archeological treasures, from the ancient walls of Céide Fields in Sligo to bog bodies and gold jewellery held in national museums in Dublin and London. The Wild Atlantic Nature programme is now helping farmers and local communities to restore, preserve and use these landscapes in a sustainable way, and some places are designated Special Areas of Conservation (SACs) or Special Protected Areas (SPAs). These include some of Ireland's remaining ancient forests and

Moyne Abbey, p105

mature estate woodlands. At the heart of the country lies the Shannon, Ireland's largest river and the eastern limit of this book, which rises in Cavan and flows south before turning west through Limerick city to a broad tidal estuary. In the 1920s the Ardnacrusha hydroelectric dam permanently raised the level of the river upstream, creating broad floodplains that are used by migrating birds in autumn.

People & Ruins

The earliest evidence of humans in Ireland comes from the west and dates back over 30,000 years. Most of the marks left on the landscape by human hands are from much later, but many modern names still go back to ancient tribes or figures from legend, as if the landscape were a living manuscript.

Megalithic tombs built by shifting populations and reused through the ages are scattered through quiet valleys and on bare hilltops, from the extraordinary cluster of Neolithic cairns at Carrowmore in Sligo to the Bronze Age Labbacallee wedge tomb in Cork. Stone circles from the Bronze Age are concentrated in the south-west, as are early medieval ogham stones with their unique writing system. Ireland's famed ringforts also date from the Bronze Age through to early medieval times and number in their thousands; 'fairy fort' legends of retribution for damage helped to preserve them after they fell out of use. Some are associated with Ireland's greatest myth cycles, like the Táin Bó Cúailnge or Cattle Raid of Cooley. That story starts at Rathcroghan, where Owenygat cave is still respected for its reputation as a portal to the Otherworld; there are countless recorded legends of other 'thin places' where people or creatures might slip from the Otherworld into ours. In legends of the Fianna such visitors also arrived from magical islands off the western coast, like Tír na nÓg where you could remain forever young.

Beehive 'clochán' huts, tiny churches and boat-shaped oratories survive from an extraordinary cultural flowering of early Christianity, when saints like Colmcille and Brendan set off from these shores for the rest of Europe and (if the legends are true) North America. Later came elaborately carved high crosses with ringed heads and tall, round bell towers that marked out a church of importance. Visible from a distance, the towers also

Upper Lake, Killarney, p256

guided pilgrims who followed ancient routes that still link sacred wells, holy mountains and ruined monasteries; today some paths are waymarked with a pilgrim figure and walked by people on their personal spiritual journeys. Often an old churchyard is the home of the local 'cloch nirt' or strength stone, lifted by local men in days when funerals were the occasion of traditional ritual contests.

From the late 12th century occupation left its mark, as fortresses like the mighty King John's Castle were built in an attempt to control this western edge of Europe. Both Irish and English gentry built countless smaller tower houses, taken and retaken by the opposing sides in the centuries of local wars that followed, some fallen to ruins long ago, others still lived in today. From the Great Famine of the 1840s on, death and mass emigration left more of the landscape dotted with abandoned homes that hold little more than stories of resilience and loss.

Travel Wild and Well

This *Wild Guide* is a celebration of wild and storied places – from cliff-top walks to tangled woods, waterfall pools and deserted islands to intriguing ruins. It's also a guide to slow food, warm firesides and welcoming places to stay – from seaweed baths and thatched cottages to wild campsites and music-filled pubs. If you travel with a spirit of adventure, taking the boreen less travelled and the time to chat with locals, you will have a richer journey wherever you go. The Irish language, used on road signs and still spoken daily in several Gaeltacht regions along the west coast, is not needed but holds history in place names and its very constructions. Try a 'Dia duit' greeting, a 'slán go fóill' farewell or a 'go raibh maith agat' for thank you, and certainly a 'sláinte' toast when you raise a glass.

Candida and Daniel

adventure@wildthingspublishing.com

Downpatrick Head, p49

Finding your way & using the book

Ireland has very few official public rights of way over private land: even waymarked paths exist almost entirely by the specific agreement of the landowner, which is sometimes withdrawn. This is usually over a safety concern, either for visitors or for livestock spooked or harried by dogs, so be careful and respectful. That said, informal access does exist in most places, established through long use over time, or readily granted by the landowner. Even where there may be a forbidding looking sign, these are more often related to insurance issues. Access to graveyards and other religious sites is usually safe to assume, as many are still visited on particular holy days. You will need to make your own judgment about whether to proceed or seek permission from the landowner, especially if none is obvious; a knock at the nearest farm usually wins a positive response, except for dogs.

There are overview maps and basic directions but please use the coordinates provided (WGS84 latitude, longitude). Enter them into any online map site, such as Google, Apple, Bing, Streetmap and most trail apps (Outdoor Active, Komoot, Hiiker, AllTrails, Wikloc etc). For places with parking adjacent, the main coordinate given is the parking. For multiple locations, it is the first place in the title/description. For favourites, we added a star. Print out the map before you go, or save a screen grab; in case you lose mobile signal or even GPS. Eircodes are used in some directions, specific to individual buildings. If a parking place is mentioned, use your own judgment and be considerate. Walk-in times are one way only, allowing 15 mins per km on the flat, which is quite brisk. For L and R river banks, this is facing downstream. Abbreviations include left and right (L, R); north, east, south and west (N, E, S, W), direction (dir), opposite (opp), low/high tide (LT, HT), National Parks and Wildlife Service (NPWS), Office of Public Works (OPW), Special Area of Conservation (SAC) and Special Protections Area (SPA).

Wild & responsible

1. Fasten all gates and only climb them at the hinged end.
2. Keep dogs under close control, especially around livestock and in nature reserves. Respect 'no dogs' signs.
3. Take your litter home, and collect litter you might see.
4. Take special care on country roads and park considerately, to allow room for a tractor or truck.
5. Take a map, compass, whistle, proper boots and waterproof clothing when venturing into remote or high areas.
6. Always tell someone where you are going, and do not rely on your mobile phone.
7. Rip currents may form in surf conditions, on long beaches, near cove edges and at river mouths. Swim parallel to the shore if caught.
8. Rivers banks may be private; do not disturb anglers if you swim.

Glossary of Irish place terms

Ard *high/tall*

Bán/bawn *white/pale*

Beag/beg *small*

Buí *yellow*

Caiseal/cashel *stone ringfort/castle*

Cathair/caher *stone ringfort/castle*

Cill/kill *church*

Cillín *unconsecrated cemetery*

Clochán *small domed stone building*

Cnoc/knock *hill*

Darach/dara/derreen *oak*

Demesne *old estate park/wood*

Dolmen *exposed single tomb chamber*

Dubh *black*

Dún *fort/castle*

Eas *waterfall*

Fir *mens (w.r.t a WC)*

Glas *green*

Gorm *blue*

Inis/innis/inis *island*

Lios/lis *earthen ringfort, like rath*

Machair *coral dune ecosystem*

Mór *big*

Mná *ladies (w.r.t a WC)*

Ór *gold*

Owen/abháinn *river*

Poll/poull *hole, eg pool, small cave*

Also see historical glossary on p335

Mount Muckish, p55

Best for
Secret beaches & coasteering

Ireland's Atlantic coast is dotted with beaches that regularly appear in movies and 'visit before you die' lists. But often there is an equally beautiful place nearby that just hasn't been 'discovered'. Some might be trickier to access, or require a longer walk from the nearest reasonable parking, but the reward for effort is a magical seclusion. If you always have your swimming gear, you may find more spots near many of the other listings, with more coves than we could possibly include tucked below headland views or ruined fortifications.

Much of the Atlantic coast of Ireland is wild in every sense, exhilarating but prone to rips, especially on long, straight beaches, so don't overlook the charms of the less invigorating bays for family swims. There are many little harbours and quays, which provide some of the best jumps from pier ends. We've marked where this is usually possible with , but always check the depth first. We've also included some of our favourite coasteering locations, for sea caves and rock jumps. It's also worth knowing that increasing numbers of the summer-lifeguarded spots we don't generally list now have beach wheelchairs; county councils can tell you which.

Before setting off, check the tides times carefully, as many hidden coves only reveal their sand at low tide (LT). Remember also that tides are much larger during full and new moons – the so-called 'spring' tides that occur every fortnight. Smaller 'neaps' are the half moons in between.

Be safe

1 Don't swim alone.

2 Be aware that rip currents can form when there is heavy swell or surf. These circulate water out to the back of the breaking waves.

3 Rips occur along the edge of coves or stacks, or between surf breaks on longer beaches.

4 To exit a rip current swim parallel to the shore.

5 Caves amplify swell as they narrow, sometimes bumping you on their ceiling, so enter only when the sea is calm.

6 Never jump or dive into water unless you have checked it for depth and obstructions.

Best for
River & lake swimming

In the uplands of the western regions the rivers are lively and pure with some of the finest pools and waterfalls in Europe. However, these are also prime locations for trout and salmon fishing, and many stretches may well be considered private. Show respect and never disturb people fishing; they have usually paid for the right. In the middle of the island the many loughs and the peaty Shannon are generally lazy waters, great for a relaxed swim, although the waters may be shared with boaters. Many villages and small towns have quays or floating pontoons at their most convenient spot, so you can always join the locals for a quick jump. If you always have your togs with you, you may also find swims near other locations: castles and monasteries especially often used nearby rivers for transport.

Some river stretches and most of the still loughs have sharp stony shores, and a pair of water shoes makes a huge difference. Always pay attention to water temperature: smaller loughs and tarns are shallow and warm up quickly, but some larger ones are deep right to the edge and cold enough to take your breath away. Unless you are used to cold-water swimming you may be surprised to find it can reduce your stamina to just 10% of your usual distance. We've marked where jumping is usually possible with a but always check the depth first and never jump into the middle of a waterfall, where currents can be very powerful.

Be safe

1 Never swim alone, and keep a constant watch on weak swimmers.

2 Cold water can dramatically decrease swimming ability, create cold shock and cause drowning through panic. Know your limits, enter slowly and stay close to the shoreline.

3 Never jump into water unless you have thoroughly checked for depth and obstructions.

4 Avoid strong currents, such as those directly under large waterfalls or weirs, or those found in river rapids during floods: they can drag you under.

5 Always make sure you know how you will get out before you get in.

6 Wear footwear if you can.

7 Avoid direct contact with blue-green algae, and be wary of water quality in lowland areas during droughts and heavy rain. Cover cuts with plasters if worried, and if you develop flu-like symptoms tell your doctor you have been in a river.

Best for
Lost ruins

Ireland is one of the most 'castled' countries in Europe, with some 30,000 fortified buildings. But the mighty walls with multiple watchtowers around extensive buildings this may conjure in your mind are a small share of the total. The long history of occupation and conflict meant that the many smaller, fortified medieval 'tower houses' of the elite remained in use far longer than they did in more peaceful places, with some even lived in through the 19th century. Most of these and the grand houses burned in the War of Independence or abandoned after now stand as fascinating shells or skeletal ruins.

Other remains from later times also tell a tale of conflict, this time continental. In the Napoleonic era, a line-of-sight chain of signal towers was built along the coast and an array of batteries covering the waters of the Shannon estuary against French forces. There are often Second World War lookouts near the signal towers, and numbered navigation markings from the same time with the word EIRE writ large to tell pilots which coast they were over.

The saddest remnants are the smallest and most everyday, the deserted cottages or even whole villages. Many date from the Great Famine of the 1840s, when some places lost more than half their population within a decade, but others are much more recent; there are islands abandoned just within living memory where the homes still have eerily familiar furnishings inside.

Best for
Sacred sites & ancient places

Ireland's most famous ancient structure is the ringfort or 'fairy fort'. Much mythologised, these were homesteads and small industrial sites built from the Bronze Age to the early medieval as either earth-banked raths or stone-walled cashels. There are also many megalithic tombs with local names like the Giant's Grave or Diarmuid and Graine's bed, after the legendary lovers' doomed flight across Ireland. The earliest are Neolithic passage graves with a central undivided dolmen chamber, often now uncovered but originally surrounded or covered by a massive stone cairn; those on hilltops could be seen across a whole region. Multi-chambered court cairns are found almost entirely north of Galway, usually grouped in valley settings. Sloping wedge tombs are the most numerous, with many examples in Clare, built at the end of the Neolithic and into the Bronze Age. Ireland's stone circles also date from the Bronze Age, and are concentrated in west Cork and Kerry. For really in-depth information from the experts, tuatha.ie is a great place to start, with articles on individual sites, and occasional guided visits.

Later sacred ruins include typically picturesque monastic sites, but also many little churches. Some fell derelict in the 18th and 19th centuries, when the Penal Laws forbade Catholic worship and congregations gathered in secret at hidden 'mass rocks'; more were lost when populations plummeted in the Great Famine of the 1840s. In an echo of the distant past, many atmospheric cemeteries and unconsecrated cillíns for unbaptised infants are on hilltop sites, with some even re-occupying ringforts.

Dunlewey Church, Poisoned Glen, p54

Kilclooney Dolmens, p65

Creevykeel Court Tomb, p91

Moyne Abbey, p105

Inishmaine Abbey, p134

Cleggan Court Tomb, Tower, Cove, p157

Ross Errilly Friary, p169

Corcomroe Abbey, p200

Grange Stone Circle, Lough Gur, p228

Kilmalkedar complex, p241

Derrynablaha rock art, p258

Uragh Stone Circle, p274 (Uragh West pictured)

Drombeg Stone Circle, p295

Best for
Hilltops & headlands

The west coast is a geological showcase of quartzite and granite cliffs and peaks, rounded limestone summits, and contorted sandstone strata. Some headlands have blowholes, others military ruins all the way back to ancient promontory forts, and these are often among the most accessible high points. There are also plenty of mountains in the far west – the midlands are flatter – haunted by the Irish hare, deer in some locations, and birds of prey. You could choose a peak type to conquer: there are 400 Arderins (over 500m in height with a prominence of at least 30m), and 275 Vandeleur-Lynams (over 600m elevation with a prominence of at least 15m). We've also included some scrambling ideas (see with safety tips opposite).

If we mention a walk with capitals, it is a defined route that you can find on local tourist sites, or on sportireland.ie with downloadable maps. Don't assume that any path is a right of way; there is almost never a right to cross private land in Ireland, and even named, waymarked paths to peaks usually exist only with landowners' permission. This is sometimes withdrawn when heedless visitors bring dogs onto farmland with livestock. Access can be nuanced, even where there are signs; landowners have waved us past printed 'no trespassing' signs (really there to say any misadventure is on our own heads). Play it by ear, especially obey handwritten signs, and be polite if access really is denied.

Be safe

1 On high ground be prepared for the weather to deteriorate, faster than you can retreat.

2 On high ground be prepared with waterproofs, warm clothes, whistle, compass, map, torch, snacks and water. A 'group shelter' and GPS are also useful.

3 Always be prepared to turn back if you don't feel confident on a scramble or climb.

4 Many scrambles are in high and remote locations; be especially cautious on wet and windy days, when some scrambles will feel even more exposed.

5 Research the scramble route thoroughly before you leave – there is much information online.

Best for
Woods, wetlands & wildlife

It's said that a squirrel could cross ancient Ireland branch to branch, but it has long been one of Europe's least wooded nations. Fragments of native forest contain jewels like Killarney's strawberry trees and shelter red squirrels, pine martens, and bats, but many 'champion' trees are in planted demesnes. Wildlife pockets survive in riverside flood areas and on coastal upland soils or dune machairs, and the old practice of leaving the 'hare's corner' of a field to nature is still practised by conscientious farmers. You will sometimes even find a mini-reserve of wildflowers and insects within the banks of a ringfort, protected from direct sprays and cultivation. But Ireland's greatest ecological treasures are its 10,000-year-old bogs, which contain more than half of western Europe's active raised bog. Drained or 'cutaway' bogs are being restored with dams to act as carbon sinks, and their capacity as reservoirs of rare flora and fauna grows as their water levels rise.

Of course, the rivers and seas also support an extraordinary array of life. Anglers love the salmon and trout rivers of the west, but plenty of leaping fish evade their hooks. Huge migrating flocks of geese and ducks stop off on river loughs, and coastal birds range from raucous choughs and ravens to perky puffins. Porpoises are frequently seen off the coast, there are resident dolphins in the Shannon estuary and several species of whales visit Irish waters seasonally; watch from the headlands or take a boat trip to get a closer look.

Tramore, Downings/Rosapenna, p49 (pictured)

Tor Mór puffins, Tory Island, p56

Cladagh Glen & Hanging Rock, p81

The Glen, Knocknarea, p95

Erriff Woods, Owenmore, p122

Derreen Wood bluebells, p145

Murvey Machair, p158

Carrownagappul Bog, p182

Inis Oírr seals, p190

Curraghchase Forest Park, p230

Glanageenty Forest, p242

Derrycunnihy Woods & Falls, p261

Roaringwater wildlife, p298

The Gearagh, p330

Best for
Slow food & local produce

Ireland is renowned as a farming nation, with superb produce and grass-fed livestock. The food culture has been expanding since a wave of continental cheese makers arrived in the 1970s, with more recent arrivals bringing sourdough baking and a tradition of fermentation and preservation that wasn't historically needed in the mild maritime climate. The curious visitor will find plenty to keep them well provisioned wherever they travel, from Michelin-starred restaurants to bright cafés and cosy pubs.

Of course, surf is as important as turf. Seafood chowder is a staple on menus in the west and a contender for Ireland's national dish, usually with a side of home-made soda bread. Festivals showcase oysters and mussels, and award-winning regional smokehouses produce firm and tangy salmon and hot-smoked trout and mackerel. Seaweed, once seen as a famine food, is increasingly appreciated as a gourmet ingredient, and chefs like JP McMahon at Michelin-starred Aniar in Galway or Max Jones at Up There The Last in Cork passionately promote local and foraged ingredients.

Recently there has been a resurgence in brewing. Almost every county has a craft brewery, some with their own bars or taprooms, others only available in local pbs, all worth trying. There are local examples of the 'black stuff', IPAs, Belgian-style brews, and ales for every palate. Distilleries have also multiplied, and alongside a wide variety of pot still and malt whiskies, you can find gins flavoured with fresh juniper, local herbs, and Atlantic salt (there's even a peated one from Lough Ree, with turf in the mix) and legal versions of traditional poitín.

Nancy's Barn, p44

Andersons Boathouse Restaurant, p68 (pictured)

Organic Centre, Rossinver, p82

Nook Café & Restaurant, p96

An Port Mór Restaurant, p124

The Hidden Corner Cheese Shop, p146

Connemara Smokehouse & Café, p159

Unglert's Bakery, Health Shop, p202

1826 Adare, p231

Manning's Emporium, p280

Restaurant Chestnut, Ballydehob, p300

Dede at the Customs House, p300

Best for
Rustic retreats & wilder camping

There have always been B&Bs, cottage rentals and country house hotels catering to the slower traveller, river cruisers for those who want to leave roads behind, converted castles offering the ultimate holiday fantasy at a price, and campsites for explorers looking to tread lightly on their travels. Today these more individual places are increasingly in demand; indeed in some places holiday rentals have put pressure on local housing, as in many tourist destinations. We have tried to recommend holiday rentals that do not pose this problem: renovated and converted buildings on working farms, purpose-built lodges, and cottages that are impractical for everyday life today but perfect for short escapes.

Of course, camping is the ultimate low-impact way to travel. For us, camping by the beach or lakeside is the dream; to watch the sunset across the water and wake up with a plunge. There are more – and more individual – campsites opening. Many campsites do close over the winter months, even for camper vans, but there are now 'aires' opening to accommodate this increasingly popular way of travelling, some private, others run by county councils or bodies like Waterways Ireland. Responsible wild camping at the coast and on wild ground is likely to be accepted; check the websites of the national parks for their individual rules about exclusions and notification. Many beach car parks are fine for camper vans, but some have height restrictions; stay out of sight of private homes. There are further tips opposite.

Wild camping

1 On moorland, camp away from livestock beyond the highest wall and away from dwellings.

2 Be prepared to leave if asked to.

3 Avoid reservoir catchment areas or archaeological sites.

4 Leave no litter, remove other people's.

5 Do not light any beach fires, except below the high-tide line.

6 Pitch late, leave early. Stay for only one night.

7 Be discreet, one or two tents max.

8 Poo at least 30m (100ft) from water and bury. Take toilet paper home in a dog poo bag.

NORTH EAST DONEGAL

Our perfect weekend

- → **Stroll** up to Glenevin Waterfall for a swim and fuel up on world-class chowder at Nancy's Barn.
- → **Choose** between a sandy bay or a pier for jumps at Ballyhoorisky Point, and visit the poignant monument at the very tip of the rocks.
- → **Marvel** at the greylag geese on on the lagoon at Inch, or visit woodland wolves at Wild Ireland.
- → **Escape** the crowds at Malin Head for a thrift-covered wild clifftop beyond booming chasms.
- → **Shine** a torch at Beltany Stone Circle at dusk and seek constellations in the markings.
- → **Trace** the Tree of Life and Celtic knotwork on the exquisite carved cross slab at Fahan Mura.
- → **Find** local producers on the map at the Lemon Tree, and stock up at The Counter deli before heading out on your next adventures.
- → **Laze** by the dunes on Ballymastocker Beach and paddle around to the wreck of the Horizon
- → **Gaze** over to Islay from the Little White Bay of Stroove, or walk up to the restored EIRE marker for even better views.

2

3

5

Before there was a Wild Atlantic Way, there was the Inishowen 100 route around this region's highlights, many of them on smaller roads and lanes: Ireland's most northerly point at towering Malin Head, mighty peaks, sweeping sands, and some of Ireland's most important early Christian remains. To the west lies the Fanad peninsula, with one of the world's most beautiful lighthouses, and between them is mighty Lough Swilly, a deep-water port with abundant sandy shores and military remains.

Buncrana is a busy holiday hub, but even here a walk on the coast path takes you past Ned's Point Fort to quieter Stragill Beach. But the best beaches are further out, beyond the Urris Hills – perfect little Lenan, curving Tullagh, and vast Pollan. The same is true on Fanad: quiet shores lie west of the lighthouse towards Ballyhoorisky Point. The rockier coast is home to fascinating features too, like the Great Pollet Arch or the caves of the Seven Arches, a wonderful kayak trip. Inland are loughs large and small – perhaps the most perfect are the twin Knockalla Loughs, hidden at the end of a hike.

The highest peak here is Slieve Snaght, named for the snow that can clothe it almost into summer. Above the famous Mamore Gap scenic road the Urris Hills have majestic sunset views, while over on Fanad the 'Devil's Backbone' of Knockalla Ridge is a classic tough hike for serious walkers, but with some more accessible shorter stretches. Here and there native woodland clings to the windswept slopes and lingers in the valleys, like beautiful Ballyarr, or the temperate rainforest that has welcomed once-native wildlife home at Wild Ireland.

The literal high points among the monuments here are the famous Grianan of Aileach cashel and the vast Beltany circle with its cup-marked stones. But there is also a wealth of crosses, found from rural fields at Carrowmore and Clonca to a village graveyard at Fahan, which show the development of the iconic 'ringed' and decorated Celtic cross. More recent remains have a military bias: Lough Swilly was vital to the navy, and remained under British control right through to 1938. Defences ranged from the rambling Napoleonic-era Dunree to the 20th-century tunnels of remote Lenan Fort.

A place apart, this corner of the island has a solid vein of self-reliance and proud local culture. Drop in at a seaside bar or restaurant and you'll usually find local produce from cheeses to Kinnegar beers and Muff Liquor gin on the menu. The same goes for local delis, so pack a picnic supper and enjoy the glorious long sunsets – or maybe even the Northern Lights.

SECRET COVES - INISHOWEN

1 LITTLE WHITE BAY, STROOVE

Stroove's Big White Bay is often very busy, but there's a smaller, emptier cove called Little White Bay on the S side of the handsome lighthouse, with views to Scotland's Islay on a good day. Park along road or walk 150m S from main car park. Nearby is the Inishowen Loop trail (parking 55.2354, -6.9285) with big coastal views, passing a Second World War lookout post at the start and a recently restored EIRE marker (55.2380, -6.9355).

5 mins, 55.2252, -6.9302

2 KINNAGOE BAY

Although remote, this sandy beach backed by verdant slopes is popular in summer, but a small car park does limit numbers. People sometimes park or even pitch on the beach overnight. The sand-buried wreck of La Trinidad Valencera, a Spanish Armada ship from 1588, was found by divers in 1971 and is 250m offshore at the W end; possible to snorkel over at spring low tide (55.2597, -7.0101).

1 mins, 55.2583, -7.01264

3 FIVE FINGER STRAND *

Iconic sweep of golden estuarine sand, sensationally beautiful, with five stubby sea stacks visible at the N end. Strong rips. Signed from the R242 past the church – you can park right by the sand between the dunes.

1 min, 55.3240, -7.3315

4 DOAGH STRAND & CASTLE

Remote estuarine beach facing the dunes of Five Finger Strand. It lies below the thatched cottages of the Famine Village (€). Follow the coast road NW for the remote ruin of Carrickabraghy Castle (55.3162, -7.3727) by a farm and a beach where a sea mine exploded in 1940. Just beyond lies the N end of Pollan Strand, popular for wild camping (see entry).

2 mins, 55.3129, -7.3378

5 POLLAN STRAND

Also called Ballyliffin Beach, truly vast, wild and remote, with over 3km of sand with some stony stretches. Perfect for big rollers and sunsets, but also rip currents. The N end is wildest, from Doagh Strand via Carrickabraghy Castle (see entry) and park on the grass. Or car park with coffee truck at S end (55.29018, -7.3912).

2 mins, 55.3108, -7.3732

6 TULLAGH STRAND *

Sheltered, dune-backed horseshoe of golden sands under the summit of Binn on. From the small dune car park to SE, at the end of a lane from Clonmany, you can follow the river to the beach in a long, beautiful loop. There's also a rough track to the NW end, where you can park overnight (55.2888, -7.4505). Along the road between is a lane to Roxton Bay, for wild camping and sunset views (55.2861, -7.4648).

5 mins, 55.2785, -7.4355

7 LENAN BEACH & PIER

This beautiful golden beach (also known as Leenakeel) is on a remote bay below the rugged Urris Hills and the legendary Mamore Gap (see entry). Turn L at the crossroads below the WAW viewpoint on the Gap for parking at S end of the beach, also the trailhead for walks into the hills. The N headland has ruined Lenan Fort and pier (see entry).

2 mins, 55.2432, -7.5242

8 STRAGILL BEACH

A long, flat strand with panoramic views across Lough Swilly, one of Donegal's hidden gems. Walk 2km from Ned's Point (see entry) or find small parking area at 55.1602, -7.4901. Also a lovely remote spot at the N end for two cars (55.1666, -7.5018).

2 mins, 55.1602, -7.4901

SECRET BEACHES - FANAD

9 KINNEGAR BEACH

An excellent local brewery is named after this dune-backed beach of red-gold sands. It's a much wilder alternative to Rathmullan, and you might see horses being galloped. Turn off the R247 to the coast at F92 Y264; you can pull off R almost immediately and walk the sand road opp to the shore or continue 650m to a height-restricted car park L (coffee van in season).

2 mins, 55.1116, -7.5328

10 BALLYMASTOCKER BEACH & WRECK

Despite their wild beauty these roadside dunes and sands, also called Portsalon or Knockalla beach, are surprisingly desolate. About 300m S along the dramatic cliffs and caves of Saldana Head lies the 2008 wreck of the Horizon crabbing boat (55.1865, -7.5855); you need a kayak or paddle board unless you are a confident coasteerer, and several local companies offer kayak trips. Knockalla caravan and camping park is set well back from the beach.

1 mins, 55.1884, -7.6095

11 ARRYHEERNA BEACH

You'll spot this perfect sand cove below the road on the R on the way to Fanad lighthouse. Go through the field gate at 55.2720, -7.6386, and then a second gate at the bottom of the field. It's private land so be respectful and don't park on lane but walk back 500m from lighthouse (see entry).

12 mins, 55.2715, -7.6363

12 BALLYHIERNAN BAY

This long Green Coast beach is something of a surprise, hidden behind a bank of grassy dunes until you are on it. Watch for rip currents. Quietest by the rocks in the middle. Or there's the the WAW viewpoint, far W end (55.2470, -7.7275) or the far E end (55.2550, -7.6905).

2 mins, 55.2475, -7.7021

13 BALLYHOORISKY POINT

A tiny lane leads past two quiet curved beaches on the E side to a pier on the rocky W side. Coasteer or take a walk over the rocks to the N tip, where there is a small tower-like monument to four fishermen who died in a storm in 1927.

2 mins, 55.2504, -7.7506

14 DOAGH MORE & COVES

This wild W-facing coast has three white-sand sunset beaches overlooking Melmore Head and Gortnalughoge Bay. They're well worth the effort of reaching on foot. At the S end a long track leads to a small parking/camping area at 55.2212, -7.7896 and a 10-min walk NE to

Doagh More. From the N end, park at 55.2354, -7.7489, climb gate and follow left bank of stream to Sessiagh Bay, and SW to Gortnatraw. Also good overnight campervan parking 1km NE from this on the road to Ballyhoorisky (55.2446, -7.7549).

5 mins, 55.2371, -7.7529

SEA CAVES & ARCHES

15 FORT DUNREE PIER

A super spot for pier jumping, coasteering or kayaking, just below the Napoleonic fort (see entry). Both the fort promontory to the R and the lookout island to the L can be encircled at shore level, with a narrow gully beneath the pedestrian bridges and various jumps to try. Large car park by fort. Kayak trips with Inish Adventures (+353 87 2202577).

3 mins, 55.1958, -7.5530

16 SEVEN ARCHES, PORTSALON

A fantastical complex of sea caves and sea tunnels. Companies like Eco Atlantic Adventures (+353 86 2250599) offer tours of this and more, or those with a kayak could venture 2.5km N from popular Portsalon Pier with its little beach, overlooked by the Stores Bar. Can also be viewed from above, ask at the farm to cross two fields (55.2282, -7.6093).

15 mins, 55.2269, -7.6056

17 GREAT POLLET ARCH ^

A huge sea arch, dry at low tide, with many rock pools, caves and formations. It's well known, with a car park and path down (55.2551, -7.6308), but you can also walk in along the cliffs from a lovely hidden beach to the S. Doagh Beg beach is down a short green track from a gate opp O'Doherty's shop (55.2497, -7.6235), and has good offshore rocks for snorkelling.

15 mins, 55.2576, -7.6196

LAKES & WATERFALLS

18 LOUGH FAD

A wild, high lake perfect for kayaking, fishing, swimming or a wild camp. Set in an NHA of intact blanket bog – look out for golden plover, hen harrier and red grouse, and you may even find cranberries, rare in Ireland.

2 mins, 55.2348, -7.3764

19 GLENEVIN WATERFALL

Tall, slender fall with a deep pool. It's a short, easy walk along the stream on a surfaced path from a large car park. More family friendly than wild, and popular in season, but people do regularly dip here.

10 mins, 55.2676, -7.4357

21

20 CRANA RIVER, RUINS & NED'S POINT

Cross Castle Bridge and explore the ruins of O'Doherty's keep and swim in the deep pools of the Crana River. Park in one of the car parks at the end of Cahir O'Doherty Avenue (55.1387, -7.4613). The bridge is to the L but the deepest pools are straight on upstream 300m, by the concrete quays. After, follow the Buncrana shore path to Ned's Point Fort, one of several Napoleonic batteries built to protect the deep water ports of Lough Swilly and Lough Foyle against French invasion (it's locked but locals climb inside). There's a pier here too, popular with swimmers. Head onwards on the surfaced path N 300m to Porthaw beach or another 1.3km to remote Stragill beach (see entry).

10 mins, 55.1414, -7.4603

21 KNOCKALLA LOUGHS

A perfect pair of lakes tucked between the twin quartzite peaks of the 'Devils Backbone'. There's a simple track from the road end in Glenvar (55.1525, -7.6181), or a higher, more scenic start from the Way of the Cross (limited parking on track, 55.1651, -7.5938), ascending 100m W from open-air chapel to follow a wall 1km SW to 55.1597, -7.6117, where a track ascends to the lakes. The full 9km Knockalla Ridge hike is challenging and windy, but rewarding.

20 mins, 55.1602, -7.6211

22 WOODQUARTER PIER, BROAD WATER

Pier with parking, perfect for a swim, or a kayak out to one of the many small islands on this inland end of Mulroy Bay sea lough. There are walks in woods of oak, alder, holly, and birch as well. Coillte sign on R245.

1 min, 55.1218, -7.7019

LOST RUINS

23 OLD REDCASTLE CHURCH

There's an eerie feel to this 18th-century ruin, set in a quiet rural graveyard with an unusual vaulted tomb and the shell of a small schoolhouse. It was replaced by the 19th-century St. Finian's Church, also now disused. Park near the road corner and walk down track SE 100m.

1 min, 55.1642, -7.1251

24 LENAN FORT *

Extraordinary remains of a fort complex built in 1902 to defend Lough Swilly, abandoned in 1952. Sunken gun placements, bunkers, tunnels, bridges and a row of six chimney stacks, atop high cliffs with big W views. Reached on a bumpy track R shortly before the fishing pier by Lenan Beach (see entry).

2 mins, 55.2458, -7.5297

25 BURT CASTLE

Hidden on a hilltop amid fields, this 16th-century tower shell has remains of a spiral staircase. Access is through the farmyard 250m NE, so you will need to ask permission there.

5 mins, 55.0195, -7.5021

26 FORT DUNREE & DUNREE BAY

Originally built against Napoleon, this was one of the last three British outposts in Ireland, held to defend the deep-water ports until 1938. Fort museum is paid entry, but spread over the hillside are abandoned metal barracks, concrete bunkers, and three spectacular cliff-top stone emplacements with sunken chambers. From the NE one, scramble down to Dunree Bay or Portbane, a beautiful sheltered bay of deep golden sand – or park on lane and walk across the dunes (55.2010, -7.5427). Also a pier below the fort (see entry)

2 mins, 55.1984, -7.5475

27 FANAD HEAD

Explore the ruined coastguard station and lookout post, spot whales and dolphins from the popular headland cliffs, and descend to the pebble beach 400m to the W. You can also climb the 1817 lighthouse tower for €12. Car park L at end of R247.

2 mins, 55.2762, -7.6344

28 RAPHOE CASTLE RUINS

17th-century fortress with corner towers built by Bishop John Leslie atop a grassy knoll with oak tree. Accessed through a woodland area on the edge of town, by the roadside layby with mural. Sometimes fenced, but viewable from the road too.

2 mins, 54.8732, -7.5976

SACRED & ANCIENT

29 COOLEY CROSS & SKULL HOUSE

All that remains of a 6th-century monastery founded by St Finian are this rural graveyard with views to Lough Foyle, the ancient high cross at the gate, and the Skull House where he is said to lie. Bones can still be seen within the little windowless cell, which resembles an oratory. Pull off by the gate.

1 min, 55.1888, -7.0616

30 BOCAN STONE CIRCLE

This 20m Bronze Age circle now has seven standing stones, some of them sinuously shaped, but there is a jumble of fallen and broken stones, so it may have had up to 30 stones originally. Magnificent views, particularly fine at sunset. Unsigned but limited parking on lane at 55.2704, -7.1491. Temple of Deen wedge tomb is 1km SW (55.2667, -7.1569); park by houses or at end of track, then 100m.

4 mins, 55.2721, -7.1481

28

31 CLONCA CHURCH & HIGH CROSSES

Inside the ruined church is a 16th-century tomb slab bearing the earliest known image of hurling, and outside are two fascinating high crosses. The 10th-century St Boudan's Cross stands about 4m tall, decorated on all sides with interlace and biblical scenes, including the loaves and fishes miracle; the 1.5m head of a 12th-century ringed cross lies to the NE (55.2679, -7.1750). Layby parking by sign/gate.

1 min, 55.2687, -7.1751

26

32 CARROWMORE & CARNDONAGH CROSS

Two stone crosses remain from a 7th-century monastic site attributed to St Patrick's brother-in-law: a tall, plain one on the NW side of the road, and a shorter cross over the road inscribed with Christ and an angel. Other important stones are 5km W from here by the side of the R238 in Carndonagh (55.2499, -7.2720) including a cross decorated with birds and a tree of life like those at Clonca or Fahan Mura (see entry), and in the middle of the little graveyard next door is the Marigold Stone, a pillar carved on all four sides.

1 min, 55.2561, -7.1896

30

35

35

33 GRIANAN OF AILEACH *

The views from this impressive cashel take in two sea loughs and three counties, and the walls with their steps and terraces are magnificent to climb. The site was probably fortified from about the 1st century – a tumulus at the site may even be Neolithic – but the cashel itself was first built around the 6th or 7th century. On the equinoxes, the rising sun throws a beam of light through the entrance right across the interior. Open 9am–7pm so come early/late to have it to yourself. Signed from the N13 at Burt, with a car park near the summit and sloped boardwalks up.

3 mins, 55.0236, -7.4275

34 FAHAN MURA GRAVEYARD

The graveyard of this roofless church has several treasures, including a beautifully decorated stone that may be a precursor to the iconic Celtic cross design. Interlaced lines trace a tree of life with two figures standing either side of it. On the reverse the cross is punctuated by five circular motifs, with two birds above and a sun shining down on it. Also find the curious stones in the wall on either side of the entrance – a carved wheeled cross and one with a hole. By the side of the R238 with a large car park.

1 min, 55.0832, -7.4605

33

33

35 BELTANY STONE CIRCLE

This wide and enigmatic circle has 64 stones, but once had as many as 80. Several bear cup marks, especially visible on the triangle stone to the NE, that may replicate constellations. The size and history suggest that rather than being a true stone circle, Beltany is the kerb of an ancient cairn. Well signed from surrounding lanes to small car park by farm entrance, then 350 up track and in field on L.

5 mins, 54.8503, -7.6046

SUNSET VIEWPOINTS

36 SLIEVE SNAGHT

The traditional day to climb Inishowen's highest peak (615m) is Lughnasa, 1st August; since snow can lie here into May and the path is always boggy, late summer is certainly best. The walls on the summit were built for camping shelter by Ireland's first mapping team in the 19th century, and S of the trig point is the stone-lined 'well of the eyes'. Start at the track crossroads to the W (55.2065, -7.3800); the less-travelled N ridge ascent from the track-end at 55.2156, -7.3322 has no real path and is just as boggy, but has less ascent and better views, and takes in the minor 'wee' summit too.

135 mins, 55.1964, -7.3342

37 MALIN HEAD

Most people visit this popular and dramatic headland just for the Napoleonic signal tower and EIRE 80 pilots' marker. For a classic sunset walk, follow the broad path W past Hell's Hole, 500m, cairns and ravines, another 500m, to otherworldly views at the end – especially with hummocks of thrift underfoot in early summer. Explore beyond the EIRE for a deep tidal chasm slicing across the most N point in Ireland; in calm seas coasteering here could be awesome. Another 500m E lies the colourful shingle of quiet Portmór/Kitters beach (or park at 55.3766, -7.3573 and walk down track).

25 mins, 55.3792, -7.3901

38 MAMORE GAP & URRIS RIDGE

This mountain pass is one of five Irish 'magic roads' where an optical illusion makes a slight downward slope appear to be sloping up. It has a superb coastal viewpoint, and a Marian shrine (55.2345, -7.4994) that's a good starting point to hike up Croaghcarragh (417m) on the Urris Ridge. This gives huge coastal views with two secret swimming lakes just below, Fad and Crunlogh (2km, 55.2244, -7.5227), and is a good place to see the northern lights and star gaze. There is a better-made, signed path to the lakes from the Lenan Beach (see entry), but with more ascent.

2 mins, 55.2337, -7.4991

37

WILDLIFE WONDERS

39 WILD ALPACA WAY

On one level this looks daft: pay to take an alpaca for a walk. But you get incredible views down to Five Finger Strand, and the cute camelids are perfect for a family outing. Three walks daily, €8, +353 87 6665106, book to get location up narrow lane. If you don't fancy the walk, the car park also has a huge view W and is a good place to park overnight.

30 mins, 55.3279, -7.3319

40 WILD IRELAND, BURNFOOT

This extraordinary passion project brought wolves, lynx and brown bears back to an Irish rainforest. While not fully wild, it offers family-friendly education, quality of life to rescued animals, and the chance to see once-native species and a few exotics living in a natural habitat. Dundrain, Burnfoot, F93 KN7X, book on wildireland.org

1 min, 55.0522, -7.3386

41 INCH WILDFOWL RESERVE

Over 3,000 greylag geese and hundreds of whooper swans overwinter here, making an impressive sight at Ireland's premier wetland reserve. During the summer, noisy colonies of

39

40

53

43

43

48

54

sandwich terns and black-headed gulls nest and raise their young. Two long causeways enclose the lagoon and create an 8km circular route with three hides.

15 mins, 55.0429, -7.4762

42 BALLYARR WOOD

One of the best and largest examples of a semi-natural deciduous woodland in the region, and a NNR, with a circular path through the oldest part. Mostly old sessile oak with holly and hazel. Ponies graze in winter to open up the understorey, the hazel is coppiced, and natives such as rowan are regenerating. There are resident badgers, foxes and stoats, visiting deer, and the usual small woodland birds are supplemented by buzzards and ravens. Parking on the road SE by the gated track in (55.0283, -7.7061).

4 mins, 55.0283, -7.7061

LOCAL FOOD

43 SEAVIEW TAVERN

Ireland most northerly inn, with a superb coastal setting. Emphasis on local produce including fresh seafood from the local pier. Along beach E is Wee House of Malin, a holy well and cave said to accommodate all who enter (55.3681, -7.3179); there's beach parking and people do wild camp here. Ballygorman, Malin Head, F93 ED30, +353 74 9370117

55.3672, -7.3311

44 THE BLUE GOAT, RAMELTON

Delightful artisan food store with a wide variety of local products: fresh Irish cheeses, including raw milk, and smoked salmon. Closed Tues-Weds. The Quays, Ramelton, F92 D9KE

55.0383, -7.6439

45 MALIN HEAD CRAB

Straight from the sea, crab and lobster plain, dressed, or in rolls, from a little food trailer. Ballyhillion, F93 CH50, + 353 83 4038038.

55.3754, -7.3620

46 KEALY'S SEAFOOD BAR

It looks plain on the outside but inside the wood-panelled dining room serves locally sourced fish and shellfish, with local beers and craft gin, in a super seafront location. The Harbour, Greencastle, F93 R588, +353 74 9381010. The ivy-clad ruins of the original Green Castle nearby (55.2052, -6.9753) can be reached through a gate at the Castle Inn.

55.2035, -6.9815

47 CÚL A TÍ

Vegetarian-leaning bistro and deli café with tapas and high-quality burgers. 12–4pm Weds–Sun, 6.30–8.30pm Fri–Sun. Main Street, Culdaff, F93V8XN, +353 87 100 9771

55.2872, -7.16771

48 NANCY'S BARN

The chowder made by the owner-chef of this bistro in a converted stone barn has won both national and World Champion status; we found it excellent with the Kinnegar beer. Plenty of other seafood and local produce to choose from, including vegan options from breakfast to dinner. Main Street, Ballyliffin, F93 VY75, +353 74 9376556

55.2807, -7.39178

49 RATHMULLAN HOUSE

Georgian country house hotel overlooking Lough Swilly, with two award-winning restaurants and the lovely Rathmullan beach below. Fresh fruit and vegetables from their own walled garden and fresh fish and seafood caught locally. Rathmullan, F92 YA0F, +353 74 9158188

55.1007, -7.52926

50 THE COUNTER DELI

Excellent bakery, cheese counter and café, with gluten-free options. Canal Road, Letterkenny, F92 PN40, +353 74 9120075

54.9474, -7.7320

51 THE LEMON TREE

This Michelin-recommended family restaurant showcases Donegal produce – there's even a map showing where their ingredients are from. The Courtyard Shopping Centre, Lower Main Street, Letterkenny, F92 EK13, +353 74 9125788

54.9487, -7.73682

WILDER STAYS

52 BINION BAY CAMPING, TULLAGH

Small grass field for tents with basic facilities, below the summit of Binion and above beautiful Tullagh Strand – you can walk down to it via the river. Fire-pits allowed, closed in winter. Bunacrick, Clonmany, F93 F381, +353 74 9376800

55.2760, -7.4250

53 FANAD LIGHTHOUSE COTTAGES

Start and end your days with views from this beautiful and iconic headland, where three cottages make up the lighthouse complex. The rooms are cosy, country-chic style with stoves and wooden floors. Fanad, Portsalon, F92 YC03, +353 74 9116020, book on fanadlighthouse.com

55.2759, -7.6320

54 PORTSALON LUXURY CAMPING

A small adults-only glamping site with five large and luxurious yurts on the southern slope of Dargan Hill. King size beds and sweeping views make it a dream couples site – choose a yurt further down the hill closer to the shared facilities, or splendid isolation at the summit with sunrise and sunset vistas. Campfires allowed, but no pets. Cashelpreaghan, Portsalon, F92 V8X2, +353 876 016654

55.2101 -7.6566

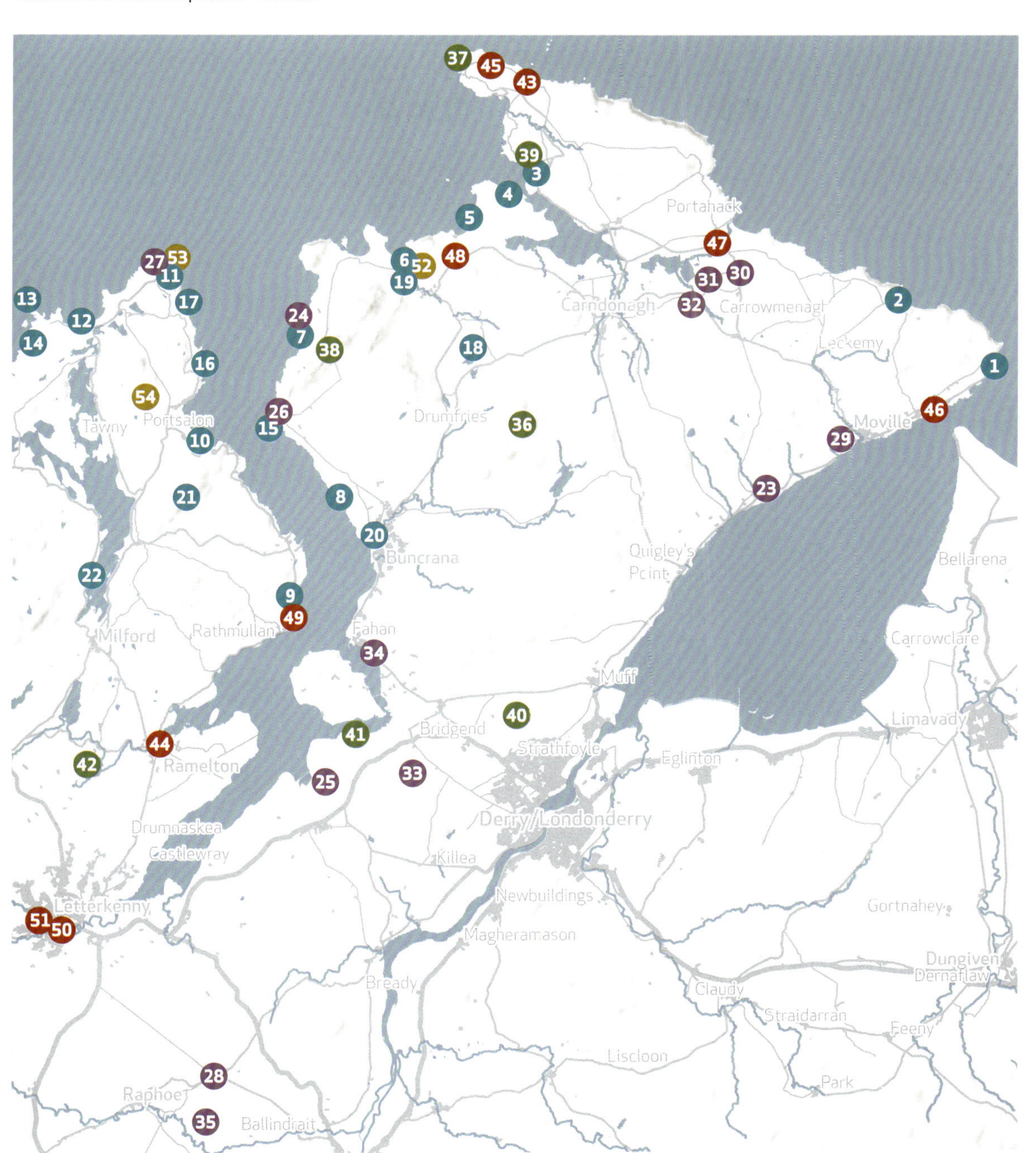

7

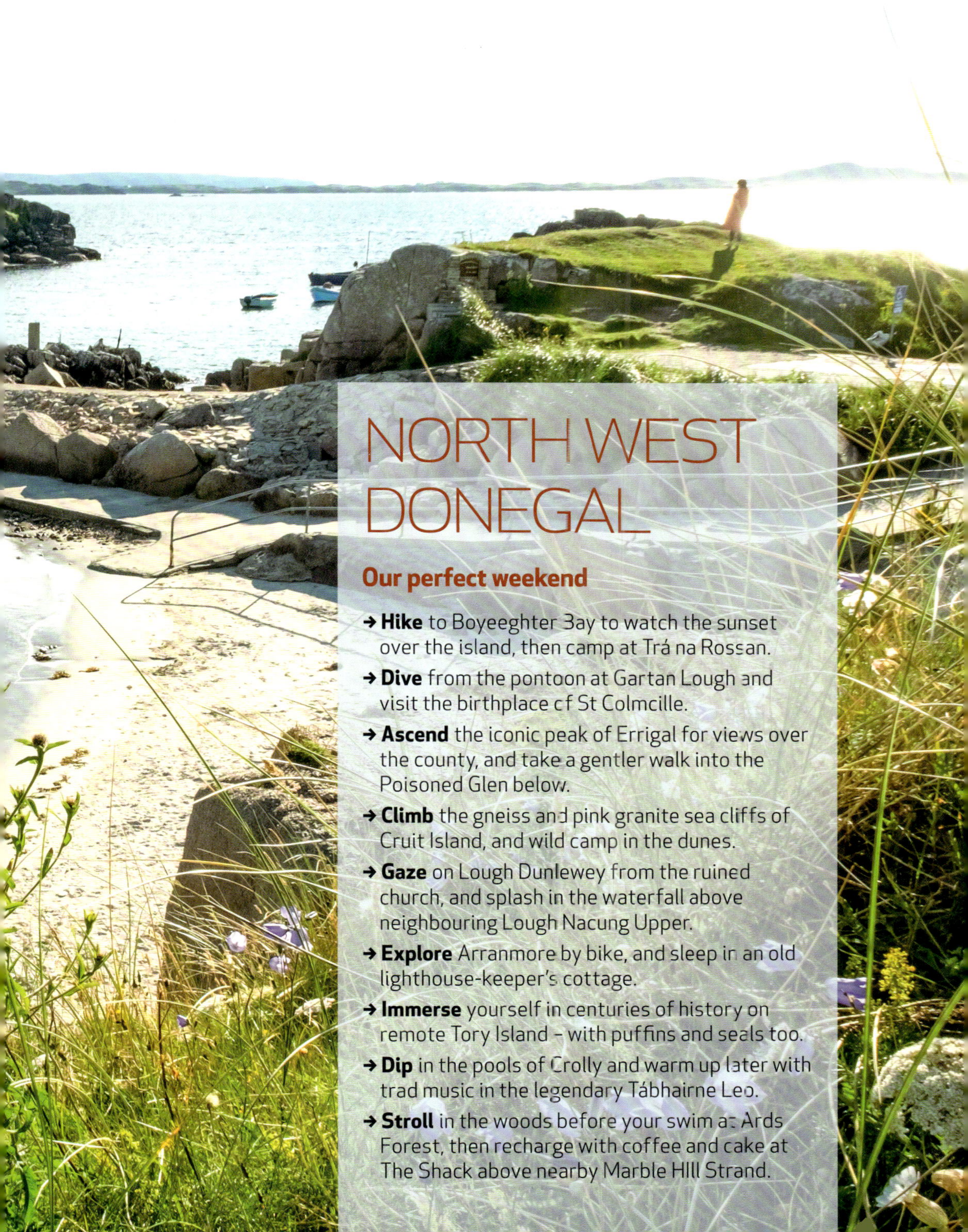

NORTH WEST DONEGAL

Our perfect weekend

- → **Hike** to Boyeeghter Bay to watch the sunset over the island, then camp at Trá na Rossan.
- → **Dive** from the pontoon at Gartan Lough and visit the birthplace of St Colmcille.
- → **Ascend** the iconic peak of Errigal for views over the county, and take a gentler walk into the Poisoned Glen below.
- → **Climb** the gneiss and pink granite sea cliffs of Cruit Island, and wild camp in the dunes.
- → **Gaze** on Lough Dunlewey from the ruined church, and splash in the waterfall above neighbouring Lough Nacung Upper.
- → **Explore** Arranmore by bike, and sleep in an old lighthouse-keeper's cottage.
- → **Immerse** yourself in centuries of history on remote Tory Island – with puffins and seals too.
- → **Dip** in the pools of Crolly and warm up later with trad music in the legendary Tábhairne Leo.
- → **Stroll** in the woods before your swim at Ards Forest, then recharge with coffee and cake at The Shack above nearby Marble Hill Strand.

A region of raw beauty, where the rugged Derryveagh Mountains sweep down to the Atlantic at some of the island's finest beaches, this wild corner of Ireland is defined by its dramatic geology and unspoiled landscape.

The coastline of Donegal has everything: jagged headlands and towering sea cliffs, vast golden beaches and hidden coves. Around Sheephaven Bay sandy beaches are tucked between rocky headlands, while to the west, the coastline rises and Horn Head towers 180m above the waves, a haven for seabirds and home to forts and lookouts spanning millennia. Árainn Mhór/ Arranmore is the largest of the many islands, a stronghold of the Irish language with dramatic westward cliffs, sheltered easterly beaches.

Inland, rivers tumble in energetic falls or linger in loughs, both in deep glens and on high bogland, all perfect for swims. Jump in the fun Sphinx Pool on the Clady near Bunbeg, or the series of deep pools on the Gweebarra River; for still waters, seek out the remote loughs under vast skies above Doocharry, or the bowl of Lough Barra. Swim with salmon, trout, otters and falcons.

The spine of the region is the Derryveagh Mountains range or 'Seven Sisters', whose quartzite heights have a pale, almost spectral appearance in a certain light, reminiscent of the lower Alps. Errigal, Donegal's highest mountain at 751m, is one of Ireland's most distinctive peaks; its steep slopes and sharp summit glow pink in evening light and offer breathtaking views. To its east, Glenveagh National Park encompasses some of Ireland's most remote terrain: Glenveagh Castle dominating the main glen and Dunlewey Church standing sentinel at the entrance to the Poisoned Glen. The woods are home to pine martens, bats and the rare wood warbler. Elsewhere, native trees such as birch, rowan and hazel cling to sheltered valleys, particularly around Dunlewey and Gweedore, and Ards where forest sweeps down to the shore at Sheephaven Bay.

Human history in this landscape stretches back millennia, to Neolithic tombs and Bronze Age strongholds like the dramatic Balor's Fort on Tory Island. King of the Formorians, Balor of the Evil Eye is a legendary figure; more real is St Colmcille, who founded monasteries here in his native Donegal and in Scotland, where he is known as St Columba. Abandoned sites from later centuries include a derelict mine and kelp works, and even a 19th-century holiday home by Altan Lough that's often mistaken for a medieval ruin. For all these human intrusions, this part of Donegal remains one of Ireland's wildest, and the remnants of our past are dwarfed by the beauty of the timeless landscape.

3

SECRET BEACHES

1 BOYEEGHTER BAY/MURDER HOLE

Famously beautiful, and once quite inaccessible, this beach of tawny gold sand and rugged cliffs has a tidal island and sea caves, but also rip currents. There's now a car park (€5) and gravelled track across the farmland, where an EIRE 78 pilots' marker (55.2412, -7.7995) may be visible from the high point. The adventurous can try the spectacular 45 mins hike over the headland from N end of neighbouring Trá na Rossan (55.2246, -7.8140) and descend the gulley at the S end. The car park is just beyond Melmore Holiday Park (55.2386, -7.8074).

25 mins, 55.2386, -7.8074

2 TRAMORE, DOWNINGS/ROSAPENNA

Trá Mór means big beach, and this 4km of dunes and sand with its magnificent mountain backdrop certainly earns it. From the R248 the N access is an unmarked lane past the golf club to some parking at the very end. The S access from the R245 is via the Boardwalk Resort restaurant car park (F92 X3WP), then 15 mins walk.

2 mins, 55.1837, -7.8273

3 BINNAGORM BEACH, ARDS FRIARY

This cove, also called Monks' Beach or Lucky Shell Beach, is reached through the beautiful Ards Forest on the estuary shore trail. Return in an anticlockwise loop around the peninsula for further coves 150m W, all good for swimming. Pay car park and coffee shop in the friary canteen, off N56 (55.1582, -7.8639).

30 mins, 55.1657, -7.8605

4 BALLYNESS PIER & DRUMNATINNY

This quiet little pier provides access into the heart of shimmering estuarine sands of Ballyness Bay. At high tide there's good jumping and swimming to the L and at low tide you may find seals on the central sandflats. Signed Cé at F92 R3P4 on the lane from Falcarragh to Drumatinney. For Drumatinny beach, continue past this turning; the lane ends at the beach car park in the dunes (55.1586, -8.0834).

2 mins, 55.1494, -8.1228

5 MAGHERAROARTY BEACH & INISHBOFIN

A full 3km sweep of almost pink sand and machair dunes rounds the headland and almost touches Inishbofin island, home to peregrine falcons and two further beaches. At low tide you feel you could wade over, but it's actually a deep channel with currents. Seasonal ferries head to Inishbofin and Tory Island from the large car park at the W end (signed off the R257 in Meenlaragh) but follow the dune tracks E past this and you can park in S end of dunes (some even camp). The tidal sands and their surrounding grasslands are home to a rich variety of birds all year round, from terns and swans in winter to skylarks, yellowhammers, cuckoos and corncrakes in summer. Birds of prey wheel above, the calls of choughs and ravens contrasting with the song of the skylarks.

5 mins, 55.1591, -8.1503

6 GLASSAGH LOWER BAY & PORT ARTHUR

Quietest of three beautiful beaches sheltered by Inishsirrer and Inishmeane, at the end of tiny L5293 past Lough Aninver and with plenty of space to park overnight. Glassagh is a good place to launch a canoe for Inishsirrer (400m) with its abandoned village of about 20 buildings, empty since the 1950s (55.1171, -8.3349), or little Umfin with its thrilling sea cave tunnel and blowhole (55.1011, -8.3649). Walk S 500m for Carrickboyle and then Port Arthur, reached by road along a lane that ends with a pier for jumping (55.1015, -8.3163) and a huge stretch of accessible grassed dune S as far as Lunniagh beach at the river mouth.

1 min, 55.1122, -8.3154

7 BOAT STRAND & DUNMORE

Few reach this perfect swimming beach, idyllic in summer with some campervans. Where the R266 turns L for Donegal airport and beautiful Carrickfinn beach, follow the little L1393 straight up the E side of the runway, turn L

6

along Carnboy Loch, and L again to the little cove and pier at Boat Strand (the older name is Trá na Marbh, beach of the dead, for the cemetery on the tidal island). Walk N 500m for a hidden cove overlooking Gola. Continuing R at the end of the runway leads to Dunmore beach, which overlooks Bád Eddie wreck (see listing) and from where you can walk to Inishinny island at LT.

2 mins, 55.0560, -8.3445

8 MULLAGHDERG BEACH

A boardwalk leads down to the sandy bay at N end, but it has rips in swell. So walk NE over the grass headland to more sheltered coves between the rocky outcrops. The best is Ballymanus below the monument (55.0410, -8.3654); a sea mine washed up on the beach and exploded in 1943. People also drive up and wild camp.

10 mins, 55.0373, -8.3692

9 CLOUGHGLASS STRAND & COVES

One of the most beautiful hidden beaches in Donegal, but if you walk SW over the headland there are even more secluded shelving coves among granite outcrops. There's also a little pier called Log an tSean Tí (old house pier); you can canoe out to Lahan Island. Signed Tra off the R259 on the L1513, then turn L to car park at T junction. Or turn R instead, for the exquisite sandy islets and inlets to the E by Inishinny, some of the least touched coves in Donegal; try parking at 55.0032, -8.4502 or 55.0041, -8.4354.

5 mins, 54.9996, -8.4471

10 WHITE STRAND, ARRANMORE

Perhaps the quietest and sandiest beach on the island, with a pier to jump from too. Walk 300m along road from the ferry pier.

7 mins, 54.9927, -8.4975

SEA ARCHES & CAVES

11 GOLA ISLAND SEA ARCH & CAVE

Once on the brink of complete desertion, this island now has new houses scattered out from the harbour among the ruins. The rocky N coast is popular with sea-cliff climbers, and has an impressive sea arch you can scramble down to and swim/coasteer through in calm water. There are sandy beaches at the S tip, and a touchingly well-kept and named cillín, the Cliabhán na bPáistí or Cradle of Children (55.0820, -8.3602). You can wild camp on the W side by Loch Machaire na nGall (55.0892, -8.3696). Daily ferry in summer with more crossings at weekends (+353 87 2245881) from the pier at Trá Dhearg, Magheragallon, itself a lovely beach (55.0869, -8.3240).

16 mins, 55.0948, -8.3704

12 CRUIT ISLAND COAST

With perfect gneiss and pink granite sea cliffs above little sandy beaches and azure waters, Cruit is one of the best places in Ireland for easyish climbing and great for bouldering and coasteering. A classic boulder route is Albatross Zawn, just S of Traderg Bay, a spot where you can park and people often wild camp, and 200m S of this is a large sea arch and sea cave. There are also two good piers for canoeing, both with beaches: Gortnasade at the N end by the golf club car park (55.0481, -8.4321) faces Owey Island 800m away, which has a great inlet for coasteering (55.0528, -8.4406); pier on the E side (55.0372, -8.4165) is good for reaching Inis Oileantraigh, a magical islet 800m away with a beach and cliff walls for deep water soloing or jumping (55.0433, -8.4133), and a deep fissure on the N side. For guided climbs book with Iain Miller at Unique Ascent (uniqueascent.ie).

1 min, 55.0334, -8.4211

13 NA BRISTÍ, CROHY HEAD *

The name of this dramatic sea arch means 'the breeches' and it does resemble a pair of legs rising from the sea; at high tide you can swim through the middle. It's a fascinating 2km coast walk from above quiet Maghery Strand cliff parking (54.9266, -8.4464) past the Red House, the ruin of a late 18th-century kelp factory, then an early 19th-century signal tower, one of the chain that ran all around the coast (54.9220, -8.4539). On the next large promontory is a recently restored EIRE 74 navigation marker (54.9197, -8.4572) and several blowholes. Finally you come to the remains of a soapstone workings, abandoned in the 1940s, and a steep descent to the little cove with the sea arch. Or park on the lane at 54.9156, -8.4531 and cross the stile by the soapstone sign (300m).

45 mins, 54.9146, -8.4563

14 LIGHTHOUSE STEPS, ARRANMORE

This flight of exciting steps leads down the steep crag to a tiny inlet 30m below the cliffs; on a flat calm day adventurers could coasteer to the huge sea arch or caves. Others can admire the views and then visit the lighthouse, the ruined coastguard station or EIRE marker (55.0121, -8.5491). Park at the road end by lighthouse entrance and follow wall down on L. The steps and railings are deteriorating, so take great care and be prepared to scramble if need be; alternatively take a kayak tour from Cumann na mBád (+353 74 9520024).

10 mins, 55.0122, -8.5615

RIVER, LAKE & WATERFALL

15 RIVER LACKAGH

Explore pools and rapids on the river below Glen Lough from the upstream fishing car park off L5272; follow the boardwalk and give

11

12

13

14

precedence to anglers. You can also dip from the R upstream bank by the road bridge itself (55.1265, -7.8509).

2 mins, 55.1202, -7.8498

16 LEANNAN RIVER

Pretty river pool beneath quiet road bridge with wooden stile and fishing path down. Downstream you can also gain access to a very exciting gorge stretch from the track to the old farm buildings (55.0180, -7.7898).

2 mins, 55.0061, -7.8061

17 GARTAN LOUGH PONTOON

This little-known pontoon at the N end of the lake is great for swimming and canoeing, with parking adjacent and Glebe House gallery with a summer tea room next door. Nearby is St. Colmcille's traditional birthplace with a cup-marked stone in a mound and parking at the gate (55.0083, -7.9162). Another access point to the lake is on SE shore behind St. Colmcille's church (54.9863, -7.9176).

1 min, 55.0033, -7.9056

18 ASTELLEEN WATERFALL & GLENVEAGH

From Glenveagh Castle (walk or bus from visitor centre) follow the lane along Lough Beagh shore under the ancient oaks of Mullangore woods and onto the popular Bridle Path up the glen from the lake head; this place is the best for a paddle. Walk beside the pretty Owenacoo burn to the falls cascading down the far slope. The ground is boggy, but real adventurers can cross and bushwhack 1 mile up the falls to the granite crags of Staghall Mountain with the islanded Lough Naweeloge (55.0138, -8.0421) and other small tarns. Alternatively, park on the R254 mountain road (54.9898, -8.0461) and descend the Bridle Path to end up at the castle for lunch (3 miles). Wild camping is allowed in Glenveagh NP, just stay 500m away from the lough and burn.

60 mins, 55.0160, -8.0104

19 LOUGH BARRA & GLENVEAGH

A quiet lake by the remote glen road. Small car park with spectacular glacial valley views and a slipway into the lake. Good for overnights. 5km NE, take the Bridle Path down towards Glenveagh to Astellen waterfall (see entry).

2 mins, 54.9589, -8.1105

20 GLENTORNAN CASCADES & LOUGH NACUNG

Loughside lane with pretty waterfall to S, small pools and super views over Errigal. Continues E with easy access to the Lough Nacung Upper shore, but this is a hydroelectric reservoir and can have sudden level or flow changes, so use caution; take a guided kayak trip with Joseph McFadden (+353 86 3066825, dunleweykayaking@gmail.com).

1 min, 55.0171, -8.1549

21 GWEEBARRA RIVER POOLS

A super series of deep pools, popular for paid fly fishing, so just enjoy the scenery if there are anglers. Park in the fishery car park (54.9175, -8.1616) and walk down 100m. There are more pools upstream for 500m, and downstream.

2 mins, 54.9164, -8.1616

22 DOOCHARRY UPLAND LOUGHS

Big views and lonely lakes on the wild R252 W from Doocharry. First is Lough More, with rounded boulders and heather; park in the small layby and bushwhack 50m down to the shore (54.9132, -8.2139). Next is Lough Nasnahida, along a rough and unmarked bog road R that crosses the lough on a causeway; you could wild camp here. At Lough Anillanowennamarve a short track R leads to a little peninsula facing an island (54.9198, -8.2529).

5 mins, 54.9183, -8.2259

23 CROLLY WATERFALLS & DISTILLERY

Pretty roadside pools with glacial boulders in ancient woods, and you can explore downstream (private fishing). On the doorstep of Criothlí, Donegal's first licensed working

whiskey distillery in 180 years, in a much-storied building (tours, thecrollydistillery.com). Park outside distillery car park and walk up N56 main road 200m to fishing gate on L, and falls visible below (250m). For a bigger fall and a deep pool, park 650m further S in gate splay (55.0186, -8.2673), cross bridge, go through the gap in the wall and follow river 20m down.
10 mins, 55.0197, -8.2684

24 SPHINX POOL, CLADY WATERFALLS

The boisterous river meets the sea at Bunbeg with a beach, a stone river quay and a small tidal estuary below rounded granite stacks, perfect for boats and dips. There are fun waterfalls just upstream, best reached by the 'Licence and permit required' signed fishing path off the road; do not disturb river fishing. The name is also spelled Spinc – Irish for a pointed rock, not a feline monument. Park where the road widens.
5 mins, 55.0605, -8.3060

25 BEAVER ISLAND, ARRANMORE

Swim out to this stone monument with beavers, a memorial to several hundred evicted tenants from the island who emigrated to the US and settled on Beaver Island in Lake Michigan. There are still exchange visits, and the islands are now twinned. You can hire bikes from the island co-operative CFFAM (+353 87 0983749) and ride out (2 miles from harbour).
40 mins, 55.0023, -8.536

LOST RUINS

26 HORN HEAD SIGNAL TOWER

This fine headland with massive views is naturally home to a Napoleonic-era signal tower, and at the very tip there is also an ancient promontory fort. On the W side of the tip is an indistinct EIRE 77 marker (55.2237, -7.9847) made to guide Second World War pilots, and a pillbox lookout post from the same era sits on a rise close to the car park.
25 mins, 55.2228, -7.9791

27 OWENCARROW VIADUCT & RIVER

Built in 1893, the viaduct had iron lattice spans resting on stone abutments, it once carried the Londonderry and Lough Swilly Railway over the windswept Owencarrow River and valley. But in 1925 a fierce gale derailed a train, killing four. The railway line closed in 1947, but the haunting ruins remain. There's a viewpoint and parking on L1332 lane but adventurers and swimmers can reach it following the river fishing path from pretty Owencarrow Bridge, 1.5km S (55.07935, -7.9034).
20 mins, 55.0839, -7.8920

25

26

28 ALTAN 'FARM' & LOUGH

A ruined 19th-century castellated summer house at the head of the wild and beautiful Altan Lough under Mount Errigal (see entry), with a stream and waterfalls tumbling down the glen. Reached by a 2.5km hike over wet bogland from the trailhead on R251 (parking for one, 55.0319, -8.0748), it would make a fine long-day circular with Errigal summit.

60 mins, 55.0511, -8.0731

29 DUNLEWEY CHURCH, POISONED GLEN*

This picturesque and pointy Gothic church, a rich widow's memorial, fell to ruin and the roof was removed in the 1950s. The dramatic slopes of Mount Errigal tower above and a track leads down to the lonely lough for a dip. The beautiful Poisoned Glen (which might really be called the Heavenly Glen, as in Irish heaven is neamh and poison is neimhe) can be walked from here over an old stone bridge. Signed off the R251 immediately below Mount Errigal; the church can't be missed.

5 mins, 55.0193, -8.1117

30 GLENTORNAN LOST VILLAGE *

Abandoned and poignant by Lough Nacung Upper, with views to Errigal, 50 people on average lived in this small village between 1841 to 1911. Park at the road end on way to football pitch.

2 mins, 55.0203, -8.1644

31 TAU CROSS, TORY ISLAND

The moment you get off the ferry in West Town, you are greeted by medieval history. The mysterious Tau cross, a T-shaped version of the crucifix that goes back to early Christian Egypt, stands by the dock, cut from mica slate not found on the island. Next to it is the old graveyard where an early monastery once stood, and the only round tower still standing in Donegal. 300m W along the road are the low remains of the Mhórsheisir, the Church of the Seven, said to hold the sons of an Indian king who came to the island to hear St Colmcille preach in the 6th century. The path continues to the lighthouse and the Foreigners' Graveyard (55.2743, -8.2486), final resting place of many sailors. Several are from the sinking of HMS Wasp in 1884, on its way to collect rents and evict tenants for Lord Leitrim.

1 min, 55.2647 -8.22693

32 BÁD EDDIE WRECK, MAGHERACLOGHER

The wooden hull of Bád Eddie, or Eddie's Boat, has served as both sculpture and climbing frame in the sand; there is less of it with each storm now. There's a car park above, and an empty hotel that may be redeveloped. Walk out when the popular beach becomes shimmering sandflats and lagoons at LT, and keep walking over the dunes around the mini-headland N for quieter Trá Mór/Bunbeg Beach. There are strong tidal cross currents along the estuary, so it's only safe to swim at slack water (HT or LT) and at LT it's deepest from the little headland.

6 mins, 55.0679, -8.3134

33 RUTLAND ISLAND LOST VILLAGE

This island was uninhabited until local landlord and MP William Burton Conyngham built a fishing station and entire village on it in the 1780s to exploit large herring shoals. The shoals declined, and by 1837 the station had vanished under the sands, but the last two islanders left in 1963. The terraces of grassed-

35

35

35

over Duck Street are now renovated and a striking sight, but there are ruins around the quay. The W coast has superb wild beaches.

5 mins, 54.9806, -8.4564

WILD HILLS & VIEWPOINTS

34 MOUNT MUCKISH

The most popular way up to the legendary views from the highest peak in Donegal is from the N, via the ruins of Muckish Quarry (55.1087, -8.0020), and a steep switchback path up the cliff. On the return, take the route of the old railway around Lough Agher back to the car park (55.1260, -7.9860). An alternative approach is the rougher S ascent (small car park at 55.0897, -8.0028). 600m W on the R256 is the Bridge of Tears, immortalised by Clannad and older folk songs; at this confluence of routes emigrants from west Donegal said goodbye to family, almost certainly forever, before walking the long road to the docks of London/Derry.

90 mins, 55.1005, -8.0040

35 ERRIGAL

It's just 5.5km out-and-back to climb this strikingly conical hill, with a good path all the way up and along the summit ridge, but at 510m elevation gain it's steep and not a quick walk. The views over the Poisoned Glen and surrounding peaks from the top on a clear day are reward enough, and this is a popular climb in summer, so if the weather looks right, get there early. Car park is at 55.0249, -8.0899 on the R251 at the SE side of the peak and can fill up on good days, with cars also parking along the verges.

90 mins, 55.0336, -8.1133

36 BÓTHÓG DONNELLY

Enjoy the sunset over the ocean or even wild camp by this cute bothy (bóthóg), a wee stone cabin built into a crag on the boggy hills at the island edge by one turf-cutter, who carried in all the stone. It's open to weary walkers and even has a tiny hearth. In the morning you could dip in little Lough Ashesky, 400m SE along the road from the start of the 350m bothy track at 54.9946, -8.5376.

5 mins, 54.9962 -8.5447

WILDLIFE WONDERS

37 TRAMORE, LURGABRACK RESERVE *

A beautiful 2km walk among dunes and wild orchids leads to this remote and usually empty beach. Look out for white-fronted geese, cinnabar moths, and possibly friendly horses. Rip tides, so be careful swimming. The small car park is at 55.1854, -7.9871. For safer swimming, Dunfanaghy village beach

33

32

37

36

41

50

(Killahoey) is better and has a 1925 shipwreck (55.1910, -7.9550).

30 mins, 55.1771, -8.023

38 TOR MÓR PUFFINS, TORY ISLAND

From the harbour, walk E 2km to Port Doon, a pebble swimming cove, then N to the Iron Age Balor's Fort embankments, supposedly built by the Formorians, the mythical first settlers of Ireland. They defend a narrow entrance onto a spectacular promontory with standing cairns and 100m vertical sea cliffs, ending in the Leac na Leannán (wishing stone) that juts out from the top over the Atlantic. In summer look for the colony of puffins off the N coast, and as darkness falls listen for rare corncrakes near East Town; divert along the coast around the reservoir to the SE to look for seals.

45 mins, 55.2602, -8.1943

CLASSIC EATS

39 THE SHACK, MARBLE HILL STRAND

Tom and Min serve home-roasted coffee and sweets with a view from their cheerful wooden shack on the little coast road above lovely Marble Hill beach (with the high tide jumping spot of Harry's Hole at 55.1835, -7.8964). Enjoy them at upcycled pallet tables above the white sands. Portnablagh, F92 A4W8, +353 86 7238318

55.1761 -7.902

40 THE RUSTY OVEN, DUNFANAGHY

In the back garden of Patsy Dan's pub (a legend in itself) is this wood-fired, sourdough-based pizzeria. Evenings from March to December; book online or just turn up (therustyoven.ie). Adjacent is Muck'n'Muffins, a pottery studio and great coffee shop. Every Saturday from March to October you can also find local crafts and produce, home-made foods and preserves. F92 A6NA

55.1834 -7.97271

41 COFFEE TIME, KILMACRENAN

You can't miss this cutesy red and white thatched byre as you pass through on the N56, but the coffee is superb, the bread wheaten, the butter home-churned and the brisket organic. F92 W935, @tiscoffeetime

55.0314, -7.7817

42 TÁBHAIRNE LEO

Leo and his wife Máire opened this pub (more famous outside the Gaeltacht as Leo's Tavern) in 1968 and held trad sessions every night. Their children grew up to become the Celtic folk band Clannad; awards and memorabilia fill the walls, and many Irish legends have played here. Now run by son Bartley, the pub still has regular ballad, ceilídh and trad nights, and a solid reputation for seafood and local produce – you can book a glamping pod next door (meenaleckglamping.com) if you want to stay late. Meenaleck, Crolly, F92 RK75, +353 74 9548143

55.0276, -8.2712

43 THE LOBSTER POT, BURTONPORT

There's a giant lobster on the wall outside and a lively maritime bar inside with pirates, sharks

and plenty of the promised seafood on the menu. Locals know it and love it as Kelly's. F94 HD91, +353 74 9542012
54.9838, -8.4401

44 THE OLDE GLEN, CARRICKART

Dating back to the 1760s, this traditional cosy pub is one of Donegal's oldest, with open fire, stone floors, local brews, and live music. There's a superb Michelin-guide restaurant and a 'Bia Box' food truck out the back. Glenmenagh, F92 KR23, +353 83 1585777
55.1264 -7.81215

45 DANNY MINNIES

Proudly Irish-speaking, award-winning, locally sourced, garden-grown, gastro dining from an old fashioned oak-panelled dining room with tapestries and antiques. Rooms too. Teach Killindarragh, Anagaire/Annagry, F94 Y48R, +353 74 9548201
55.0213 -8.31483

BEACH CAMPSITES

46 QUIET MOMENTS CAMPING SITE

Super simple beachside campsite right on the estuarine waters of Invermore Bay. Dun-dooan Lower, Downings. Call Anthony +353 86 0727045
55.2268, -7.7984

47 ROSSAN CARAVAN & CAMPING

This is a small, basic site, set into the hillside. Facilities all work, and the sensational views plus beautiful beach make up for any shortcomings. +353 86 2539201
55.2237, -7.8138

48 THE MILL

Classic family-run country B&B with seven rooms, two of them dog-friendly, and one the former studio of artist Frank Eggington. Award-winning breakfasts set you up for the day, and there's an honesty bar to enjoy in the lakeside gardens in summer or by the open fire in winter. Figart, Dunfanaghy, F92 RK79, +353 74 9136985
55.1767 -7.97953

RUSTIC RETREATS

49 DONEGAL THATCHED COTTAGES

Five thatched cottages superbly placed above a lovely cove on Cruit island (reached by bridge). Visitors also sometimes park/wild camp at 55.0334, -8.4212. donegalthatchcottages.com
55.0362, -8.4189

50 LIGHTHOUSE DWELLINGS, ARRANMORE

Two holiday lets in the former keeper's accommodation are furnished in an unpretentious, old-fashioned way, as if you've walked into someone's house from 50 years ago. Search Airbnb.
55.0143, -3.5601

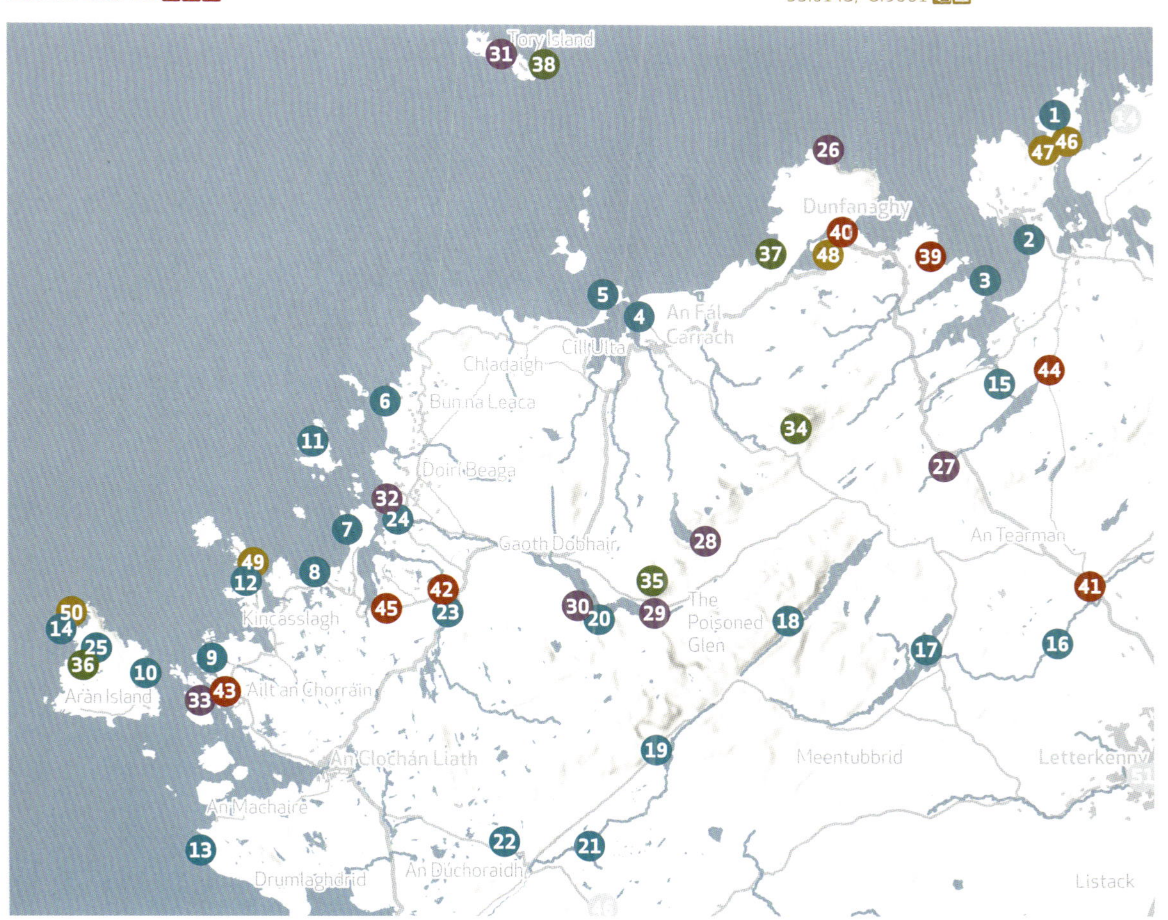

2

SOUTH DONEGAL

Our perfect weekend

- **Climb** even higher from mighty Slieve League cliffs, then refuel with local seafood at the Rusty Mackerel in Teelin.
- **Wander** through the poetic 'rushy glen' of Ardnamona Wood on the shore of Lough Eske, and swim in the rapids of the river flowing out.
- **Watch** the salmon leap at 18th-century Cloghan stone bridge on the River Finn.
- **Swim** in fjord-like Loch Finne and sleep in a treehouse 'nest' at Neadú.
- **Follow** the old bog railway to Lough Machugh or the Owenea before a fine dinner at The Thatch.
- **Explore** rare machair and wildlife at Sheskinmore, and camp by the shore at Tramore Beach.
- **Jump** from the pier at Rosbeg, kayak the rocky shore of the Dawros headland, then dine at Joe's Seafood Bar above.
- **Retreat** off-grid in remote An Port, and explore the magnificent cliffs of the Sturrall.
- **Find** the hidden loughs of Bonryglen, and dusk-walk to Kilclooney dolmens with the red deer.

2

4

9

This is perhaps the most accessible part of Donegal, with the family-favourite sands of Portnoo, world-renowned locations like the Slieve League cliffs, and one of Ireland's oldest attractions, Glencolmcille Folk Village. All have something to offer in themselves, but just a little way beyond them lie hidden treasures – an island monastic site with medieval carvings, a headland signal tower or an ancient pilgrim path.

The coast here is dramatically variable. Along the southern stretch is Killybegs, Ireland's biggest fishing port. There is no better place to eat seafood, especially from the Seafood Shack on the harbour, but this is a region to sample seafood wherever you go. Nearby lies 'Donegal's secret waterfall' – no longer secret, but still beautiful and just tricky enough to reach so that many don't make the trip. The cliffs become more dramatic as you head west to the massive Slieve League cliffs, where you can reach the even higher summit beyond by braving the narrow 'One Man's Pass'. As the coast faces into the full force of the Atlantic, you find yourself on mighty cliffs with dramatic headlands like the Sturrall, tiny fishing piers tucked into sheltering inlets, and a scattering of remote bays. As you reach Ardara town the scene changes to broad sandy estuaries, curving white bays and machair headlands.

Much of the inland landscape is boggy and unforgiving; you will find yourself on dramatic cliff walks rather than inland peak climbs and ridge hikes. But the absence of intensive farming means the region boasts some of Ireland's best rivers for salmon fishing, with waters clean enough to host the rare freshwater pearl mussel. There are bubbling waterfalls with deep pools in the valleys and quiet loughs between the rugged mountains – some, like Loch Finne, large enough to be taken for a fjord, others small and remote. The mosaic of the landscape also includes important protected areas full of wildlife, like the ancient Ardnamona Wood, or the dunes and wetlands of Sheskinmore, alive with butterflies and birdsong.

Despite the toughness of this wild landscape, this is a truly ancient human landscape. The dolmens at Kilclooney may be the best-known ancient remains, but the classic monument here is the court tomb, built by the first farmers almost 4,000 years ago and concentrated in the north-west. Even in recent history, the countryside was more populated than it is today, and there are villages that were abandoned within living memory. The past can seem very close here and the power of the elements is real; it makes one even more grateful for the warm comfort of a local bar with good food at the end of a day.

SECRET BEACHES

1 DOOEY BEACH, LETTERMACAWARD

Almost 3km of silver sand faces the sunset at this Green Coast beach. Despite having good surf and a little beach sauna (Wild Atlantic +353 83 8477373), it is off the beaten track and limited parking helps keep the numbers down in summer.

2 mins, 54.8734, -8.3818

2 WHITE STRAND, GWEEBARRA *

A curve of white sands on the meandering Gweebarra estuary, reached from SE along 1km of farm track (R261 at 54.8375, -8.3920) or from W 1.8km across golf course, lane end L7543 (54.8442, -8.4257).

20 mins, 54.8449, -8.3993

3 TRAMORE BEACH, MAGHERAMORE *

This beautiful remote beach has glorious sunset views to the distant bulk of Slievetooey. At the S end the sands round the Magheramore dunes and become the white curves of Ballinreavy Strand. There is very little signage, and parking is along a track by the caravan park (with tent field, F94 RW66, +353 86 8337123).

8 mins, 54.8100, -8.4970

4 TRABANE, LOUGHROS POINT

Tiny lanes lead onto the little-visited headland N of Maghera Strand and this quiet sandy beach with streams, rock pools, and easy access from parking for two cars. Or seek out the spectacular hidden Liskeeraghan Strand, looking over to Ballinreavy Strand; park before the house at 54.7852, -8.4913 and ask permission to follow the track 200m over private land.

1 min, 54.7848, -8.5167

5 ROSSBEG PIER

Swim or kayak out among the skerries of this quiet bay from the pier, and stay for superb sunsets. The L7713 loops around the coast and passes the pier, where there is space to park.

1 min, 54.8206, -8.5251

6 THE SILVER STRAND *

Stunning curve of beach in a horseshoe of cliffs, with 174 steps down from the car park. Adventurous kayakers can leave from here to explore under Slieve League cliffs; try Sea Kayaking Donegal (seakayakingdonegal.com) for a trip. There's even a perfectly located Silver Strand B&B above (F94 X47P, +353 74 9730899).

4 mins, 54.6645, -8.7762

7 ST JOHN'S POINT BEACH

At the far end of this sinuous peninsula is a quiet, white sand beach with a small car park; this is the end of the road, unless you are staying at the lighthouse (see entry). Also 1km before the beach is a L turn to a fun pier, popular for snorkelling due to its marine life (54.5854, -8.4297).

1 min, 54.5780, -8.4394

8 MURVAGH BEACH

Almost 4km of calm and sheltered sand, with an extensive SAC dune system. Well signed from the N15 on the road past Murvagh Links House B&B (F94 E179).

2 mins, 54.6041, -8.1612

SEA CAVES & ISLANDS

9 PORTNOO & INISHKEEL ISLAND

Big family beach with easy parking, also called Narin, but walk 500m over the LT sandbar to contemplate the ancient Inishkeel monastic site. There are two church ruins and a holy well above the beach, with a beautifully carved 9th-century cross slab and shaft of a high cross. Head to the far NE end for solitude and further coves (or White Strand, see entry).

2 mins, 54.8416, -8.4454

10

13

12

13

10 MAGHERA & ASSARANCA WATERFALL

Despite its popularity, this vast beautiful sweep of pale sand is like a desert landscape backed by dune grasses. At LT head around the far L to find some good sea caves in the dramatically tilting strata. Cash-only parking €4. Combine with a quick stop or dip at the even more popular roadside waterfall 1km E along with parking (54.7584, -8.5135).

5 mins, 54.7624, -8.5272

11 AN PORT, GLENLOUGH & STURRALL

Sheltered by imposing headlands with dramatic coasteering and kayaking, this shingle bay and pier are glorious in fine weather, dramatic in storms. They lie below an abandoned village, still inhabited in the 1920s when American artist Rockwell Kent painted magnificent coastal scenes here. Walk 3km NE for sea stacks and pyramids at Glenlough Bay (descend via stream and scree scramble), then inland to a now-ruined cottage where Dylan Thomas retreated in 1935 to conquer his alcoholism – only to find himself in the heart of poitín country (54.7603, -8.6576). Along cliffs 2.5km SW from An Port is the legendary Sturrall, a knife-edge headland ridge nearly 200m high, which can be scrambled with extreme care in fine conditions (54.7370, -8.7437). Sea kayakers will find arches below; try Iain Miller (uniqueascent.ie) for trips.

1 min, 54.7475, -8.7022

12 LARGY 'SECRET' WATERFALL, FINTRA

This waterfall cascades into a collapsed sea cave, accessible at LT. Park at Largy viewpoint (54.6297, -8.5118) and walk E on road 250m to a gated gravel track R to coast. Scramble R over rocky, slippery foreshore for 300m to a headland with three cave openings; you hear the waterfall before you see it. Nearby Fintra beach is sheltered and sandy, with good swimming and a small car park (54.6352, -8.4882).

20 mins, 54.6263 -8.5134

13 MUCKROSS HEAD

Drop down from the headland onto huge wave-cut rock platforms, popular for bouldering, orcoasteering and jumping in calm seas. On the the clifftops above is an EIRE marker and more platforms beyond. Signed from L1215 coast road. Parking area at end of lane. Follow the other L lane 100m for safe little swimming cove of Trá Bán with small car park (54.6145, -8.5771); the W cove develops rips.

2 mins, 54.6096, -8.5901

RIVER, LAKE & WATERFALL

14 LOCH FINNE

This narrow, quiet lough set below rugged Aghla Mountain does a passable impression of a Norwegian fjord. A gravel path leads to the shore for easy access where the River Finn leaves the lough. Families might enjoy the narrow-gauge steam train that runs through breathtaking scenery along the shore from Fintown village – the only railway running in all of Donegal (F94 FR90,+353 74 9546280).

3 mins, 54.8681, -8.1081

15 BONNYGLEN LOUGH & DOON FORT

A short walk leads to this lake; the felled forestry is being replanted with more native species, but will be open for some time. The forest track leads on to more hidden lakes including Lough Namanlagh after 1.6km. Coillte signs on L2463 S of Clooney.

5 mins, 54.8318, -8.4006

16 DOON LAKE, ISLAND & FORT

For something very hidden, Doon Lake is about 4km W, with a remarkable high-walled cashel on an island, 150m off shore. It used to be possible to rent a rowboat from the nearby house, but the cashel is now being restored and is closed. You could view it from the shore by bushwhacking 800m across rough land from the tiny lane at 54.8345, -8.4695.

20 mins, 54.8290, -8.46401

17 OWENEA RIVER & LOUGH MACHUGH

The Owenea has deep sandy pools and waterfalls, but is one of the best salmon rivers in Donegal, so only dip away from anglers. From the small parking area off N56 E of Adara (54.7794, -8.3282) follow the GAP cycle trail along the old Bord na Móna railway route 400m to the river and over the old railway bridge; it continues 1km up to remote and shallow Lough Machugh. There is a good path to explore waterfalls downstream for up to 4km (also accessible from Ardara, 1.5km on bog road R beyond F94 VY83 to 54.7766, -8.3916, or 1km upstream from the R216 river bridge, 54.7756, -8.4093). For something right by the road, just W of Glenties on R56 pull off on hard shoulder at 54.7861, -8.3028 and cross down to the footbridge from Owenea Fishery sign.

10 mins, 54.7833, -8.3396

18 DONAGH EAST WATERFALL

The Corabber river has some of the best waterfalls in the county, like this huge remote cascade into a deep, black pool. Upstream towards Lough Belshade lie more, with a good but boggy track. Follow lane from Lough Eske car park (54.7201, -8.0552) 1.7km to the farm at end – you could ask to park here. Take the track L of the new barn for 1.7km, crossing several tributaries. The R track from farm descends to amazing pools at 54.7303, -8.0359 and many more upstream (bring river shoes).

45 mins, 54.7387, -8.0348

19 LOUGHS NAHOORY & FAD

Two in a cluster of four remote lakes with big views, nestled amid the Blue Stack Mountains; the other two are reached from these. (Nahoory is also found as Lahoory.) An easy walk up a rough track under Benson's Hill from parking at lane end by water treatment unit (54.7128, -8.0123).

20 mins, 54.7208, -8.0017

20 RIVER ESKE

Flowing S from Lough Eske, this is a beautiful stretch of fly fishing river, and an SAC for the endangered freshwater pearl mussel. Follow the R bank anglers' path down from the stone bridge to a weir (200m) at the bend, followed by islands and then rapids/waterfalls (400m).

10 mins, 54.6850, -8.0471

21 LIMM-NA-MHILLE, EANY MORE

A deep pool and sandy river beach on a tight meander, shaded by woods. There's a layby and fishing stile, then 50m N along the forestry path; popular with anglers, so swimming may not be possible.

2 mins, 54.6842, -8.1927

24

28

29

22 BONNYGLEN FALLS, EANY WATER

A wide waterfall creates a long, deep pool overhung by ancient oaks. Eany Water is popular with fly fishers (day permits €30) so don't swim near anglers. Park at the lane end (54.66729, -8.2636) and follow the fisheries signs down to the riverside path. Falls are 150m upstream, a footbridge 100m beyond, and Burns Falls after another 800m (two sets); downstream 300m is a weir. Also lovely riverside meadow with a stile just above the road bridge N of Frosses (54.6805, -8.2477).

10 mins, 54.6691, -8.2659

23 SALMON LEAP, RIVER GLEN, CARRICK *

A huge pool with jumps below a waterfall, easily accessible from the riverside path upstream from the small car park, and a good place to watch salmon migrating from the sea meet their first obstacle. Quite popular in summer, and with anglers. On Teelin Rd just S of Carrick.

1 min, 54.6504, -8.6427

SACRED & ANCIENT

24 KILCLOONEY DOLMENS *

Two dolmens surrounded by scattered stones from the cairn that once covered both. The larger one carries one of the biggest capstones in Ireland at a jaunty angle; the smaller one is partly collapsed. The flat, open land gives a huge sky, and if you visit early or late you might meet red deer. Park at the Dolmen Centre (has a café), cross the bridge and follow the trail L of the church 500m along sometimes soggy fields with sheep and some stiles; this is private property, so be respectful, keep R and be careful with all gates.

10 mins, 54.8175, -8.4330

25 GLENCOLMCILLE FOLK VILLAGE

Small, white-washed, thatched cottages in a small settlement known as a 'clachan', built and furnished as a living museum in the 1960s. They replicate homes of the 17th–19th centuries with a schoolhouse and pub-shop to round out the scene, and there are demonstrations of traditional crafts, workshops and cultural events in the summer months. Entry €7. Below the car park are flower-studded dunes perfect for a picnic, and a superb beach.

2 mins, 54.7070, -8.7409 €

26 CLOGHANMORE COURT TOMB

Beautifully set in a peaceful valley bowl, this is one of Ireland's largest court tomb cairns. Two stones, next to the N and S galleries, are marked with curved lines and concentric circles. Path in from small parking area on L1025 to SE at 54.6886, -8.74396, just NE of F94 E9K5.

5 mins, 54.6891, -8.7465

25

26

31

31

31

27 INVER OLD CHURCH & GRAVEYARD

This ruined 17th-century church is beautifully set on a meander in the small sandy estuary of Eany Water, thought to be a monastic site dating back to St Colmcille. From the N56 follow L1565 signed for Inver and then beach, park at quay and follow rough track to the ruin. The Rising Tide by the quay is a plain but popular locals' pub.

3 mins, 54.6470, -8.2804

28 SHALWY COURT TOMBS

This remote valley has three court tombs within 500m of each other: Shalwy, Bavan and Croaghbeg. Excavations found stone arrowheads and sherds of a large decorated bowl, but for visitors it is the massive roof slabs and entrance stones that impress. Park by R263 at Tobar Naomh Ciaran (54.6261, -8.5404) and take the path through the circular burial ground (look for the cross-marked slab and bullaun) then 800m SW to Shalwy. Croaghbeg is further SW (54.6235, -8.5484), while Bavan is N along the road and through a field gate L (54.62707, -8.5406).

15 mins, 54.6230, -8.5512

VIEWPOINTS & HILLTOPS

29 GRANNY PASS & OWENWEE FALLS

This small road follows the glacial scoop of the Owenwee valley up for big, empty views back to Maghera Strand; photographers scramble up the rocks behind for the best shots. There are small waterfall pools to explore below the viewpoint. It's one of the best mountain passes, but lesser known and quieter than Glengesh to the E (54.7205, -8.4846).

2 mins, 54.7477, -8.5573

30 GLEN SIGNAL TOWER

This Napoleonic-era tower on the cliff edge has terrific views of the Sturrall ridge (see An Port entry) with sea stacks and rock arches in the swirling ocean below. The walk up is part of the fascinating Glencolumbkille Loop walk, a pilgrim route passing St Colmcille's church and bed (54.7180, -8.7388) and a cairn created by centuries of pilgrims bringing stones to his holy well (54.7205, -8.7383). Start from parking opposite the church (F94 AC92), head W on the road past the standing stone to the corner and follow signs.

30 mins, 54.7281, -8.7470

31 SLIEVE LEAGUE *

These cliffs are nearly three times the height of those at Moher, yet have far fewer visitors. From the main car park you can open the gate and drive to the viewing platform at very end, or walk up to spot the the well-restored EIRE 71 marker (54.6242, -8.6772) or find the lesser-visited Carrigan Head signal tower (54.6202, -8.6794, a 600m walk from a small layby about half way up). If conditions are fine, take the 2km cliff walk from the top up to Shanbally (435m) and another 2km to the true Sliabh Liag summit (595m) including the spectacular and precipitous 'One Man's Pass' ridge, possibly the most dramatic coastal walk in Ireland. You can also take a boat around the stunning coast to the foot of the cliffs, sometimes spotting dolphins, basking sharks or even Minke whales; try Sliabh Liag Boats from Killybegs (+353 87 6284688) or Atlantic Coastal Cruises from Teelin (+353 87 2214497).

2 mins, 54.6277, -8.6839

WILDLIFE WONDERS

32 CLOGHAN BRIDGE SALMON LEAP

This 18th-century humpback bridge over the River Finn is a good spot to see spawning salmon leap, with a popular fishery just above. Riverside paths lead downstream through gates on both banks, giving views of the graceful stone arch rising directly from bedrock, above many pools and cascades popular with anglers; if no one is fishing and levels are low you could have a dip. Signed 'Gort an Easa' from the R252, with parking on NE side of bridge.

2 mins, 54.8280, -7.9309

33 SHESKINMORE MACHAIR/ BALLINREAVY STRAND *

A glorious machair meadows nature reserve including a lough and dunes with marsh, bee and Irish orchids and helleborines in spring, home to 20 species of butterflies, plus dragonflies and damselflies. Listen out for melodious skylarks in summer, croaking choughs in winter, and look up for birds of prey. Small car park at end of L7763 off R261 or walk in from Tramore beach to the N (see listing). Be sure to keep dogs on leads and leave gates as you find them.

5 mins, 54.7976, -8.4479

34 ARDNAMONA WOOD & LOUGH ESKE

A looped trail leads through an enchanted, moss-carpeted forest dominated by rare mature oak trees on the picturesque shores of Lough Eske. Sometimes called the 'Fairy Glen', it is punctuated by fern-fringed waterfalls, and thought to be the inspiration for the 'Up the airy mountain, Down the rushy glen' opening of The Faeries by local poet William Allingham. Brown signs lead to small car park (54.7064, -8.0599).

Follow the forest trail 150m to a small gate L by a house, and cross little bridge into forest. The rushy shore is 300m E.

15 mins, 54.7072, -8.0577

TRADITIONAL PUBS

35 NANCY'S BAR

At least seven generations of the same family have owned and run this award-winning pub and seafood restaurant, packed with cosy nooks and atmosphere. Check food times through the year. Front Street, Ardara, F94 AC04, +353 74 954 1187

54.7625, -8.4121

36 RUSTY MACKEREL

Atmospheric maximalist bar serving a menu with plenty of locally caught seafood. Music on weekends, and impromptu trad sessions. Teelin Road, Croaghlin, Carrick, F94 VP99, +353 74 9739101

54.6368, -8.6427

LOCAL PRODUCE

37 THE BAKERY SHACK

A mother-and-son team run this roadside artisan food shop and excellent bakery, serving single-origin barista coffees. Some outside seating. Friary, Cool Beg, F94 V402

54.5466, -8.2053

38 ANDERSONS BOATHOUSE RESTAURANT

Offering the freshest local seafood, as well as other Irish produce, and stocking local craft beers to wash it all down. In summer opt for a table out in the cobbled courtyard, or get a takeaway from the near-legendary Seafood Shack by the harbour, which Garry and Mairead also run. There's a four-person flat above if you fancy staying in this fishing village. Main Street, Killybegs, F94 X21X, +353 74 9731730

54.6365, -8.4427

39 JOE'S SEAFOOD, DAWROS BAY HOUSE

Popular family-run seafood restaurant, bar and takeaway with super sea views. Open Fri–Sun early evening only, book in advance. Eden, Portnoo, F94 XR66, +353 74 9545252, tormore2@gmail.com or joesseafoodbar@icloud.com

54.8248, -8.5234

ORGANIC & GASTRO

40 THE THATCH BAR & RESTAURANT

Firm local favourite for good food and atmosphere with highly praised vegetarian options and atmosphere. Scraggy Bay from local brewery Kinnegar on draught. Main Street, Glenties, F94 C3CD, +353 74 9551050

54.7958, -8.2810

41 BLUEBERRY TEAROOMS

This cute and award-winning café has been family run since 1993, with an especially good reputation for its breakfasts and sweet baked treats. Open 9am–6pm, closed Sundays. Castle Street, Donegal, F94 AH75, +353 74 9723663

54.6543, -8.1105

42 QUAY WEST

Chef-owners Debbie O Reilly and Jo Roarty are committed to local produce for their repeatedly award-winning upscale restaurant. The upstairs tables have massive views over the bay. Quay Street, Glebe, F94 E2A2, +353 74 9721590

54.6520, -8.1112

43 AROMA COFFEE SHOP & MINI BAKERY

Food prepared and baked fresh daily on a Mediterranean-influenced menu, with legendary Tunisian orange cake, in a cheery little café set among artisan craft shops. Opening times vary, closed Jan–Mar. Donegal Craft Village, F94 YHT0, +353 74 9723222

54.6411, -8.11534

BEACH CAMPING

44 TRAMORE BEACH CAMPING & CARAVAN

Low-key site above the beach, open May to Sept. Kiltoorish, Portnoo, F94 RW66, +353 86 8337123, eimear.tramorebeach@gmail.com

54.8090, -8.4957

45 KILLYBEGS HOLIDAY PARK

Big sea views from several terraces of an old coastal quarry, with hardstanding above and a grassy area near the private shore reserved for tents. Patsy and Rose have been welcoming people to this quiet site for two decades, with glowing reviews. Roshine, Killybegs, F94 X06W, +353 872769765

54.6219, -8.4527

RUSTIC RETREATS

46 NEADÚ, BAILE NA FINNE

Three quirky-chic hideaways, including a Cosy Converted Cowshed and Birdbox tree-house, at the end of a winding track with big views. Glenlieghan, Baile na Finne (Fintown), F94 D6X3, airbnb.com

54.8891, -8.1512

47 PORT ECO COTTAGE *

This off-grid, off-beat cottage and a few neighbouring ruins are all that remains of the vanished fishing village of Port (see entry). Solar panels provide enough power for lighting but no sockets or fridge (chill your milk and beers in the stream); two stoves heat water and keep the chill away. Back to basics experience – far from even neighbouring houses, but minutes from the shore. Sleeping four, it is usually only available for full weeks, but occasional weekends out of season. An Port, F94 X009, airbnb.ie

54.7478, -8.6989

48 ST JOHN'S POINT LIGHTHOUSE

Open fires, panoramic sea views, an EIRE marker on the headland and a lookout post nearby, and a sandy beach down the single-track lane. Each apartment sleeps four. Be prepared to disconnect – there is virtually no wifi and the nearest shop is quite a drive. Killultan, F94 F5H6, irishlandmark.com

54.5694, -8.4594

30

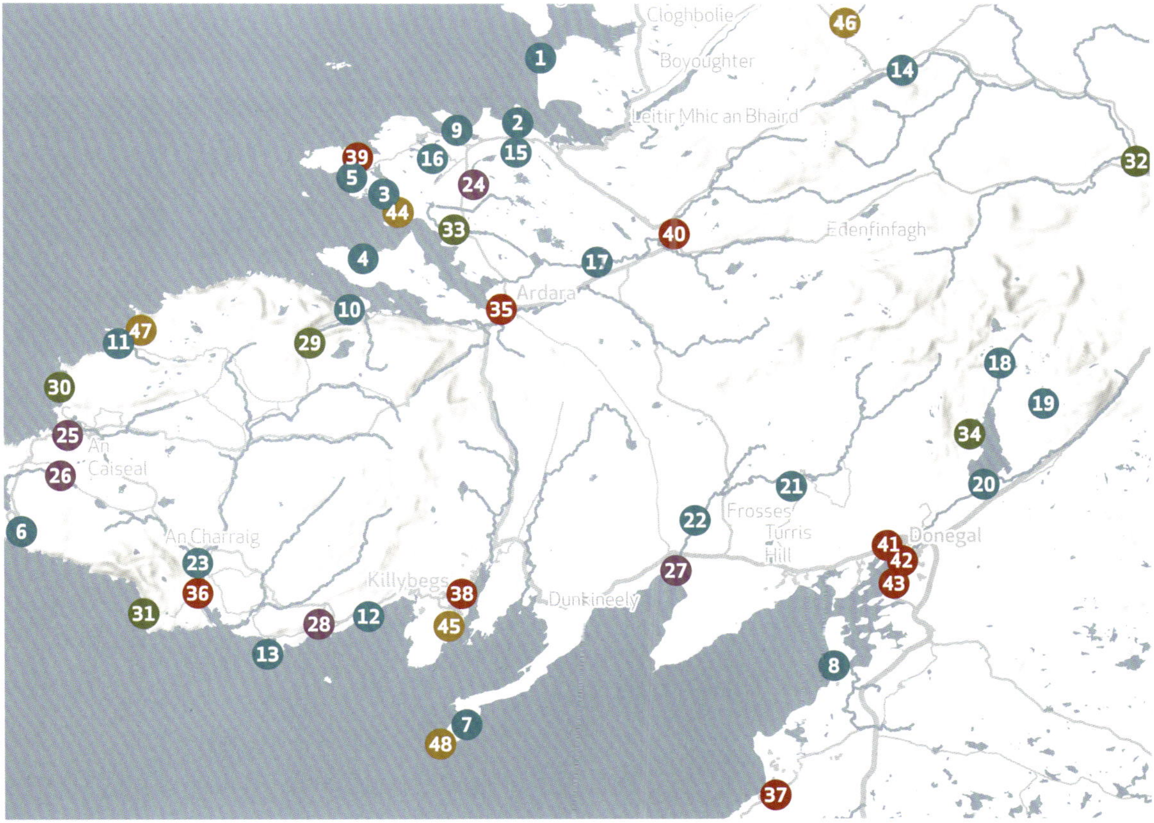

LEITRIM TO LOUGH ERNE

Our perfect weekend

- → **Explore** the Lough Erne shore and Castle Caldwell ruins, then forest bathe and sleep in your own bubble dome at Finn Lough.
- → **Fuel** up at Rossinver's Organic, and take a streamside walk to the tumbling Fowley's Falls.
- → **Hike** up Keeloges to dip in stunning Tin Whistle Lake, with infinity-pool view.
- → **Look** for the white trout in Ireland's coldest waters at St Patrick's Holy Well, then dine on one at superb MacNean House restaurant.
- → **Cross** the river to Creevelea Friary and warm up with a pint by the fire in Stanford Village Inn.
- → **Climb** the Stairway to Heaven for the magnificent views from the summit of Cuilcagh, or plunge into the ferny Cladagh Glen below.
- → **Paddle** into the sinuous White Fathers Cave with its rare bats and zombie spiders, then visit the cursing stones at ruined Killinagh Church.
- → **Trace** the ancient rock art or the 10th-century cross carvings at Boho, and pick up local tips from Dessie in his unique bar, The Linnet.

1

2

2

Browsing this chapter you may be struck by how many entries for woodlands or ancient tombs end with some variation of 'also a short walk to a jetty'. Although we have left the coast, it can feel as if there is more water than land here. North of the border lie two Lough Ernes, and you can take an international dip in Lough Melvin. A little further south Ireland's longest river rises at Shannon Pot, soon broadening into Lough Allen.

Connecting the loughs are sinuous rivers, and there are mountaintop tarns like the glorious Tin Whistle to find. The limestone geology favours waterfalls, like swimmable Pól an Eas, and formed the basis of what is now the Cuilcagh Lakelands Geopark. All this water was perfect for a thriving local linen industry until the end of the 18th century, when industrialised competition proved too much.

This was also once a heavily forested region, with an 18th-century survey noting that from Drumshanbo to Drumkeeran 'one could travel the whole way from tree to tree by branches'. Much of this was cut to make charcoal for iron works on mighty Sliabh an Iarainn. When the wood was gone, they tried to use coal from mines at Arigna, and then the foundries fell silent. Scraps of the old forests remain, some along northern scarps of the Geopark and into Cladagh Glen.

With local industries wiped out, the final blow to the local population was the Famine in the 1840s, when the population here fell by over a quarter, leading to over 100 years of steady emigration and a quiet, empty landscape. Only recently has the tide begun to turn.

There are ruins from lost local industries to see, like the shoreline lime kiln in Castle Caldwell demesne that fed Belleek pottery, the many churches that lost congregations, and ruined tower houses from troubled times.

Among more ancient relics, the court tombs that this corner of Ireland is known for can be seen almost en masse at the geopark or in splendid isolation at Aghanaglack. Most enigmatic are the carved figures on Boa Island, one with two faces forever gazing in opposite directions, like Janus; nobody can even be sure whether they are pagan or Christian. They seem a fitting emblem for this region, poised between past and future, one nation and another, and even solid and liquid.

SEA POOLS & CAVES

1 FAIRY BRIDGES & TULLAN STRAND

Tullan is a popular surfing beach; there are dangerous rips, but on a calm day at HT you can wade/swim into the Fairy Bridge caves at the S end near the car park. This remarkable group of blowholes with bridge-like arches to the sea have been drawing visitors for 200 years. Sit in the rock-cut Wishing Chair above, tap it twice and tell nobody what you wished for; results are not guaranteed, but a fine view is. You can follow the Rougey Walk S to Bundoran; look for traces of an EIRE marker by the shelter, and maybe take a turn on the Dancing by the Sea platform (54.4850, -8.2790), once used for daytime dances.

5 mins, 54.4904, -8.2719

2 BUNDORAN TIDAL POOLS

This popular town and seaside beach has smooth rocks and little coves. At the N end is a HT diving board and jumps off Rougey Rocks (54.4851, -8.2813), and the cliff path leads onto the Fairy Bridges (see entry). At the SW is the West End and smaller Nun's tidal pools.

5 mins, 54.4778, -8.2920

LOUGH ERNE

3 DRUMMONEY FALLS

A deep pool beneath a wide, picturesque waterfall in a wooded setting. You can climb up and explore the flat strata above. A good path leads down from the little car park with steps right into the water – best to change at your car.

5 mins, 54.5565, -7.7417

4 ELY LODGE, LOWER LOUGH ERNE

Easy roadside lakeshore paths for woodland walks or swimming. There are two islands just 50m offshore. Park in the large layby on A46.

5 mins, 54.4117, -7.7220

5 TRORY JETTY, LOWER LOUGH ERNE

There are several old stone jetties, meant for fishing/boating but also decent for a swim with views to the ruins of Devenish Island (see entry). Further S is the main modern floating pontoon which tends to be a bit busy. Parking on the lakeshore lanes, or in a bigger car park and picnic site 200m back.

1 min, 54.3799, -7.6533

6 CLOONATRIG QUAY, RIVER ERNE

Floating quay in a pretty location, good for canoes and swimming, but on a narrow stretch

5

5

of the river, so watch out for boat traffic. Follow Shore Guest House sign from A509 at Killywillen to the end.

1 min, 54.2832, -7.5960

7 ROSSDONEY QUAY, RIVER ERNE

Little lanes come to an end at a remote, wide meander of the river – a lovely spot for canoeing, swimming or overnights. Signed for anglers from the A509 S of Bellanaleck.

1 min, 54.2706, -7.6113

8 NAAN ISLAND, UPPER LOUGH ERNE

Canoe out to wild Naan Island with its own little jetty (on the opp N shore), or just swim and overnight from this tiny lane-end lakeshore spot. 2km NW along the shore by the road is Knockninny Quay (54.2301, -7.5734).

1 min, 54.2296, -7.5475

9 TIRAROE QUAY, LOUGH ERNE

Dive into the deep, dark waters of Upper Lough Erne at this quiet, remote floating pontoon and boardwalk, good for an overnight camp. At the end of tiny lanes off the A509 near Derrylin.

1 min, 54.2177, -7.5323

LAKE, RIVER & WATERFALL

10 LOUGH MELVIN PIER & PARK

A concrete pier for fishing, boating and swimming, with trails to walk in the woodland Lough Melvin Eco Park. Just 100m NW from the car park entrance on R281 is a green track to the old graveyard and ruined church, a more secluded place for a peaceful picnic (54.4463, -8.2778).

2 mins, 54.4470, -8.2716

11 ABHORNALEHA BRIDGE, LOUGH MELVIN

This shallow, sandy shore with a little slipway, jetty, and parking for a few cars, is one of those curious places where you can swim between two countries. The border follows a stream to enter the clear, clean waters of Lough Melvin and pass between the jetty and the wooded peninsula.

1 min, 54.4448, -8.1577

12 GLENANIFF WATERFALLS

This magical hidden glen has a string of waterfalls below a remote, narrow mountain road with big views. The track down to the river (walk straight on where it bends R) is at 54.4040, -8.2166, and you may be able to park at the end of it, or there is a proper pull-off area 300m N at the brow of the hill.

15 mins, 54.4000, -8.2188

13 FOWLEY'S FALLS, ROSSINVER

Four picturesque cascades over crisp steps of rock, with no really big pools, but tiers that are fun for paddling and wet-scrambling in summer; it can be quite a torrent in winter. Park on roadside by wooden fenced entrance (turn off R282 W over the bridge at Rossinver and follow 1.8km). Or there is a lovely 3km out-and-back walk up the Glenaniff River from the Organic Centre (see entry) in Rossinver, passing the Mass rock used in Penal times.

2 mins, 54.3808, -8.1335

14 LOUGH GLENADE

Swim in one of the finest glacial valley lakes in Europe, a conservation area home to rare crayfish and water plants, from a pier that leads out past the reeds. The Dobhar Chú (pronounced Dowarcoo) or water dog is said to have lived in the depths, emerging in 1722 to kill Grainne Ni Conalai; it is carved on her grave in the middle of nearby Conwall old cemetery (54.4083, -8.3132). Signed off the R280 9km NW of Manorhamilton.

1 min, 54.3597, -8.2600

15 LOUGH MACNEAN UPPER, GLENFARNE

Little slipway and forested picnic area at the start point for the Glenfarne Forest Walk. Seek out Myles' Big Stone (54.3080, -7.9744), a glacial erratic and a nearby oval enclosure that may be an old fort and burial ground (54.3077, -7.9745). From N16/R281 go through the demesne gate house (F91 R8YT) and follow 'boat quay' signs. 100m before the quay a delightful little lakeshore lane branches off to the L, worth exploring or overnighting.

1 min, 54.2999, -7.9636

16 TULLYDERMOT FALLS

Most people stop at the easy access from the roadside parking down to the viewpoint, but exploring downstream through woodland will reward you with more pools.

2 mins, 54.1719, -7.7717

17 CORRY STRAND, LOUGH ALLEN

This small sandy strand above a mostly stony shore has parking on the lane in and is one of the surprisingly few easily accessible spots on the Lough Ree shore. It is visited by locals in the summer, and a few wild camping tents appear. Signed R from the R200 about 4.6km E from Drumkeeran, then entrance R after 400m.

1 min, 54.1643, -8.0821

18 SPENCER HARBOUR, LOUGH ALLEN

In the 19th century, this was a working harbour where 200 people were employed shipping bricks and iron up the canal. A tall brick chimney and ruins stand as a reminder of that

past in what is now a peaceful cove with large floating boat quay and picnic tables under the trees. Corry island is offshore for kayakers. From Drumkeerin follow the R280 SW dir Drumshanbo 4km, signed on L.

1 min, 54.1411, -8.0986

19 CORMONGAN PIER, LOUGH ALLEN

Sheltered swimming with wonderful views across the lake, a sandy shore, a pier (no depth for jumping), and space for a handful of cars. There's another slipway 50m to the N. Signed 5km N of Drumshanbo, off the R207.

1 min, 54.0921, -8.0359

20 PÓL AN EAS, YELLOW RIVER *

Double cascades tumble into the deep, wooded 'pool of the falls'. Locals swim despite the signs or there is paddling downstream with a grassy picnic area. A beautiful and easy spot for a quick dip, perhaps after the exertion of climbing Sliabh an Iarainn (see entry). Follow the L1313 for Aghacashel from Ballinamore 5.4km, through Aughnasheelin, and the falls are signed R with a car park by the road.

1 min, 54.0666, -7.8769

21 LOUGH MEELAGH, CRANNÓG & TOMBS

Swim out to the crannóg island near the shore from the little jetty (with car park), or follow the loop trail through native Knockranny Woods to the court tomb remains (54.0544, -8.1554) – you can circumnavigate the whole lake (see walk entry).

1 min, 54.0545, -8.1510

22 ACRES LAKE, SHANNON BLUEWAY

From Lough Allen kayakers can paddle some 70km on the Shannon Blueway all the way down to Lanesborough (water quality variable after heavy rain). Walkers and cyclists can follow alongside some sections that also offer easy access for swims, like this gentle start on the Lough Allen Canal, rejoining the river at Battlebridge. The picnic area with parking and pier on the edge of picturesque Drumshanbo also has a fun 600m floating boardwalk. Walkers can cross at Drumhauver Bridge or Drumleague Lock to loop back via the country lane. Electric Bike Trails in Leitrim village offers half or whole day e-bike hire (N41 T6V6, +353 71 9623609).

2 mins, 54.0383, -8.0488

23 KEELDRA LAKE

A popular family swimming spot with parking on the quiet road, toilets, and a long jetty. Follow the trail away around the lake edge R to pick your own swimming spot, with more jetties to discover; you can loop the lake on the path and the lane. Follow L1566 S from Cloone village

GAA ground 2km, then turn L at crossroads for lake after 800m.

1 min, 53.9190, -7.7728

LOST RUINS

24 CASTLE CALDWELL, BELLEEK

A walk out to Rossergole Point point passes through old walled gardens and around the ruins of the ivy-clad 17th-century chapel and Gothic castle, with red squirrels above and bluebells in late spring. In the 1840s deposits of kaolin and feldspar from here were used in the iconic Belleek china; near the tip of the peninsula is a lime kiln, and quicklime was shipped out by barge. Signed E of Belleek on the A47 (BT93 2AH); go through a set of castle gates to park on the corner after 750m.

5 mins, 54.4929, -7.9738

25 TULLY CASTLE

Popular but beautiful ruined plantation castle with a short, bloody history; built in 1615, it was burned in the Rebellion of 1641 and those in it killed. Inside accessible in summer, with a lovely barrel-vaulted undercroft and an exhibition at the gate, but the site and views are open all year. A short shore walk leads through broadleaf woodlands to a jetty. Well-signed from A46.

2 mins, 54.4577, -7.8054

26 MONEA CASTLE

A beautiful avenue of beeches leads to this dramatic tower house shell with round turrets and stepped parapets, designed with a distinct Scottish feel for an immigrant prelate. It was gutted by fire in the mid-18th century and abandoned. In the 20th century 'a weird woman named Bell McCabe' lived in a vault under one of the towers until she was evicted by the owner, to avoid the possible inconvenience of her dying there. Turn off B81 onto Castletown Road through Monea for 1km; castle is signed right down driveway.

1 min, 54.3927, -7.7472

27 AGHANAGLACK TOMB

An impressive tomb with twin galleries and a court at each end, set on a remote hillside amid forestry. Sadly, the roof stones were removed in the 19th century and used in buildings nearby. Signed on narrow lane from Boho Road to Ballintempo forest gate. Continue 800m along track (on foot if closed) to find sign on R.

1 min, 54.3405, -7.8515

28 CREEVELEA FRIARY *

This ruined Franciscan friary was founded in 1508, accidentally burned in 1536, and suppressed in 1541. The church is almost intact, with an assortment of ornate windows

and a wonderful arcaded cloister with carved pillars – look for Saint Francis of Assisi preaching to birds under one of the northern arches. You can drive right to it (signed off the R287, 1.4km W from the S end of Dromahair), but the path over the river from the centre of Dromahair, signed at the right of F91 AT22, is a nicer approach.

2 mins, 54.2309, -8.3095

29 KILRONAN GROTTO & DOON POINT

A little-visited but gorgeous romantic grotto ruin to explore, once a gatehouse to Kilronan House (now a hotel). From the main road look out for the old triple archway entrance. There's a little picnic spot with parking and direct access to Meelagh Lough (see entry), or head along the path R along the shore for the magically tangled Annagh Wood and Doon Wood – it's worth walking 1.5km out to the tip of Doon Point, an ancient promontory fort, for the view back down the lake (54.0591, -8.1821).

2 mins, 54.0614, -8.1661

SACRED & ANCIENT

30 JANUS FIGURES, BOA ISLAND

Often called the Janus stone, the larger of these two enigmatic figures in a small Caldragh Cemetery on Boa Island has a double-faced triangular head and crossed arms. People leave offerings in a groove on the top. Probably early medieval, it may represent Badhbh, the Celtic war goddess for whom the island is named; the lower body was recently found nearby. The smaller single-sided figure was brought from an early Christian site on the nearby island of Lustymore. Signed lane off the A47, 1.6km from the W island bridge (where there are pontoons with easy parking, 54.5121, -7.9047).

2 mins, 54.5061, -7.8692

31 DEVENISH ISLAND *

Saint Molaise founded a monastery here in the 6th century; it lies on a pilgrimage route to Croagh Patrick, but there are older earthworks from pagan times too. The island setting is serene today, but it was raided by Vikings in 837 and burned twice; the oldest ruins are from the 12th century. These are a small tomb shrine known as St Molaise's House, which may hold his remains, and a fine round tower with a conical cap, both with typical Romanesque decoration. The later church and priory also have some fine carvings, including a detailed head of St Brigid. But the most ornate is the high cross, reduced to a shaft and the centre of the head, covered with figures, plants and dense knotwork. Several local boat companies run trips, daily in summer, weekends in winter; try ernetours.com or ernewatertaxi.com.

2 mins, 54.3705, -7.6560

35

36

36

32 BOHO HIGH CROSS & ROCK ART

In the graveyard of the Sacred Heart Chapel stands the ornate shaft of a 10th-century high cross decorated with biblical scenes. Far more ancient is the Neolithic Reyfad rock art – clear cup and ring markings covering five boulders. The chapel is on the Carrickbeg Road, 2.3km N of Boho, with parking; the rocks are up the lane beside the graveyard, L after 450m and in a field L after another 400m near 54.3642, -7.8282.

1 min, 54.3646, -7.8206

33 ST PATRICK'S HOLY WELL, BELCOO

The village takes its name from this very pretty spring and stream, with steps down to the bullaun stones and shallow bubbling pool beneath raggedy trees. Almost certainly an ancient pagan site, traditionally visited over Lughnasa at the start of August, it is said to cure nervous disorders in those who see a white trout there or take the water, reputed to be the coldest in Ireland.

2 mins, 54.3060, -7.8838

34 KILLINAGH CHURCHYARD & LOUGH

This ruined church and graveyard are easily overlooked on the shores of Lough Macnean. According to local tradition, Saints Brigid and Laighne founded a church here in the early 6th century on a site sacred to a pagan idol known as Crom Cruaich – bullauns with cursing-stones and a possible megalithic mound behind support the idea. It was badly damaged on the 'Night of the Big Wind' in 1839, which destroyed buildings all over Ireland. The signed (may point wrong way) path is through a field gate on N16 (54.2873, -7.9100). Park on verge, or 400m E is a car park with toilets at the slipway; you could kayak over the border in the middle of the lake.

4 mins, 54.2892, -7.9100

35 CAVAN BURREN TOMBS

Explore a boulder landscape of portal and wedge tombs among the woods. The Burren in Clare is world famous, but the name means 'rocky place' and the Cuilcagh Lakelands Geopark has its own Burren of limestone dotted with sandstone glacial erratics. There's a big car park and good gravel paths through the Giant's Leap dry river valley, boulder fields and sinkholes to slab tombs like the Calf House, Giant's Grave, Boulder Grave and Cairn Dolmen, as well as a cup-and-ring marked boulder and a promontory fort. The 26km Cavan Way passes through. Take the R206 just W of Blacklion, entrance is L after 4km.

5 mins, 54.2647, -7.8886

CAVES & CAVERNS

36 POLNAGOLLUM COOLARKIN, BELMORE

This picturesque waterfall streaming 12m down a cliff face into a mossy crater to vanish into a river cave was used as a location in Games of Thrones; you can scramble down from the viewing platform to stone steps a the mouth of the cavern, which is blocked by a fall a short way in. Park at Belmore Forest car park (54.3383, -7.8143, signed off Boho Road); 30m S is the barred forest track, continue and find path L by tall cliff with climbing bolts.

5 mins, 54.3366, -7.8128

37 WHITE FATHERS CAVE, BLACKLION

The river disappears for 400m through three large caverns under a once-Franciscan monastery, hence the name. The little stone gorge is sinuously undercut, clean and sculpted. The third chamber is exceptionally beautiful, but is chest-deep with a 'sump' that can trap people in high water levels so full exploration is limited to experienced cavers please. This is also a protected area for Daubenton's bats, which roost in the ceiling and hunt above the water – so just admire it from near the mouth with a bit of a paddle, maybe staying to see the bats at dusk. Follow N16 W from Blacklion 3km and turn L dir Glangevlin; the cave is signed

40

44

44

42

almost immediately R. Pull off carefully after about 100m before the sign and gate R.

3 mins, 54.2865, -7.9210

38 CARROWMORE CAVERNS & VIEWS

A remote and beautiful mountain road leads up into the Geevagh karst area, with old quarry ledges, sinkholes, and views to Knocknarea and the Ox Mountains above the road to S. Experienced cavers can seek out what the first explorer here in the 1950s called 'the horrors of Carrowmore' via a deep pothole or a horizontal passage (54.1368, -8.2605), some way on a snaking track NE from the stone sign by the lane.

10 mins, 54.1355, -8.2634

SUNSET HILLS & VIEWS

39 KEELOGES MOUNTAIN

Cliffs rear up into an escarpment dominating the landscape with far-reaching W views from the plateau top, which also conceals beautiful Tin Whistle Lake with a shale sand beach and infinity-pool view. The only access is 1.2km up the steep side, through the field gate on the R280 (54.3976, -8.3039, park at church 300m N or junction 150m S), aiming for a zig-zag path to the R of the eroded gully. There was a longer, easier route, the Arroo Trail, but it is closed due to abuse. No dogs.

25 mins, 54.3963, -8.2898

39

40 EAGLE'S ROCK, GLENADE

A stack of rocks carved by two colliding glaciers, Eagle's Rock or Hag's Leap is a fantastical jumble of geology dominated by a sheer cliff escarpment and great towering stack, so sheer it was only first climbed in the 1970s. The walk takes you along the ridge for superb views. There is a car park, and a good gravel track at the start SW up towards the escarpment – but then you need a map and proper walking gear. There is also a warning sign against trespassing, but usually no access issues; no dogs.

60 mins, 54.3884, -8.3358 ?

41 STAIRWAY TO HEAVEN, CUILCAGH

This popular gravel and boardwalk trail leads 6km across blanket bog and up a wooden staircase to breathtaking panoramic views at the boggy and stone-strewn summit of Cuilcagh Mountain. Changeable weather and poor mobile reception; no dogs allowed. Medium-sized car park, well signed from the Marble Arch Road (54.2500, -7.8157).

120 mins, 54.2066, -7.8247

42 MULLAGHGARVE MASS ROCK & SLIABH AN IARAINN *

One of Ireland's most dramatically sited Mass Rocks, hidden in a deep rock chasm between

41

43

45

towering cliffs. For many the views from here are good enough to make further climbing unnecessary, but the main hill beckons above, looming over Lough Allen. Sliabh an Iarainn, the 'Iron Mountain', was mined from prehistory until deforestation exhausted supplies of charcoal for smelting in the 18th century. Ancient legend says the magical Tuatha Dé Danann landed in 'cloud-ships' on the summit – obscuring cloud can arrive rapidly, and it is boggy all year. Head SW from the small parking area at the end of the forestry road (54.0870, -7.9624).

60 mins, 54.0841, -7.9667

ANCIENT FOREST

43 OLD CASTLE ARCHDALE & PARK

This easy country park boasts a well-maintained ruined castle and forest paths to a boat jetty (600m W, 54.4880, -7.7217). Distance swimmers could cross 500m to White Island, where the ruined church has intriguing 9th-century carved figures (54.4881, -7.7303). Well signed from A46, 1.6km N of Lisnarick.

2 mins, 54.4870, -7.7129

44 CLADAGH GLEN & HANGING ROCK

This limestone gorge with exposed strata, dramatic cascades, caves and occasional pools is filled with a relic ancient wood of ash, hazels, yew and beech, with wood anemones and bluebells in spring; home to butterflies, red squirrels and pine martens. The 'arch' is a cave entrance, with a natural hole through the adjacent rock and added grottos. The well-maintained river path heads S and connects via wooden steps up to the Marble Arch Caves car park (paid entry). Park at the gate on Marble Arch Road, 5.4km SE from Blacklion (54.2697, -7.8035). On the same road 2.6km closer to Blacklion is the entrance to the magnificent 30m limestone cliffs of Hanging Rock (54.2787, -7.8400); juniper and yew trees cling to them, and one of the best ancient ash woodlands on the island lies at their base. To the W it blends into the mature oak, beech, great willow and elm of Rossaa Wood, another home to red squirrels and pine martens.

15 mins, 54.2591, -7.8150

45 DRUID'S ALTAR

Mossy stone slab tomb under an ancient oak in open woodland, possibly a folly. Just 50m from roadside, but a bit tricky to find among the undergrowth. A track from 53.8919, -7.8444 passes behind it.

5 mins, 53.8908, -7.8411

46 FARNAGHT WOOD

A new native wood with birch, oak and crab apple is growing here, the first of several established by the Native Woodland Trust. At the back corner furthest from the gate are three ancient hawthorns, the foundation of the site. No trees will ever be harvested, and the site is completely left to nature with no paths, so you will need boots. To E off tiny lane there's a field gate and space to park on the grassy verge.

10 mins, 53.8584, -7.7811

WILDLIFE WONDERS

47 BÓTHAR NA NAOMH, CLOONE

This isn't the wildest, with flat gravelled paths, but provides a very accessible and family-friendly walk through mixed woodlands and wet meadows full of flowers around Anaghmaconway Lough, where you can watch water-birds including resident swans and among the reeds lie a pier and slipways into the water. There's a recreated crannog feature, fulacht fia, and causeway that make clear things that can be obscure when looking at ancient remains, willow sculptures, extensive planting of native broadleaf trees, and a variety of looped paths. Signed L 600m N out of Cloone, then gate L after 300m; three parking areas ahead and L before the lake.

10 mins, 53.9479, -7.7973

48

53

56

57

TRADITIONAL PUBS

48 THE LINNET INN, BOHO

Known locally as McKenzie's, this unique pub has open fires and 'cave room' decor with stone walls and ceilings and artistic versions of cave paintings, in homage to the nearby limestone caves. Dessie inherited the pub from his parents and it is the heart of the village. Dog-friendly, with campervan parking. 174 Boho Road, Tullyholvin Lower, BT74 5BB, +44 286 6341218

54.3462, -7.7998

49 STANFORD VILLAGE INN & TEA ROOM

This 200-year-old tea room and pub has been run for six generations by the same family, and some of the fittings in the fascinatingly cluttered interior may have been there for its entire history. Great beers from the local Lough Gill brewery are on the bar, and there's a woodburner to warm you up in winter. Main Street, Dromahair, F91 E9E8, +353 71 9164140

54.2298, -8.3024

ORGANIC & GASTRO

50 LEITRIM HILL CREAMERY *

Tangy goat's-milk cheese, hand-made ice cream, and dairy-based sweets like fudge and cajeta caramel spread. Farm open for visits in the summer, but products are available year round at The Hidden Corner Cheese Shop (Unit 2 Market Yard, Carrick-On-Shannon, N41 CD45) and at farmers' markets in Manorhamilton on Fridays, Boyle on Saturdays, and Sligo Airport, Strandhill on Sundays. Leitrim Hill, Drumcong, N41 EH79, +353 85 1852385

54.0346, -7.9544

51 ORGANIC CENTRE, ROSSINVER

This education and training centre has gardens and an orchard you can wander around and a café with delicious food. It's a favoured refuelling stop for touring cyclists, catering well for vegetarians and vegans. You can follow a riverside walk from here up to the lovely Fowley's Falls (see entry). Sraud, Rossinver, F91 H978, +353 71 9854338

54.3926, -8.1193

52 MACNEAN HOUSE & RESTAURANT

Serious fine dining with local produce, in the lifelong home of chef, author and TV presenter Neven MacGuire. Booking highly advisable. Blacklion, F91 YK0F, +353 71 9853022

54.2913, -7.8766

WATERSIDE RETREATS

53 PINK APPLE ORCHARD GLAMPING

Choose from a grass-roofed Hobbit House, the Woodsman's teepee or several yurts, spread among apple trees, with pink blossom in spring, and fruits that are harvested for organic juice and cider, available to sample. The low-impact site has its own springs, vegetable gardens and chickens, and composting toilets, while wood fuels the heating stoves and a pizza oven that can be pre-booked. There is outdoor seating and a fire-pit, children's play area, books and games and a communal kitchen and access to the shores of Lough Allen (Canadian canoe rides can be booked). Corry, Drumkeeran, N41 AC03, +353 83 4886645, irelandglamping.com

54.1666, -8.062

54 MCGUIRE'S RED DOOR COTTAGES

A quirky close of traditional-style cottages, built for holidays in the 1970s with old-fashioned flagstones and open fires. It's on a roadside, but the family also run an artisan bakery and tea room on site and the Acres Lake Boardwalk (see entry) is opposite. Carrick Road, Drumshanbo, N41 V306, +353 71 9641033, selfcateringleitrim.ie

54.0366, -8.0479

55 LOUGH RINN CARAVAN & CAMPING

This small council-run lakeside site has bays for campervans or caravans but also tent space. This is also the public access point to the lough for swimming and canoeing. Clooncahir, Mohill, N41 KH22, +353 86 8254428

53.8994 -7.8551

56 FOREST BUBBLE DOMES, FINN LOUGH

Forest bathe while taking a bath and fall asleep with the stars as your ceiling. These clear bubble lodges hidden in the forest offer spa trails with lake swimming, saunas, and floatation and bubble pools. Seasonal local produce is used for meals in the Barn restaurant and breakfast hampers delivered to your door. Upscale pricing, but truly unique; the whole Finn Lough site is adults only. 33 Letter Road, Aghnablaney, BT93 2BB, +44 286 8380360

54.5163, -7.8891

57 FLOATING BOATHOUSE, CARRICKREAGH

Modern-build, fully-floating cabin on Lough Erne, perfect for those who like to start the day with a dip or paddle. airbnb.co.uk/rooms/52613383

54.4199, -7.7353

58 SHANNON RIVER BOAT HIRE

For a complete immersion into the green and silver heart of Ireland, hire a river boat and sleep on the open water. A good place to start looking is the simply named Shannon River, who have a very informative website with maps and company listings, and can handle bookings. +353 71 9658964, shannon-river.com

54.3003, -7.6370

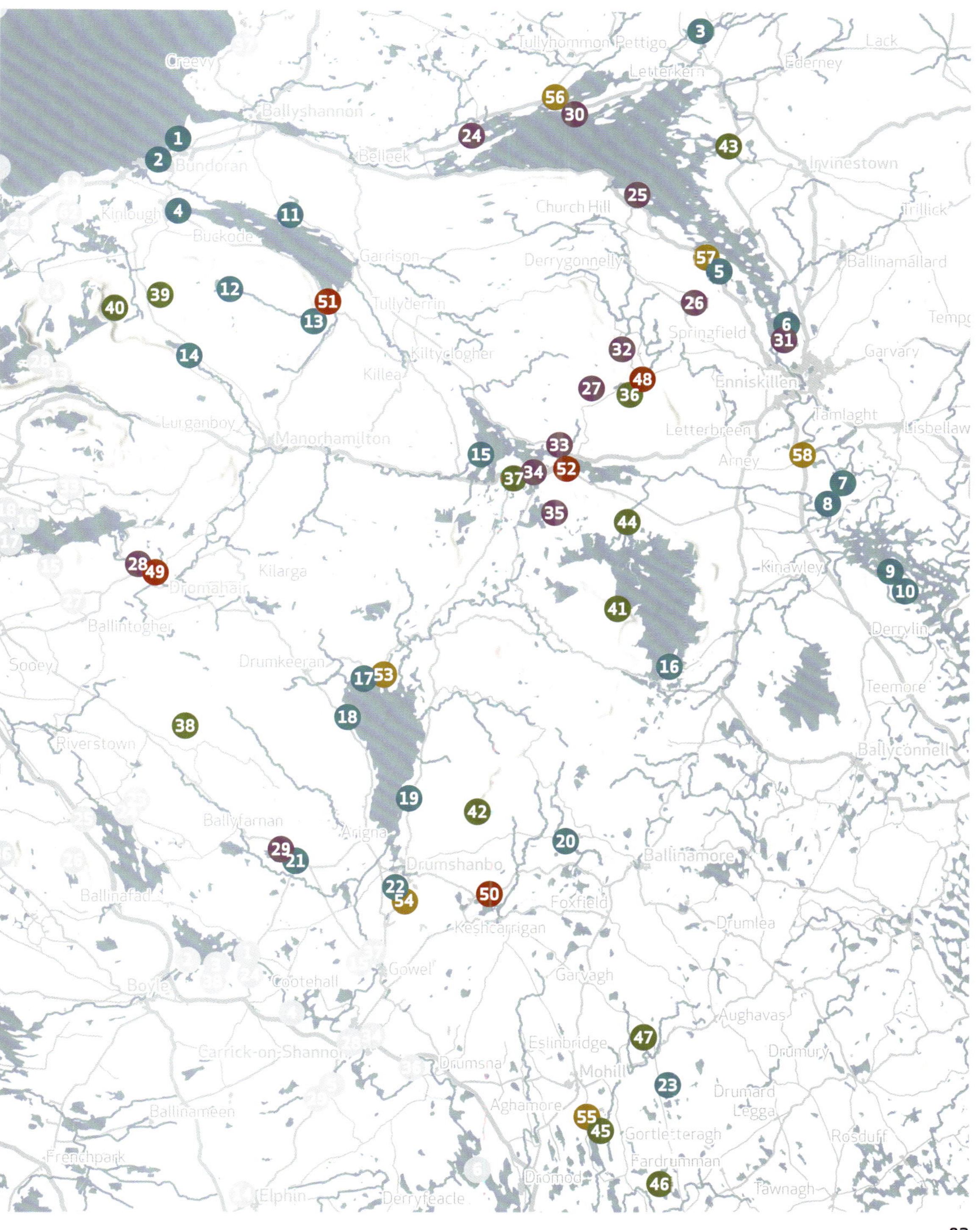

Creevy
Tullyhommon
Pettigo
Lack
Letterkern
Ederney
Ballyshannon
Belleek
Bundoran
Irvinestown
Kinlough
Buckode
Church Hill
Trillick
Garrison
Derrygonnelly
Ballinamallard
Tullyderrin
Springfield
Kiltyclogher
Garvary
Killea
Enniskillen
Lurganboy
Manorhamilton
Tamlaght
Letterbreen
Lisbellaw
Arney
Kilarga
Dromahair
Kinawley
Ballintogher
Derrylin
Sooey
Drumkeeran
Teemore
Riverstown
Ballyconnell
Ballyfarnan
Arigna
Ballinamore
Drumshanbo
Ballinafad
Foxfield
Drumlea
Keshcarrigan
Gowel
Garvagh
Boyle
Cootehall
Aughavas
Eslinbridge
Carrick-on-Shannon
Drumsna
Drumury
Mohill
Drumard
Aghamore
Legga
Ballinameen
Gortletteragh
Rosduff
Frenchpark
Fardrumman
Dromod
Tawnagh
Elphin
Derryfeacle
1
2
3
4
5
6
7
8
9
10
11
12
13
14
15
16
17
18
19
20
21
22
23
24
25
26
27
28
29
30
31
32
33
34
35
36
37
38
39
40
41
42
43
44
45
46
47
48
49
50
51
52
53
54
55
56
57
58

SLIGO

Our perfect weekend

- → **Cross** the causeway to Coney Island to find the wishing chair and perfect beach, but leave before the tide covers the causeway again!
- → **Drift** around Lough Gill on a kayak, seeking your own perfect lake isle, with picnic supplies from Kate's Kitchen in Sligo town.
- → **Swim** at the Rosses beaches, favourites of W.B. Yeats, and camp almost on the shore at Greenlands campsite.
- → **Stroll** around the wild, flower-studded headland to Killaspugbrone church and take a dip at the deserted crescent of Nuns' Beach below.
- → **Jump** in the glorious Poll Gorm rock pool, climb the secret stairs in Easkey Castle for the sunset.
- → **Walk** the Duneill riverbank and country lanes from Dromore West Waterfall to lovely little Pollnadivva pier, dipping on the way.
- → **Take** a 'rockpool ramble' with Prannie Rhatigan to find fantastic seaweeds, or walk out on Streedagh Beach at low tide to find the last remains of the wrecked 'Butter Boat'.
- → **Explore** up through stands of old sessile oak, to great views from Union Rock where the landlord flew a Union Jack on rent days.

1

2

7

Sligo is associated with two iconic names: Benbulbin and the poet buried 'under' it, W.B. Yeats. The mountain's ice-carved shape looks a little like an Irish Uluru, and it can be as contentious to climb; past conflicts have seen farmers patrolling with shotguns around the famous Gleniff Horseshoe. A more approachable summit is the classic and popular Knocknarea, topped by 'Queen Maeve's Grave', but there are other hilltop cairns like Carrowkeel that are far less visited, perhaps just because nobody has made up a royal story for them.

W.B. Yeats lies in Drumcliffe graveyard, but his presence is strong across the county. 'The Lake Isle of Innisfree' arose from memories of sparkling Lough Gill, with several islands to choose from. He immortalised Glencar Waterfall – although in spate, the Devil's Chimney next door is even more spectacular. For swimming waters, the biggest draw is Strandhill, but around the corner Ballysadare Bay estuary is quieter.

Armada ships foundered off this coast, and Streedagh has wrecks far below, as well as a later skeleton on the sands. To the west the shore is rockier, with piers and pools like lovely Poll Gorm. You can even cross a tidal causeway to the original Coney Island that gave its name to the New York one.

Easkey bog dominates the interior, so woodland walks here are relatively few, but Sligo has one of the most curious in the country, the unique Glen below Knocknarea. An arrow-straight limestone rift, it feels like a lost-world jungle. Easier to wander are the woods on the shores of Lough Gill, including the old parkland of Hazelwood House, now being restored.

The county ruins range from Carrowmore's ancient Neolithic cairns to churches that feel almost modern in comparison. Boyle Abbey, in the heart of the town that grew up around it, has medieval carvings of fantastical animals and dancing figures, while tiny Killaspugbrone, visited by St Patrick, is vanishing into remote coastal dunes. Later remains tell of troubled times, with castles and signal towers all along the coast.

The Irish name Sligeach means 'abounding in shells', and this county is famed for oysters. Great food culture is spread across the whole region: you can take a seaweed foraging tour, eat local venison, and sample great beers from two craft breweries, Lough Gill and the highly adventurous White Hag.

You may not find Yeats' silver apples of the moon, or golden apples of the sun, but there is plenty to satisfy the most ardent foodie.

6

SECRET BEACHES

1 TRAWALUA STRAND, CLIFFONY

Perhaps Sligo's best wild beach, a 1km walk across fields to huge dunes with mountain views. Strong rip currents in surf conditions. Naturist to the R. Turn off N15 at O'Donnells and after 500m park on gravel/grass R, opp wooden gates (54.4343, -8.4575). Follow track and stream. The far L end, 2km S opp Dernish Island, can be reached from the lane end at 54.4230, -8.4821, but you will have to park back at the houses and walk 700m.

20 mins, 54.4392, -8.4682

2 STREEDAGH BEACH & CONOR'S ISLAND

Park on the sand/mudflat for this beach, or walk 30 mins to the far end to explore the white sands of Conor's Island. Low tides reveal vestiges of the 'Butter Boat', a ship called the Greyhound that foundered in 1770. On the W side of the point 1km before the main beach (54.3974, -8.5665) is a small, secret grey sand cove, with a sunken wedge tomb on the little headland beyond (54.4007, -8.5721). Signed off L3203.

2 mins, 54.4042, -8.5597

3 YELLOW STRAND, RAGHLY

These white sands backed by high dunes are wild and unfrequented, unless you are a surfer, in which case they are legendary – beware of rips. There's almost no parking at the end of the narrow lanes (F91 XH52), so it may be a longer walk than you expect; the Raghly Blowholes are a nearby alternative (see entry).

2 mins, 54.3469, -8.6675

4 CULLEENAMORE STRAND

Around the headland S from the popular Strandhill, sheltered by the dunes, lies a vast crescent of estuarine beach and tidal sands, with delicious salty samphire growing above the tide and a chance of seeing harbour seals resting on the sandbanks. Small car park, good for dogs.

1 min, 54.2592, -8.6010

5 PORTAVADE BEACH

You'll share this estuarine beach with local sheep, but the views are superb. At the end of the lane next to a farm, with room for a few cars. Watch for estuary/tidal currents – best swimming at high tide.

1 min, 54.2554, -8.6408

6 AUGHRIS HEAD PIER & COVE

A popular family beaches with fun pier jumping too. Follow the well-made Aughris Coastal Walk to a hidden shale cove, best for swimming at HT. There's a promontory fort above and a holy well further along (54.2779, -8.7638). Park at the lane end by the slipway and Beach Bar (54.2722, -8.7564, signed 'coastal walk'). Dunmoran Strand on lanes to the E is also popular with car park at 54.2626, -8.7241.

15 mins, 54.2775, -8.7545

7 POLLNADIVVA PIER & TRÁ BHUÍ

Unexpected and beautiful little harbour with long quay, good for swimming when the tide is up, and for sunsets and overnights. Signed off the R297, 8km E from Easkey. The wild Trá Bhuí/Trawwee is a bit further E on the road (54.2608, -8.7932) with grassy beachside parking, perfect for surfing and wild camping.

1 min, 54.2578, -8.8445

CAVES, POOLS & ISLANDS

8 BISHOP'S POOL, MULLAGHMORE

On the tip of the Mullaghmore Head, a large tidal rock pool (actually a small inlet) lies hidden just below the road and a scrappy layby; it's a wonderful place for summer sunsets, swims and campouts. From Mullaghmore/Bunduff Strand (itself beautiful, and backed by machair dunes and rich in shells) continue N 1.5km, one bend beyond the memorial with benches.

15 mins, 54.4728, -8.4554

10

10

8

9

12

9 RAGHLY POINT BLOWHOLE

Follow lane signed Raghly Harbour from parking at 54.3310, -8.6473 to the cliff walk path, and then W 400m to the blowhole; locals jump from the arch into the lagoon below. The remote harbour at the far S of the point is good for sunsets and overnights.

10 mins, 54.3294, -8.6559

10 POLL GORM, EASKEY *

Superb tidal pool with jumps, mostly natural rock with a holding wall built by a handful of dedicated locals in the 1960s. Find the sign board on the lane and descend to the rock ledges below. Continue 300m W to the flat pavement of the headland to see the huge Temple Rock erratic, and views to Easkey Castle; 750m E people overnight/wild camp on Cooanmore Point.

1 min, 54.2932, -8.9420

11 CONEY ISLAND

Drive or cycle the tidal 3km causeway across to this quiet island and remote beach on the W side. There's a little parking above, or park by the E pier, with the low outline of a bastioned fort on the headland S over the bay, and take a coastal walk with a pause to sit in the huge Wishing Chair stone (54.3035, -8.5928). On a summer weekend you might even take a pint from local brewer Lough Gill at Michael J Ward's island pub before leaving. From Scarden (54.2792, -8.5517) there's a six-hour crossing window; text 'Coney' to 51155 to receive the current day's times from the RNLI.

5 mins, 54.2994, -8.5940

WATERFALLS & LAKES

12 DUFF/BANDUFF RIVER WATERFALL

A gravelled path leads up the L bank of the river from the N15 for a total of 3.5km out and back, with pools between rapids and wooded shores. Park in the layby W from bridge. However, by far the best waterfalls – big cascades with huge plunge pools – are actually downstream, towards the sea; climb over the crash barrier and follow a rough path down the L bank.

10 mins, 54.4629, -8.3805

13 DEVIL'S CHIMNEY & GLENCAR

Ireland's tallest waterfall (150m) is only spectacular after heavy rain, when the mist blows up into the air like smoke from a chimney, but it's always a nice woodland walk with ancient yew trees at the base of the cliff. Layby parking and gate at 54.3405, -8.3933 then 700m; if you can't see the falls from the road, they're not running. There's the lakeshore for a dip or just 1.7km E is busier Glencar Waterfall, more reliable and made famous by W.B. Yeats' poem 'The Stolen Child'. There's a tarmac trail

17

15

15

and large car park and café (54.3385, -8.3689).
10 mins, 54.3475 -8.3930

14 GLENIFF BARYTES MILL WATERFALLS

At the start of the beautiful Gleniff Horseshoe loop road, this charming old mill site processed ore from the Glencarbury mine (see entry). There are remains of old processors, several ruined buildings, and a waterwheel beneath a cascade and leat. The stream has a number of waterfalls, particularly at the far end of the riverside path. The mill covered both sides of the road, and across the road is another river with deeper pools, falls and rope swings.
1 min, 54.3977, -8.3998

15 SLISHWOOD & INNISFREE

Wooded lakeshore paths lead E to small coves, a stream for paddling, and views to islands, including one supposed to be W.B. Yeats' famous Innisfree (54.2464, -8.3582). For more lakeshore follow the road further W on R278 for Dooney Rock (54.2383, -8.4281) or Tobernalt pier (see entry), but all locations are shallow and rocky for quite a long way out – bring water shoes or a paddle board!
5 mins, 54.2308, -8.4012

16 HAZELWOOD DEMESNE, LOUGH GILL

The woods of the lakeshore estate land surrounding Hazelwood House and the whiskey distillery are now Coillte forest, full of oaks, bluebells and rare orchids. Follow the sign to the lakeside car park to find the grotto and numerous places to get in the water. For something more secret, park at the turn-off for the car park and walk W 1km for the Garvoge riverside with old boathouse and lime kiln (54.2564, -8.4378).
5 mins, 54.2581, -8.4258

17 TOBERNALT PIER & HOLY WELL

This little concrete jetty is an easy roadside stop to get into the lough for a swim or kayak, although the water is shallow for a long way out. Signed from here is Tobernalt Holy Well, a maintained site with an altar, benches, statues and devotional candles, by a stream with waterfall pools (54.2439, -8.4460). There are entry points on the S shore too, such as in Slishwood (see entry).
2 mins, 54.2454, -8.4424

18 DOORLY PARK, RIVER GARVOGE

An easy launch point for canoes or swimmers, giving access to the wide tree-lined reaches of the majestic Garvoge (sometimes Garavogue) River upstream to Lough Gill. Car park off The Back Avenue.
2 mins, 54.2647, -8.4457

13

14

19

19

20

22

19 MILL FALLS, COLLOONEY

A waterfall thunders down into a pool below the derelict mill, with cascading salmon steps at the side where children play in summer. There are little river beaches downstream. Park in Collooney streets and walk in through the housing estate, which has towing signs.

1 min, 54.1861, -8.4931

20 LADIES BRAE, OWENBOY RIVER

High in the heather-clad Ox Mountains, this charming roadside picnic area has a pretty mountain stream and deep, long pool below rapids. The views on the road up here are some of the best in Sligo. Just SE there's a small roadside lake (54.1569, -8.6779). If coming S from Skreen also stop for a dip at Lough Achree, reputedly made by an earthquake in 1490 (gate at 54.2119, -8.7289 then 600m)

1 min, 54.1662, -8.6989

21 EASKY LOUGH & COOPER'S LODGE

This otherworldly lake shimmers below big skies by a lonely road through a bowl of heathery hills. As well as a swim (stony going in), you can walk all around the shore; the blanket bog here hosts Ireland's only native reptile, the common lizard, and threatened birds like the Greenland white-fronted goose. Turn S off N59 on the L63072 at crossroads just W of Dromore West; the long, straight lane passes the ruins of Cooper's Lodge (54.1920, -8.8587), supposedly abandoned by its owner because of a fearsome spectral horse – a tale probably invented to keep people away from an illicit poitín still nearby.

1 min, 54.1596, -8.8441

22 DROMORE WEST FALLS, RIVER DUNEILL

This graceful stepped cascade hides below the road bridge in Dromore West, above the derelict Old Mill. Across the road 100m E is the Duneill River Walk, which follows the course of the river through mature woods to the coast road. It's a beautiful route, although disappointing that it doesn't run all the way to the sea; 1.8km on the quiet lanes at the end will get you to Pollnadivva Pier (see entry).

1 min, 54.2489, -8.8723

LOST RUINS

23 LABBY ROCK & LUGH'S SEAT

With an extraordinary grass-topped 65-tonne capstone, this is the grave of the magical king Nuada of the Silver Arm (the original inspiration for the prosthetics of Darth Vader). Park on lane in small pull-in at 54.0885, -8.3066 and follow footpath sign through field gate opp, then 500m NW. Combine with a walk to the circular grassy hilltop cairn of Lugh's Seat on the plateau. Continue 200m N along the lane to find marked footpath on R through pedestrian gate.

15 mins, 54.0905, -8.3128

24 BALLINDOON ABBEY

Beautifully situated on a rise overlooking Lough Arrow, this Dominican ruin has arches galore, tracery windows, and the remains of an external cantilever staircase. It was built around 1507 and dissolved in 1585, but the attached graveyard remains in use, keeping access open. Park on the lane and cross field via kissing gate.

2 mins, 54.0833, -8.3224

25 CASTLEBALDWIN FORTIFIED HOUSE

Little known, obscure in history, and lost in fields, this early 17th-century shell shows several defensive features such as gun slits, a machicolation above the door, and a return socket for a drawbar in the frame. It can be freely explored from the lane (access from the kissing gate and sign at 54.0789, -8.3668). According to unfounded local tradition, Baldwin was a soldier of Cromwell (in fact he owned it in a century later) and the house was burned by his servants; however it met its end, it was certainly unroofed by the 19th century.

4 mins, 54.0789, -8.3668

26 CARROWKEEL PASSAGE TOMBS

An atmospheric hilltop with over 14 Neolithic burial cairns, some of which you can crawl into. The first (Cairn G) even has a 'roofbox' slot that captures the midsummer sunset against the summit of Doomore. Like many, these cairns once included chunks of white quartz, but sadly souvenir hunters have long since taken it all. The panoramic views from the summit are glorious, and in evening light you may make out the 160 hut circles of Ireland's oldest known Neolithic village, Mullaghfarna, on a plateau to the E (54.0564, -8.3699) with another cairn on the summit above them; other cairns at Carrowmore and above Keshcorran Caves (see entries) were built by the same population. Signed from the L1404 3km SW from Castlebaldwin dir Ballymote. Follow the rough track 'cul de sac' to a small parking area at the end (54.0571, -8.3793) then walk R uphill 200m.

3 mins, 54.0542, -8.3773

27 CASHELORE STONE FORT

There are old walls and plenty to see at this little-known Iron Age fort. Caiseal Óir means the fort of gold, and local legend says this is buried below and guarded by an eel, but can only be retrieved by a party of three, two of whom would be killed by the eel. It's a pleasant 300m walk along a signed footpath from the S (54.2066, -8.3791, from Ballintogher turn N opp church, then 1.2km).

5 mins, 54.2099, -8.3779

24

25

23

28 GLENCARBURY MINE & GLENIFF HORSESHOE

When this barytes mine closed in 1975 the whole complex was abandoned: a miners' hostel, crushers, dynamite storage and a cable car system – plus underground railways and tunnels that you can peer into. Historic access along the old miners' track from the beautiful Horsehoe loop road to the N (54.3708, -8.4150) also gave direct access to the high level Gleniff Horseshoe walk, but is now disputed and aggressively defended by the owners, particularly if you have dogs. Diarmuid and Grainne's Caves in the cliff face above (54.3735 -8.4255) are therefore also off limits, but visible from road. The longer, less dramatic but locally agreed route to the mine is from Glencar Lough side, starting at 54.3409, -8.3752 near Glencar Falls parking, and across commonage on the summit; no dogs. Once you are up there, the views from Annacoona and Benwiskin summits are easily as dramatic as Benbulbin. Group treks with highhopesmountaintreks.com

60 mins, 54.3551, -8.4119

29 CREEVYKEEL COURT TOMB

The finest example of a Neolithic court tomb in Ireland, thought to be 5,500 years old, and so substantial at 55m long that it was once called the Fort of Bhaoisgin. Wedge-shaped in outline, its oval court, a burial gallery and three subsidiary chambers are clear to see. In early Christian times it was re-used as an iron foundry, in the 19th century as a poitín distillery, and most recently as a cillín. Look for the signed layby on the busy N15, 1.7m E of Cliffoney.

1 min, 54.4386, -8.4333

30 QUEEN MAEVE'S GRAVE, KNOCKNAREA

Good paths and plenty of people go to the top of this iconic hill, whose cairn-topped peak dominates the landscape with massive views in all directions. There are several more tombs on the hill, and if you start from the SE car park (54.2532, -8.5576) you will also pass the site of a deserted village on L.

45 mins, 54.2586, -8.5740

31 CARROWMABLA SIGNAL TOWER

One of the best-preserved signal towers in the west, built within a large oval enclosure that may be Neolithic. It still has vast views in all directions, although none of the adjacent signal stations can now be seen. Take the L2302 WAW/coast road sign from the R297 5km SE of Easkey, then immediately L (unsigned lane). Follow 450m to the last house and ask permission from the nice farmer, as this is on private land.

3 mins, 54.2613, -8.8799

26

28

32 EASKY CASTLE & RUINED CHURCH

Sited on the shore by the pier, this 13th-century tower shell (aka Roslee or O'Dowd Castle) has a secret 'intra-mural' staircase (crouch down and go through what appears to be a fireplace) up to the top. Easky village itself is lovely and is reached via pretty riverside walk with pools. In the village, find door in wall which leads to the ruined church. It ran out of space to put bodies below ground so families had to bring their own cart-load of clay for any burial – hence the number of table top tombs. Signed Easky Beach from R297.

1 min, 54.2918, -8.9566

SACRED & ANCIENT

33 DEER PARK COURT TOMB *

A marked woodland walk winds up to this hilltop. The 30m tomb (also called Magheraghanrush) is still clear: half-oval court in the centre, with a passage entrance, and galleries at either end. Even with some non-native forestry around, the siting remains majestic, with views to Lough GIll and surrounding peaks and tombs. Car park is signed off the R278 4.5km E from Sligo (54.2820, -8.3758).

10 mins, 54.2791, -8.3815

34 CARROWMORE TOMB COMPLEX

There are 30 surviving tombs in this vast Neolithic complex, the most ancient heart of the dense ritual landscape here, so the car park and small visitor centre are only to be expected. The mighty Listoghil has a 34m-diameter cairn with a corridor into the uncovered central chamber, and the smaller satellite tombs and circles lie both within and beyond sight. Best in early summer when it is meadowy. 10am–5pm, €5. Well signed S off the L3507 just W of Sligo.

3 mins, 54.2507, -8.5197

35 KILLASPUGBRONE CHURCH & BEACH

A threadlike path around a headland carpeted with wildflowers in summer leads to a hidden church, almost engulfed by the sands with views to Coney Island (see entry). An elderly St Patrick lost a tooth here, now in reliquary in the National Museum. Below lie the quiet crescent sands and shallow waters of Nuns' Beach. Park at the tiny airport (54.2783, -8.5988) and walk W then R along the coast. There is a long looped route, so you could continue, or walk back and – if you visit on a Sunday – refuel at the farmers' vmarket in the old hangars.

20 mins, 54.2828, -8.6023

36

38

36

GLENS & CAVERNS

36 KESHCORRAN CAVES, KEASH

Sixteen interconnecting limestone caves in the escarpment, with superb W views. Bones of brown bear and arctic lemming have been found here, as well as signs of human use since the Neolithic. Mentioned in the legends of the Fianna, their name comes from a tale that the harpist Corran put a huge magical sow to sleep here with his enchanted music. Those in search of a higher challenge can continue up to the cairn on the summit, but there is no path to this; the peak rises in a set of tough terraces, requiring proper shoes and a couple of hours. There is parking on the lane below, 1km N of Keash village (54.0584, -8.4535).

15 mins, 54.0579, -8.4500

37 THE GLEN, KNOCKNAREA *

This fern-hung canyon between sheer limestone walls is cool, damp and muddy. It is an entirely natural feature, a rift in the mountainside, 1km long and generally 20m deep with no phone signal. There is a glade of beech trees and rope swing at the start, and from here each section feels more magical than the last. On L3507 1.3km W from the signs for Knocknarea (see entry), park in a gravelled layby L; 200m beyond, downhill, is a white well on R. Look for the gap in the hedge opposite (54.2483, -8.5763). Follow the path down, and when the wall on your R becomes solid and there's a fallen tree ahead, turn L. No signs.

5 mins, 54.2477, -8.5742

HIGHPOINTS & WILDLIFE

38 BENBULBIN

Dominating the surrounding landscape, this is perhaps the most recognisable mountain in Ireland, with its flat top and towering glacier-carved limestone cliffs rising above shale slopes; ascent is by one route, strictly no dogs. Park at Luke's Bridge (54.3735, -8.4659) signed from the N15 2km S of Grange. Walk over the bridge and follow R fork up the river 700m. Cross the river R and follow L fork, which heads pretty straight to a dip in the ridge. The path follows the stream up the slope, then R along the ridge to the trig point, iconic plateau edge and spectacular views (400m ascent). The competent could combine with a loop to King's Mountain on S side of plateau. Its jagged and rifted escarpment hides the Annach Re Mhor canyon, a narrow fissure splitting the limestone hillside in two – exploring it requires a mix of scrambling and abseiling through narrow natural passageways.

90 mins, 54.3649, -8.47419

39 UNION ROCK

Large smooth rock crag, reached by a good looped trail with boardwalks through a nature reserve, where an area of old sessile oak woodland is fenced off from the mixed forestry and deer for another walk. Plenty of wildlife to look out for on the way up, and huge views at the top, where the landlord used to hoist a Union Jack on rent day. Car park signed off R284 (54.2136, -8.4713).

30 mins, 54.2055, -8.4853

40 KNOCKNASHEE HILLFORT & FRIARY

There are huge panoramas from this hillfort – to the W lie the Ox Mountains, to the N and E Knocknarea with Queen Maeve's Grave and the Keshcorran Caves (see entries). On a really clear day you can see Croagh Patrick far to the SW. Within the earth and stone ramparts of the vast enclosure are a rock slab shelter, two cairns at the N end and 30 circular hut sites. Leave the N17 5km E of Tobercurry on the L8403 and follow 3km to layby parking R and good path up L (54.1172, -8.6690). The ruins of Lavagh (Court) Friary are nearby, but may be under repair (54.1124, -8.6682).

0 mins, 54.1199, -8.6797

41 EAGLES FLYING

This wildlife sanctuary set on a farm also has hawks, owls, falcons and vultures flying in two daily shows, as well as macaw parrots to chat with and furry and farm animals to pet as well. €15/€5 admission (adult/child); Portinch, Ballymote, F56 P089, +353 85 2690717

1 min, 54.1033, -8.5683

TRADITIONAL PUBS

42 THOMAS CONNOLLY BAR

Connolly's is 'the real deal' as Irish pubs go, trading since 1780 and visited by Charles Stuart Parnell, with venerable flagstone floors, long bar and glazed timber 'snug' partitions. Alongside over 100 whiskies, there is a growing list of craft beers from locals like White Hag and Lough Gill, including gluten-free brews. Bar bites available, and regular music sessions in the evenings. 1 Markievicz Road, Sligo, F91 HC04, +353 71 9194920

54.2727, -8.4739

43 ELLEN'S BAR, MAUGHEROW

This roadside thatched pub is renowned for its old-school atmosphere, with a pool table, darts board and character to spare. There are regular events but no food; campervan parking available. Maugherow, F91 WE04, +353 71 9163761

54.3547, -8.6454

44 THE BEACH BAR, AUGHRIS

This cosy and colourful thatched beachside pub is almost an institution, with local history on the walls. Campsite/campervan parking (first come, first served) next door. Aughris, F91 YE98, +353 71 9176465

54.2689, -8.7572

LOCAL PRODUCE

45 OYSTER EXPERIENCE

Sligo is the natural home of Irish oyster production, and its name literally means 'abounding in shells'. Take a tour to see how they are grown and harvested on the shore of the vast bay under the iconic peaks of Benbulbin and Knocknarea, including a tasting in the courtyard with a local craft beer. Tours June–October; you can also book a tasting at WB's Coffee House in Sligo town (11 Stephen Street, F91 V2XR, +353 71 9141883). Tours start from Bree's Bar car park, Larass, F91 P650, sligooysterexperience.ie

54.2714, -8.5816

46 PINK CLOVER, DRUMCLIFFE

Guinness and treacle soda bread and seasalt and rosemary focaccia are made on site, together with the scones and jams, quiches and sausage rolls for the café, and the produce used is locally sourced. As a bonus, you can visit the grave of W.B. Yeats and check out the camel on the medieval high cross outside. Drumcliffe Churchyard, F91 ECF5, +353 71 9144956

54.3259, -8.4943

47 SEAWEED EXPERIENCE

Prannie Rhatigan is a long-standing champion of Irish seaweeds, running summer identification walks and 'rockpool rambles'. Even if you can't make one of these, it's worth buying her pocket-sized seaweed guide from her website to inform your own foraging; it comes complete with QR code links to videos for extra help. Various shoreline locations, irishseaweedkitchen@gmail.com or irishseaweedkitchen.ie

54.4056, -8.5623

48 MAMMY JOHNSTON'S, STRANDHILL

Three generations of the same family have made and sold gelato ice cream on the seafront, starting with the original Mammy Johnston in the 1930s. Her grandson Neil still visits Italy every year to brush up his skills. Shore Road, Strandhill, F91 W673, +353 71 9168005

54.2704, -8.6089

49 BELTRA COUNTRY MARKET

Small and friendly traditional country market held in an old red-painted community hall with plenty of parking. Delicious home baking, seasonal produce, eggs, preserves and local arts and crafts, together with a coffee shop

42

44

49

54

60

and fresh crepes. Saturdays 10am–noon. Beltra Hall, Beltra, F91 VX97, +353 87 2172104
54.2211, -8.6244

ORGANIC & GASTRO

50 NEANTÓG KITCHEN GARDEN SCHOOL

This organic farm is named after the nettles that had overrun it when Gaby and Hans Wieland arrived here from Germany in the 1980s. They have been offering courses since 1996 in growing, processing and cooking your own plant-based foods, or you can book a foraging trip or Sligo Food Trail Tour. Ballincastle, Cliffoney, F91 HW82, neantog.com
54.4221, -8.4586

51 NOOK CAFÉ & RESTAURANT

This distinctive modern venture from award-winning chef Ethna Reynolds focuses on using local and Irish produce to create upmarket comfort food. The menu changes frequently to offer the best of seasonal produce and the chance to try new cheeses, charcuterie and quality meats from artisan producers. Gluten-free and vegan/vegetarian needs are well looked after. Lower Main Street, Collooney, F91 X7T1, +353 87 3522135
54.1851, -8.4921

52 EALA BHÁN, SLIGO

Just one of the town's many fine-dining restaurants on the bank of the Garvoge specialising in locally sourced Irish produce. Their more casual restaurant, Hooked, is just next door (+353 71 9138591). 5 Rockwood Parade, Sligo, F91 YX52, +353 71 9145823
54.2712, -8.4728

53 KATE'S KITCHEN, SLIGO

Gourmet groceries and other good things abound, including their own pickles and jams, cheeses and meats, and fresh baked bread. 3 Castle Street, Sligo, F91 YK2E, +353 71 9143022
54.2705, -8.4729

54 HONESTLY FARM KITCHEN *

Top quality Drumanilra Farm burgers, deli and organic food served by passionate staff proud of the their sustainable, regnerative produce. Shore Rd, F91 HH31, +353 71 9317387
54.2705, -8.6076

55 THE GOURMET PARLOUR COFFEE SHOP,

The roadside setting is not promising, but the food is: good vegan and vegetarian options and everything can be take-away. There's another branch in Sligo town. N4 Roundabout, Collooney, F91 CKF8, +353 86 1732154.
54.1829, -8.4844

62

56 THE JAM POT, GRANGE

This much-loved local institution has good vegan and gluten-free choices and local ice cream. The Diamond, Grange, F91 D9CH, +353 87 1644228
54.3926, -8.523

57 THE LITTLE COTTAGE CAFÉ

Healthy and vegetarian options at an excellent seafront café. Rosses Point, F91 NC01, +353 71 9117766
54.3059, -8.5552

58 FROM THE GROUND UP 2020

Sligo native Jenny French started with an honesty box selling her home-grown veg, then progressed to a market stall and eco grocery store, now transformed into this beautiful café, with another branch in Charlestown, Mayo (F12H9AO). Tubbercurry, F91 CX61, +353 87 9135030
54.0537, -8.7297

BEACH CAMPING & HOSTELS

59 ROSSES POINT/GREENLANDS CAMPING

Modern and well-maintained facilities for caravans, campervans and tents, just back from the beach. Tourist Association-run site, book well in advance. Rosses Point, F91 TC64, +353 71 9177113, sligocaravanandcamping.ie
54.3070, -8.5694

60 STRANDHILL CAMPING

Tourist Association-run site on the beach, for caravans, campervans and tents. Book ahead +353 71 9168111, sligocaravanandcamping.ie
54.2720, -8.6055

61 EASKEY HOSTEL

Quirky historic townhouse hostel in popular Easkey seaside village, with sea views from yard and hot tub. Main Street, Easkey, F26 F728, +353 85 1706060, easkeyhostel.com
54.2862, -8.9616

RUSTIC RETREATS

62 TEAPOT LANE

Adult-only stylish glampsite with three geodesic dome tents, a treehouse and a country cottage (over-14s allowed). Wild surroundings give you a good chance to spot foxes, badgers, deer or hares nearby. Mallanyduff, F91 D363, glampingireland.ie

54.4453, -8.383

63 ISLAND VIEW RIDING

Stay and trek at this equestrian farm which specialises in beach and island riding. The Lookout, Mount Temple, F91 N4T1, +353 71 9166156, islandviewridingstables.com

54.4169, -8.4839

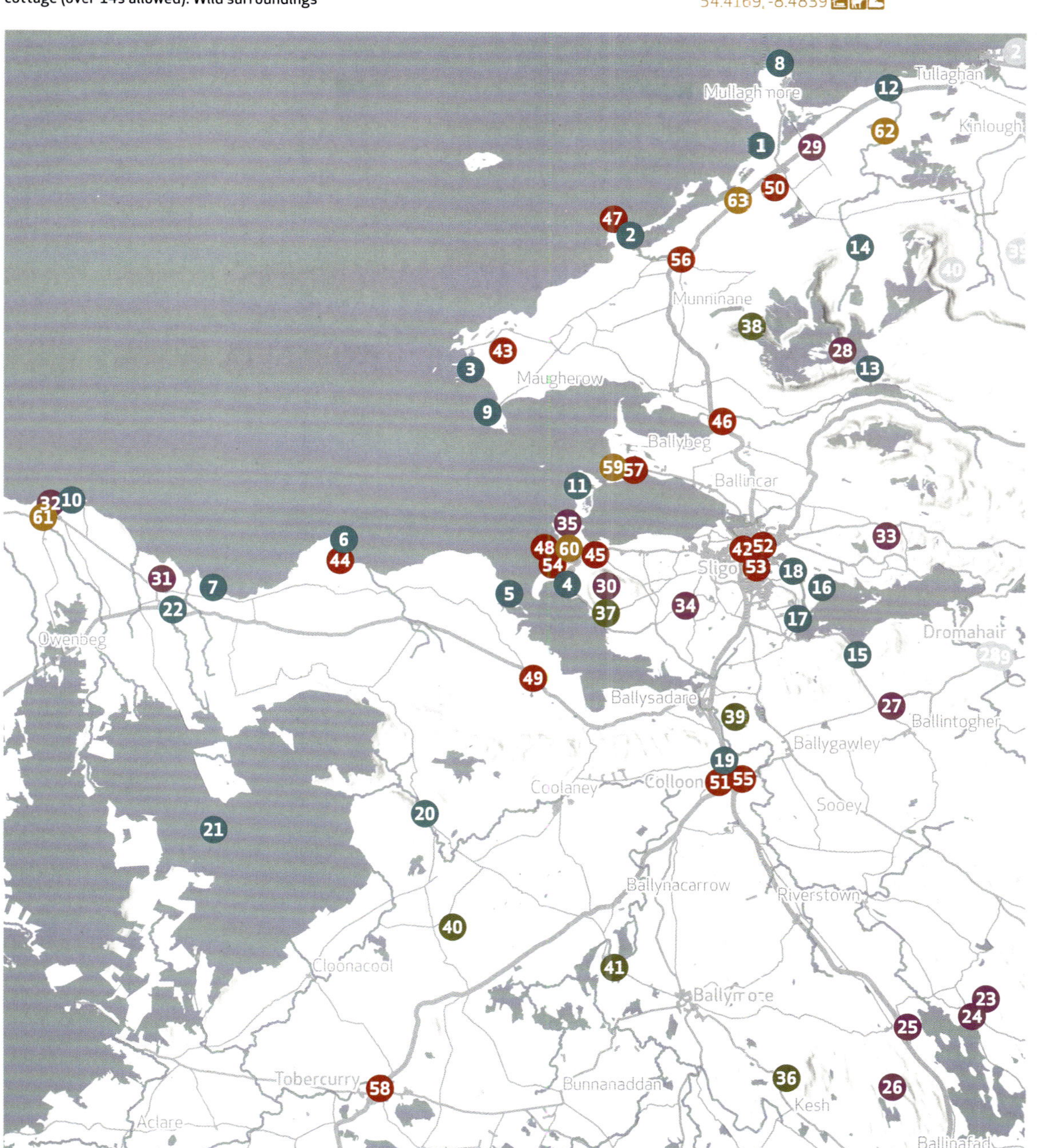

NORTH WEST MAYO

Our perfect weekend

- → **Hunt** for curious carvings on the walls of Rosserk Abbey, and find magical Moyne, rarely visited with intact cloisters.
- → **Walk** from ancient Kilcummin Church past the bothy sculpture on the headland to 'back strand' beach, with a pint in Bessie's Bar afterwards.
- → **Drift** in the rock pool at Belderrig, or peer into the blowholes on the headland across the bay.
- → **Gaze** from the magnificent Dun Chaocháin cliffs near Portacloy beach on a walk to the poignant Children of Lír sculpture.
- → **Cross** the dune causeway to Claggan Island to visit the vast beaches and cillín sculpture.
- → **Scan** for bottlenose dolphins from the clifftops of Erris Head, and descend to swim in the sandy estuarine lagoon at Tipp Pier.
- → **Tour** the wild beaches of the Mullet and take a walk around the spiral stones of Deirbhle's Twist.
- → **Explore** the wilds of Knockmoyle/Sheskin on the Western Way, with home-made supplies from Mary's Bakery.

1

1

3

The wild landscapes here can look untouched by human hand, but looks are deceptive. Céide Fields, the world's oldest and most extensive network of Neolithic field boundaries, was found here by a local teacher in the 1930s. The walls still lie hidden and protected below the peat, but surveys show they stretch over the horizon and down to the cliff edge; all the land here and some that has eroded was once farmed in this now-empty coastal corner.

The Belmullet peninsula, or Mullet, is the star of the coast, a long arm thrown out around Blacksod Bay as if to shield it from the Atlantic storms; weather reports from the lighthouse here were critical to the timing of D-Day. It stands next to the old stone pier, where you can catch a boat trip to the empty Inishkea islands, abandoned in the 1930s after a lethal storm. On the eastern side of the peninsula are sheltered sands and safe waters; the western beaches are just as pale and beautiful, but more suited to surfing.

This area is home to Tír Sáile, or The North Mayo Sculpture Trail, with many landscape pieces in magical locations. Our favourites are on Annagh Head, where the coast rises from the sandy dunes of the Mullet. From here eastwards, the coast has fewer beaches and more cliffs, with rock pools, blowholes, and mighty views. They pass Céide Fields to reach their most dramatic point at the magnificent Dún Briste sea stack, which broke from the land some six centuries ago.

The shore gives way to sands again at Killala Bay. This estuary contains a few intriguing wrecks, including the very recent Shingle, a 60m drug smugglers' ship seized by the state and deliberately sunk in the middle of the bay in 2024 as an artificial reef for divers and wildlife. On the estuary shore, the old Belleek Castle estate has parkland woods to wander and curious follies to find within. The river valley has ancient tombs and wonderful ruins, from one of Ireland's oldest churches at Kilcummin to Rathfran Abbey 'of the sweet bells'.

Further west, the boggy landscape supports important wildlife: Irish hare, red grouse, and golden plover on upland Inagh, and willow ptarmigan on the wet lowland of Knockmoyle/Sheskin, a Ramsar wetland. You can skirt this on the Western Way, and visit the crumbling lodge where Arthurian novelist T. H. White once wrote. The rivers are peaty and brown but provide beautiful swimming spots as they wind slowly through these flat lands; take your cue from them and explore at a leisurely pace.

SECRET BEACHES

1 RATHFRAN BAY, ROSS POINT

Nameless stretch of empty white sand with dunes and orchids. There's a small parking area at 54.2413, -9.2033. Turn L on unsigned lane just before better-known Ross beach.

10 mins, 54.2466, -9.2043

2 GORTMELLIA STRAND

Remote sandy estuary with the ribs of a shipwreck at LT. Shallow, warm swimming at HT. Unsigned at a crossroads on L1202, then track.

2 mins, 54.2346, -9.8680

3 SRAH/CLAGGAN BEACH

The Irish name 'sraith' or 'swath' perfectly describes this long curve of fine, straw-gold sand, forming a dune causeway to Claggan Island and empty even in high summer. Follow R313 about 11km E from Belmullet, turn R at crossroads at Bunnahowen, then R at the Marian shrine, both signed WAW.

5 mins, 54.1731, -9.9526

4 DOHOOMA BEACH

Long, wild golden sands and views across to the mountains of Achill. Grassy parking with a picnic table for overnights.

2 mins, 54.0716, -9.9620

5 TERMONCARRAGH BEACH & BLOWHOLE

A cobble storm beach at the head of a deep slot bay, just made for a secluded dip and evening light. A stone building above and if you're lucky a curragh upturned and weighted with stones complete the scene perfectly. It's a good start point for snorkelling, kayaking and coasteering, and Steve and Mikey run Wavesweeper Sea Adventures here +353 97 81096. Park on road edge. 1km N along the coast road, WAW signed, is Dún na mBó, the dramatic blowhole enclosed by stone-wall sculpture 54.2644, -10.0759. Inland E 1km in a field just off the lane are the remains of a fortified house with gun-loops 54.2509, -10.0637.

2 mins, 54.2552, -10.0731

6 IMLEACH BEAG/EMLYBEG BEACH

Dune-backed wild sunset beach. The last 800m is track access (No Dumping sign) and then room for only a few cars to park. Signed Golf Course from R313.

2 mins, 54.2221, -10.0539

7 MULLACH RUA/MULLAGHROE BEACH

Long sheltered beach with soft white-pink sand and dunes. Popular among swimmers (despite signs). Car park for 14 and portaloo.

2 mins, 54.1386 -10.0768

13

12

8 CROSS LAKE/LOCH NA CROISE

The longest and possibly the whitest strand on the peninsula, with the remains of Cross Abbey at the N end by the parking area, and the Cross Lake loop walk around the tarn. You'll pass layby parking for Belderra Strand 1km to the E on the way in.

3 mins, 54.2089, -10.0826

9 TARMON/FEORIN BEACH

Tarmon – or Termon – is one of many sheltered bays on the E side of Erris Head with white sand but little beach at HT. Parking layby for a couple of cars.

2 mins, 54.1144, -10.0930

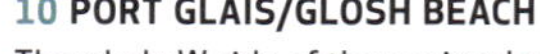

10 PORT GLAIS/GLOSH BEACH

The whole W side of the peninsula is one dune-backed white sand beach after another, all with little lanes, all prone to rips but favoured for surfing. This one has Tonn Nua surf school on the sandy lane leading in (+353 83 3074659). An obscure circle of 28 stones stands on the headland at the S end (54.1109, -10.1255), leading on to the ruined signal tower (54.1059, -10.1279), while on the road to the beach someone has built a modern circle sculpture in an enclosure by the road (54.1124, -10.1145). Follow the R313 down the peninsula, turn R in Aghleam onto L5321, signed Bóthar an Chósta. Follow 1.4km to hairpin turn R down to beach.

2 mins, 54.11365, -10.1227

11 FAULMORE BEACH

Also called Portmore; a beautiful white beach overlooking the peaks of Achill Island. If you are lucky, you may see dolphins in the bay. Facing S it's relatively sheltered for swimming. There is space to park at either end, but more parking to the E, just after the ruined church.

1 min, 54.0960, -10.1110

12 DOONA BEACH & WILD NEPHIN

Vast sands and dunes, with shallow warm water and SW views over Achill's mountains. A remote paradise reached via tiny lanes and a long sandy track which ends at common land. The E side of the peninsula faces the estuarine beach of the Owenduff. Nearby on N59 is the Ballycroy Visitor Centre, the W gateway to Wild Nephin.

5 mins, 54.0607, -9.8826

SEA CAVES & COASTEERING

13 BELDERRIG POOL & BLOWHOLE

The little harbour has a popular tidal pool, reached by steps behind the pier. For an altogether bigger adventure, seek out the giant blowholes in the wild headland to the E. It's a rough track up to some parking at 54.3116,

-9.5403 then 500m NE. It's beautiful up here and exciting to peer down into the holes from a safe distance. We actually swam into Poll na Gaoithe via the steep grass banks to the rocks, and a tricky scramble down into swirling water (54.3148, -9.5335). Best in morning light.
2 mins, 54.3118, -9.5527

14 PORTACLOY BEACH & CLIFF WALK

This beautiful sand and dune beach is sheltered at the back of a slot-like bay, off the beaten track but perfect for families. From here, take on the mighty Dun Chaocháin cliffs, at 255m far higher than famous Moher and with caves and tilted strata for coasteering/kayaking if calm. Search Carrowteige Loop Walks but the walk starts along a sculpted promontory bearing a dramatically sited EIRE navigation marker falling into the sea (54.3420, -9.7809), with views to the Stags (Na Stacaí) of Broadhaven islands. The beach and cave below can be reached with a tricky scramble on SE corner. After 5km arrive at a shelter-like sculpture and Benwee/Bhinn Bhuí WAW parking area (campervans possible, 54.3243, -9.8402).
2 mins, 54.3237, -9.8403

15 RINROE STRAND, CARROWTEIGE

The tiny lane descends to a remote machair isthmus, with Rinroad Point and pier beyond, and beaches on either side. The N cove has a fun network of caves to explore at the far end. Popular for overnights.
2 mins, 54.3036, -9.8447

16 TIPP PIER

A narrow rock channel leads into Blind Harbour, a sandy lagoon with Tipp Pier. There's beautiful clear water at higher tides but it dries to sandflats at low. A little further NW (turn L on unmarked lane just before) is a very remote rock cove, slipway and cliffs, perfect for adventurers (Muingcreena/Illanbaun, 54.2709, -9.9575).
2 mins, 54.2655, -9.9306

17 BELMULLET TIDAL POOL

Beautiful views over Erris Head and perfect for a sunset 'infinity' swim. Locally loved and maintained, with coffee van.
2 mins, 54.2174, -9.9899

TINY ISLANDS

18 BARTRAGH ISLAND

A sandy tombolo with dunes, a long sweep of beach on the seaward side, and a neglected but not derelict 19th-century house. Cross the sandflats barefoot from 2 hours before LT to allow enough time for return. Park at lane end 54.1976, -9.1592. Or paddle board access from

19

17

22

22

24

W end of Enniscrone Beach. NB access to the island may be restricted by a new owner.
15 mins, 54.2032 -9.1416

19 INISHKEA ISLANDS

Abandoned in 1935 after most of the young fishermen were drowned by a sudden storm. Visit the haunting remains of the main village on a perfect shell-white beach. These deserted machair islands host peregrine falcons, Ireland's biggest autumn breeding population of grey seals, and half its wintering barnacle geese. As well as the remains of the main village there are medieval religious sites like the shelly mounds of Bailey Mor and Beg with a crucifix-inscribed grave slab, beehive hut remains (54.1322, -10.1885) and a whaling station (54.1192, -10.2032). Both islands have perfect white beaches and on the south island walk to the navigation marker on the summit of Knocknaskea or Alt Mór and marvel at the western cliffs. A few restored homes are lived in seasonally, but that is all, so bring your own picnic; the NPWS prohibits wild camping on the island. Boats from Blacksod Pier with Belmullet Boat Charters (+353 86 8365983) or Blacksod Sea Safari (+353 83 0263100).
10 mins, 54.1189, -10.2070

25

RIVER, LAKE & WATERFALL

20 MOY RIVER, DRUMREVAGH

Well-maintained banks for fishing, but if all is quiet then a dip is possible, although the banks are steep. Turn off N26 opp the Mt Falcon estate entrance. Find track on R after 500m, park and walk past the ruined lodge to find river at end, 200m.
5 mins, 54.0676, -9.1500

21 GORTNOR ABBEY PIER

Views of Nephin Mt across Lough Conn. Quiet and easy for overnight parking with facilities, perfect for a sunset swim or canoe launch.
2 mins, 54.0932, -9.2988

22 CARROWMORE LAKE & BANGOR TRAIL

A tiny lane runs the entire 4-mile length of this freshwater lake in the wildlands N of Nephin. It's relatively shallow and warm (only 6m at its deepest) and a good spot for brown trout, particularly in early summer, but it's so vast and remote you should have no problem finding a quiet spot for a swim or overnight without disturbing fishermen (this spot has parking and a small jetty). The surrounding landscape supports breeding merlin and golden plover and there are several Iron Age crannog islands. Signed Carrowmore Drive off the R313. Nearby is the start point for perhaps the wildest hike in Ireland, the Bangor Trail (54.1405, -9.73625), 26km of wilderness S into the heart of Nephin Beg, passing Slieve Carr (721m).
2 mins, 54.1905, -9.7927

23 VERA FALLS & OWENINY RIVER

Pretty woodland falls with small pools plus access to the main river below. Park in a small layby area on S side of N59. Cross and enter new double wooden gate for falls N, or bushwhack S through the overgrown fields for the river banks, 200m. There is another river access point at the layby E at 54.1347, -9.6493.
5 mins, 54.1389, -9.6754

24 OWENDUFF RIVER, LAGDUFF

A beautiful secret river swim in warm, whiskey water above a weir. With only the Wild Nephin mountains upstream, this is some of the purest water in Mayo. Signed NPWS off N59, then see track to river on R, 1km. Park a further 100m down the road.
1 min, 54.0718, -9.7950

LOST RUINS

25 ROSSERK ABBEY

Standing on a peaceful river bank, but on a smaller scale than nearby Moyne Abbey (see entry), it has much more decorative stonework: plants, animals and angels appear on or below arches. NB 400m back from the car park a path

25

leads 500m to the secluded 18th-century stone wellhouse of Tobar Mhuire (54.1687, -9.1445).
2 mins, 54.1714, -9.1433

26 MOYNE ABBEY *

Overlooking the Moy estuary, this is one of the best-preserved abbeys in the country, with columns, lancet and tracery windows, cloisters and extensive buildings, yet it's rarely visited. An enchanting approach along an avenue of old trees with a pretty mill race. Legend tells of rooms full of bones, and a young chapel clerk who bet his friends a guinea he could fetch a skull from the abbey one night. Abbey is signed at a farm gate (54.2016, -9.1832). Park very

26

28

28

33

respectfully; this is a working farm and there are 'beware of bull' signs but you have full rights to access without dogs.

5 mins, 54.2022 -9.1770

27 KILCUMMIN CHURCH & BEACH

One of the oldest stone churches in Ireland, on a 700AD graveyard site, with a holy well, carved crosses and a vertical sundial. 1.5km further W along lane is big, wild Carrowmore beach 54.2788, -9.2319 or turn R for the headland and Tearmann na Gaoithe, a cliff-top, lean-to bothy sculpture 54.2862, -9.2198.

3 mins, 54.2777, -9.2112

28 RATHFRAN ABBEY & GRAVEYARD

Exquisite lancet windows, tomb niches and intricately carved grave slabs, this 13th-century Dominican abbey was burned in 1592 by Sir Richard Bingham, the hated Governor of Connacht. Parking for one by gate (54.2385, -9.2423). Afterwards: 500m NW along lane you'll see the grand ruins of Summerhill House on R (54.2422, -9.2433). Then, at junction, turn L 300m for Rathfranpark wedge tomb, roadside L (54.2419, -9.2526) or R 300m for Breastagh ogham stone, in field L (54.2465, -9.25366).

5 mins, 54.2380, -9.2443

29 CASTLE GORE & RIVER POOL

This ivy-clad ruined mansion has a service tunnel from the lane, so the owners didn't have to see arriving servants traipsing across the lawns. 200m S, on the edge of the farmyard and river, is the impressive 16th-century stronghouse (the original Deel Castle, 54.1083, -9.2535). 200m N steps lead down to a deep pool beneath Deelcastle Bridge. Park at the junction to the bridge for all the above.

2 mins, 54.1109, -9.2529

30 ERREW ABBEY, LOUGH CONN

Set on a remote isthmus in Lough Conn, a ruined abbey with vaults and archways. Beyond is a tomb. Well signposted but sadly the farmer has stopped parking at the lane end, so come by cycle only.

30 mins, 54.0530, -9.2632

31 SHESKIN LODGE RUINS

Find the poignant remains of Sheskin Lodge, once a picturesque hunting residence where Arthurian novelist T.H. White stayed. After it was abandoned, coniferous forestry was planted right up to its boundaries and it's now a mysterious mossy ruin. The lowland bog here is an important Ramsar wetland site: willow ptarmigan feed on the heather, and golden plover in the acidic pools. The Western Way long-distance route skirts NW. Follow the N59 4km W from Bellacorick, turn R onto L52926 and continue 5km as it becomes a forest track (sometimes gated). On the side of N59 take L52929 for the access to the River Oweniny from the bridge, 200m.

45 mins, 54.1719, -9.6135

SACRED & ANCIENT

32 CARROWCROM WEDGE TOMB

Although small, this tomb is large enough to crawl inside and a great example of the type, with four large upright blocks and overlapping roof stones. There's a stile straight into the field from the lane, but limited parking.

3 mins, 54.0899, -9.0478

33 RATHLACKEN COURT TOMB

Above sandflats of Lacken Bay, one of the best court tombs in the country, part of a wider landscape of tombs, dwellings, and enclosures that are now mostly under the bog. You can park on the lane verge or walk the whole 8km 'Lackan Trail', starting at Lacken Church (F26 P9P1), following green/blue markers (8km or 11km options). The return passes Lacken Gazebo, a 1794 eye-catcher with views to Donegal on a clear day (54.2788, -9.2710, park at 54.2787, -9.2810). To the S are the ruins of Lacken Castle; on private land but 200m E from

29

33

35

36

37

access gap in the wall (54.2722, -9.2674). Vast, clean sandy bay, for walks at LT or shallow, or warm afternoon swimming if the tide has come in over warm sands.

2 mins, 54.2906, -9.2810

34 BLANEMORE FOREST

6,000 years of history among regenerating coniferous woodland, on wheel-friendly gravelled tracks. There's a low boulder outline of a court tomb and a Bronze Age standing stone known as The False Man, which dominated the skyline for millennia. The Celestial Stones row then leads to a forest lake (swimmable but signs say do not approach). Signed from the R315 1km N of Moygownagh, follow 3.6km to car park and trailhead. 3.7km loop

10 mins, 54.1743, -9.3981

HEADLANDS & VIEWS

35 DOWNPATRICK HEAD

This popular and magnificent headland is home to puffins, kittiwakes, and cormorants and feels within touching distance of Dún Briste sea stack. There's also the Tír Sáile sculpture, The Crossing, which encircles a terrifyingly huge blowhole – apparently troublemakers met their end in it. Also find the old lookout, statue and EIRE stone marker (54.3269, -9.3459). Adventurers sometimes try to make their way into the huge sea caverns below the lookout, and blowhole, opp the stack. They descend at 54.3235, -9.3473 to the LT rock ledges and continue 400m along, but it's all too easy to get cut off by the tide or washed off the rocks by a freak wave. NB a boat sculpture, Battling Forces, is also by the road just before the car park.

5 mins, 54.3254, -9.3467

36 DEIRBHLE'S TWIST SCULPTURE

Evoking an ancient stone circle, granite pieces from the landscape were erected in this tightening spiral with magnificent views over to Achill. Turn R on the WAW along L5230 from the approach to Blacksod Lighthouse, parking and path to sculpture L after 1.3km.

2 mins, 54.0950, -10.0849

37 ANNAGH HEAD

Walk on the oldest rocks in Ireland; 1,753 million years old. Find the Thin Places sculpture inspired by Irish monastic beehive huts, up on the top of the headland and down to R. In summer there is a carpet of thrift, bladder campion, and other meadow flowers, and if you listen out you may hear the call of a corncrake. There's also an EIRE 61 marker 500m before to S (54.2392, -10.0947) and a pier for swimming or overnighting, 1km before to N (take unmarked lane to 54.2405, -10.0814) or the wild remote beach itself; very sheltered but shallow (54.2338, -10.0669).

3 mins, 54.2418, -10.1044

FOREST & WILDLIFE

38 BELLEEK FOREST PARK

Follow good paths to the spired folly-mausoleum of Sir Knox-Gore among mixed woodlands awash with bluebells in the spring and home to foxes, pine martens, and red squirrels. Then along the riverside with two sunken boats: the concrete barge SS Crete Boom, once intended to support a sandbank at the river mouth, and the 19th-century Floweret or Florette (54.1354, -9.1384). The original estate entrance is an arch over the road immediately after F26 E7C9. The woodland car park is on R about 900m or take next R for Belleek Castle hotel itself.

60 mins, 54.1324, -9.1417

39 CÉIDE FIELDS

This reserve is rich in orchids and wild flowers but below the peat lies a vast network of Neolithic field boundaries of a now buried agricultural settlement. A smart new visitor centre illustrates and explains what lies beneath, but the real value here lies in the guided tours out over some uncovered sections of wall and a large hut circle on the heathery slope. On the R314 coast road, 8km W of Ballycastle, closed Nov to Feb (€5).

5 mins, 54.3055, -9.4588

40 ERRIS HEAD

Headland loop walk with gannets, fulmars and guillemots circling and sightings of bottlenose dolphins, porpoises and seals. Views over Eagle Island with its lighthouse off the western side. The cliffs themselves are full of dramatic chasms far and near, while on the springy grasslands you may see red-legged choughs and Irish hares, as well as a Second World War lookout post and EIRE navigation marker in stones (54.3001, -10.0025). 5km loop walk. WAW viewpoint car park. Signed Ceann Lorrais from the L1201, 3km N of Belmullet, then 5km to car park at end.

45 mins, 54.2886, -9.9888

TRADITIONAL PUBS

41 ROUSES BAR, BALLINA

Run by the Rouse family since 1947, this quintessentially traditional pub has live Irish music on Saturday nights, and a good selection of Irish whiskies on the back bar. 53 Pearse St, Ballina, F26 T042, +353 96 21083

54.1137, -9.1547

42 BESSIE'S BAR, KILCUMMIN

New owners Nollag and Michael are keeping the local tradition with a rejuvenated bar in the style and spirit of a traditional Irish rural pub. Music nights on weekends, community events, and local food trucks. Closed Tues & Wed but check social media. Kilcummin, Carrowmore Lacken, F26 WY82

54.2735, -9.2101

43 P. HEALY'S PUB, BELMULLET

If it's open, go in; you won't find a more authentic little Irish snug bar anywhere. Some of the stuff on the walls has probably been there since the foundation of the state, but if you want to see an almost vanished Ireland, this is it. Main Street, Belmullet, F26 YY45

54.2237, -9.9880

LOCAL PRODUCE

44 MARY'S BAKERY

Home-made everything, from a tiny stone cottage, from soda bread to chowder. Main St, Ballycastle, +353 85 2514125

54.2798, -9.3729

45 POACHER, BALLINA

Inventive, contemporary dishes from local producers, with plenty of excellent vegetarian options. 4 Market Square, Ballina, F26 Y5D1, +353 96 77982

54.1148, -9.1560

PUB CAMPING

46 HEALY'S BAR, BALLYCASTLE

This proper village pub, spread over three colourful house fronts, has good pub food, a welcoming atmosphere (not for nothing is the owner Padraic known as Smiler), and camping out back, with pastoral views. Main Street, Ballycastle, F26 C3X2, +353 87 2033101

54.2793, -9.3697

RUSTIC RETREATS

47 THE COTTAGE, KILCUMMIN

A renovated 18th-century cottage on a tiny country lane a short walk or cycle down to Kilcummin Back Strand and Bessie's Bar (see entries). There's a woodburner in the sitting room, two double bedrooms, and a secure yard for bikes or kayaks. Kilcummin, Ballina, F26 H7D2, Airbnb.

54.2794, -9.2178

48 BELMULLET COASTGUARD STATION

Modern 3-bed cottage, but set on its own almost-island with incredible views. With flowery fields all around, a poignant land art sculpture in the field below, and vast sandy beaches either side of the narrow linking causeway (see Srah entry), this is an idyllic spot with great hosts right on site. Claggan Island, Bunnahowen, Ballina, F26 A9C5, +353 87 6833985, belmulletcgs.com zo65g

54.1806, -9.972

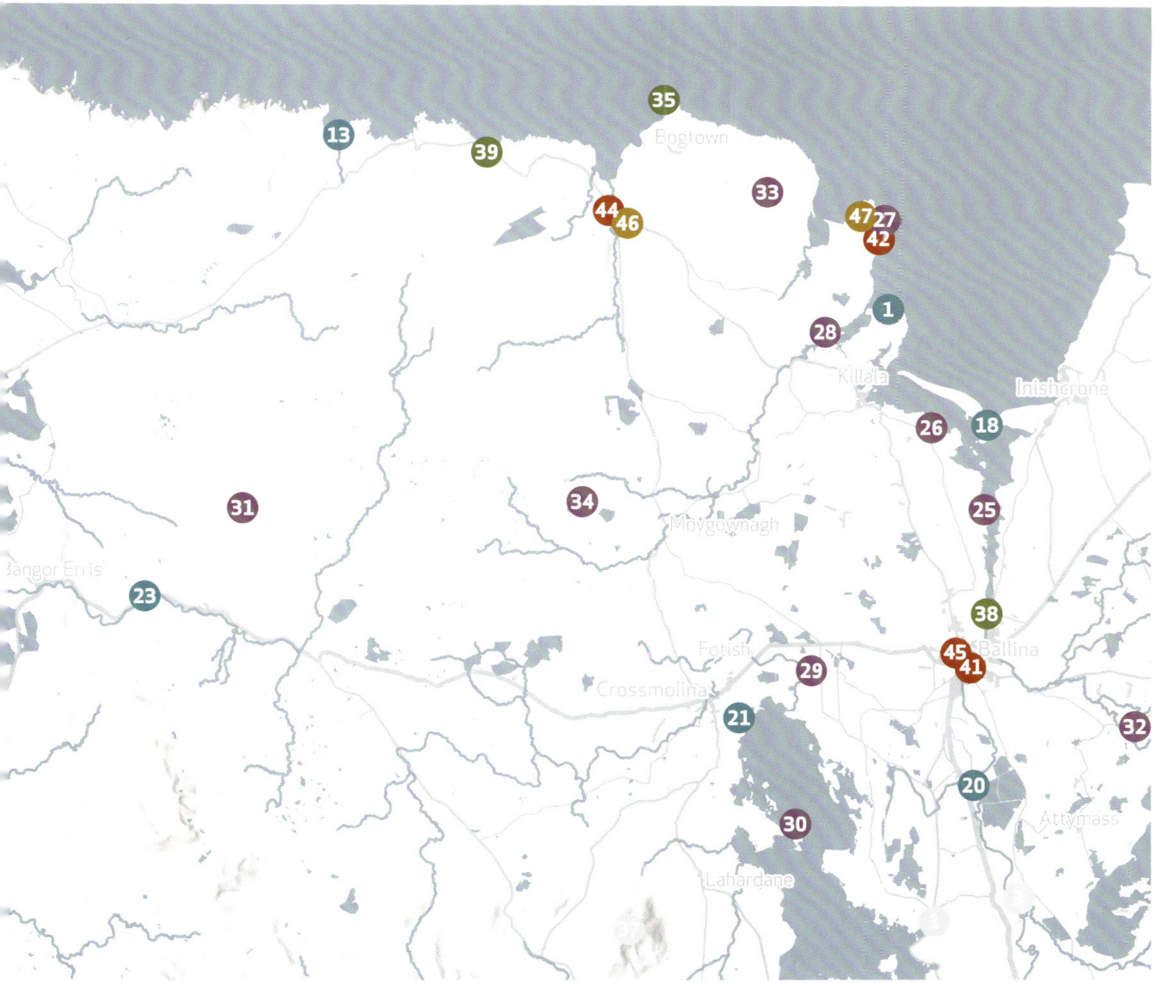

3

SOUTH WEST MAYO

Our perfect weekend

- **Explore** the empty lanes and flowery fields of Inishbiggle, ferry hopping with a bike from the mainland on to Achill Isalnd.
- **Swim** with the morning sun at Keem Beach, setting from The Banshees of Inisherin, and climb to the lookout and lost village.
- **Learn** to brew Belgian-style at one of the Mescan workshops, then drink their beers with a fabulous meal of local produce at An Port Mór.
- **Climb** Mweelrea from the seaward side, and take a refreshing dip at the Silver Strand.
- **Trace** the cross on Srahwee wedge tomb, then take the clapper bridge to Cross Beach.
- **Tackle** the tough ascent to the ridge of Ben Lugmore, with a dip in beautiful Doo Lough as a bonus on your return.
- **Descend** the Erriff in stages, exploring sessile oak woods, a vast river pool at Houston's Bridge, ending at Aasleagh Falls, backdrop in The Field.
- **Venture** out among the drumlins on the tip of the Rossmore peninsula, and taste fresh Clew Bay oysters at Croagh Patrick Seafoods.

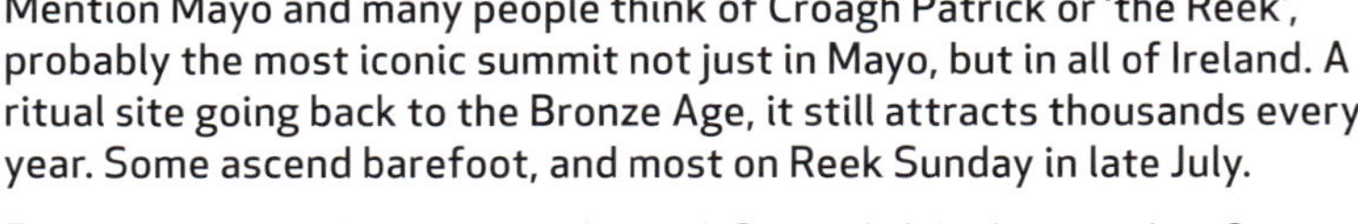

Mention Mayo and many people think of Croagh Patrick or 'the Reek', probably the most iconic summit not just in Mayo, but in all of Ireland. A ritual site going back to the Bronze Age, it still attracts thousands every year. Some ascend barefoot, and most on Reek Sunday in late July.

For others mighty Mweelrea is the goal, Connacht's highest peak at 814m and a classic climb, with many routes up and relatively few people. This is also the home of Wild Nephin National Park, a Dark Sky Park of wild, empty places; hardcore hikers wild camp here (notify the park in advance).

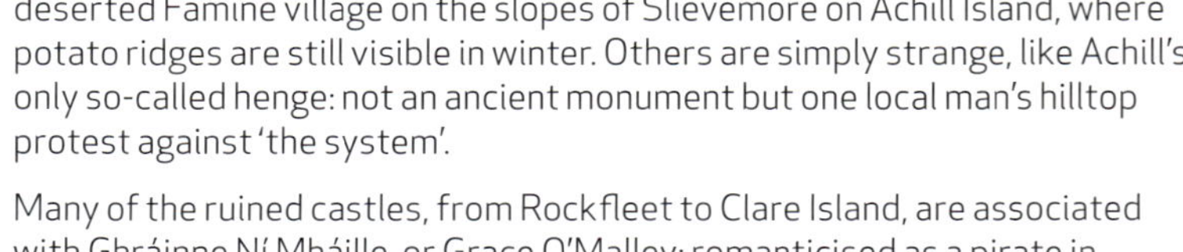

There are plenty of ruins and relics here. Some are poignant, like the deserted Famine village on the slopes of Slievemore on Achill Island, where potato ridges are still visible in winter. Others are simply strange, like Achill's only so-called henge: not an ancient monument but one local man's hilltop protest against 'the system'.

Many of the ruined castles, from Rockfleet to Clare Island, are associated with Ghráinne Ní Mháille, or Grace O'Malley; romanticised as a pirate in popular legend, she was the most famous leader of the clan that controlled the waters of Clew Bay for generations. The bay is famous for its islands, drumlins of gravel deposited by ancient glaciers. On land these make eerily perfect, oval hills; here they are half-drowned, dreamlike islands, and legend says there is one for every day of the year, each with a quiet sandy edge.

There are bigger islands too: Clare Island is an adventure in itself, with dramatic sea cliffs, hidden coves, an abbey with the O'Malley tomb, and the choice of camping or going for luxury in an old lighthouse. Achill sits so close to the mainland you may not realise it is an island at all – it is even reachable on a car-free greenway from Westport – and has pretty beaches, some easy, some hidden on a hike, and one with movie-star status.

Back on the mainland, there are loughs between the rugged peaks and rivers like the Bundorragha, tumbling through the glacial Delphi Valley down to the dramatic fjord of Killary Harbour.

In Westport, created when the old village was taken to make a woodland park for Westport House (now free to walk and with a campsite), the town's autumn 'Westival' turns 50 in 2025, and has helped the growth of great cafés to start the morning and excellent restaurants and welcoming bars with music for an evening. The culture has spread across the wider area, from an excellent local microbrewery to quirky hostels; so this makes a great pitstop for the weekend's gourmet picnic supplies.

SECRET BEACHES

1 GOLDEN STRAND, DUGORT

Idyllic, sheltered sweep of pale sand backed by cobble and machair dunes (some wild camping in the flatter parts, and a handy pub over the road) haunted by snipe and blackheaded gulls. Its local name of Barnyaguppal, from the Irish Bhearna nagCapall or 'horse's gap', recalls the days when horses carried seaweed from here to the fields; today you can walk alpacas instead (Achill Island Alpacas +353 89 2030418). There's WAW roadside car park at the S end or 'wild' parking in the dunes by the soccer pitch on E side (54.0134, -9.9855). The main Dugort beach is Silver (Pollawaddy) Strand 2km W, dominated by dramatic Slievemore with wood-fired sauna (sabhna.ie). Seal Caves campsite is over the road, mostly static with a tent area to rear (F28 P273, +353 87 3536379). Explore around the E face of the E headland to find the real seal caves (54.0159, -10.0123).

2 mins, 54.0139, -9.9916

2 ANNAGH STRAND 'SECRET BEACH'

Remote, spectacular LT cove below an ancient tomb and the glacial Lough Nakeeroge, with no marked trail in. Start from the end of Slievemore Road, past the famine village (see entry), head W to the ruined signal tower and 2km beyond. Alternatively start from Lough Acorrymore as for the Cliffs of Croaghaun (see entry) and continue N and E at the ridge, descending L around the lough. Both routes are serious walks.

120 mins, 53.9998, -10.1340

3 KEEM BEACH & BENMORE CLIFFS

At the far tip of Achill and always popular with wild campers (despite signs), this picturesque bay is E facing so best visited in the morning. Made world-famous as a location in The Banshees of Inisheerin. A steep trail leads up to the lookout on Moytoge Head (53.9627, -10.1975) and then a dramatic coastal ridge walk about 2km NW along the Benmore Cliffs (332m, 53.9715, -10.2185). The infamous Croaghaun sea cliff/summit (664m, 53.9815, -10.2061) is beyond, but difficult, so return to Keem down the valley through a village emptied in the 19th century (53.9700, -10.2003).

2 mins, 53.9674, -10.19561

4 ASHLEAM BAY & WHITE CLIFFS

Below the shard-like stacks and white cliffs that give it the name Port na hAille, this cove is one of those where the sand comes and goes. With or without its top-dressing, it is a favoured traditional spot to view New Year's Eve sunsets, and the water is always an ethereal blue. Park at the N end, maybe walk W to view the stacks, then head down to the beach. There are

numerous options for coasteering/jumps along the coast. Try the inlets on headland SW of Dooega (53.9152, -10.0404, pictured).
7 mins, 53.9027, -9.9922

5 MURREVAGH BEACH *

A nearly empty sweep of sand, with the foundation outlines of a lost village and graveyard blurring into the flowery fields behind. Perfect sundown beach, with wild overnight parking on the machair. Take the very bumpy track through Mulranny Golf Links car park, or ask to park at clubhouse and walk. Links signed on the road through the village.
7 mins, 53.8963, -9.7521

6 BERTRA BEACH

Long spit of sand and shingle that broadens to a triangular tip, like a pennant on a pole; you can walk to the end for views over the drowned drumlins of Clew Bay. Swim off either side depending on the wind. Increasing winter storms may destroy the bar and leave the end an island, so visit it while you can.
2 mins, 53.7899, -9.6586

7 FALDUFF STRAND & OLD HEAD

A long stretch of gently shelving sand, good for children, with sheltering cliffs and great views to Croagh Patrick. A small parking area, good

for overnights, signed L18282 off the R335 towards Kilsallagh. The W end is Old Head with all the facilities, a pier for jumping, a mobile sauna (slaintesaunas.ie) and kayak hire/classes (summersup.ie).
2 mins, 53.7746, -9.7533

8 CROSS/SRUHIR BEACH

One of the most popular surfing beaches in Ireland, and home to horse races one day in July. Majestic views of Croagh Patrick, Mweelrea, and the islands of Clew Bay in front, and Lough Roonach along a sandy meandering stream in the dunes behind. Wild parking on the pebbly ground. The N end, from Carrownisky (also used as a name for the strand), tends to be a little busier (53.7354, -9.8931).
1 min, 53.7219, -9.8997

9 WHITE STRAND, CORRAGAUN

These flat sands, also called Tullaghbawn, constantly shift; depending on recent storms, much of the vast expanse may be under a thin glaze of water even at LT, and right under this latlong is a lost graveyard marked on old maps. There is a car park at the end of the lane past F28 XN97, but perhaps the best way to experience this beach is with Horse Back West (F28 W226, +353 87 6104306, horsebackwest@gmail.com).
10 mins, 53.6713, -9.9044

10 SILVER STRAND, DOOVILRA

A less-visited WAW viewpoint beach, narrow and dramatic, nestled under Mweelrea at the end of a long single-track lane and perfect for sunsets. Just before is the entrance to the Lost Valley, a fascinating historical site where a whole village of 17 households were evicted in 1851. Gerard Bourke, descendant of a tenant, now leads brilliant 90-min walking tours, including a sheepdog demonstration; pre-booking essential (€25, F28 D651, +353 85 1139977, thelostvalley.ie).
2 mins, 53.6499, -9.8809

TINY ISLANDS

11 INIS BIGIL/INISHBIGGLE

Walk on vanishing lanes past the old church and dozens of cottages falling or fallen to ruin, between flowery meadows and bogs haunted by choughs. Only a handful of older residents remain; in winter ferocious currents often isolate the island. In fair weather there is a ferry from Doran's Point to the E (Micheal Leneghan, +353 87 1269618) or from Dooniver, Achill to the W (Joe O'Malley, +353 86 0612482/+353 86 0612482) making the island a great stepping stone on a cycle tour.

30 mins, 53.9941, -9.8939

12 ROSSMORE, CLEW BAY

These sunken drumlins create an archipelago of tiny sandy islands, said to be one for every day of the year. Head out onto the remote spit of Rossmore to find yourself among some of them, and Rabbit Island 300m opp. If you have your own kayak, you could explore more. Signed L14023 from the N59. Or take a boat trip from Rosmoney Pier (53.8256, -9.6204).

2 mins, 53.8846, -9.5913

13 TRÁNAUN, INISHTURK

A small white sand cove with turquoise waters and views of the mainland mountains beyond. From the harbour (ferries from Roonagh Pier, F28 W8P3, +353 87 2413783) walk S to the Community Centre and shop then through the field, where potato ridges are still clearly visible under the grass.

20 mins, 53.7004, -10.0884

CLARE ISLAND

14 CLARE ISLAND LIGHTHOUSE

If you're looking to treat yourself, there is boutique accommodation in Clare Island's converted lighthouse complex. One option is a detached cottage with a private patio and sauna with a view, and if you don't fancy cooking for yourself (limited shopping on the island, so plan and shop before crossing) there is a private chef for hire. Ballytoughey, F28 X073, +353 87 6689758, clareislandlighthouse.com

53.8274, -9.9829

15 THE COVE, CLARE ISLAND

A tiny fishing harbour used by local currach fishermen, with a waterfall flowing down the cliff, this is an ideal place for a quiet swim. There's a mostly straight path starting from the road at 53.8177, -9.9761. Reached from Cloughmore pier, 9.30am every Wed & Sun, advance bookings only (+353 98 23737).

60 mins, 53.8210, -9.9712

11

16 KNOCKMORE CLIFFS

Unparalleled views and cliffs populated by fulmars, gulls, cormorants, gannets, and great skuas. Inland sheep-nibbled fields host wheatears and meadow pipits. A good area for wild camping, and you can walk a loop of the western island in a couple of days. Path ascends NW for about 2km from the lane across the middle of the island at 53.8086, -9.9864; continuing W there's a trig point on Knockmore (53.8080, -10.0205) and 'Mackenzies Monument' (53.8055, -10.0240), a maritime marker from the 1770s atop an ancient cairn.

60 mins, 53.8128, -10.0007

17 LECARROW COURT TOMB

Clare Island is famed for its medieval sites, but in the hummocky bog to the N lie more ancient remains including this roofless Neolithic tomb with views to Croagh Patrick, traces of a court and the low remains of a cairn. Site 20 on the signed Clew Bay Archaeological Trail; from the harbour follow the N part of Knockaveen walking loop or the road N to the lighthouse; a signed trail between them passes the tomb.

45 mins, 53.8058, -9.9644

18 SHIVEL HEAD SIGNAL TOWER

This gaunt ruin brooding over the western cliffs is simply called the Napoleonic Tower by

13

12

16

16

18

20

the residents of Clare Island. The neighbours in the chain, on Achill to the N and Inishturk to the S, are still standing and visible in good weather. Follow the road W from the harbour, becoming a track then a path, at the W coast, turn N. Serious hikers can take a day and walk a full loop of the island via Knockmore sea cliffs (see entry).

120 mins, 53.8003, -10.0464

19 SEA ARCH COVE

Clare Island coast is full of caves and arches, and the small cove 200m S of the harbour and castle is one of the easiest and quickest to reach, on track beyond Shoreline Pursuits (e-bike hire, +353 87 2684312) below barn.

5 mins, 53.7982, -9.9517

20 CLARE ISLAND ABBEY

Grace O'Malley is sometimes claimed to have died on the island; she is certainly buried here below the elegant tracery arch of the family tomb in this 12th-century Cistercian abbey. Above the tomb are Ireland's best remaining medieval ceiling paintings; only a handful of examples exist at all, and no flash photography is allowed. Look for dragons, a cockerel, stags, men on foot and on horseback, a harper, birds and trees. Signed from the harbour, collect the key from the local post office, O'Malley's Foodstore, just before you reach it.

30 mins, 53.7932, -9.9889

LOUGHS, RIVERS & FALLS

21 LOCH GEAL/GAR, WESTERN GREENWAY

With little beaches and easy access this lake is super stop off along the R319 to/from Achill. It's even better reached by cycle on the Westport–Achill 42km old railway, which could make a fantastic car-free weekend. The route takes in coastline and mountain and Sea Breeze bike hire is at both ends (+353 83 845 7337).

2 mins, 53.9371, -9.8225

22 ROCKFLEET CASTLE & RAIGH PIER

This imposing 15th-century tower house (also called Carraigahowley), which may be where legendary chieftain Grace O'Malley died, stands by a small inlet of Newport Bay. You can swim from here or a pier further W on the lane with HT jumps (53.8945, -9.6381). Signed L off the N59 17km N of Newport. Follow about 850m and pull off at castle.

1 min, 53.8960, -9.6270

23 LOUGH FEEAGH & WILD NEPHIN

Fed by the pure, peaty waters of Nephin Beg, there's no formal access, but people do swim from the beach at the N end. There's some verge parking by the field gate, then 50m to the shore. The lane leads on to the bothy and Letterkeen trailhead parking where there's also the stream for paddling (53.9893, -9.5727).

3 mins, 53.9578, -9.5705

24 DOO LOUGH & BEN LUGMORE

Stop for a dip at the shale cove on the impressively scenic R335 and take a moment to read about the 1849 famine walk, a desperate and deadly 20-mile return trip in a storm. Quieter beaches, away from the road, are at the N end, also the start point for the tough, steep ascent of Ben Lugmore (803m) to the SW. Park on verge at 53.6621, -9.7726. Another ascent is from the S end of the lake (53.6417, -9.7464) where wild camping also seems to be popular.

1 min, 53.6526, -9.7588

25 BUNDORRAGHA RIVER, DELPHI VALLEY

A glacial valley carries this popular fly-fishing river from Fin Lough to Killary Harbour with glorious pools, weirs and neat river banks. It's all private land, so the best option for a dip is the rarely fished pool above the road bridge, just N of the Delphi resort, with parking for two cars. Downstream are pools with laybys, tempting for a picnic or a dip when no-one is fishing; 500m along the road below the waterfall (53.6183, -9.7526); or another 1km down, through a gate, is a bit more private (53.6096, -9.7511).

1 min, 53.6236, -9.7524

21

23

28

26 KILLARY HARBOUR PIER

Dip in the round, sheltered river pool, or jump into Ireland's only fjord from the pier. The views S across the water are superb.

1 min, 53.6062, -9.7522

27 HOUSTON'S BRIDGE, ERRIFF RIVER

Super, huge river pool below bridge and waterfalls, with views over Glennacally peak, with more pools upstream. Parking by bridge.

0 mins, 53.6352, -9.6081

28 AASLEAGH FALLS, ERRIF RIVER

Popular but beautiful waterfalls where you can watch salmon leap, and maybe recognise the setting for the pivotal fight scene from The Field. A riverside path leads up to them, and you can swim in the deep river pools just upstream.

2 mins, 53.6196, -9.6705

LOST RUINS

29 GRACE O'MALLEY'S CASTLE

Caisleán Ghráinne is a solid 15th-century tower house, properly called Kildavnet. It stands by the road with stunning views over Achill Sound and access to the water's edge. You can see why it was such a valuable site for the O'Malley clan, who controlled the waters of Clew Bay for generations, although Grace is romanticised as a pirate. Follow the L1405 and WAW signs L after crossing to the island, park at Cloughmore Small Pier after 7km and walk back 100m.

3 mins, 53.8808, -9.9458

30 FAMINE VILLAGE, SLIEVEMORE, ACHILL

The village lasted from at least the 12th century until it was almost entirely emptied by the Famine in the 1840s. Of the 137 houses mapped in 1837, just 80 can be made out today, full of ferns and wild flowers. The village and old cemetery (with parking) are signed from a bend in the road between Keel and Dugort. Much can be easily explored just above the cemetery, but the last ruin is about 1km to the W on the track; the scant remains of a Napoleonic signal tower and an overgrown lime kiln stand on Saddle Hill beyond (53.9967, -10.1085), although there is no proper path.

5 mins, 53.9971, -10.0769

31 ACHILL HENGE

Far from ancient, this hilltop monument with massive views was built from concrete slabs over one weekend in 2011 by local Joe McNamara, as a protest against government policies. He lost a long legal battle, but won local support, and the structure remains, a monument to sheer stubbornness. Heading W through Pollagh turn R just after the church, then R again after 230m (at F28 FA47). This

31

29

34

road becomes a track and impassable to normal cars at about 700m, so pull over where you can and walk the last 400m or so.

7 mins, 53.9786, -10.0995

32 BURRISHOOLE FRIARY

Lovely 15th-century priory ruin on the river mouth. The living quarters have gone, replaced by graves, but most of the church remains, with a tower, tracery windows, and a buttressed cloister wall. From Newport, head N on N59 for 1.8km. Take signed L for abbey at F28 X981 and follow narrow lane 600m to parking at end. 78Q

2 mins, 53.8987, -9.5721

33 BUNLAHINCH CLAPPER BRIDGE

The 37 slabbed sections of this impressive pedestrian crossing span 50m, making it the longest clapper bridge in Ireland. Although an ancient form, it was built in the 1840s for a Protestant mission that gave out soup in exchange for conversion during the Famine (the church gates remain at 53.7181, -9.8850). Cars must drive through the ford when the water is low enough. Unsigned lane R off the R378 6.5km S from Louisburgh with space to pull off L before ford; the lane continues to Bunlough Strand.

1 min, 53.7182, -9.8886

SACRED & ANCIENT

34 KEEL EAST TOMB, ACHILL

Handsome monument with a striking flat roof slab, a circular court outlined by stones, and magnificent views from mighty Slievemore. A curious earthwork, the 'Danish Ditch', extends W 200m to a shelter once thought to be another ancient monument. There is another less-distinct tomb on the way in (53.9989, -10.0602). Path signed R 3km W from Dugort, parking just beyond on L.

10 mins, 53.9999, -10.0600

35 MURRISK ABBEY

This small 15th-century Augustinian ruin is beautifully sited on the seashore and is a traditional starting point for the pilgrimage up Croagh Patrick (see entry), as the site was reputed to be originally one of his churches. The long, narrow church has vaulted chambers and a fine Irish Gothic window to the E, with carved heads on the wall outside probably representing wealthy patrons. Bus 450 from Westport stops in Murrisk, or there is parking right by the abbey.

5 mins, 53.7819, -9.6395

36 OLD KILGEEVER ABBEY

Picturesque ruin with medieval pillar and slabs with incised crosses in the graveyard; pilgrims on Reek Sunday deepen the scratched crosses on the rocks. Some visit the holy well at the graveyard entrance on July 15th and complete the daunting 'pattern' of 70 prayers. From the centre of Louisburgh follow Chapel Street SE 2.8km, then Archaeological Trail sign R to park at the new graveyard and walk down to the old.

2 mins, 53.7629, -9.7646

37 SRAHWEE WEDGE TOMB

Perhaps Ireland's best-preserved wedge tomb, with a large flat stone covering the double-walled chamber, this is called Altóir by the locals, who used it as an altar in Penal times; there is a cross cut into the surface. It was also honoured as a holy spring called Tobernahaltora, for Lough Nahaltora over the road – where the preserved stumps of Scots pine that grew when the tomb was built 4,500 years ago can be seen in the cutaway bog. Follow R335 N 6km from Doo Lough (see entry) and turn L onto R378; after 1.3km the tomb is R at a sharp turn with space to pull off.

1 min, 53.7061, -9.8249

WILDS HILL & CLIFFS

38 SLIEVEMORE, ACHILL

An imposing peak with mighty views both out to sea and inland down to the deserted village on its southern flank. There is a short, steep walk

40

38

39

up from Dugort to the E, but the approach from the W is slightly less tough; there's no real trail either way. From the cemetery parking for the deserted village (see entry) walk W and turn R as the houses peter out (53.9965, -10.0897). Head up and slightly R to the ridge and follow this up to the summit.

90 mins, 54.0098, -10.0595

39 MINAUN HEIGHTS, ACHILL

Right in the middle of the island, the views from this 403m peak are worth the 3km mountain lane, even if you do share them with a transmitter. It can get windy, but it's also an exciting spot for overnights.

1 min, 53.9570, -10.0268

40 CLIFFS OF CROAGHAUN, ACHILL

The highest sea cliffs in Ireland offer 18km of unmatched views, with peregrine falcons soaring above whales, dolphins, porpoises, and basking sharks. Start from Lough Acorrymore, signed R on the R319 W of Dooagh. Cross the dam and head NE for about 1km (poor GPS) before turning W to ascend the cliffs above the perfect glacial corrie of Bunnafreva Lough West; always stay inland of the eroding ridge. The goal is spectacular Southwest Top (53.9816, -10.2056), an almost sheer 664m drop, then back around the SW of the lough past the site of a 1950 plane crash (white rock at 53.9827, -10.1874) to the road and L back to the car park. The experienced may try from the N end of Benmore Cliffs above Keem Bay (see entry), but the tough, sustained ascent defeats most walkers.

150 mins, 53.9815, -10.1673

41 CROAGH PATRICK

Ireland's holiest mountain, where St Patrick is said to have fasted for 40 days and nights, has been a site of worship for over five millennia. It has some of the best views in Ireland, encompassing Mayo to the Partry Mountains around the south, and the many drumlins of Clew Bay to the north. Thousands walk the steep, stony historic path to the 764m summit on Reek Sunday (the last Sunday in July) as a life marker, a pilgrimage of tradition or of faith; a few will walk it barefoot. There's a very large pay car park (€3) for this in Murrisk on the R335, but those looking for wildness more than tradition can bushwhack the W ridge, via Ben Goram (park on lane at 53.7642, -9.7060) with better views from the start. Or another good track from R335, but with tricky parking, at 53.7796, -9.6748.

140 mins, 53.7599, -9.6597

42 MWEELREA MOUNTAIN

Of the several routes up Connacht's highest mountain, the seaward side has some of the best views even before the summit panorama. Start up a dead-end lane about 1km before Silver Strand (see entry), with some space to park at the end (53.6547, -9.8692). Beyond the gate there is no real trail, just head R aiming for the stream visible coming down from the ridge (53.6452, -9.8378) and follow it up, then R along the ridge to the summit. Steep scree slopes at the top. Alternative approaches from NE at Doo Lough (see entry) takes in Ben Lugmore on a long, tough horsehoe trail.

120 mins, 53.6371, -9.8316

FOREST & WILDLIFE

43 ERRIFF WOODS, OWENMORE

This is a rare and magical stretch of old riparian sessile oak woods, carpeted with ferns. Path leads in from the layby on S side (L bank), with a ruin and a waterfall along the way. River access is better downstream, by anglers' path on the other bank.

0 mins, 53.6544, -9.5718

44 CLAGGAN MOUNTAIN COASTAL TRAIL

Between a quiet sea inlet and Claggan Mountain, this boardwalk leads over heathers, bog cotton and sundews, with darting butterflies and dragonflies; you can return along a shore dotted with bog oak stumps like strange sculptures. Lies within the dark skies

43

44

43

area if you fancy an easy night viewing spot. Trailhead and car park 6.3km N of Mulranny on N59, 800m after F28 EH32 on the R.

12 mins, 53.94998, -9.7958

45 MULRANNY CAUSEWAY

Follow the causeway from the beach to a wide expanse of shallow sands for paddling on R. On the L side is salt marsh, with orchids in spring, thrift in summer, native birds all year and huge flocks of Brent geese in autumn. Park along the road by the beach, on the road to the pier. Or to walk in from N, take steps below the Mulranny Park Hotel on N59.

2 mins, 53.8975, -9.7822

CLASSIC PUBS

46 PURE MAGIC *

Founded by Alex LeVieux, this legendary and madcap restaurant, lodge, and adventure centre has great views, quirky rooms and prize-winning pizzas – the place to go to eat and talk outdoor adventure. Slievemore Rd, F28 HN27, +353 85 2439782

53.9961, -10.0542

47 LYNOTT'S PUB

Tiny thatched stone pub with open fire, locals playing music sessions, and lively atmosphere within. Cashel, Achill, F28 YV24, +353 86 0843137

53.9632, -9.9767

48 MATT MOLLOY'S

When a pub is owned by a member of The Cheiftans, you don't really need to know much else: proper old-fashioned Irish bar with a buzzing atmosphere and live music every night, but no food. Bridge Street, Westport, F28 FV40, +353 98 26655

53.7992, -9.52262

49 CRONIN'S SHEEBEEN

Traditional pub looking out over one of Westport Bay's many inlets. Dog friendly, cosy fires in the winter, and a solid reputation for food prepared from fresh local ingredients. Closed Mon and Tues. Rosbeg, Westport, F28 VK70, +353 98 26528

53.7940, -9.56095

LOCAL PRODUCE

50 KELLY'S KITCHEN, NEWPORT

Farm to fork cafe and deli: all their food is sourced from local farmers, via the family's own artisan butchers next door. Crumbles, scones and pickles are home-made and there's a grab-and-go deli in the form of a fridge stocked with

45

everything from local kombuchas to regional cheeses. Main Steet, +353 9841647

53.8858, -9.5465

51 CROAGH PATRICK SEAFOODS

Taste the freshest of oysters at this family-run farm, which also sells mussels and clams and offers tours. Open Wed–Sun, Roslaher, Westport, F28 AV96, +353 87 2497570

53.8576, -9.5625

52 KRÊM GELATERIA & CAFÉ

Four generations of pastry and gelato making lie behind the extraordinary range of flavours

47

53

55

55

56

at Graham Byrne's award-winning café. Irish porter and whiskey, brown bread, and blue cheese are on the menu alongside more typical fruit and sweet flavours; vegan sorbet options too. Bridge Street, Westport, F28 XD43
53.7992, -9.5223

53 MESCAN BREWERY

More microbrewery than craft brewery, Mescan has a small but excellent range of Belgian-style beers that are available in many of the best bars and restaurants locally, but barely seen outside the area. It is the passion project of two ex-vets, Belgian Bart Adons and local Cillian Ó Móráin, and named after the monk who was St Patrick's friend and personal brewer. Tours most Fris through the summer. Kilsallagh, Westport, F28 FW70, +353 86 8320320
53.7472, -9.7283

ORGANIC & GASTRO

54 STONE BARN CAFÉ

Vegetarian restaurant that is part of Macalla Farm but open to passing customers in the summer months only (occasional pop-up in shoulder seasons), serving food that is almost entirely organic and homegrown or locally sourced. There are also seasonal cooking courses you can book in advance. Open 11.30am to 4pm, Thurs–Sun, Ballytoohey More, F28 DN82, +353 87 2504845.
53.8151, -9.9753

55 AN PORT MÓR RESTAURANT *

Frankie Mallon has a mantra of 'keep it fresh, keep it simple, keep it consistent' but also keeps it seasonal and original. The restaurant is a quirky maze of atmospheric rooms, from jazzy to refined, and this is the place to come for the very best of Mayo produce; no under 12s or vegan options. 1 Brewery Place (off Bridge Street), Westport, F28 KP70, +353 98 26730
53.7990, -9.5218

56 THIS MUST BE THE PLACE

Cool bistro-style gastro lunches, breakfast and groceries from local produce, right on the corner of the High Street, Westport, F28 Y440, +353 98 44871
53.7983, -9.5233

57 THE TAVERN BAR & RESTAURANT

The front wall of this roadside gastropub is crammed with awards. Inside you find a cosy, traditional bar-restaurant serving local produce in generous portions with amazing oysters, chowder and organic smoked salmon. Murrisk, Westport, +353 98 64060
53.7782, -9.6309

BEACH CAMPING

58 KEEL SANDYBANKS CAMPING PARK

There aren't many campsites on Achill, so unless you're going fully wild, this site with the beach in front and the hills behind is clean and friendly if a little dated, and very busy in summer; Keel Beach is popular with surfers. The Sandybanks, Keel East, Achill, F28 EA47, +353 98 43211, achillcamping.com
53.9747, -10.0770

59 MULRANNY CAMPING & GLAMPING

Simple camping right on the beach near the Causeway (see entry), with firepits and basic facilities provided by Ciara and Pádraig. +353 87 6385071
53.8982, -9.7864

WILD NEPHIN BOTHIES

60 LETTERKEEN BOTHY

Wild Nephin National Park encompasses the Nephin Beg mountains and some of the most remote landscapes in Ireland, and by night it becomes Mayo Dark Sky Park. There are shelters and designated wild-camping spots, which can only be used by those who have pre-registered at the website – a process requested for all visitors, but essential for camping. The Letterkeen trailhead (four looped trails start from here) is the darkest and most remote site still accessible by car, and this stone bothy, also called the Brogan Carroll Bothy, is open for shelter, if notified; you can hike to wild-camping spots and the Altnabrocky Shelter (54.0453, -9.5868), Tarsaghaun Cottage (54.0821, -9.7305) or Lough Avoher Shelter (54.0042, -9.6202). Signed off the L1402 from Newport to Furnace, campingwildnephin.com
53.9893, -9.5728

RUSTIC RETREATS

61 THE VALLEY HOUSE, ACHILL

Popular hostel, bar and restaurant in old country house with castle parapets and archway. Opposite is a beautiful woodland, with a 'faerie trail' perfect for kids although there is a small entrance fee. Tonatanvally, F28 D8F7, +353 85 2167688
54.0126, -9.9697

62 MULRANNY HOUSE

Established over a century ago, this family B&B also served as the village post office and garda station in the past; all the rooms look out over Clew Bay below and are simply furnished. Sarah and Nick offer breakfasts from local produce including home-made jams, and will make up picnics, a great option for those travelling on the

greenway. Mulranny Garda Station, Murrevagh, Westport, F28 P285, +353 98 36953
53.9064, -9.7781

63 MACALLA FARM

Ciara and Christophe have been running this organic, regenerative farm for two decades, and offer Sati yoga retreats, vegetarian cookery courses, and volunteering farm placements with accommodation (mostly but not entirely from Easter to autumn). Ballytoohey More, F28 TR96, +353 87 2621832, calendar at macallafarm.ie
53.8162, -9.9754

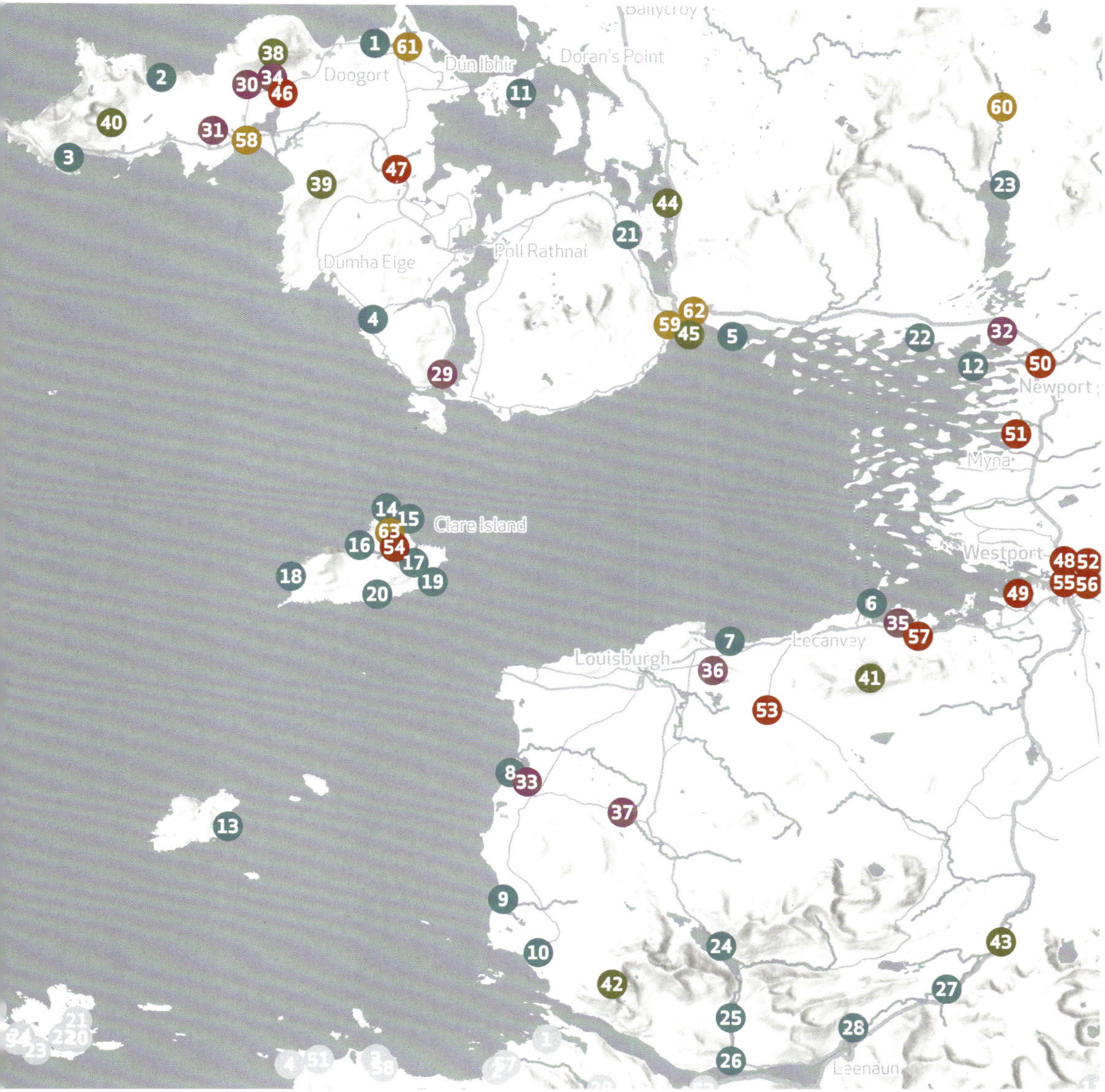

EAST MAYO

Our perfect weekend

- ➔ **Pack** a picnic from Café Rua & deli and take a day to climb Nephin for panoramic views.
- ➔ **Watch** the bats stream out of Moore Hall on a summer dusk, or the starlings swirl above the waters on a winter evening.
- ➔ **Follow** woodland paths to swim at lovely Tourmakeady Waterfall, and visit the Gothic church across the road on your return.
- ➔ **Bask** on the amber sands of Lough Nafooey, or seek out the towering waterfall upstream.
- ➔ **Climb** the Guinness Tower and descend into the Pigeon Hole cave in the Cong woods, and refuel with home-baked treats at McHughs.
- ➔ **Follow** the ill-fated Cong Canal, from the dry lock to the other worldly shore of Lough Mask.
- ➔ **Stand** in the grove of trees at Glebe stone circle then visit the thorn-clad and hare-haunted slopes of Ballymacgibbon Cairn.
- ➔ **Walk** in the Ard Na Gaoithe woods, owned by the Guinness family, swim by their chalet, then take tea in their old home, Ashford Castle.
- ➔ **Explore** mysterious Cregduff ringfort, then seek out hidden Kilmaine Church and the lonely ruin of Kilmaine Castle.

This inland region is dominated by loughs, all renowned for trout fishing and all with swimming spots, some with limestone pavement shores, others with tree-lined beaches like Drummin Wood.

In the north are Cullin and Conn, named for Fionn mac Cumhaill's hounds, which flow out through the Moy to Ballina. In the south the shallow, warm waters of Lough Carra flow into mighty Lough Mask, the second-largest lake in Ireland, before continuing south into Galway.

Castlebar is centred between these two lough systems, an old military base turned university town. It has been hosting a walking festival in early July since 1967, including a full-day Ramble over three routes in spectacular wilderness. The former linen hall is now an arts centre, and the town is a hub for great food and drink, including the historic John McHale pub where you can uniquely buy a 'meejum' Guinness if you fancy something between a glass and a pint.

The village of Cong may attract as many tourists as the rest of the region put together. Some come for the filming locations in the classic movie The Quiet Man, from the local Pat Cohan's bar to estate offices at Ashford Castle. Others come for Cong Abbey, original home of the stunning 12th-century processional Cross of Cong; richly decorated with carvings, the abbey is also the gateway to wonderful woodlands (just over the river in Galway).

There are plenty of other religious ruins to explore, from partly restored Ballintubber with a 500-year-old crucifix that was hidden locally through dangerous times, to Inishmaine dreaming on a remote lough shore. Older remains include some imposing and strangely unvisited tombs like Daithi's Cairn, and a whole set of stone circles at Glebe.

For those who love to stretch their legs, there is only one peak, the 806m Nephin, a surprising distance east from Nephin Beg and the national park, in splendid isolation that makes it Ireland's highest standalone summit. But important landed estates here left some beautiful mature woodlands behind when they declined, now open to all for shady walks. The mighty Ashford Castle, once home of the Guinness family, had not only the woods around Cong Abbey but also Clonbur, with a hidden castle among the trees. On the shores of Lough Carra, the Moore Hall estate is smaller but also has its own grand house ruin, now a protected home for lesser horseshoe bats. Other woods are scraps of ancient native forest, like Drummin.

RIVER MOY & LOUGHS

1 MAGGIE'S BAY, LOUGH CONN

Follow the gravel track 100m to the shore of this easy, sheltered bay, behind Knockmore picnic parking area on the R310. Simply SUP run lessons here (+353 87 9090625). There are wilder beaches W of Knockmore, signed Lisdovogue House: 2km (turn L for Calladashan 54.0140, -9.1913) and 5km (Sandy Bay, shallow coves with parking off tracks 54.0415, -9.2289).

2 mins, 54.0160, -9.1750

2 DRUMMIN WOOD, LOUGH CULLIN

Rare delight of sandy lakeshore beaches, not one but three, set among limestone boulders. Perfect summer fun for families, and never too deep. Behind the mossy old-growth sessile oaks of Drummin Wood SAC rises, with about 4km of walks within.

2 mins, 53.9842, -9.1611

3 WOOD POOL, RIVER MOY

A stretch of fine salmon river, with access from lane end, signed 'Wood Pool' from N26; minimal parking at end. Managed by Knockmore Salmon Anglers, so do not disturb.

5 mins, 54.0246, -9.1216

4 CLOONGEE, RIVER MOY

A remote meander of the old River Moy has created an oxbow lake, with a small anglers' car park. Follow the bank path N 300m for the main river and junction pool, and do not disturb anglers. Signed L53523 off the N58, then sharp R after 800m to parking (with height barrier). For a second anglers' car park upstream, continue 800m on L53523 past the sharp R to 53.9520, -9.1237.

2 mins, 53.9634, -9.1261

5 OLDCASTLE, RIVER MOY

The fishing is private along the deep, dark pools of Mayo's finest salmon fishing river, but you can park up and walk the beautiful banks if you don't disturb anyone. Signed East Mayo Angling from the Oldcastle Road, off N26.

2 mins, 53.9480, -9.0282

LOUGH MASK

6 BALLYGARRY, LOUGH MASK

Secret shoreline with rather shallow, reedy rocky shore, but can warm up nicely. Found down narrow lanes, signed Ballygarry, off the R330 near N84 junction.

2 mins, 53.6842, -9.2944

12

13

13

9

10

7 TOURMAKEADY WATERFALL

Large waterfall with a perfect, deep woodland plunge pool, as if made for swimming. Signed Tourmakeady Woods on R300, with parking at 53.6526, -9.3758. A lovely 1km path up the stream through old estate woodland and Millennium Forest planting continues on around to a lake and back to the parking.

15 mins, 53.6507, -9.3889

8 CAHER PIER, LOUGH MASK

This little pier with verge parking is one of the better spots for a deeper, clearer water swim among the rocky limestone landscape of the lough. Follow Caher signs from W side of Ballinrobe.

2 mins, 53.6113, -9.2993

9 DRINGEEN BAY & CONG CANAL

This is a fascinating limestone pavement shore with smooth rock ledges and deep, clear water, wonderful for swimming and diving, off the L1613, turn at the 'Isham' accommodation sign. There may be anglers, but you can follow the rock shore N for 1.5km and find the end of the Cong Canal, cut to link 8km S to Lough Corrib. The project failed, as water leaked through the limestone strata, but gates and sluices can still be seen, and the dry bed followed in summer (also accessible 1.5km along the old towpath from the L1613 at 53.5737, -9.2898). NB you can also dip in the River Cong in town where a huge spring bubbles up: 50m up from Top garage on the main road (53.5427, -9.2859).

2 mins, 53.5631, -9.3261 ?

10 BIG ISLAND, CLONBUR WOODS

Walk out to the wooded island; from the N tip the water is a little deeper. Turn through semi-circular gateway at Clonbur sign and park by walkers-only gate on L at bend 53.5546, -9.3764.

10 mins, 53.5586, -9.3738

11 SRAHNALONG RIVER FALLS

A long series of narrow pools and waterfalls tumbles from the Partry Mountains through a dramatic glacial U-shaped valley with big views over Loch Mask. Go through the gate at lane end and park near the bridge after 200m. Cross and explore the riverside track upstream for up to 1km.

10 mins, 53.5949, -9.5105 ?

12 LOUGH NAFOOEY WATERFALL

Spectacular cascade over a rockface, with a large, deep pool enclosed in a steep glen. There's not much room to change once you arrive, there may be midges and the path is tricky, but it's worth the expedition. Park at

53.5740, -9.5949 on the L1301 just S of the river bridge and walk upstream on river's R bank for 500m.

15 mins, 53.5729, -9.6021

13 LOUGH NAFOOEY

This sandy lakeshore beach has a gentle slope in at first, then drops off deeper, so careful with kids. People do camp on the shores. Can be popular with locals in summer, with cars parked all along the little L1601. Further along the lane to the E, pass the lakeside pub The Larches (F12 H104, +353 94 9547992), and 200m beyond is a car park viewpoint with potential shore access.

2 mins, 53.5785, -9.5816

14 FINNY RIVER

For something more hidden, follow the fishing track straight down to the river for rapids and pools, with more upstream. On R300 at the L16005 turning.

4 mins, 53.5749, -9.5051

LOUGH CORRIB

15 CHALET BEACH, LOUGH CORRIB

This lake beach sits among the Ard Na Gaoithe woods (with loop walks) and was made famous by the Guinness family, who lived in nearby Ashford Castle up to 1939 and built a summerhouse chalet, hence the name. From the parking walk 50m E along the shore for the beach.

2 mins, 53.5248, -9.3076

16 DERRY QUAY, LOUGH CORRIB

Quiet parking area and slipways on a wooded shore for canoes and swimming, although shallow in summer. Signed Bayview B&B from R346 W of Cross village.

2 mins, 53.5197, -9.2378

LOST RUINS

17 BALLYLAHAN CASTLE

Circular ruins of Anglo-Norman curtain wall and gatehouse towers, once a stronghold at a fording point for the deep waters of the River Moy. Take the R321 for Kiltimagh off the N58 and park on junction after 100m, next to ruins. Another 300m W along N58 on R is turning to a layby by a field gate (53.9364, -9.1119) with anglers' field path to the beautiful river, one of Mayo's finest for salmon and trout.

2 mins, 53.9345, -9.1047

18 MACPHILBIN'S CASTLE & CHURCH

This tower house atop a mound has atmosphere and views but almost no known history; pull

17

18

over by gate on lane (53.7764, -9.4227) and walk up. To the E are the overgrown ruins of St Patrick's church; there is said to be a tunnel between them, but the tower was a ruin before the church was built. It is by a home, do ask to visit, but the interior is closed off for safety.

2 mins, 53.7762, -9.4255

19 DAITHI'S CAIRN

Daithi was a legendary Mayo giant, and despite being robbed of stone for local field walls this is still a giant cairn; at some 60m in diameter it rivals that of Queen Meave atop Knocknarea (see Sligo). It has an unusual enclosing circular wall about 20m out from the kerb, like nearby Eochy's cairn (see entry or 53.5884, -9.2634). Take the lane off the L1612 SW of Ballinrobe at F31 F434 and after 250m pull off R by stone ruin and follow track in along field edges.

2 mins, 53.6099, -9.2549

20 KILMAINE CHURCH & CASTLE

This hidden ivy-clad 19th-century ruin of the Holy Trinity Church still has its bellcote, and below it not only Gothic window openings but a striking heraldic stained-glass window. It lies incongruously behind Burke's Garage N84; follow the driveway to the R. Also, 1km NE in fields are remnants of Cregduff Castle with spiral staircase, zig-zag entrance passage and vaulted cellars (53.5858, -9.1090).

2 mins, 53.5788, -9.1231

21 NEALE HOUSE & FOLLIES

The ruins of the colourful Browne family's house can be found in a field by the woods, and a 2km-loop walk leads to further curiosities. Park outside the Neale school, L5659 signed off R334, and go through the black kissing gate in the wall and 120m NE for the house. On the way, on the R in the woods, is a peculiar monument built with salvaged medieval carvings: an angel, a unicorn and a lion, and an inscription of fanciful Druidic history calling them the 'Gods of Neale' (53.5740, -9.2243). Beneath is a vaulted cellar, built to support a planned tower. Back to road, walk E and first L up the lane to 53.5760, -9.2208 to find a curious hole inside a circular wall by the road L. Opp, 200m E in the field, is a 19th-century Doric temple gazebo on a mound 53.5765, -9.2179 (access dependent on livestock). Continue to lane end and turn L and you'll pass the stone Pyramid in field on R, probably built as famine-relief work in the 1740s. The church they endowed is opp, now a shell. It's on the main road R334, and worth a detour before returning to the school.

40 mins, 53.5746, -9.2232

22 BALLYKINE CASTLE, CLONBUR WOODS

Deep in the woods, mostly visited by deer, lies a little 13th-century castle ruin with a four-storey tower and a mural staircase, colonised by moss, ivy, and small trees, very romantic, slightly spooky. There's a gravel track through the woods from the Coillte car park on the R345 on the E edge of Clonbur village (53.5455, -9.3612), or a quicker approach from very small layby on R345 at 53.5484, -9.3386.

30 mins, 53.5556, -9.3385

23 CONG CANAL LOCK

This curious hidden canyon is a dressed limestone lock, never completed; nearby is a wall over the river, possibly intended for an aqueduct. Both were part of a canal, started in

25

the 1840s to link two loughs through Ashford Castle. It was never completed, due to 'leaky' geology or the advent of railways or both; this is the most accessible part, a short walk down from the car park past the aqueduct R to a house gate (F31 NY57) and then R along the grassy track. The other end can be found 5km upstream at Dringeen Bay (see entry).

5 mins, 53.5427, -9.2846

SACRED & ANCIENT

24 STRAIDE ABBEY

This 13th-century friary ruin houses a flamboyant 15th-century canopy tomb, one of the finest in Ireland: flowing tracery, pinnacles, a cross-shaped finial, a dog for loyalty and faithfulness. The front has two fabulously detailed panels, depicting the birth and death of Christ, and enigmatically a kneeling weaver, a bishop, and saints Peter and Paul. Also a lovely window and an arch decorated with a pelican and eagle. Park at adjoining 19th-century church, now a museum to locally born land reform campaigner Michael Davitt.

2 mins, 53.9214, -9.1287

25 TURLOUGH TOWER

Cycle the greenway from Castlebar through rolling countryside to the Museum of Country Life (or park here, Turlough Park House, F23 HY31, +353 16 777444) and then up to this monastic site with round tower, its cap restored in the 1880s. It almost touches the 17th-century church ruin with two crucifixion plaques on the walls facing W. On fairly high ground, and a ringfort visible on brow of hill across the road.

90 mins, 53.8887, -9.2083

26 AUGHAGOWER CHURCHYARD

Ruined church and 10th-century round tower church now in the centre of a village, built on the site of a wooden church built by St Patrick. In the graveyard is a stone supposedly dented where he knelt, and 'Patrick's tub', a circular bath where pilgrims probably washed their feet. Across the road between the benches is Cloughundra, a 150kg lifting stone marked by the fingers of a giant. At the NW corner are two holy wells; there is a sheelagh na gig in the wall around the one over the road.

2 mins, 53.7640, -9.4647

27 BALLINTUBBER ABBEY

Now restored, this beautiful building, the start of the Tochár Phádraig pilgrim route up Croagh Patrick (see entry), is 'the abbey that refused to die'; mass has been said here for 800 years without a break, even after it was burned and left roofless by Cromwellian soldiers in 1653 and mass was illegal. S from Castlebar on the

30

32

33

38

N84 for 9km and turn L, signed Attavally, then 2km, F12 W584.

2 mins, 53.7566, -9.2828

28 BURRISCARRA FRIARY

Most extensive 13th-century Augustinian ruin in Ireland, with carvings including a piscina and tracery window, in a beautiful hillside setting hidden below a 14th-century parish church ruin. Signed W from Carnacon village, follow lane 1.7km to cemetery with parking. Ruin hunters could seek out Clogher House mansion, lost ancient estate oak, 2km N, but on private land, so ask first (53.7489, -9.2432 with access from lane end 53.7481, -9.2362).

2 mins, 53.7309, -9.2457

29 CHRIST CHURCH, TOURMAKEADY

This elegant Gothic church is peaceful and picturesque now, but was built in the 1850s by a Church of Ireland bishop – buried in the overgrown graveyard – who then forcibly evicted every Catholic within a mile of it. Inside, the unusual slate-hung walls are still partly intact. Signed L and visible from the R300 S of Tourmakeady.

2 mins, 53.6533, -9.3636

30 INISHMAINE ABBEY

Beautiful lost ruin of early-13th-century Benedictine abbey by the lakeshore. Lovely carvings on the chancel arch, and internal stairs to climb. The site, founded in the 7th century, was originally an island (inish), and the stony-terraced lakeshore is a serene spot for a picnic. Turn off the L1612 4km SW of Ballinrobe, at sign for Ballinchalla Cemetery. Follow 2km, turn R immediately after gate, then R again before houses and pull off near abbey in field L.

2 mins, 53.5980, -9.3012

31 CREGDUFF RINGFORT

The history of this 100m structure, with 135 low standing stones and concentric walled banks, is unclear; it could be defensive, or ritualistic. Easily seen from N84, but on private land adjacent to a new house, so ask there first. Julian Cope didn't, but parked at 53.5704, -9.1198, scurried along the N field hedge and found a clear opening into the henge interior on the N.

2 mins, 53.5696, -9.1178

32 GLEBE STONE CIRCLE

Atmospheric circle of 20 stones on a hillock under trees, the largest of four grouped circles. Park carefully by the gate of the Deanery (F31 HX61), walk 100m N to the concrete stile (Heritage Trail 9 sign), and cross the field. The cattle fence can be stepped over at the far side. The other circles are at Tonleeaun with no access (53.5480, -9.2621), and Nymphsfield (53.5473, -9.2635 and 53.5477, -9.2647) on a track to the S of the Deanery (ask permission). NB 2km SW is Kelly's Cave, signed through woods at a red wall stile at 53.5444 -9.2793, but it is usually gated and locked.

3 mins, 53.5485, -9.2636

33 BALLYMACGIBBON CAIRN

Impressive, unopened limestone cairn, 45m across and 10m high, with the remains of a lime kiln at the N side and trees growing on the lower slopes. It provides cover for wildlife, so approach quietly; we got close to hares in the scrub. Pull off the R346 at the end of the track 3.3km E of Cong, walk up the track to a stile and across the field, 250m.

3 mins, 53.5421, -9.2371

CAVES & CAVERNS

34 CARRAIG AILLE & AILLE LOUGH

The Aille River disappears into a cavern and runs E for 3km underground. It's a bit of a mission, but a pleasant walk on part of Tóchar Phádraig, the longest and most ancient of the pilgrim paths to Croagh Patrick. Park at the lane end, 53.7688, -9.41089, by the cottage and lake where you can picnic and swim. Back up the lane 220m is a waymark L over the wall and a stair-stile visible across the field (if there is livestock to avoid, the track L further up the lane also leads to this). About 75m beyond the stile, drop down into the valley L and wade up the sandy stream. The entrance is under the cliff but prone to rock falls and fast-rising floods, so do not enter.

15 mins, 53.7706, -9.4129

35 PIGEON HOLE & CAVES, CONG WOOD

Stream cave reached by a flight of stone steps down a deep, narrow fissure. In folklore this is home to a woman transformed into a magic trout and waiting for her lost love. For shortest route park off the R345 at the entrance marked Pigeon Woods (53.5420, -9.3088) then path 100m E or walk 2km through woods from Cong Abbey. To the E is Dog's Cave in a cliff (53.5415, -9.2996) but much easier is Teach Aille cave/ice house (pictured) just 50m from the footbridge into the woods (53.5391, -9.2904).

2 mins, 53.5422, -9.3069

HILLTOPS & VIEWS

36 GUINNESS TOWER, CONG WOODS

Superb stone tower in the woods, built by the Guinness family in 1864, when they owned Ashdown Castle. It is usually open, not often visited and can be climbed for great views. About 800m S then W from Cong Abbey (see entry).

15 mins, 53.5371, -9.2952

34

36

35

37 NEPHIN, GLEANN NÉIFINNE

Fabulous panoramic views from the 806m peak, over Lough Conn to the E and the wilds of the Dark Sky Park to the W. Best route up is on the N slopes, a strenous 8km marked trail that starts gravel but becomes a serious boggy hike. Starts opp Nephin car park, 2.5km W from Lahardane, turning off the R315 at F26 E3H5.

120 mins, 54.0131, -9.3687

WOODS & WILDLIFE

38 MOORE HALL & WOODS

Famous ivy-clad ruins of a grand 18th-century house, once home of the novelist George Moore, which was burned out in the civil war. No access to protect resident bats, but you can peer in through the windows and explore a servants' tunnel. The woods are forestry with native trees regenerating and home to red squirrels; the walled garden is now a wild native meadow. WCs and often a food truck in the car park, and a swimming beach 1km NE along the road on shore of Lough Carra.

6 mins, 53.7133, -9.2262

39 CONG ABBEY & WOODS

Original home of the exquisite gold-decorated Cross of Cong, now in the National Museum, and some of Ireland's finest early-Gothic

36

39

architecture. Over the stream are the woods, once part of the Ashford Castle estate, with fine specimens of coast redwoods, yews and sequoias among the deciduous broadleaves. As well as the caves and tower (see entries) there's the ruined Priest's House (53.5400, -9.2968). All the walks start over the bridge past the adorable Monk's Fishing House, with access to beautiful river bank for paddling and swimming (best upstream, may be anglers).

5 mins, 53.5397, -9.2901

40 LOUGH CARRA MURMURATIONS

A wonderful place to see birds any time, but from late autumn to spring, starlings flock and swirl over the waters in the evening twilight, and near Moore Hall, you can watch them in a picture-perfect setting, reflected in the water with the last of the light behind them. In summer, swallows roost in the bulrushes, there are resident swans and many species of duck, and white-tailed sea eagles have been filmed here in recent years. Watch from shore car park, or kayak out beneath them.

1 min, 53.7114, -9.2229

LOCAL PRODUCE

41 CAFÉ RUA & DELI

Funky bistro-style café serving fine local produce since 1995, now run by the second generation. Closed Sun but they also have a deli 10 mins' walk S on Spencer Street (F23 P302), open every day, so you can take gorgeous local stuff home with you. 2 New Antrim St, Castlebar, F23 E177, +353 94 9023376

53.8589, -9.2980

42 RYAN'S FOOD EMPORIUM, CONG

Deli, traditional butcher, and wine shop in the heart of Cong village. Main St, Cong, F31 XF75, +353 94 9546035

53.5414, -9.2867

ORGANIC & GASTRO

43 BAR ONE, CADDENS

Good GF, vegetarian and vegan options, and a big focus on local ingredients. Rush Street, Castlebar, F23 RW68, +353 94 9034800

53.8580, -9.2967

44 HOUSE OF PLATES

Casual, excellent, contemporary Irish food, and a menu full of surprises. Wed–Sat dinner, Sun lunch and dinner. Upper Chapel Street, Castlebar, F23 XC56, +353 94 9250742

53.8576, -9.3015

45 DEVOUR BAKERY

Colourful bakery, food shop and café with great patisserie, always busy. 3 Church Ln, Friarsquarter West, Ballinrobe, F31 CK64, +353 94 9521626

53.6226, -9.2203

46 MCHUGH'S CAFÉ

McHugh's began with a van in the 1950s, and now have seven great cafés across Mayo run by the third generation. Loose-leaf tea, fresh-ground coffee, and home-made sandwiches and pastries. Abbey Street, Cong, F31 YE37, +353 87 1525004

53.5407, -9.2875

WATERSIDE CAMPING

47 CARROWKEEL CAMPING & CARAVAN

Family and dog friendly, grassy site sheltered by trees and bordered by the tumbling little Clydagh River. There's a small shop, children's playground equipment, one of the showers is wheelchair accessible, and all the usual facilities including a games room and clubhouse. Ballyvary, Castlebar, F23 NX74, +353 94 9031264

53.9077, -9.1828

48 CARRA CARAVAN & CAMPING PARK

Hardstanding for caravans, simple grass pitching for tents, a row of bright bow-topped caravans and simple facilites (coin-operated showers) on this summer site. There's a village convenience store, children's playground and pubs on the doorstep, and loop walks to the river nearby. Dogs welcome, on leads. Glebe, Belcarra, F23 TW02, +353 85 2535288, bookings online carracaravanpark.com

53.7995, -9.2166

RUSTIC RETREATS

49 MAYO GLAMPING, BALLYVARY

Stay in a stone-fronted hobbit hut built into a bank – complete with circular door – an A-frame wooden cabin, or the converted railway freight car. A pizza oven, bar, hot tub and sauna on site take it all up a notch. Keelogues Old, Ballyvary, F23 A446, +353 91 442765

53.8760, -9.1702

50 ASHFORD CASTLE HOTEL

If you want to indulge in an Irish castle, this is the classic, once home to the Guinness family. Non-residents can also visit the woodland demesne, with Victorian gardens, for an entrance charge. Cong, F31 CA48, +353 94 9546003

53.5345, -9.2848

42

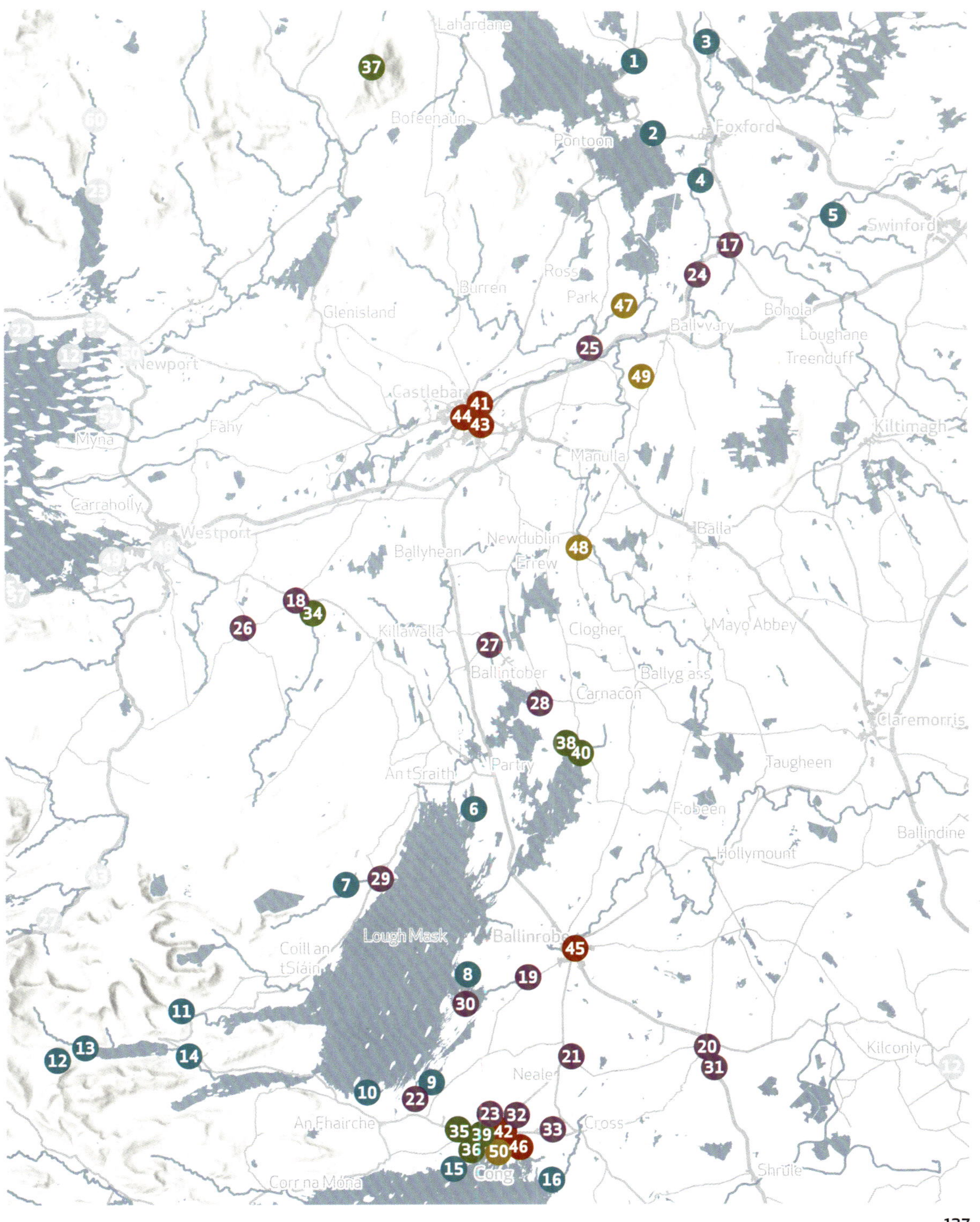
Lahardane
Bofeenaun
Pontoon
Foxford
Swinford
Ross
Burren
Park
Glenisland
Bohola
Ballyvary
Loughane
Treenduff
Newport
Castlebar
Fahy
Myna
Kiltimagh
Manulla
Carraholly
Westport
Balla
Newdublin
Ballyhean
Errew
Mayo Abbey
Killawalla
Clogher
Ballintober
Ballyglass
Carnacon
Claremorris
Partry
An tSraith
Taugheen
Robeen
Ballindine
Hollymount
Lough Mask
Ballinrobe
Coill an tSiáin
Kilconly
Neale
An Fhairche
Cross
Cong
Shrule
Corr na Móna

3

ROSCOMMON & SHANNON

Our perfect weekend

- → **Plunge** into the Boyle below Knockvicar Bridge, and take a stroll through the old oaks at nearby Derreen, especially at bluebell time.
- → **Paddle** to the crannóg island on Lough Eidin, look for deer at Toomna Church and enjoy local brews and riverside camping at Battlebridge.
- → **Find** hidden piers in Derrycarne Woods, and dine on local produce at The Cottage on the shore.
- → **Wonder** at massive Rathra fort with its souterrain entrance, then Drummin Rath among old trees, with two entrance ogham stones.
- → **Follow** the track up to Kiltullagh Church, hidden on a hilltop, and marvel at the views from a site used for burials since pagan times.
- → **Stroll** the Frass Englishtown Green Way through beautiful bog lands full of rare plants, and look out for delightful field mice.
- → **Trace** the swirling patterns on Castlestrange scribed stone, then camp and swim at Galey Bay.
- → **Swim** under Urlaur Abbey, keeping an eye out for the dancing devil, and spend the night in a colourful yurt at lovely Willowbrook.

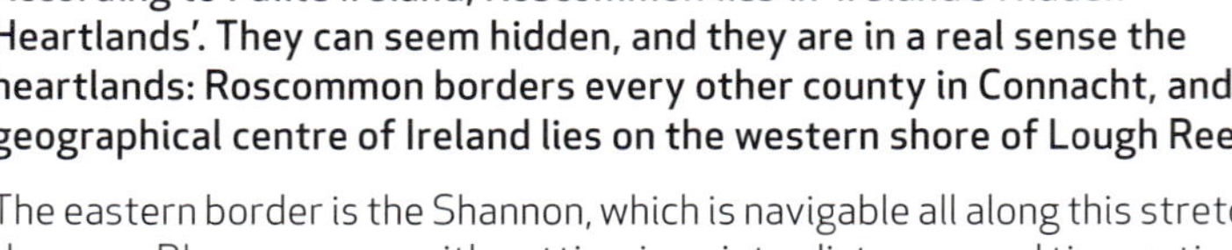

According to Fáilte Ireland, Roscommon lies in 'Ireland's Hidden Heartlands'. They can seem hidden, and they are in a real sense the heartlands: Roscommon borders every other county in Connacht, and the geographical centre of Ireland lies on the western shore of Lough Ree.

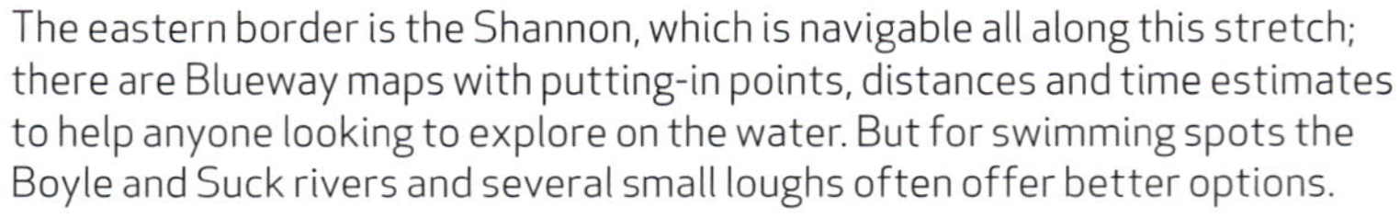

The eastern border is the Shannon, which is navigable all along this stretch; there are Blueway maps with putting-in points, distances and time estimates to help anyone looking to explore on the water. But for swimming spots the Boyle and Suck rivers and several small loughs often offer better options.

This place wasn't always so quiet. The wide, flat plains supported Iron Age cattle-farmers, and Roscommon is the birthplace of the great Irish epic of the Táin Bó Cúailgne, or Cattle Raid of Cooley. It is bound up with the ritual sites of the sprawling Rathcroghan complex, which has simply too much to detail here: aside from the main ceremonial mound, there are 28 burial mounds, plus other earthworks and stones. The best overview is found at the visitor centre in Tulsk (F45 HH51), worth a visit before making your own explorations. But whatever you do, make time and wear your oldest gear to slide into Owenygat Cave. Of course there are plenty of younger remains, monastic and military, including Glinsk Castle, possibly the last true castle built in Ireland.

The woodlands of old landed estates have become the centre of leisure here: Lough Key forest park is commercially developed but huge enough to lose yourself in and with the lough to paddle out on, while Mote Park demesne has bluebells in spring and the relics of the grand estate scattered around it, including a lion-topped gateway.

Bogs are also a big part of the landscape, many now being restored from extraction to their natural flowery, wildlife-rich state, with boardwalks to explore them. Once you learn to look closer they are fascinating, supporting rare birds and small mammals.

When the day is done, there are local bars with music to visit, riverside cafés and restaurants, and laid-back lakeside campsites to sleep in. Roscommon may lack the eye-catching drama beloved of 'see before you die' lists and influencers, but fewer WAW tourists means a more natural pace, and you can explore the landscapes and ruins or swim the peaty waters in a deeper peace.

LAKE, RIVER & WATERFALL

1 KNOCKVICAR BRIDGE, R BOYLE

Pleasant spot for a picnic and a dip, tucked below the road and a handsome 19th-century bridge giving access to the Shannon Blueway. Quay with picnic table on the downriver side on L bank, steps down from the grassy bank to the water on the upstream side, both with parking.

2 mins, 53.9988, -8.1948

2 DOON SHORE AMENITY & ISLAND

On the W shore of Lough Key there's parking and easy access with a concrete pier for jumping. If you have a kayak, it's only 400m to Church Island (on the R) to explore the ruin. You could even camp there. Signed off L1013.

10 mins, 53.9944, -8.2609

3 MCDERMOTT'S CASTLE, LOUGH KEY *

Swim or canoe 300m across to this perfectly romantic ruined castle on a lake island. A stronghold of the McDermotts in the 13th century (when the magical Hag of Lough Key visited for a full year), it was rebuilt and reimagined by renowned architect John Nash in the Gothic revival of the 19th century, before burning down in the 1940s. Parking near the quay.

10 mins, 53.9893, -8.2325

4 LOCH EIDIN, R BOYLE

A quiet lough on the River Boyle navigation, also called Drumharlow, and this tiny parking area and slipway provide a perfect entry point for swimming, or perhaps canoeing to the little crannóg-like island. Signed off the N4 at Hughestown.

2 mins, 53.9623, -8.1550

5 KILLUKIN CASCADE WATERFALLS

An easy, prety place for paddling. Below an old stone road bridge with small car park and more cascades upstream. Signed off R368.

2 mins, 53.9185, -8.1142

6 LOUGH BODERG, DERRYCARNE WOODS*

This old lakeshore estate of beech, oak, holly, and conifer woodland has several swimming points, including a slipway and rustic stone pier. The scant remains of the grand house, at the end of its once-drive, are at 53.8689, -7.9667 but the undergrowth is dense in summer. Bikes, pushchairs and some wheelchairs can get at least to slipway from parking at 53.87204, -7.9572.

20 mins, 53.8670, -7.9664

7 URLAUR LOUGH & ABBEY

Popular but peaceful swimming spot at a quay and a shale beach, below little-known 15th-

6

2

7

9

3

12

13

11

century monastic ruins with steps up to the roofline. A comical tale of the friars of Urlaur tells of the devil and a black boar dancing on the lake and tormenting the friars, who enlisted the musical aid of a drunken piper. Signed from the lane to E.

2 mins, 53.8515, -8.7469

8 LOUGH ERRIT, GORTHAGANNY

The designated bathing spot, very popular in summer, has a concrete jetty, barrel sauna and a kayak centre (Errit Kayaking Club, Jimmy Kelly +353 87 7581227). There's a lakeshore loop walk W for exploring quieter areas.

2 mins, 53.8076, -8.6917

9 RINDOON CASTLE & JETTY *

In the 13th century there was a short-lived Norman town here with 1,000 people, a church, a mill (53.5371, -7.9888), a castle above a harbour, and a defensive wall with towers across the Warren peninsula. There's even a pontoon/bathing deck with ladder offshore from the harbour. Some road parking, gate and signboard 3km E of Lecarrow at 53.5435, -8.0054, then 1.2km walk on farm track. Or more parking (and swimming) from Judy's harbour, just 250m further S along lane (53.5412, -8.006). You could also kayak from here. Contact St John's Parish Heritage Group, Lecarrow, on Facebook about access, they will sometimes guide trips.

20 mins, 53.5389, -7.9912

LOST RUINS

10 MOYGARA CASTLE

This unique site, a huge square bawn with four residential towers and a gatehouse, dates from the 16th century. It has been undergoing badly needed conservation since 2023, with an aim of reopening public access to parts as they are finished, while work will likely continue for years. You may not get access to much at first, but will see the impressive work to keep the walls standing. Signed from R294 at Redhill, L after 1.2km on a narrow lane; pull off at corner by farm buildings if entrance is full.

2 mins, 53.9716, -8.4746

11 BALLINTOBER CASTLE

Built around 1300 by the powerful (and unruly) Red Earl, Richard Óg de Burgh, this vast keepless complex is much overgrown with ivy and it demands some imagination to see the towers and fill the interior with the buildings it once held. Although on the edge of the village (here since the castle was built) it remains atmospheric and impressive. In private ownership, you may encounter 'dangerous structure, keep out' signs, due to liability; easy parking opp SE corner.

2 mins, 53.7222, -8.4148

12 GLINSK CASTLE

Fine remains of possibly the last true castle built in Ireland, around 1628. It can be viewed from the Suck Way path that runs alongside, or the road, but is accessible if you ask for key at the farm above, entrance 100m S from car park for the pretty streamside.

5 mins, 53.6519, -8.4319

13 MOTE PARK LION, DEMESNE

This magnificent Doric arch topped by a Coade stone lion was the entrance to long-lost Mote Park house, demolished by the 1960s. The lion is hollow and for many years housed a colony of bees; it was restored in 2016. Old estate oaks and other broadleaf species can still be found amid the Coillte plantations, creating a habitat where you might see red squirrels and pine martens. Ballymurray Wood, on your L as you head S from the parking on the original Broad Walk, is full of bluebells in the spring, and also holds a 30m rath (53.5996, -8.1416). Signed from the N61 in Ballymurray, opp F42 HW08. Follow the road 1km and park by the gates (53.6007, -8.1434).

25 mins, 53.5903, -8.1431

19

20

22

22

14 ELPHIN WINDMILL

The only windmill in the west of Ireland; totally delightful with a reed-thatched roof that is rotated to catch the wind by a 'circumscribing' wheel. Storm damage from Éowyn in 2025 will be costly to fix, so consider the €8 to visit the agricultural museum. Opposite is a community wildlife park with ponds, wild flowers, fruit trees and a modern-day 'passage tomb'.

2 mins, 53.8518, -8.2054

SACRED & ANCIENT

15 TOOMNA CHURCH

Lost in the woods, this atmospheric derelict church was in use until the 1980s. The stained glass was removed to another church some years ago, and ivy is gradually clothing the walls inside. If you are lucky, and quiet, you may see deer. Limited parking on the roadside by the old wrought iron gates (53.9923, -8.0849).

3 mins, 53.9936, -8.0848

16 THE FOUR ALTARS, BALLAGHADERREEN

An unusually visible relic of Penal times, this monument shelters altars in four arched niches facing the cardinal compass points, to allow for mass whatever the weather might be. Built around 1750, with a much later enclosing wall. On private land, pull off carefully on the R293 and ask at Four Altars Cottage.

4 mins, 53.9238, -8.5308

17 KILCASHEL STONE FORT

One of the largest and best-preserved cashels in the west of Ireland, 30m across, with great views from the heathery top. The impressively tight drystone walls are mostly well over 2m high and have internal steps and low creepways to chambers within them, and the entrance passage still has its paving slabs and a lintel in place. Inside are the low remains of round huts and a possible souterrain. Layby on lane off R325 S of Kilmovee.

2 mins, 53.8834, -8.6802

18 DRUMMIN RATH *

A pair of inscribed ogham stones lead into a rath with a deep fosse and outer bank. Lovely hidden rural setting for picnics among old trees. Park Drummin Cemetery (signed from N5) and walk 100m E up farm lane to the kissing gate on L.

3 mins, 53.8343, -8.3698

19 RATHRA HILLFORT, RATHBARNA

This massive enclosure, with a full four banks and commanding views all around, as far as Croagh Patrick in the west, was an important ceremonial and political site for the Ciarraige Aí, who dominated this area in the 4th–8th

14

centuries. The barrow and earthen platform are still easily discernable in the centre, with a souterrain about halfway between them; local legend held this was the entrance to a tunnel all the way to Rathcroghan. Pull off the road by the gate at 53.7555, -8.4194 and cross the stile, following the hedge W to the ramparts.

2 mins, 53.7560, -8.4219

20 KILTULLAGH CHURCH

This small roofless 15th-century church in a walled graveyard is hidden atop a pretty hill with beautiful views. Still used for outdoor mass, this is a truly ancient site: Christian since the 5th century, it has foundations of an earlier wooden church to the W and evidence of earlier pagan burials. Some parking by a field gate with a track up, sometimes flooded (53.7129, -8.7033). Keen ruin hunters in the area can also find Lowberry House ruins 3km S, by the lane (53.6870, -8.6804).

7 mins, 53.7128, -8.7076

21 CASTLESTRANGE STONE & RIVER SUCK

A rounded boulder with swirling ornate patterns in the La Tene style, similar to Galway's more famous Turoe stone, beneath trees by a driveway. Park at the corner just N of Castlestrange Bridge (53.5855, -8.2715) then 150m N. From the bridge a rough path leads 2.5km downstream over wooden stiles along the beautiful, wide, wild River Suck to Athleague village, where there's deep river access above the weir by the church Riverside Centre.

2 mins, 53.5869, -8.2718

CAVES & CAVERNS

22 OWENYGAT CAVE, RATHCROGHAN

Uaimh na gCat, the cave of the cat, was once an obscure site. Old texts call it a gate to the underworld, home of the war-goddess Morrigan and magical beasts that emerged to wither the countryside on the winter festival of Samhain, and it has gained fame as 'the birthplace of Halloween'. Slithering under an ogham

stone lintel and through the low souterrain entrance into the natural rift cave certainly feels otherworldly, and is something of a rite for anyone into pagan mythology. It lies in the hedge near the gate, and parking on the lane is tight. Two raths are by the road nearby: Rath Beag at 53.8065, -8.3079 and Rath na dTarbh at 53.8021, -8.3130.

2 mins, 53.7972, -8.3105

ANCIENT FOREST

23 FAIRY BRIDGE, LOUGH KEY

The old Rockingham estate is a popular lake and woodland area with relics from many ages, from ancient forts to an ice house, a ruined church, treetop walkways, and an unexpectedly Brutalist 1970s tower with views to McDermott's Castle in the lake (see entry). Our favourite is the ornate Fairy Bridge leading through woodland to Drummans Island, where bluebells flower in late spring. There is a large pay car park, café and activity centre. Signed Lough Key park from several points on N4 and R285.

20 mins, 53.9856, -8.2436

24 DERREEN WOOD BLUEBELLS

Among the old oaks there are sheets of bluebells in May. Their fame has made them popular, with a new track and car park, but the woods are large. There are also three lakes and the bank of the River Boyle, in which you can swim. Gates are signed on R285.

5 mins, 53.9852, -8.1974

25 ST JOHN'S WOOD, LOUGH REE

A rare remnant of original ancient Irish woodland, this enchanting pocket on the shores of Lough Ree has a canopy of pedunculate oaks, native crab apple trees and Irish whitebeam, and below them a thriving understorey of hazel – the largest population in Ireland. Come for the blossom and catkins in spring, the cool shade in summer, or the fruit and nuts in autumn. The further end of the woods is unmanaged, from the car park there is a looped gravel track around the nearer end, with narrower trodden paths off it; one leads to an opening in the trees at a shore strewn with strange bubbly-looking rocks, where you can wade out into the lake (53.5574, -7.9996). At the end of lanes E of Lecarrow, car park shortly before F42 X362.

10 mins, 53.5522, -8.0040

WILDLIFE WONDERS

26 DERRYDONNELL FOREST

The old Mote Park estate, replanted since the 1930s, is now a haven for red squirrels and pine martens, and birdlife includes ravens and long-eared owls, with visiting redwings, fieldfares, and chiffchaffs. There are orchids

and cowslips in season. You can also trace the old Monk's Walk through the woods to the river (53.6058, -8.1716). Signed Mote Park from N61 at Ballymurray then first R (3.5t limit) passing the old coach house R and through the stone archway on the bridge.

5 mins, 53.6064, -8.1702

27 FRASS ENGLISHTOWN BOG & HEATH

Beautiful 5km figure-of-eight walk through a bog on track and boardwalk, with magnificent heathland views and abundant flora and fauna - you may spot fieldmice. Dogs on leads. Small car park at the start of the walk, and places to picnic. Signed from R362 E of Glenamaddy. Also

29

29

37

30km N lies Carrowbehy re-wetted bog, site of an EU LIFE project, where you might even spot rare red grouse (53.8005, -8.6759).
60 mins, 53.6036, -8.5132

TRADITIONAL PUBS

28 THE OARSMAN BAR

This multiple award-winning restaurant comes with history: the premises dates back to 1780s, and the family has been in the hospitality business for seven generations. Specialising in local, organic, and wild food, they source as much as possible from producers within a 60km radius. Bridge Street, Carrick-on-Shannon, N41 AK19, +353 71 9621733
53.9439, -8.0948

29 ANDERSON'S THATCH PUB

If you ask about the photos and mementoes on the walls and beams of this three-centuries-old thatched building, you get their backstory – and then another story, and another. Music has taken owner Gene around the world, and brought trad musicians from all over the world to play here. Popular, with live unplugged music spontaneously, and regularly Wed, Fri in summer and Sat in winter. Overnight campervan parking. Ballindrehid, Carrick-on-Shannon, N41 WP46, +353 71 9620142
53.9098, -8.1295

30 COFFEY'S, LECARROW

This typical eye-catching country pub and grocery store is family-run, with regular music, pizzas, and a buzzing atmosphere. Galeybeg, F42 AV22, +353 90 6661118
53.5466, -8.0545

LOCAL PRODUCE

31 THE HIDDEN CORNER CHEESE SHOP

An emporium for Irish cheeses of all kinds – goat, sheep, cow, mellow, or sharp, plus home-made ice cream, olives, pesto, and more. St George's Terrace, Carrick-On-Shannon, N41 CD45, +353 85 1852385
53.9450, -8.0962

32 PURPLE ONION KITCHEN

There's a relaxed welcome in this café-restaurant, delicatessen, and art gallery in the heart of a Shannonside town. Fresh local foods, bottled craft beers including local brews, and an ever-changing selection of Irish artists' paintings to peruse. Takeaway available. Tarmonbarry, N39 FY94, +353 43 3359919
53.7422, -7.9191

ORGANIC & GASTRO

33 KNOCKVICAR ORGANIC GARDEN

Sells freshly harvested produce (salad bags, veg etc) and has a freely accessible walk through bogland and bluebell woods. F52 YA44, +353 86 0667962
53.9982, -8.2006

34 HONESTLY FARM KITCHEN, CARRICK *

Organic Dexter beef burgers raised on their own organic farm (Drumanilra) . Farm shop has veg and bakery plus Irish artisan chocolate, locally roasted coffee and organic smoked salmon, cheeses, olives and charcuterie. Retail Park, Castlecara Rd, Carrick-On-Shannon, N41 VK33, +353 71 9317388
53.9460, -8.0786

35 THE RED BANK RESTAURANT

Award-winning head chef Michelle McGowan works closely with a host of amazing local producers and artisan suppliers to create modern European dishes. Elegant setting in an old bank. St George's Terrace, Carrick-On-Shannon, N41 CK00, +353 71 9671392
53.9449, -8.09642

36 THE COTTAGE RESTAURANT

Right on the banks of the beautiful Shannon, this is literally a cottage, with parking on the road. Eastern-style food from Sham Hanifa, with the best local ingredients. You can buy his sauces, cooked here in small batches, at the Synergy Café in Carrick itself. Jamestown, Carrick-on-Shannon, N41 EK63, +353 71 962 5933
53.9291, -8.0330

WATERSIDE CAMPING

37 BATTLEBRIDGE CARAVAN & CAMPING

The riverside camping field and wider caravan site at this friendly pub are at the upper limit of the Shannon navigation, with slipway access for canoeing (or swimming, but watch out for boats). Beirne's pub has been in the family for generations. This is a lively site, with a playground, dogs and ball games welcome; the local road alongside is a bit noisy in the day but quiet overnight. There's also a marina and

sauna. Beirne's Pub, Battlebridge, N41 Y462, +353 71 9650824
53.9956, -8.0807

38 LOUGH KEY CARAVAN & CAMPING

Park a camper in a secluded pitch with a hook-up among the trees, or pitch your tent on one of the three open grassed areas to have the whole forest park on your doorstep and the lough 500m away. Dogs welcome, fires allowed in raised firepits, and forest park facilities and activities nearby (best booked in advance). Boyle, F52 HE06, +353 71 9662212
53.9812, -8.2356

39 WILLOWBROOK GLAMPING HIDEAWAYS

Wes and Tuesday are the second generation to run this 15-pitch field with a few colourful yurts and an old farm building. They are planting a woodland, and the site runs down to a gentle river. This is a family-friendly place, offering creative classes, alpacas, and evening activities for the young ones – but also a pizza oven, spa centre, hot tubs, and yoga retreats. Kiltybranks, Ballaghaderreen, F45 YE27, +353 94 9861307
53.8668, -8.6023

40 GALEY BAY CAMPING

Right on the shores of Lough Ree, this small, family-run site hire out boats to campers, and can arrange kayak hire for groups. The tent field is separated from hardstanding pitches and there's a teetering ruined tower house across the road. Apr–Oct. Cash only. Knockcroghery, F42 RP20, +353 90 6661058
53.5778, -8.0674

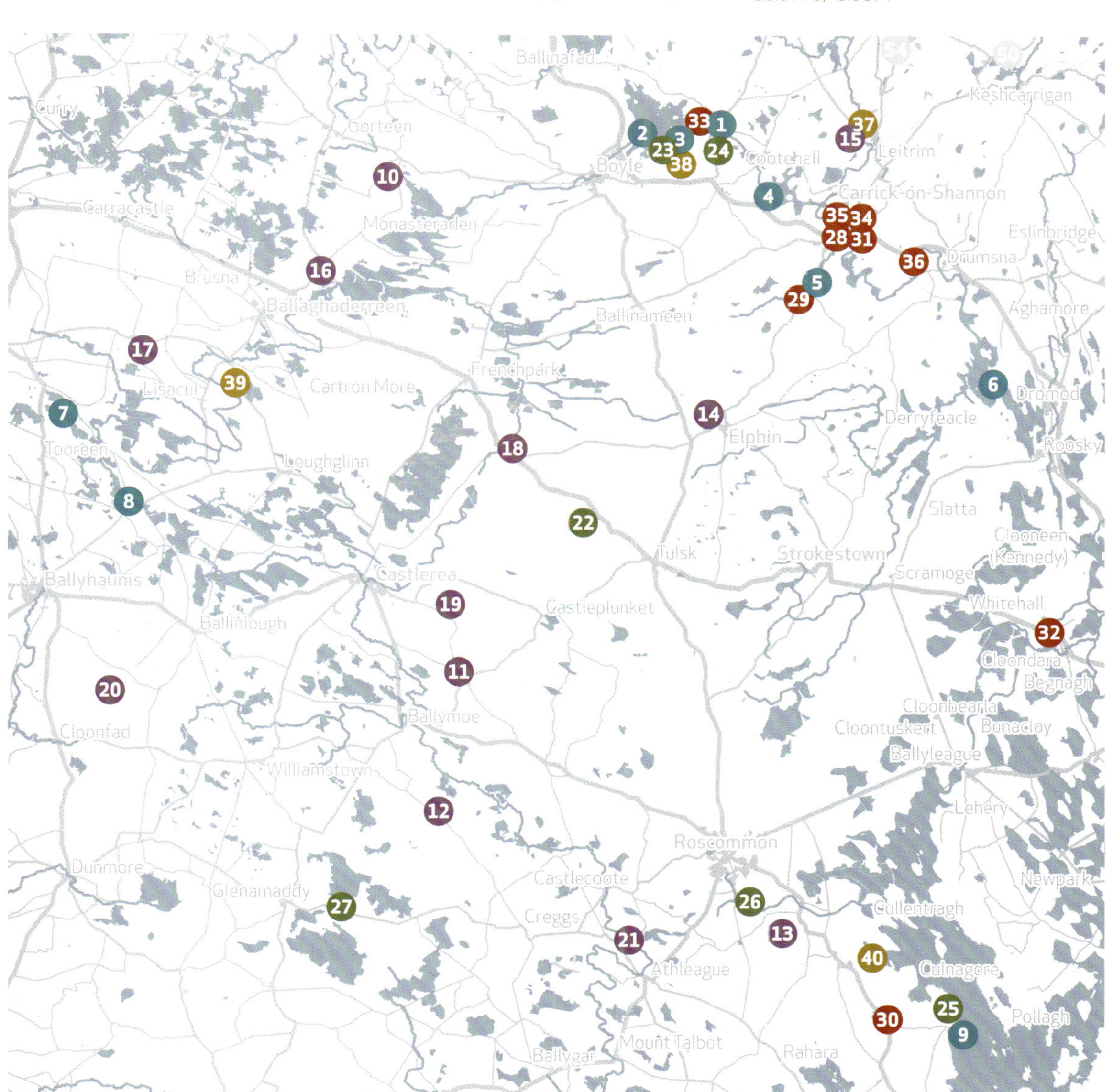

CONNEMARA

Our perfect weekend

- **Climb** Errisbeg for glorious coastal views, then refuel at O'Dowd's with classic seafood.
- **Laze** on the sands of Aillebrack with a delicious picnic from the Conneramara Smokehouse.
- **Pitch** your tent in the dunes at Clifden Eco and discover the sinking church of Omey island.
- **Pack** a picnic and walk to the hidden beach and holy well on Cleggan Head, visiting the watchtower and beautiful court tomb on the way.
- **Swim** in sparkling waters under the ruins of two once-warring churches on the headland walk from Moyrus Beach.
- **Pick** wild bilberries and jump on the quaking blanket bog at Carna Heath, and walk over to the deserted village on Fínish Island at low tide.
- **Test** your strength on the bullaun in St Colman's Monastery on Inishbofin and stay out late to listen for the corncrakes.
- **Scramble** up Derryclare from the wild woods and return for a dip in the lough.
- **Marvel** at Clifden Castle, then follow the famous Sky Road to Eyrephort Beach and park up for the night facing the sunset.

3

4

7

Connemara is one of Ireland's most awe-inspiring regions; a landscape of extremes, where mountains rear up almost from sea level, bogs seem more water than land, and the sea relentlessly harries the shore.

This is a place on the edge of the world, shaped by the sea – the 'mara' of the name means 'of the sea'. Stretching from the slopes of Killary Fjord in the north to the white beaches near Roundstone in the south, the island-studded coastline is deeply fissured, with sandy coves and rocky inlets tucked between headlands that defy the Atlantic swells. Offshore, the island of Inishbofin and its deserted neighbour Inishark merit a weekend to explore their breathtaking cliffs, ancient monastic sites, empty beaches, and the call of rare corncrakes late on a summer's night. Smaller and closer islands, such as tidal Omey, give a feeling of remoteness in a far shorter visit. Inland waters here tend to be small but renowned for their fish, with old stone bridges and tree-lined banks perfect for a dip. The most substantial bodies of water are Loughs Inagh and Derryclare to the east, while in the west lie the ecological riches of vast, pool-mottled Roundstone Bog.

Mountains define the landscape, none more striking than the Twelve Bens – there are in fact almost 20 'Bens' and the name may mean just those that were visible to sailors for navigation. These mostly quartzite peaks are not Ireland's highest, but rise from a low, coastal plain to create a formidable skyline visible from almost everywhere in Connemara. The hikes here are classic challenges, rewarding strenuous efforts with vast panoramas.

Forests are scarce, but important. Native oak, birch, and hazel cling to sheltered valleys and riverbanks, while remnants of ancient woodland clothe the shores of Derryclare. Other woodlands are the legacy of wealthy landed estates, such as those around popular Kylemore Abbey or Ballynahinch Castle, and include more exotic specimens that thrive in the Atlantic climate, and provide a welcome contrast to the expanses of open bog and mountain.

Scattered across this landscape are remnants of Connemara's past, from ancient to modern. There are tombs with coastal views, such as Cleggan, and hardy medieval churches, such as St Colman's on Inishbofin with its tale of stolen skulls; there are signal towers from times of war, deserted villages with still-visible potato ridges, and even incongruous industrial remains, such as Marconi's mighty telegraph station deep in Derrygimlagh bog. It's also a place of vibrant life today, with arts festivals in Clifden and on Inishbofin, excellent local produce, and a wealth of places to eat or stay.

SECRET BEACHES

1 GLASSILAUN BEACH

Sensational white strand with tidal island and views to the beacon in Inish Bearna and summit of Mweelrea beyond. Easy access with small car park, so arrive early as it can get busy on summer days.

2 mins, 53.6149, -9.8750

2 LETTERGESH BEACH

Beautiful expanse of white sand below dunes with distant peaks behind and easy parking signed at S end. The views don't quite compare to Glassilaun, but it's quieter and you can overnight.

5 mins, 53.6022, -9.9085

3 RENVYLE BEACH & GURTEEN PIER

Fine silver-sand beach, sheltered and safe, with mountain views to distant Inishturk and Mweelrea. Explore to L for more coves and a cillín (53.6100, -9.9942). On roads 2km S is Tully Beach with Gurteen Pier (turn by petrol station); smaller, just as white and perfect for high tide jumps, with a barrel sauna excellent for cooler days (sweathouse.ie).

2 mins, 53.6070, -9.9892

4 TRAWMORE, CURRAGH & INISHBROON

This long, remote strand of sand and pebble is backed by cliffs, and looks over to little Inishbroon, a possible kayak mission (500m). There's parking for one car at the track end. 250m up on the headland to the L, through field gate, is a lookout hut and earthworks of Cathair an Dúin (53.6031, -10.0503); see if you can make out the very faded EIRE 55 pilots' marker (53.6041, -10.0497)

2 mins, 53.6047, -10.0469

5 ROSS BEACH, ARDKYLE

A curve of white cobbles, sand at low tide and a little island to cross to, all at the end of fuchsia-filled lanes with space for a couple of cars at the end, and possible overnights. Freaghillaun South island is 500m offshore, for kayakers and hopeful divers; the Falcón Blanco Menor of the Spanish Armada may have foundered here in 1588 and left traces below.

1 min, 53.5693 -10.0288

6 ROSSADILLISK BEACH

The W side of the headland is a vast flat bay, all white sand at LT, shallow water at HT, dotted with rock outcrops, below machair that is carpeted with wild flowers in summer. Park in small gravel layby opposite house H71 VW57. Or walk 220m N to end of the lane, and through field gate to the headland and sandy tombolo of Gooreen Island, and loop back L over the sands. On the E side is smaller Emlagh, where you can rent a renovated beach cottage (see entry).

1 min, 53.5630, -10.1501

7 SELLERNA BEACH

This sheltered crescent of pale sand is a locals' secret, quieter and not overlooked, with flower-filled grassland above it and easy parking. At the far R end you can scramble up and step over the fence to visit lonely little Knockbrack tomb (53.5588, -10.1290).

1 min 53.5573, -10.1319

8 AUGHRUSBEG & ANCHOR BEACHES

Perfect for sunsets, this golden beach with its teeming rockpools is one of the most westerly in Ireland, and invisible from the road as you pass Aughrusbeg Lough on little lanes. Cyclists can use the field gate at 53.5513, -10.1851 but drivers must park in small layby by house at 53.5483, -10.1824, walk N 100m to lane on L and take grassy track on R after 500m (opp H71 F857). 1km N on road, with direct access, is picturesque Anchor Beach with a rusty anchor buried in the sand (53.5586, -10.1768) while 1.4km S along lanes is Aughrus pier for HT jumping (53.5402, -10.1765).

10 mins, 53.5503, -10.1882

9 OMEY STRAND & ISLAND*

At low tide, some of the biggest sands in Connemara, the scene for the Omey races in July or August, and wind karting, kite sailing, dolphin watching and swimming the rest of the time. You can walk or drive to Omey Island at LT, but you will only have a few hours unless you wild camp in the dunes, so follow the only lane 2.5km for the W beach (53.5285, -10.1647 with grass parking) overlooked by a holy well to N, and then find St Feichin's ancient church sunk in a grassy bowl in the bird- and rabbit-filled dunes 800m N (53.5357, -10.1679); beaches here are sheep fenced.

35 mins, 53.5388, -10.1446

10 EYREPHORT BEACH

Perfect end-of-the-world slice of white sand facing W to Inishturk (only 200m for kayakers) with possible tidal jumps from rocks at N end. Small car park, good for overnights, down narrow unsigned lane W from H71 VF51.

1 min, 53.5122, -10.1362

11 CORAL BEACHES, DERRYEIGHTER

A curious crunchy beach of white maerl peppered with yellow snail shells, and continuing W for 2km. Parking for one at 53.4644, -10.0501. Carry on W up lane passing Lough Usk for lovely places to stop and swim 53.4667, -10.0629

1 min, 53.4636, -10.0498

12 MANNIN BAY BEACHES

A series of dreamy, white maerl beaches with high dunes and flower-filled machair, sometimes called the 'Irish Seychelles', but also like the Outer Hebrides. Best on a bike as almost no parking; try corner at 53.4460, -10.0998; climb over the gate to walk down. Or the lane to the S, take rough track and park through gate, at 53.4482, -10.1098. There are coves on both sides – take your pick.

5 mins, 53.4496, -10.1050

13 DOONLOUGHAN BEACHES*

Perfect white coves on the peninsula beyond Ballyconneely. Follow unsigned lanes NW from crossroads on the lane to Bunowen and park or follow dune tracks at 53.4388, -10.1337 or 800m farther on at the bridge. Some wild camp in hollows.

10 mins, 53.4455, -10.1360

14 AILLEBRACK BEACH

Icing-sugar soft sands, azure waters and few people. Follow signs for Connemara golf course then bear L to park at 53.4193, -10.1434 with several more verge spots beyond. There are about three main areas to park, which can be good overnight.

5 mins, 53.4173 -10.1417

15 INISHDAWROS, CALLOW STRAND

This island has a very secluded beach on the seaward side perfect for sunsets; it can be reached on foot at LT and waded to at most states of the tide. An unsigned lane off the R341 leads down to the beach, on which you can park.

5 mins, 53.3988, -10.0360

16 DOG'S BAY AND GORTEEN

The two glorious back-to-back white beaches are well known and incredibly popular. Arrive early and explore the headland beyond, populated by placid cattle: Trá Mhartog is a hidden slice of sand about 200m beyond the end of Dog's Bay, and 350m due S following a dip in the hill lies Trá Garbh. The machair grass is speckled with wild flowers including harebells and sea holly, and you may see ringed plovers, lapwing, small blue butterflies and stoats. Limited parking signed off the R341, or via Gorteen side, signed Port na Feadoige slightly further E.

1 min, 53.3809, -9.9632

17 MOYRUS BEACH

One of Connemara's most beautiful beaches, Trá Mhaírois in Irish, with shallow, turquoise waters over the white sand making it a safe haven – but in the 1850s it was a scene of open religious fights. The SW end, L from the central Moyrus Cemetery with the ruined medieval Catholic church, is more visited and the starting point for the Lúibín Mhaírois looped walk around the headland. For the quieter N end, overlooked by the ruined evangelical Protestant church, walk R from the middle of the beach or follow a tiny lane to the N end opp H91 YCA3 (53.3442, -9.8808).

2 mins, 53.3410, -9.8824

18 TRA MHAIRE & FÍNISH ISLAND

A simple strip at pure white sand and shallow water around boulders at HT, but at LT you have a two-hour window to walk across the flats to Fínish Island and explore the ruins of more than 20 houses, mostly to the SW, abandoned in the last century (53.2949, -9.8173). Grass parking at end of lane.

1 min, 53.3038 -9.7952

19 MWEENISH ISLAND BEACHES

Cross the bridge to a quiet world of shallow waters and white beaches, but best by cycle

as lanes narrow and parking limited. The best beach is the far SE tip, with a second cove to the S beyond the ruined houses. Parking for only one or two cars. Alternatively, there's plenty of parking on the lane to the cemetery (53.2995, -9.8471) and a short walk W to Trá Mhór instead.

5 mins, 53.2933, -9.8401

INISHBOFIN

20 ST COLMAN'S MONASTERY

These ruins of a 13th-century chapel are thought to stand where 7th-century St Colman built his monastery after leaving Lindisfarne over a switch from the Celtic to the Roman calendar. It has a dark tale of skulls stolen in the night in 1890 by a researcher, which the university finally returned in 2023 after a long campaign from the island. The massive 177kg bullaun in front of the altar is a traditional stone of strength, lifted to the altar or windowsill. Just E where the lane bends, a path leads to quiet sands looking over to Inishlyon.

25 mins, 53.6154, -10.1888

21 EAST END BEACH

The safest and most accessible of the beaches, so the least wild but most family-friendly option. Also a nature reserve, so a snorkelling trip will show you ample wildlife under the surface including spider crabs, plaice, pollock and wrasse. Follow the lane E from the pier past St Colman's Church (see entry) 2.5km to the beach; walk or hire a bike at the pier (+353 95 45833).

45 mins, 53.6224 -10.1891

22 ISLAND HOSTEL & CAMPSITE

A cheerful and family-friendly hostel in a converted farmhouse with options from small dorms to private family rooms and a small number of tent pitches. Pre-booking essential, open Easter to October; no pets. Cloonamore, Inishbofin, H91 TW97, +353 954 5855

2 mins, 53.6158 -10.1980

23 CROMWELL'S FORT

This impressive bastioned barracks was built by Cromwell's forces in the 1650s, possibly on the site of an older fort known as Bosco's Castle, owned by one of Grainne O'Malley's allies. It was also used as a prison for Catholic clergy before transportation to the West Indies. A rugged, pathless trek around the harbour, ideally done at LT.

30 mins, 53.6103, -10.2164

24 CORNCRAKE HABITAT

Inishbofin is home to 10% of Ireland's corncrake population, and people visit just to seek these once-common farmland birds. They're hard to spot, but from April through the summer you may well hear them calling at night S of Lough Bofin, W from the harbour. Other project areas are 53.6131, -10.20264 and 53.6185, -10.1879.

20 mins, 53.6161 -10.22679

25 POLL TOLLADH BLOWHOLES

Peer down into these long fissure blowholes. On a calm day you can descend into the S hole and wade through the tunnel to the larger N chasm and arch at the seaward end. There are also rock arches along the N coast at the other end of the island, as well as Dún na h-Inine sea stack (53.6344, -10.1944).

45 mins, 53.6268, -10.2459

26 TRÁ GHEAL BEACH

Overlooked by Cnoc Mór, this beach is beautiful, but exposed and dangerous, take care. Tropical-feeling white sand, with views over to Inishark. It's easily reached, but 2.4km along the coastal track W from the pier, so one of the less-visited beaches.

35 mins, 53.6156 -10.246

27 WESTQUARTER CLIFFS

A path along the S coast passes Trá Gheal beach (see entry) to Dún Mór promontory fort at the SW corner. Only a curving dry-stone

29

wall remains but the views into the chasm are dizzying. Walk on with views to the deserted village on Inishark (see entry) to the NW corner, where the jagged rocks of The Stags reach out into the sea; often a good place to see the seal colony. In the broken cliffs here is the Poll Tolladh blowhole (see entry); back along the N coast a shingle bar offers calmer sea and lough dips (53.6207, -10.2314) before the lane descends gently to Bofin Harbour.

90 mins, 53.6270, -10.2564

28 INISHARK DESERTED VILLAGE

The last residents left in 1960, but the graveyards and ruins of Inishark have remained a place of pilgrimage. Look for Clochán Leo oratory inside an old cashel (53.6046, -10.2711); just to the E a narrow inlet has a cave and a rock well also named for St Leo. Hire a boat from Inishbofin boats ferry company (+353 95 37228, they have a rib) and maybe a local guide; we have spent a day with the excellent Tommy Burke, an Inishbofin-born archaeologist/historian (tommybofin@gmail.com).

2 mins, 53.6051, -10.2676

RIVERS & LAKES

29 LOUGH FEE & MUCK LOUGH

Surrounded by mountains high above the Killary fjord, these two loughs are linked by the lively Culfin river which takes them down to the sea at Lettergesh. The WAW runs alongside but there's only really room to stop at the far NW end of Fee at the pontoon, or the pebble beach/track on Muck Lough, another 500m.

1 min, 53.5947, -9.8384

30 TWELVE PINES ISLAND

From the iconic viewpoint on the N59, drop down to the shore to find the narrow causeway across to the island itself – sometimes under water. You can also pick up the old railway path on foot or bike along the S side of Derryclare Lough for swimming and exploring, starting 150m SE along the main road on L.

1 min, 53.4623, -9.7956

31 CLOONBEG BRIDGE & GREENWAY

The huge pools on the Owenmore River under the old railway bridge are tempting for a dip if nobody is fishing, particularly just downstream on the far bank; or walk W up the lane 200m to descend from the road bridge. There's parking across the R341, for the new Connemara Greenway, a 76km walking and cycling route along the old railway (to become part of the EuroVelo 1-cycling route along Atlantic coasts from Norway to Portugal).

2 mins, 53.4544, -9.8675

30

33

35

35

38

38

34

32 LOUGH NABRUCKA

Take the little bridge next to tiny St Bridget's church and explore the wild lakeshore behind. There's easy parking on the roadside, R341.

5 mins, 53.4584, -9.8104

33 OWENGOWLA RIVER POOLS

Deep, wide river pools flow briskly through moor and bog. There are many waterfalls and pools along the 1.5km from bridge to sea to explore, if no one is fishing. Park in gravel pull-off near bridge (L bank).

1 min, 53.3949, -9.7772

RUINS & SACRED SITES

34 CLIFDEN CASTLE

The D'Arcy family founded modern Clifden and built this fine Gothic revival manor house, complete with a fake stone circle; the Famine, bankruptcy, buyouts and feuds reduced it to a ruin within a century. Park at road and walk down drive; further along are remains of a substantial farmyard enclosed by outbuildings.

15 mins, 53.4917, -10.0567

35 MONUMENT & MARCONI STATION

Two historic sites far into an empty landscape. In 1919, the first non-stop transatlantic flight crash landed here in Derrygimlagh Bog. The 'nose cone' monument where Alcock and Brown came down is right by Marconi's transatlantic wireless station, a cutting-edge facility built in 1907, with 70m masts giving off loud high-voltage sparks. Concrete foundations and rusted machinery hint at the scale and historical photographs fill in the blanks. Park at the WAW waymarker by the main road for a good walk or cycle (bike hire and excellent local knowledge from Clifden Bike Shop +353 95 22630); those with smaller children might drive further in.

25 mins, 53.4457 -10.0218

36 AILLENACALLY VILLAGE

Home to 15 families before the Famine, a handful of the ruined houses still remain at the end of a long, remote track with a stone quay. At one point the village was considered for development as a harbour, but Roundstone was chosen instead. Twenty years ago the whole area was put up for sale, touted as 'Ireland's oldest village'. On the beach, find the anchor stone with the old groove around the middle that held the rope snug; local men lifted it as a strength test. Take small unsigned road off R341 at 53.4276, -9.8951. After 350m turn R and it's 1.5km on a rough track, best walked, R after gate at end.

25 mins, 53.4195, -9.8777

37 LOUGHACONEERA KILN & SEAWEED

Not even a century old yet; built by the present landowner's grandfather in the 1930s, this kiln is testament to how hard it was to keep land here fertile and productive. Limestone from the Aran Islands was burned into fertiliser, all with manual and animal labour. It's just N of the bridge R340, with a good metal gate and verge to pull off opposite. To the S side of the bridge you can buy nutrient-rich dried dulse and moss from Island Seaweed (+353 87 23 75983).

1 min, 53.3603 -9.70175

38 CLEGGAN COURT TOMB, TOWER, COVE*

A wonderful curved capstone with beautiful strata covers three little chambers with fine views out to sea. There's parking for walkers at 53.5610, -10.0981. Continue W along lane, dead straight, past the farm/holiday lets and a gate marked 'walkers only'. After 200m, through the next field gate, follow wall 150m down to the tomb. Take the track on W 2km for a perfect narrow swimming cove with LT sand and HT jumps, plus a holy well (53.5731, -10.1173), or climb the hill on the R for superb views and a ruined signal tower (53.5684 -10.10535).

10 mins, 53.5617, -10.1042

WILD SUMMITS & VIEWS

39 DIAMOND HILL

The classic Connemara summit, with spectacular views. The trail from the National Park Visitor Centre in Letterfrack (H91 K2Y1) has a lower and upper loop and is well maintained and signed, but steep and exposed at the top, so heed the weather warnings. Popular, so get there early and stick to the clockwise rule for the upper loop.

60 mins, 53.5475 -9.9147

40 DERRYCLARE, TWELVE BENS

The Glencoaghan Horseshoe is one of Ireland's best and most famous ridge walks, a strenuous 17km hike offering spectacular views and otherworldly landscapes of sharp quartzite peaks and ridges, taking in six to nine 600m-plus summits, depending on keenness and route. For a shorter day, our favourite is Derryclare (677m), reached from the beautiful mountain lane that winds into the valley, trailhead at 53.4773, -9.7994. It's about 3km and 650m ascent, up the spur ridge. For the more popular W end of the horseshoe, start from the Ben Lettery Hostel on N59 (53.4699, -9.8424), bearing L of the building to follow the ascent path.

110 mins, 53.4963, -9.7865

41 PAS MÁM ÉAN

At the saddle-point of this mountain pass is Tobar Phádraig well, a small chapel and a statue of St Patrick. For the quieter walk in, park at 53.5062, -9.6243 and follow path SW. You can explore scrambles up the Maumturk Mountain slopes either side, but for the very best views take the challenging hike to Corcogemore summit from the R336 (53.4926, -9.5637).

45 mins, 53.4923, -9.6528

42 CASHEL HILL

The glorious views from this summit take in the Twelve Bens and all this part of Connemara. The climb is about 300m, but it's quite steep nearer the top and not well marked, so take a map. Park at High Cashel graveyard (53.4234, -9.7956) or back at church on main road, follow stony path to L, then ascend ridge W to the twin summit with trig point on the N end, avoiding E hill face, which has many rocky escarpments.

60 mins, 53.4296, -9.8055

43 ERRISBEG

From the summit the view N over mountains and bog is almost alien, while the sea sparkles to the south. A moderately challenging and boggy, but still popular, 3km, with 300m climb from Roundstone; no dogs allowed. Nearest certain parking at 53.39598, -9.9217, follow the lane W up.

70 mins, 53.39572 -9.9579

44 THE OLD BRIDLE PATH

The last trace of a path that ran around the slopes of Errisbeg and all the way to Ballynahinch before the coast road existed. A fairly short, gentle ascent gives a rewarding coastal panorama, for those daunted by the summit (see entry). Park 5km W from Roundstone on the coast road, at a gate on a bend, with 'NO DOGS' painted on rocks (53.3914, -9.9785) – respect this. Turn R, keeping the wall on your R. The path mostly follows the wall, with stepping stones in wet places.

30 mins, 53.3903, -9.9568

WILD WOODS & WILDLIFE

45 DERRYCLARE NATURE RESERVE

Below the quartzite summits of Derryclare and Bencorr lies an old woodland of mossy sessile oaks, with rowans, ash, and birch on drier ground and alder and willow at the shore of scenic Derryclare Lough. Ferns and a hundred species of lichen thrive in the clean air, and if you look up you may see red squirrels. From R344, H91 HK5E, go through forest gate to parking area between the two bridges (53.4864, -9.7452); there are pools and rapids here, but you can dip in the lake ahead. Follow the lake-shore path 500m N, bear L at the fork and after 500m find forest trail on L into woods back the lake. To the R trails lead up Derryclare (677m).

20 mins, 53.4883, -9.7537

46 ROUNDSTONE BOG

This walk or cycle on the old bog road over common land ends at Loc Caimin, which has an ancient crannóg island in the middle (53.4288, -9.9210). Look out for plovers, merlins, and especially larks, or ptarmigans and white-fronted geese in winter. Follow the rough lane off the R341, park beyond the gate at end and head R.

30 mins, 53.4135, -9.9211

47 MURVEY MACHAIR

Beautiful Dolan Beach is surrounded by this machair conservation area, a large area of dunes and flowers for exploring on foot. There is some rocky parking for one car on the beach at 53.3859, -10.0227 just to the W.

15 mins, 53.3869 -10.0172

48 CARNA HEATH & BOG

An intricate mosaic of blanket bog and lakes between granite outcrops, a mass of purple and gold in summer. Follow the 2km green track through cottongrass, bog asphodel,

53

bogbean, and heaths, and look for sundews and bilberries. Have a jump near the small lake – it should quake. The larger Lough Sheedagh has several crannogs, one wooded and quite distinct (53.3205, -9.7945). Space to park at either end of the track.

15 mins, 53.3229, -9.7996

TRADITIONAL PUBS

49 KEOGHS OF BALLYCONNEELY

This welcoming, unpretentious roadside pub with a large beer garden is dog-friendly and popular with walkers and cyclists. The hearty menu has an emphasis on seafood. Ballyconneely, H71 PX25, +353 95 23522

53.4311, -10.0755

50 O'DOWD'S SEAFOOD BAR

Local food being served by the fourth generation, just above the pier with sea views and great atmosphere. Roundstone, H91 C853, +353 95 35809

53.3964, -9.9190

LOCAL PRODUCE

51 LOBSTER & CRAB, RENVYLE

Buy lobster and crab direct from fisherman Shane Flaherty, owner of Ireland's first registered fully electric fishing vessel. Under a traditional potting license scheme he sets traps close to the shore and helps to protect lobster stocks, through 'v-notching' and the release of breeding females. Order online or by WhatsApp and collect at the shore. +353 87 6603872, lobsterandcrab.ie

53.6067, -10.0275

52 CONNEMARA SMOKEHOUSE & CAFÉ

Three generations of Roberts family have been producing award-winning fish since 1979, and their original 'Old Smoky' is still working today. You can visit them to buy and learn about their sources and processes, and take a dip at Bunowen Beach below. Shop Monday to Friday 9am–5pm, closed 1–2pm, café open 1–3pm summer. Bunowen Pier, Ballyconneely, H71 KR29, +353 95 23739

53.4046, -10.1169

ORGANIC & GASTRO

53 MISUNDERSTOOD HERON

A wooden shack with tables by a car park – but the car park is for a trail on the shores of a spectacular fjord, and the food from the shack is 'fresh, local, never conventional'. Near legendary; closed in winter. Killary Fjord car park, Leenaan, on the dead-end road to H91 TP63.

53.5944 -9.7701

54 INISHWALLAH

Excellent Indian-Irish fusion street food offering on an incongruous red London bus, with vegetarian and vegan options. Parked in Westquarter and open during the summer season, +353 87 2874139

53.6144, -10.2293

55 STEAM CAFÉ

High-quality café, cooking local produce with a Mediterranean slant and good vegan options. Great place for breakfast or brunch. Station House, Clifden, H71 TD96, +353 95 30600

53.4882, -10.0175

56 CONNEMARA HAMPER

Long-established delicatessen with a great Irish cheese counter, local and exotic produce. Market Street, Clifden, H71 T996, +353 95 21054

53.4874, -10.0194

BEACH CAMPING

57 CONNEMARA CARAVAN & CAMPING

Sublime location right above Lettergesh Beach and friendly management compensates for motorhomes and sloping pitches. Busy in

56

52

57

summer so book ahead. Lettergesh Beach, Gowlaun, H91 NR13 +353 87 1253254
53.6048, -9.9025

58 RENVYLE BEACH CARAVAN & CAMPING
Since 1976 this little campsite has offered 30 or so summertime pitches above the beach, with tents scattered in the hollows. There are a few statics to rent. Facilities are basic but very well kept, and past customers come back time and again. Tully Beg, Renvyle, H91 EP38, +353 95 43462
53.6034, -9.9845

59 CLIFDEN ECO BEACH CAMPING *
Pre-book to pull up or pitch up in the dunes overlooking the secluded beach and hire a brazier for an evening on the sand. Facilities including showers and hairdryers, kitchens and laundry. Pet-friendly, bike and kayak hire, secure lock ups for your own – you could kayak to Omey island (see entry). Claddaghduff Road, Clifden, H71 W024, +353 95 44036, clifdenecocamping.ie
53.5237 -10.1348

60 CLIFDEN CAMPING AND CARAVAN PARK
Flower-filled traditional campsite for those who would like better facilities than the wilder nearby beach campsites offer. Dogs allowed, and a bonfire area; closed winter. Westport Rd, Shanakeever, H71 TP08, +353 95 22150
53.5018 -10.01872

61 EMLAGH BEACH COTTAGE
Renovated stone cottage sleeping six (eight at a push using two extra sofas in one bedroom) in three bedrooms. Big end window looking to sea, stove and electric heating, modern decor quite minimalist, great reviews.
53.5618, -10.1440

RUSTIC RETREATS

62 ROSLEAGUE MANOR HOTEL
Country house hotel overlooking Ballinakill Harbour, with a renowned restaurant where their own pork is on the menu along with other local produce. Letterfrack, H91 CK26, +353 95 41101
53.5487, -9.9744

63 THE OLD EXCHANGE
This renovated stone Labour Exchange is a tranquil haven of original features and pale decor, but Mari is great at accommodating walkers and cyclists (hire from Clifden Bike Shop around the corner, +353 95 22630) with wet gear if you give warning. The friendly chat over breakfast is full of local tips. Bridge St, Clifden, +353 86 0582143, H71 TW82
53.4873, -10.0191

64 THE QUAY HOUSE
Family-run hotel by the estuary, in Clifden's oldest house. Paddy and Julia offer plenty of helpful local advice, perfect period rooms, and fires in the sitting rooms in winter. Beach Road, Clifden, H71 XF76, +353 95 21369
53.4856, -10.0300

65 BALLYNAHINCH CASTLE
For ultimate luxury, it's worth staying at an Irish castle. This one has a lake in front and a mountain behind, its own spectacular 700-acre estate with woodlands, and is near the Connemara Greenway. There's a self-catering lodge and cottage. Restaurant uses local produce, including the estate's own pork, and they will make picnics for days out. Recess, Connemara, H91 F4A7, + 353 95 31006
53.4600, -9.8623

66 CALLOW SCHOOLHOUSE
This blissfully quiet converted schoolhouse above Inishdawros at Callow Strand (see entry) is a family holiday home rented out part-time and looked after by a neighbour, so it has quirky, personal decor, full of beach finds. Internet but no other reception for the tiny TV, a great incentive to switch off and watch the sunsets over the bay instead. H91 NCK8, search on Vrbo.
53.4038, -10.0316

57

57

Inishbofin
Tully Cross
Leenaun
Owenduff Bridge
Tullyconor Bridge
Clifden
Sraith Salach
Letterard
Carna
Cill Chiaráin
Leitir Móir

CENTRAL GALWAY

Our perfect weekend

- → **Beach-hop** along the shore path from Inverin to Carricknatraw, and reward your exertions with a delicious lunch at POTA café.
- → **Test** your nerve with the locals jumping from iconic Blackrock Diving Tower and warm up with coffee at Blackrock Cottage after.
- → **Wander** the woods on the way to romantic Menlo Castle ruins, and swim from the rushy shore at the nearby graveyard and pier.
- → **Take** a glorious hillside walk above Lough Invernagleragh to the lost village, lifting stone and holy well of Cnoc dhá Daimh.
- → **Sleep** in a 300-year-old thatched and stone cottage at Cnoc Suain and breakfast on supplies from White Gables in nearby Moycullen.
- → **Explore** the maze-like remains of Ross Errilly Friary, then discover forgotten Moyne Castle where you can still climb the hidden stairs.
- → **Eat** home grown fare at TamiJoy Farm or maybe indulge in a seaweed spa then venture on to the islands of Trá Dhireáin Huston.

This is one of the busier parts of the county, with a string of highly accessible beaches strung along the coast from Galway past Spideal.

There are reasons families might choose these: An Trá Mhór for example has a beach wheelchair, Céibh an Spidéil has a sauna. But there are many other little coves down threadlike lanes, and if you can leave a car or can be dropped off, you can walk from one to another.

The peninsulas and islands where the coast turns north have sands between the rocky headlands, and are where director John Huston holidayed and so fell in love with Ireland that he bought a home and became a citizen. Still, they're less visited – with the exception of the famous coral beach of Trá an Dóilin.

As if the sea shore was not enough, there's also vast Lough Corrib, a Ramsar site with more than a thousand islands and plenty of piers along its shores. Many have associated castles and there's even one inland lighthouse at Ballycurrin – built to guide either delivery boats or the tipsy returning owner, depending on who's telling it. More famous is Menlo Castle, scene of a tragic fire and once romantically engulfed in ivy, but recently uncovered for conservation work that should allow safe access.

Between these two watery shores the landscape is dominated by Moycullen bog, a quiet and largely empty expanse. Once cut and burned for energy, this area is home to wind turbines, with the county making a significant contribution to renewable power. The ground below is a Special Area of Conservation that supports Irish hares and a range of birds from lapwings to kestrels.

The gateway to all this is Galway city, a vibrant historic harbour city plagued with modern traffic. It's worth venturing in for some of the best food in the west, lively trad bars and sinful patisserie. The Corrib waters reach the harbour through the city via the fast-flowing River Corrib, whose noisy force gave Galway electric power before London; there's talk of harnessing it again. For now, kayak and rowing clubs put in on the calmer stretches near the university.

The harbour is the home of the classic red-sailed Galway hooker cargo boats that gave their name to one of Ireland's first craft breweries; today Galway Bay Brewery is a force to be reckoned with and a pint of their Full Sail is a great way to end a day's adventures.

SECRET BEACHES

1 AN DUMHAIGH BEACH & DINISH ISLAND

This end-of-the-world beach is pure white and provides the opportunity to swim or wade across to Dinish island, with further coves and some ruins. Parking is very tricky at the lane end (53.2590, -9.7463), so it would be nicer to paddle 1.5km up the W shore from the slip at 53.2493, -9.7471.

20 mins, 53.2616, -9.7482

2 TRÁ DHIREÁIN HUSTON

Little sandy cove at the end of a lane with a few parking options, houses nearby but beautiful and quiet. Signed 'Trá' from Lettermullan crossroads; named jointly for a writer born here and the film director who had a holiday home here. Tide comes in fast, be aware.

2 mins, 53.2327, -9.73342

3 AN TRÁ BHÁIN, GARUMNA

A small, white cove and slipway, just below the graveyard (space to park) and ruin of late medieval Trawbaun Church, once a gathering point from Aran pilgrims. There's a poignant memorial to four brothers all lost at sea in the 19th century. This is on the Luibin Garumna walk, you could walk it all from here, or just the (more attractive) coastal part of it as an out-and-back.

2 mins, 53.2339, -9.5494

4 AN TRÁ MÓR, GARUMNA

Not the 'big beach' the name implies, but a small cove with a quay and views across to the Twelve Bens, at the end of a tiny lane past H91 KH7K, Deirin Darach. Plenty of parking for such a secluded spot, handy for overnights, and a ruined chapel just off the lane (53.2558, -9.6439). This is one of the high points of the Luibin Garumna loop walk, along with An Trá Bháin (see entry).

2 mins, 53.2581, -9.6431

5 TRÁ AN DÓILIN, AN CHEATHRÚ RUA

Known as the Coral Beach, this unique strand is deservedly popular; the tawny maerl resembles cake sprinkles, the water has a tropical turquoise hue. At the start of August, you might catch the regatta of distinctive red-sailed Galway hooker boats. Keep walking N over the rocks for a final emptier stretch. The other name of Trá na bPaistí or the children's beach is from a cillín that lay where the car park is now. Signed along the R343 from Caifé Teac na Cúirte (H91 W573), at the end of the road.

5 mins, 53.2468, -9.6300

6 KEERAUNMORE QUAY & TRÁ NA REILIGE

Two close neighbours looking out over Cashla to a majestically turning wind turbine and Martello tower (see entry), on little lanes from Carraroe; take your pick or visit both. Keeraunmore is a fan of white sand sheltered by a pier for jumps, with space for only a couple of cars at the end of a lane from H91 N9XT, and rarely visited by anyone but locals; perhaps best for a weekend. Trá na Reilige is signed Bharr an Doire one turning further S along the road (53.2498, -9.5794): the main sands lie below a ruined church in a graveyard, providing easier parking, with a smaller cove to the L. People do make family visits to the active graveyard; maybe better for a weekday.

2 mins, 53.2546, -9.57833

7 TRÁ AN TOBAIR

Rocks and LT sands backed by flowery turf and the quiet dead. The best beach is 350m W from the older graveyard, perfect to watch the sun set, but the granite platforms are dotted with great rock pools. Also look for St Cholm Cille's well and stone boat signed outside the graveyard: the boat is a big rock at (53.229741 , -9.532051), and the tidal well is a hollow next to it. Signed Toibreacha agus Bád Cholmcille off road W leaving R336 at 53.2420, -9.5038. Quiet and remote for an overnight.

6 mins, 53.2308, -9.5366

8 CARRICKNATRAW, TRAVORE BAY

The white sand at this beach gives it incredible turquoise water and a tropical feel on a sunny day. It's popular with locals, but with space for just two cars and no parking on the lane, it's passed by most who cannot walk to it. On a bike, cycle down the lane next to POTA café (see entry); you could park at the café and walk down (about 1km), but it's more polite to drive down to the WAW point parking at Céibh Bhaile na hAbhann to the W (see entry) and follow the lane E for 900m.

20 mins, 53.22836, -9.4895

9 CARTRONKEEL BEACH

This deep, narrow beach below Minna is sandy most of the time and has flower-studded grass above. It has no name on OS maps and no sign when we visited, but the lane down to it is labelled Cartronkeel on the earliest OS; it's twisty and bumpy, so take it slowly, but it leads to a gravel car park. If you have time, you could extend a beach-hopping walk from Inverin to Pollnameeltoge (see entry) as far as this.

2 mins, 53.2338, -9.4546

10 INVERIN TO POLLNAMEELTOGE

Rocky shore and white beaches with glorious views to the Burren, gleaming white on a sunny day. Most beaches can each be visited down tiny lanes with a couple of parking spaces, but to catch them all, park at Inverin cemetery (53.2420, -9.3677) and walk W for up to 6km, along part of the Slí Chonamara walking trail. The high point is lovely Teachmore beach between two poignant crosses: one to the E end for a deadly sea mine explosion, one in a famine burial ground to the W. Further on, try to budge the 175kg lifting stone at 53.2332, -9.4288, and explore the Cor na Ron kelp kilns (53.2337, -9.4330), rare survivors of structures once found all along the coast. Next to them is Pollnameeltogue Harbour (no sign of any quay), a long slot of sand where the kelp was landed. The official path turns inland here; if you had two cars you could leave one here, or further on at Cartronkeel (see entry).

60 mins, 53.2352, -9.4091

11 TRÁ SÁILÍN, POOREEN

Lovely little white beach with limited parking down a tiny lane from Pooreen. Signed S off R336 under a height restriction at H91 FY8K. The lane may be busy on the sunniest days, because although visitors usually miss the sign, locals love this beach. There's an old burial ground in the dunes L.

2 mins, 53.2405, -9.3452

12 BLACKROCK DIVING TOWER, SALTHILL

These 100-year-old diving platforms (rebuilt in 1954, opened to women in the 1970s) have

13

14

13

become a symbol of Galway's sea-swimming culture, with the top board an intimidating 7m high. Join the hardy community in any season, but check the depth gauge on the tower before taking the plunge – and if you walk in along the prom (parking on road, car park at Galway end of the beach), it's traditional to kick the wall before you walk back.

20 mins, 53.2561, -9.0921

LAKE, RIVER & WATERFALLS

13 SCREEBE WATERFALL

Idyllic scene with waterfalls tumbling down to the white-washed stone gillie hut on the shore of Lough Aughawoolia below There are small laybys at the R336 bridge and good pools both above and below the road bridge for 50m. Don't disturb anyone fishing.

2 mins, 53.4190, -9.5450

14 HILL OF DOON PIER & VIEW

A cove and stone pier reaching into Lough Corrib at its narrowest neck, with views to the hills opposite. Walk straight down the grassy slope from the two viewpoint parking areas above, at the very end of the shore road from Oughterard.

2 mins, 53.4864, -9.4556

15 ANNAGHKEEN, LOUGH CORRIB

Beautiful spot with two ruins and a stone quay. The ivy-hung 13th-century castle shell is a rare undressed-stone construction, and passages inside the 2m-thick walls lead to the upper levels and parapet; the ruin of a later manor house stands behind it. The quay below is a great spot to swim or kayak. On little lanes W from Headford.

2 mins, 53.4467, -9.1964

16 LEAGAUN SHORE, LOUGH CORRIB

A small hidden spot to swim or kayak the wilder islands and reedy wonderlands of this shallow bay on Lough Corrib, including Inchacommaun straight across the bay, and the pony-filled shores to the N. There's some parking and a gravel beach, good for overnights, too.

2 mins, 53.3486, -9.1462

17 MENLO PIER, RIVER CORRIB

Slip out through the reeds from Menlo pier. Kayakmór (+353 87 7565578) also run half-day and dusk kayak tours of the river from here. For wilder swimming spots enter the graveyard and turn R. Little trails lead off the gravel path down to the water: the third and fourth are the best (53.3007, -9.0782). The graveyard is a great gallery of memorial history, from 19th-century Celtic crosses to recent pictorial styles,

15

17

22

22

22

20

24

and from English to Irish in names. Take the fork to shore in Menlo village at H91 DK2R. Also see Menlo Castle entry.

2 mins, 53.3012, -9.07726

18 ANNAGHDOWN PIER & SAUNA

The old pier here is perfect for swimming, with steps into the lough and a jumping point into deeper water, and popular with locals in summer. There's even a mobile sauna with lake views (Folláine Sauna +353 83 8385581 and social media). Pier signed from Annaghdown village, continue to the end past the ruined abbey (see entry).

2 mins, 53.38729, -9.0769

LOST RUINS

19 MARTELLO TOWER, RHOS AN MHÍL

This well-preserved Napoleonic era tower sits right on the rocky shore overlooking the route into Rossaveel, now used by ferries to Inishmore. Elliptical in plan externally, it was fitted with a 24-pound cannon, which is still on the roof. A well-preserved though green military road provides access across the raised bog to the tower, but the doorway is at first-floor level and would have had a ladder to lower. A fine spot to watch a sunset, and the boats going in and out.

2 mins, 53.2550, -9.5621

20 HEN'S CASTLE, CAISLEÁN NA CIRCE

Also Castlekirk, this island castle, one of the oldest mortared keeps in Ireland, was built early in the 12th-century by Irish and Anglo-Norman allies (but in folklore by a cock and a hen in a single night). The nearest kayak launch is 4km NW at Belanabrack River Pier by Maum Bridge (53.5149, -9.5604).

120 mins, 53.4925, -9.5133

21 AUGHNANURE CASTLE & PIER

This restored six-storey 15th-century castle and bawn with a later banqueting hall is a good way to see how tower houses worked, €5, Mar–Nov. O'Flahertys built their castles by water; the river here is dry, but Lough Corrib is near and 5km N is Oughterard pier (53.4384, -9.3039) for a swim or kayak and boats to Inchagoill island (see entry).

2 mins, 53.4187, -9.2757

22 MOYNE CASTLE, HEADFORD *

Little-visited, 16th-century keep with intact roof and staircases you can climb, set in the old parkland, now a hay field. There's a gate with sign in the stone wall, right on a fast section of the R334; park out of the way in the gravel area at the entrance to the farm just over the river E.

6 mins, 53.4886, -9.1204

23 MENLO CASTLE, RIVER CORRIB

This achingly beautiful riverside 18th-century Gothic castle was gutted by fire in 1910. It sits in a flowery meadow with its own tiny quay and beach, and lesser horseshoe bat colony that appear at dusk. The woodland R on the drive has more bats and a mystery stone structure. Park at school (H91 YD63), walk down past old castle gates and through the farm gate. E of the school is a decorated 17th-century pillar by the lane that was once the main road to Galway (53.3031, -9.0649).

12 mins, 53.2963, -9.0735 

SACRED & ANCIENT

24 INCHAGOILL ISLAND CHURCHES

Those with kayaks can explore these islands solo, launching from Derrymoyle (53.4551, -9.3303, 3km). Others take a trip in summer months with Lough Corrib Adventures (+353 87 3396215, sailing), Corrib Cruises (+353 87 2830799) or Corrib Safari (online booking corribsafari.ie). Teampull Phadraig was supposedly built by St Patrick and his nephew, Lugnad, but is more likely 6th or 7th century. An ancient flagged way leads from it to the 12th-century Teampull Na Naomh, Church of the Saints, with a Hiberno Romanesque doorway with several orders of arches c.12th century, decorated with a variety of ornamentation. There are bullauns, a cross-incised slab, and a 6th-century ogham stone.

60 mins, 53.4857, -9.3162

25 ROSS ERRILLY FRIARY *

Set in serene fields by the Black River, these maze-like, 15th-century Franciscan remains are some of the most impressive and complete in Ireland; even a fish tank in the kitchen has survived. This is because the Clanricard family kept it in use until the 19th century, re-establishing it after dissolution and restoring it at some personal risk after Cromwellian soldiers burned it. There is still informal use today; we visited while there was a 'handfasting' in a side chapel. Signed W at the crossroads in Headford.

2 mins, 53.4794, -9.1317

26 ANNAGHDOWN ABBEY & CATHEDRAL

Quiet Annaghdown was once busy, with not just the abbey but a nearby cathedral (53.3877, -9.0712), and 'nunnery', actually a monastery church, all built between 1140 and 1224. The Romanesque abbey ruins may have once held the fine window now seen in the cathedral, which also holds a cross with a human face, and a sheela na gig lying on the ground. Park at the graveyard or at the abbey on the road to the pier (see entry).

2 mins, 53.3867, -9.0727

25

25

25

26

26

ROCKS & MINES

27 CNOC DHÁ DAIMH & CLOCH NIRT

Beautiful walk past sparkling Lough Invernagleragh, through the remains of a deserted settlement to a cluster of large glacial erratics. One is shaped like a small coffin, and raising one end is all that has been managed on recent attempts, but legend says those who lived here could lift it. Small gravel pull off at 53.3878, -9.6132, or park at the Ionad Cultúrtha an Phiarsaigh and walk 350m E with care. Walk up 400m and fork L through gate, down hillside and across a boggy area to the lough, to pick up a track with stone culverts for the mountain streams. Further N and W (the track gives out) is a small stone shrine over a bullaun holy well (53.4080, -9.6237).

60 mins, 53.4043, -9.61309 

28 GLENGOWLA MINES, OUGHTERARD

Venture into the underground world of silver and lead mining with shafts, tunnels, and caverns shimmering with pyrites and quartz. The tours are very small scale and rather charming, the small stone entrance overhung with cotoneaster. Above ground, explore a thatched Cornish powderhouse, blacksmith's shop, and quirky museum, watch sheep-herding and turf-cutting demos, and pan for gold. €10, Mar–Nov. Oughterard, H91 PX22, +353 87 2529850, glengowlamines.ie

2 mins, 53.4181, -9.3743 

29 GALWAY WIND WAY

Close encounters with the future of energy, in a landscape of moor and bog that once provided power through the extraction and burning of turf. You can get up close below these towering, whooshing turbines on a series of walking and cycle trails with vast views. Another opportunity to walk into the Moycullen SAC, with red grouse, hare, and birds from kestrels to lapwing, is at Lettergunnet wind farm (53.2814, -9.2003).

10 mins, 53.3824, -9.3740

CLASSIC PUBS & BARS

30 POWERS THATCH, OUGHTERARD

Renowned bar and restaurant, be prepared to queue on a summer evening, especially at weekends – it's worth it. Get a pint at the bar and take in the eclectic assortment of items on the walls until you get a table for great seafood and other local produce. Main Street, Fough East, Oughterard, H91 CVY3, +353 91 557597

53.4286, -9.3188

31 PÁDRAICÍNS SEAFOOD BAR

In season, this maritime-themed local institution is open all day, so you could dip at

27

27

27

'urbo Beach below and then get breakfast. here are local brews on the bar and a strong eafood menu. Furbo, H91 YW68, +353 91 592444

3.2504 -9.2249

2 O'GRADYS ON THE PIER

)n a fine summer day it doesn't get much better han an outside table here, right on the shore f the bay, with boats bobbing in the harbour; 1 winter, enjoy the same views through the vindows with a real fire in the hearth. The mphasis is on fresh seafood simply prepared the trio of scallops, sea bass and sea trout is signature speciality. 1 Seapoint Road, Barna, 91 P8P3, +353 91 592223

3.2495, -9.1509

3 THE CRANE BAR, GALWAY

lthough this place seems a very no-frills ffering downstairs, it's widely regarded as ne of the must-visit pubs for the trad sessions pstairs every night. Get there about 9pm, it an be squeezing room only by half-past. 2 Sea oad, Galway, H91 YP97, +353 91 587419

3.2698, -9.0605

4 TIGH NEACHTAIN, GALWAY

alway's Latin Quarter has a wealth of great ars with atmosphere and music; this is one of the best, with a bohemian vibe and nooks where you can find your own space, even in a crowd. It has plenty of history: it was once machine gunned for the Irish name above the door, and was the home of 'Humanity Dick', founder of the Society for the Prevention of Cruelty to Animals. 17 Cross Street, H91 F9F7, 091 568820. For more craft brews, we also love The Salthouse on Raven Terrace, H91 D9Y2, +353 91 441550.

53.2713, -9.0539

35 TAAFFES BAR, GALWAY

Old-fashioned GAA pub in the heart of the city, noted for its trad music sessions. Order a hot port and try to get a seat by the open fire in winter. 19–20 Shop Street, H91 WF20, +353 91 564066

53.2723, -9.0531

HOME COOKING & BAKING

36 TAMIJOY FARM, LETTERMULLAN

TamiJoy cooks using local produce, including her own, for private dining meals in her restored famine cottage. She will also set up beach picnics and hosts farm tours, classes and wellness days. Ballinakill, Lettermullen, H91 YV2X,+353 87 6073492. You could combine with the Oileanra Seaweed Baths and Sauna a little further W on R374, behind the bar (behind H91 FY52, +353 87 6154740, book on oileanra.ie).

53.2430, -9.7025

37 AN GARRAÍ GLAS

Sometimes the roadside shop is open, otherwise there are honesty shelves at this super little farm growing with organic and regenerative principles. They also run farm tours with lunch on Saturdays in summer from 2pm +353 83 8071113, H91 D26R

53.2383, -9.4796

38 BUILÍN BLASTA CAFÉ & BAKERY

Spiddal Craft Village (Ceardlann an Spidéil) is a cheerfully coloured collection of craft workshops offering handmade goods and this award-winning, bright and airy café and bakery. Savouries, sweet treats, and their own range of small-batch sauces on the shop shelves. There's even a beach (but across a fast road). Bohoona East, Spiddal, H91 XPA8, +353 91 558559

53.2452, -9.3001

39 LE PETIT DELICE

Bakery, patisserie and coffee, superb hot chocolate, signature strawberry tart. 7 Mainguard Street, Galway, H91 F5TE, +353 91 500751

53.2720, -9.0539

34

36

41

48

49

52

40 WHITE GABLES

This bakery and deli sells artisan foods and wine, and its takeaway options include salads and savouries, as well as cake. Open 10am–5pm every day, and 7.30pm on Friday for takeaway fish and chips. Moycullen Village, H91 FR63, +353 91 555744

53.3379, -9.1805

ORGANIC & GASTRO

41 POTA *

Our favourite place for a cooked breakfast before a hike, an indulgent cake after a swim, and for learning what the ingredients are called 'as gaeilge'. Diarmuid Ó Mathúna opened this bilingual café (the name means a cooking pot) based on seasonal locally produced foods in 2021 and it has won fans and awards ever since. An Tulach, Baile na hAbhann, H91 A9W8, +353 85 7566963

53.2366, -9.4937

42 WEST RESTAURANT, BARNA

The Twelve Hotel has good food in the hotel bar and Pizza Dozzina, but it's the West restaurant that stands out for fine local produce, in season, presented at its best. Tasting menu, small or large plates, and an excellent west of Ireland artisan cheese board. The Twelve Hotel, Barna, H91 Y3KA, +353 91 597000

53.2513, -9.1524

43 BLACKROCK COTTAGE

With its unassuming cottage exterior (with modern, glazed extension), superb coffees, fine foods and organic ingredients, curated by award-winning French chef Mathieu Teulier, this is the place to soak up the Galway outdoor vibe post sea swim. Salthill Promenade, H91 KV9D, +353 91 399280

53.2568, -9.0923

44 ANIAR *

The name of this small, simple, Michelin-starre restaurant means 'from the west', which sums up JP McMahon's menu, largely sourced and even foraged from the local land and coast. One-day courses with the genial chef patron fill up months in advance: we met a couple who built a trip to Ireland around one. 53 Lower Dominick Street, H91 V4DP, +353 91 535947. JP also runs Cava Bodega tapas restaurant, H9 AF89, +353 91 539884

53.2710, -9.0571

45 ARD BIA AT NIMMOS

This bohemian, shabby-chic restaurant is a local legend. The walk-up lunches fill up fast, and booking for the evening is highly advisable. The menu is seasonal, with Mediterranean and Middle-Eastern inspiration. Spanish Arch, The Long Walk, H91 E9XA, +353 91 561114

53.2695, -9.0537

46 THE LIGHTHOUSE VEGETARIAN CAFÉ

Family-run café serving plant-based foods, a great place for a quick and healthy lunch seven days a week. The original café is in the busy heart of the city but this branch on the bypass is great for those just trying to get around it. Terryland Retail Park, Headford Road, H91 WR99, +353 91 568706

53.2853, -9.0452

RUSTIC RETREATS

47 CURRAGHDUFF FARM

Three unique little wooden lodges on Airbnb, two suitable for families, with shared facilities on a farm with alpacas, pygmy goats, sheep and chickens; take farm walks and even yoga classes with alpacas. Curraghduff West, Oughterard, H91 R2Y7, +353 87 3968305

53.4756, -9.40975

48 WILD ATLANTIC BUS, OUGHTERARD

Owner RIchard converted a double-decker bus into a two-bedroom holiday hideaway that sleeps six, on Airbnb. There's everything from a Belfast sink in the kitchen to a woodburner, and outside a firepit and an extra shower – though you might have an audience of cows. Derrymoyle, H91 FW3F, +353 86 2562138

53.4533, -9.3373

49 CNOC SUAIN *

'An Baile Íochtar' (The Lower Village) here is a trio of ancient stone cottages restored – really rebuilt – as a labour of love by the owners since 1995. With converted oil lamps, underfloor heating and handcrafted furnishings, two are available as blissful adults-only retreats set in their own 200 acres of blanket bog: no pets, no mobile signal and no wifi in the cottages, only in a communal building up the lane. Award-winning and booked well in advance on Airbnb. Knock, Moycullen, H91 W44N

53.2878, -9.2641

50 BALLYCURRIN LIGHTHOUSE LODGE

Right on the shore of Lough Corrib with a row boat, next to a unique inland lighthouse that you can climb (can also be visited even if you are not staying). Svleeps six, on Airbnb. H91 FKT1, +353 93 35805

53.4854, -9.2131

51 CARRAIGIN CASTLE

For a large group, it doesn't get better than a castle to yourselves. This beautifully restored 13th-century keep right on the Corrib shore has fine stone fireplaces and oak-beamed, vaulted ceilings, and sleeps 12. You can stroll out on to the parapets for the sunset views and there are seven bedrooms, one reached by a rough stone spiral staircase. +353 89 6002250, carraigincastle@gmail.com

53.4352, -9.1548

52 CATHERINA, LOUGH ATALIA

Within walking distance of the busy heart of Galway, an off-grid sailing barge for two moored on Lough Atalia. Electricity is from a combination of wind, solar and an on-board generator, and you can sit on your own deck enjoying a sunset over the city and water, or snuggle up by a turf fire in the stove if it gets chilly. Near The Huntsman at H91 D5DW, listed on Airbnb as Beautiful Boat in the Heart of Galway City.

53.2803, -9.0318

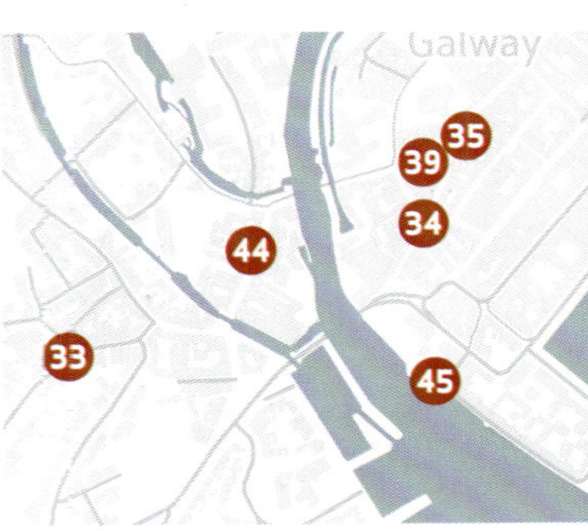

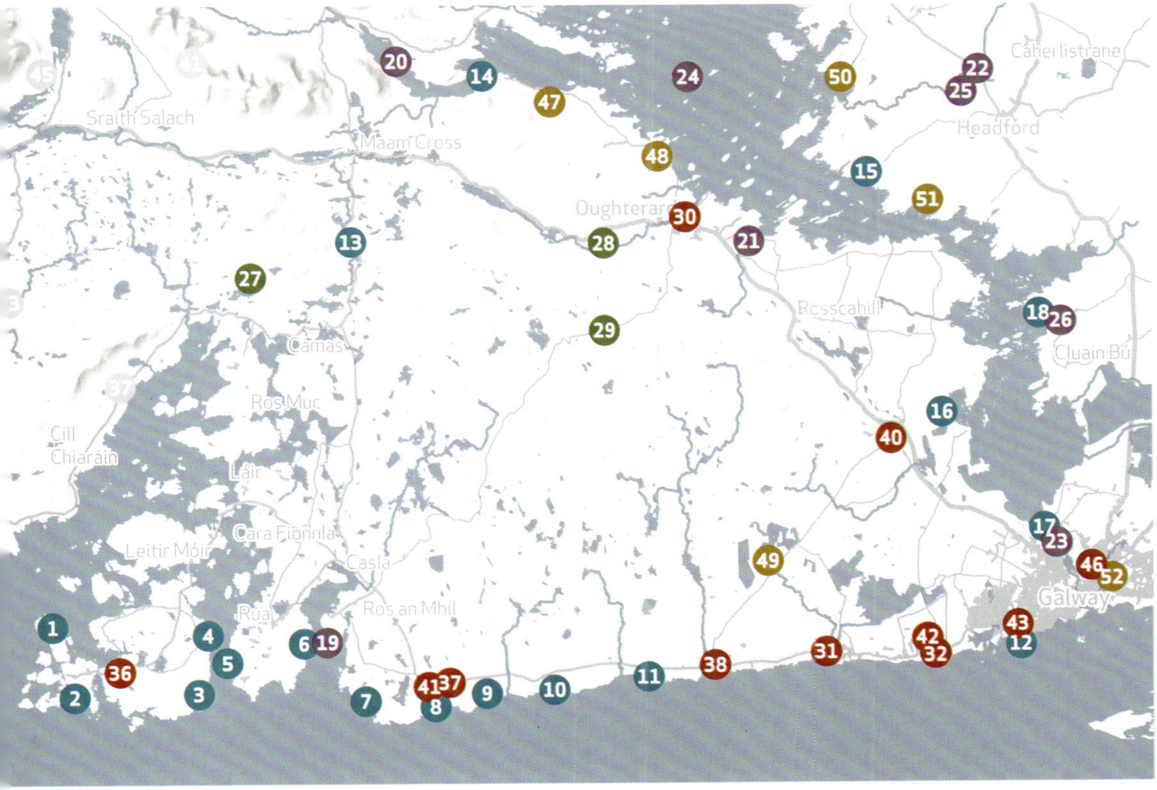

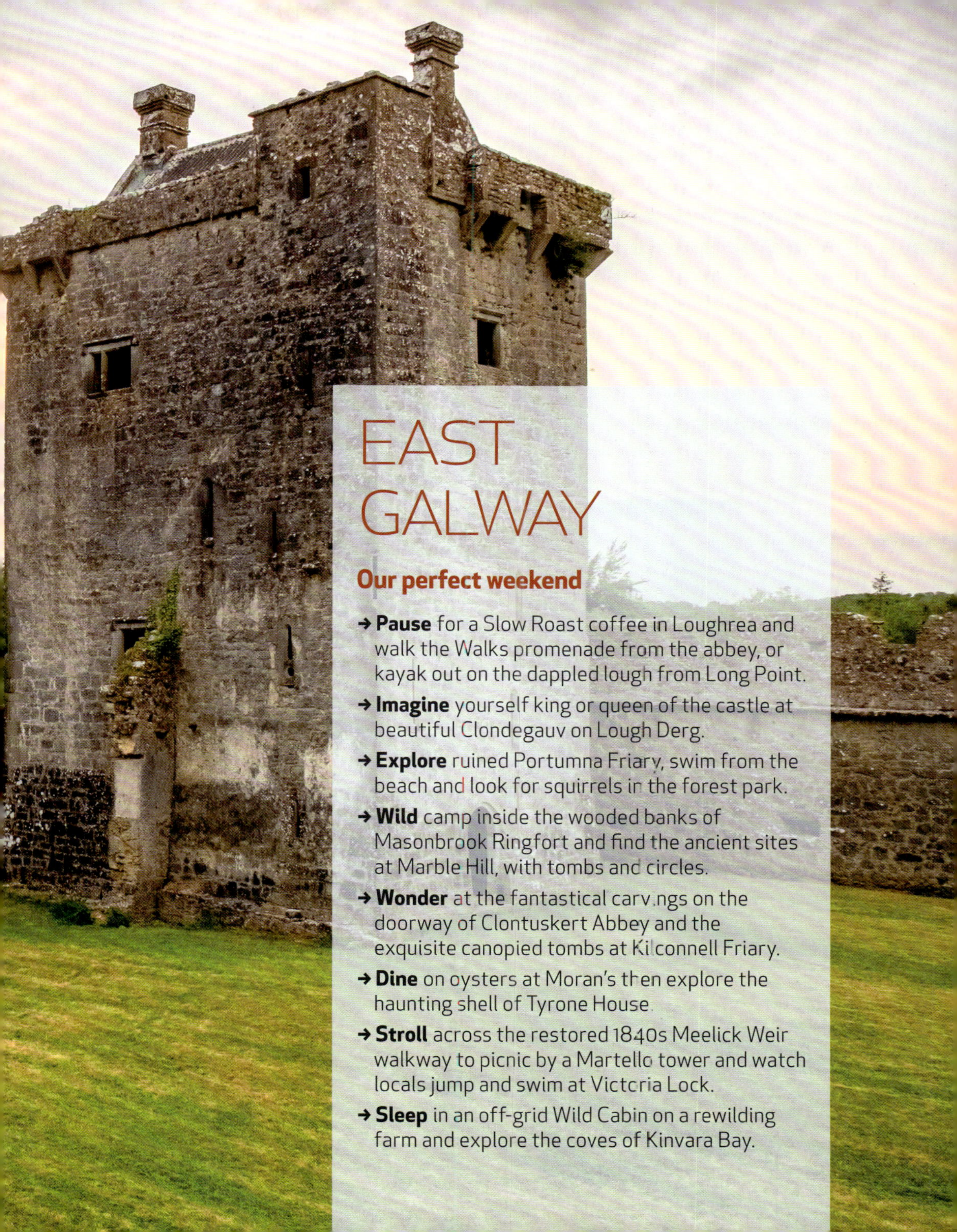

EAST GALWAY

Our perfect weekend

→ **Pause** for a Slow Roast coffee in Loughrea and walk the Walks promenade from the abbey, or kayak out on the dappled lough from Long Point.

→ **Imagine** yourself king or queen of the castle at beautiful Clondegauv on Lough Derg.

→ **Explore** ruined Portumna Friary, swim from the beach and look for squirrels in the forest park.

→ **Wild** camp inside the wooded banks of Masonbrook Ringfort and find the ancient sites at Marble Hill, with tombs and circles.

→ **Wonder** at the fantastical carvings on the doorway of Clontuskert Abbey and the exquisite canopied tombs at Kilconnell Friary.

→ **Dine** on oysters at Moran's then explore the haunting shell of Tyrone House.

→ **Stroll** across the restored 1840s Meelick Weir walkway to picnic by a Martello tower and watch locals jump and swim at Victoria Lock.

→ **Sleep** in an off-grid Wild Cabin on a rewilding farm and explore the coves of Kinvara Bay.

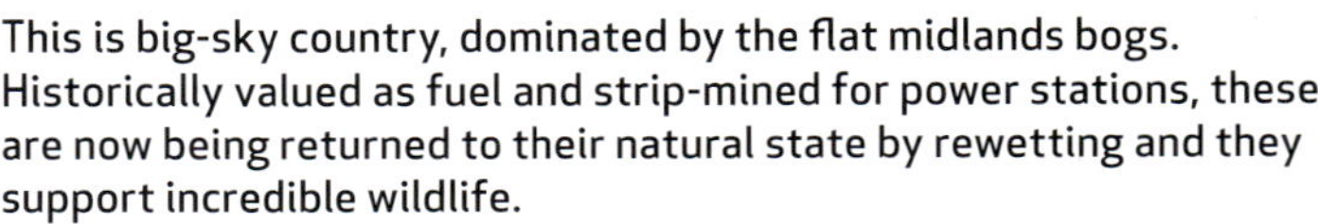

This is big-sky country, dominated by the flat midlands bogs. Historically valued as fuel and strip-mined for power stations, these are now being returned to their natural state by rewetting and they support incredible wildlife.

Many have trails to walk – Carrownagapul is the jewel. There are sparkling sundews, fluffy bog cotton and tart-berried juniper, dragonflies at pools and abundant butterflies, melodious birdlife, small mammals in the heather and birds of prey above hunting them. This is a landscape of detail that invites slow strolling rather than the energy of a hike to a mountaintop vista.

The quiet depths of the Shannon flow along the eastern border, with Lough Derg more like a long widening, not a mountain-hemmed lake. I grew up with these silky river waters: no crashing falls or waves, but plenty of little quays and piers for jumps, and banks with reeds and brandy-bottle lilies.

Since then the Shannon Blueway has been developed, with convenient putting-in points and distance maps for those who paddle their own canoe. Facilities for river travellers can benefit those on land too, with access to serviced aires. The River Suck is worth exploring: with development prevented by the broad winter-flooding 'callows' either side, it's protected for a variety of resident and migratory birds, from flocks of geese and swans to plovers and lapwings. There's a 105km Suck Valley Way through all this (no dogs), starting in Ballygar.

You may notice that you are not in stone-wall country here, but hedge country. The land, less stony and more fertile than in the far west, supported some great estates, and woods remain from these, most famously at Coole. Some have been exploited for forestry, at least in part, but in recent years there's been more mixed planting and regeneration.

The landed families also left castles and manors – some in ruins such as Pallas, others you can stay in, such as Castle Ellen. Rich families also endowed monastic foundations that now lie in ruins, along with older parish churches such as mysterious Kiltiernan.

Take your cue from the landscape here: slow down and meander. Take the unexpected turning, explore the little lanes, and don't shun the towns: they're small and often rich in history, such as medieval Athenry, famous in song, or Portumna, long one of the most important crossing points on the Shannon.

LOUGH, RIVER & ESTUARY

1 CRUSHOA PIER & TRAUGHT BEACH

Remote pier, perfect for a swim or kayak at HT, shallow otherwise. Also a peaceful place for an overnight. Continue 5km N for the long, pebble, life-guarded strand of Traught Beach (53.1712, -8.9859). On the way, you'll pass the impressive sunken basin of Patrick's Well on the roadside junction at Tawnagh West (53.1620, -8.9907).

2 mins, 53.1538, -8.9526

2 PARSON'S ISLAND, LOUGH CUTRA

A well-wooded lough with several islands; two of them once had castles and two had churches, including Parson's Island, only 400m from the shore. There's a rough parking area and beach and its very quiet apart from occasional anglers. Reached by a track with height barrier.

2 mins, 53.0364, -8.7673

3 LONG POINT, LOUGH REA

The public swimming spot for Loughrea town isn't the wildest, but it's a good place for kayaks, to explore the wilder shoreline and crannógs of the 'dappled lough'. S of the quay and there's a small stretch of more natural shore without lifeguards. Just over 1km S of Loughrea along the E shore of the lough on the R351.

2 mins, 53.1850, -8.5617

4 ROSSMORE QUAY, LOUGH DERG

Great spot for swimming, kayaking and overnights with a large concrete quay, good for jumping if you check the depth. Expect some cruisers to be moored here. Signed from R352 N of Gorteeny.

2 mins, 53.0172, -8.3108

5 CLONDEGAUV CASTLE, LOUGH DERG*

This 15th-century tower house among the trees on the Lough Derg shore is a beautiful setting for a picnic and swim. The interior is closed off. Down unsigned lanes 8km E of Woodford, pull off road at track.

2 mins, 53.0482, -8.2898

6 PORTUMNA BEACH, LOUGH DERG

Swim out from the pontoons, and you can quickly find yourself among rushes and brandy-bottle lilies in the smooth, silty brown waters. With a kayak, you can explore even further. This is an excellent place to watch for birds, especially the starling murmurations that swirl over the lough on winter evenings before roosting in the reeds. Or swim/kayak from adjacent the castle harbour just to the W (see entry).

2 mins, 53.0835 -8.2110

7 CLOONFAD, RIVER SUCK

This wide, deep river leads to the Shannon and can be swum or paddled anywhere downstream of Ballinasloe. This parking area at the end of a long lane L7601 is a lovely spot to stop and explore on a meander with a small island. and an old gun platform still discernible on the bank (53.2806, -8.1488).

2 mins, 53.2818, -8.1490

8 BANAGHER POOL, RIVER SHANNON

My main summer swim spot in childhood, below a late-medieval battery called Cromwell's Castle; a pontoon enclosure has made it less wild, but also much less muddy, and provides jumping-off points straight into the deeper waters. There is a café above in summer, too. Teenagers also jumped from the old quay walls across the river and even the bridge, but it can be busy with boats, so needs caution. Riverside park with parking, off R356 by bridge.

2 mins, 53.1935 -7.9943

9 MEELICK QUAY & WEIR WALKWAY

You can swim at the quay/riverside or take a short short diversion over the Shannon; a recently restored walkway over the weir leads to Moran Island, created by the cutting of the canal in the 19th century. Take a picnic and find your own spot. There's a rare inland Martello

16

13

14

11

11

tower, and on the far side of the island Victoria Lock is a popular locals' swimming spot with jumps, where you can swim three counties.

2 mins, 53.1763, -8.0755

LOST RUINS

10 OLD PALLAS CASTLE*

One of the largest and best-preserved 15th-century tower houses, this has an intact bawn wall you can walk, with gatehouse and turrets; the tower itself is locked. In remote countryside down unsigned lanes, but with parking once you arrive.

2 mins, 53.1265, -8.3621

11 TYRONE HOUSE RUIN*

This wonderful Georgian shell (just step over the low wire) inspired the novel The Big House of Inver, which describes a great yard, gardens, turf yard and quay; the remains of all lie down the track L, still cobbled in places, with abundant blackberries when we visited. The quay is perfect for a picnic or a HT swim. The house was burned in 1921; the imposing family mausoleum is at nearby St Sourney's church (see entry). Space to pull in at gate.

2 mins, 53.2070, -8.9097 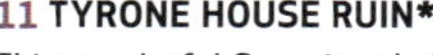

12 FEARTAGAR CASTLE & CASTLEGROVE

Also known as Jennings Castle, this 16th-century tower has hidden chambers and passages in the upper walls. It was attached to Castlegrove ruined house 100m N in woods (53.5711, -8.9419), which was lived in until 1922, when it was attacked and burned in the civil war. According to local tradition, the owner 'escaped through a secret passage and boarded a train at the local Castlegrove station and was never seen again'. Fruit trees survive in the woods around it. Castle is locked; ask at farm on the way in about the key. At end of L64502 off R332 N of Tuam.

2 mins, 53.5696, -8.9427

13 KILMACDUAGH ABBEY

This extensive site, once the seat of the diocese, is called the seven churches, though not all the structures were churches. The 10th-century round tower, with its distinctive lean, is the oldest of them and the tallest ancient structure in Ireland; most of the rest is from the 12th century on.

2 mins, 53.0479 -8.8877

14 ST MARY'S ABBEY & WALKS

The 13th-century abbey ruins have unusual carved animals on the windows (the inside is locked). It stands in a packed graveyard at one

15

15

17

end of the Walks, a promenade along the old town moat to Station Road (53.1996, -8.5656), past footbridges and doors into the burgage plots behind properties; malls such as this were fashionable in the 18th century. Detour to visit the strange head of Stoney Brennan, hanged for stealing a turnip during the Great Famine: a kiss is said to prevent hangovers or bring marriage, but a ladder would be handy (53.1991, -8.5743). Park on Main Street.

2 mins, 53.1998, -8.5701

15 ROSCAM ABBEY

By a lonely stretch of shore lies a church ruin (fenced against the cattle) and a short 11th-century round tower; unusually it has a door at ground level and window above, a weakness that would limit the height. Below is a graveyard crammed with uncut markers and two massive multiple bullauns that St Patrick is said to have washed his hands in. Room for one car between gates at 53.2650, -8.9799; you can walk through the lowest fields if you hug the walls and don't bother the cows. Some may prefer to walk the cobble shore and climb in at the graveyard.

15 mins, 53.2641 -8.9850

16 LISMORE CASTLE

Once an important O'Madden castle, built in the 16th-century, now remote and forgotten. It has four storeys with a square bartizan on the SW corner, reached by a lane then rough track.

5 mins, 53.1952, -8.0867

17 CLONTUSKERT ABBEY

The best part of these 15th-century ruins is the great west doorway, similar to the one at famous Clonmacnoise in Offaly. Carvings around it include the archangel Michael with a sword and scales, griffins, a pelican feeding her young, and a mermaid similar to one at Clonfert. There are also fine windows, arches and a cloister to the top of the pillars. Car park signed by farmyard on R355, often missed.

7 mins, 53.2825 -8.2157

18 ATHENRY PRIORY

This 13th-century foundation had a turbulent life, was re-used as a barracks, and even has a handball alley built on to the W side in the early 20th century; this happened to a surprising number of religious ruins. Houses the best collection of occupational illustrated gravestones in Ireland; if locked, you can usually get a key from the castle (a restored 13th-century keep 53.3000, -8.7444 with a medieval town gate nearby) or the Heritage Centre (St Mary's Church, H65 WC57). On-street parking.

2 mins, 53.2982 -8.7445

18

18

19 KILCONNELL FRIARY

Most of the church, with tracery windows, masses of carvings and some fine canopied tombs, survives at this 15th-century ruin, as well as large sections of the cloister. Park at 53.3316, -8.4029, and walk up the gated track from the corner. Across from the track, the Donnellan Wayside Cross was most likely a preaching cross for the displaced friars after dissolution. It was first put up in 1682, taken down in Penal times, and re-erected in 1842.

5 mins, 53.3327 -8.4009

20 ABBEYKNOCKMOY ABBEY RUINS

Rare wall paintings survive here (gated, but viewable), showing scenes including St Sebastian, and the three living and three dead kings from a 15th-century poem. These and a carved head on a capital are clearly cut in the same style as work at Boyle Abbey in Roscommon, which supplied the monks who settled here. Park at the graveyard, stiles on the way up.

7 mins, 53.4404 -8.7429

SACRED & ANCIENT

21 MARBLE HILL WEDGE TOMB

The ruins of a long narrow gallery with sloping roof stones in a mound with displaced slabs. Turn off R353 at L8206 and find track entrance on R after 700m (pull off carefully) then 30m up track. The keen can seek out another around a tree in the next fields 200m to N (53.0868, -8.4670) and to the E the hilltop Cartron South stone circle, Galway's only radial cairn (53.0860, -8.4563).

2 mins, 53.0848, -8.4667

22 PORTUMNA FRIARY & HARBOUR

This 15th-century ruin among trees had a busy life, growing from a 13th-century chapel and ending up a Protestant church in the 18th century. Tracery windows, a lovely cloister and carvings, including a curious inverted head, survive. Nearby is the restored castle with a kitchen garden and history display; you can park at the marina S along the lane, good for swimming and for starling murmurations in winter, and an official Waterways Ireland aire for overnights.

5 mins, 53.0861, -8.2176

23 MASONBROOK RINGFORT*

This magical and unusually multivallate rath is hidden in rustling trees and oddly obscure. Three substantial, ferny embankments, almost 100m across, enclose a central glade where some might wild camp. It's also called Rathsonny or Rathsoony, the ringfort of the palisade. Take the unsigned lane at H62 EH48 for parking and gate R after 200m. Head L around the banks to find openings. Bronze Age Moanmore stone circle, or the Seven Monuments, lies by the main road W of the lane (53.1884, -8.5311).

2 mins, 53.1814 -8.5106

24 KILTIERNAN CHURCH

An ancient and mysterious site with no written records, believed to have been founded by St Tiernan in the 5th century. The stone church is from the 8th century, putting it among Ireland's oldest. It sits in a large circular enclosure amid the low outlines of more than 20 structures, mostly house-sites, over 16 sub-enclosures, and a souterrain at 53.1879, -8.8435. Behind the enclosure is an even older grassed-over cairn (53.1874, -8.8417). Unsigned lane off R, small gate in; park in front of houses NE, or possibly overgrown gate to W.

2 mins, 53.1880, -8.8428

25 ST SOURNEY'S WELL & CHURCH

Founded by the 6th-century St Sarnait, whose holy well lies just W of the graveyard. The square-headed doorway is the oldest part of the church (also called Drumacoo); there's also a 13th-century doorway. Attached is the ostentatious Gothic mausoleum of the St George family (of nearby ruin Tyrone House, see entry); the closing lines of Betjeman's 'Ireland With Emily' about the family and tomb are by the door. Signed from N67.

2 mins, 53.1987 -8.9048

26 KNOCKMA CAIRNS & CASTLE

Grand panoramic views from Ceasair's Cairn on Knockma's highest summit. It's said to be the grave of Noah's granddaughter, the first woman to set foot in Ireland, bringing sheep with her. The way in passes the impressive ivied shell of 13th-century Castle Hackett, home of the Kirwans; colour-coded trails lead up the hill through ancient woods to the cairn. To the W is Finvarra's Castle cairn (53.4819, -8.9642), with a hole in the top supposedly made by Lord Kirwan to rescue his abducted wife from the king of the fairies within. Car park is on R333 at 53.4917, -8.9711, follow old drive S.

45 mins, 53.4817, -8.9623

ANCIENT FORESTS

27 PORTUMNA FOREST PARK

Look for fallow deer and red squirrels in this mix of regenerating ash and beech forest, and forestry plantation. In the birch at the lough shore is a hide: as well as water birds, you might see one of the white-tailed sea eagles recently reintroduced; a pair has raised chicks on Church Island (53.0741, -8.2446). On winter evenings, starling murmurations darken the sky over the

29

30

33

34

42

water. Walking and cycle trails, including a path into town.
2 mins, 53.0775 -8.2386

28 COOLE PARK NATURE RESERVE

Most famous for the wild swans of the WB Yeats poem, Coole also has beautiful old managed woods, seasonal turloughs, and limestone heath with a huge array of plants and plenty of other wildlife, including otters and pine martens. The whooper swans arrive in autumn, together with ducks numbering into the thousands, just when the deciduous trees are at their most colourful.
5 mins, 53.0931, -8.8359

29 MONIVEA WOODS

The old parkland woods are mainly beech, oak, ash and sycamore; there's also coniferous plantation. Find the underground icehouse (53.3766, -8.6861) and castle-like mausoleum (53.3723, -8.6876) of the Ffrench family who once owned the estate. In the village, there's also a derelict Gothic church tower by the playground (53.3739, -8.7015), next to the unusual greens that were used for drying flax for linen.
5 mins, 53.3765, -8.6918

WILDLIFE WONDERS

30 TURLOUGHMORE MURMURATIONS

The gatherings here can resemble a scene from 'The Birds', with the skies darkening before sunset rather than after, as many thousands of starlings swirl in mesmerising patterns. The location shifts a bit but is generally NE from the filling station (H65 HD59), Nov–Mar, and flocks have increased in size over the past few years. Murray's Bar or Copper Beach pubs (H65 YF82) may have space outside early in the evening, and be open for a restorative drop after the show.
20 mins, 53.3965, -8.8327

31 CARROWNAGAPPUL BOG

This internationally protected area is one of the largest raised bogs in the west, re-wetted by installing more than 3,000 dams across drains. Meadow pipit, skylark, red grouse and curlew breed here, and the dawn chorus is amazing; you might also spot hares, badgers, pine martens and many summer butterflies. A road runs to the centre, where a 'till island' of glacial material is a smallholding known as Patch's Garden. Plans for a reconstructed cottage, bird hide and turf footing demo area here have been progressing, but the bog walks will remain outside any enclosure.
5 mins, 53.5023, -8.4865

ORGANIC & GASTRO

32 THE GALLERY CAFÉ

This combination business owned by an artist is housed in a beautifully restored 19th-century building: try for the gorgeous upstairs window for a zinging brunch or lunch with local ingredients any day, or book a table for an evening meal on Fri-Sat. The Square, Gort, H91 Y279, +353 91 630630
53.0672, -8.8197

33 SLOW ROAST CAFÉ & GASTROBAR

Excellent coffee and sourdough toasties in a modern, friendly café with quirky local art on the walls. The 'slow roast' refers not to the coffee, but to how they cook the local beef for the Glade evening gastrobar from 5pm, Thur-Sun, with take-out, and a couple of craft beers on the taps. 12 Main St, Loughrea, H62 RY61
53.1984 -8.5695

34 MORAN'S OYSTER COTTAGE

This legendary quayside restaurant has been open for over a century, always offering mainly seafood. If you want to eat in the original cottage nooks, book ahead and say so. On sunny days, if you eat out front you may see horses being swum in the river; walk W on the lane and you can see Tyrone House (see entry). The Weir, Kilcolgan, H91 VP26, +353 91 796113
53.2109, -8.8951

35 SLIEVE AUGHTY CENTRE CAFE *

Home-cooked organic food using organically grown ingredients from their garden and local sources. Tapas nights, pizza parties and sourdough bread-making classes. Riding centre and 'enchanted wood' trail too. Kylebrack West, H62 DX77, +353 876871769
53.1339, -8.4727

36 ARMORICA, ORANMORE

Cosy, upscale restaurant where French cookery meets the freshest and most local Irish ingredients possible. Also has rooms . Main Street, Oranmore, H91 YA09, +353 91 388343
53.2695 -8.9285

37 THE OLD BARRACKS

Restaurant and bakery in a comfortable, handsome, old stone building. Also has crisp-looking rooms with king-size beds. Cross Street, Athenry, H65 W427, +353 91 877406
53.2982, -8.7466

RUSTIC RETREATS

38 SPA HOUSE, LOUGH DERG

Remote and cosy wood-clad lodge 10m from the shore, with its own little motorboat to hire.

Sleeps six, €110/night. Kylenamelly, Woodford, H62 HX68, ferienhaus-lough-derg.eu
53.0292, -8.2864

39 CRANN ÓG ECO FARM

This small eco-farm and community offers courses and workshops from foraging and forest school to yoga and meditation, but also has a cute off-grid A-frame cabin on the edge of the woods, which you can book on Airbnb for a wifi-free retreat. Drummin, Gort, H91XEY1, crannogecofarm.com
53.0393 -8.7325

40 WILD CABINS KINVARA

A handful of architect-designed, off-grid, off-wifi cabins with woodburners and fire pits at the Burren Nature Sanctuary. Each sleeps two, adults only, call about pets. Minimum two-night stay, three-nights on bank holidays. Cloonasee, Kinvara, H91 PTK7, booking.roomraccoon.com
53.1312, -8.9247

41 CASTLE ELLEN HOUSE, ATHENRY

Stay in the ongoing restoration of a 19th-century country house in a woodland setting: expect a quirky take on the original decor and very little in the way of mod-cons inside, the inevitable mess of work in progress outside, a fascinating host and an experience to remember. The Walter Lambert Room on Airbnb; Castlellen, H65 AX27+353 87 2747692
53.3374, -8.7626

42 CLAREGALWAY CASTLE

Sleep in a restored 15th-century tower house with the ruins of the friary just over the road (3m-thick walls deal with any road noise). At the end of August, you can get the full medieval experience over a weekend tournament in proper traditional armour. H91 E9T3, claregalwaycastle.com
53.3462, -8.9418

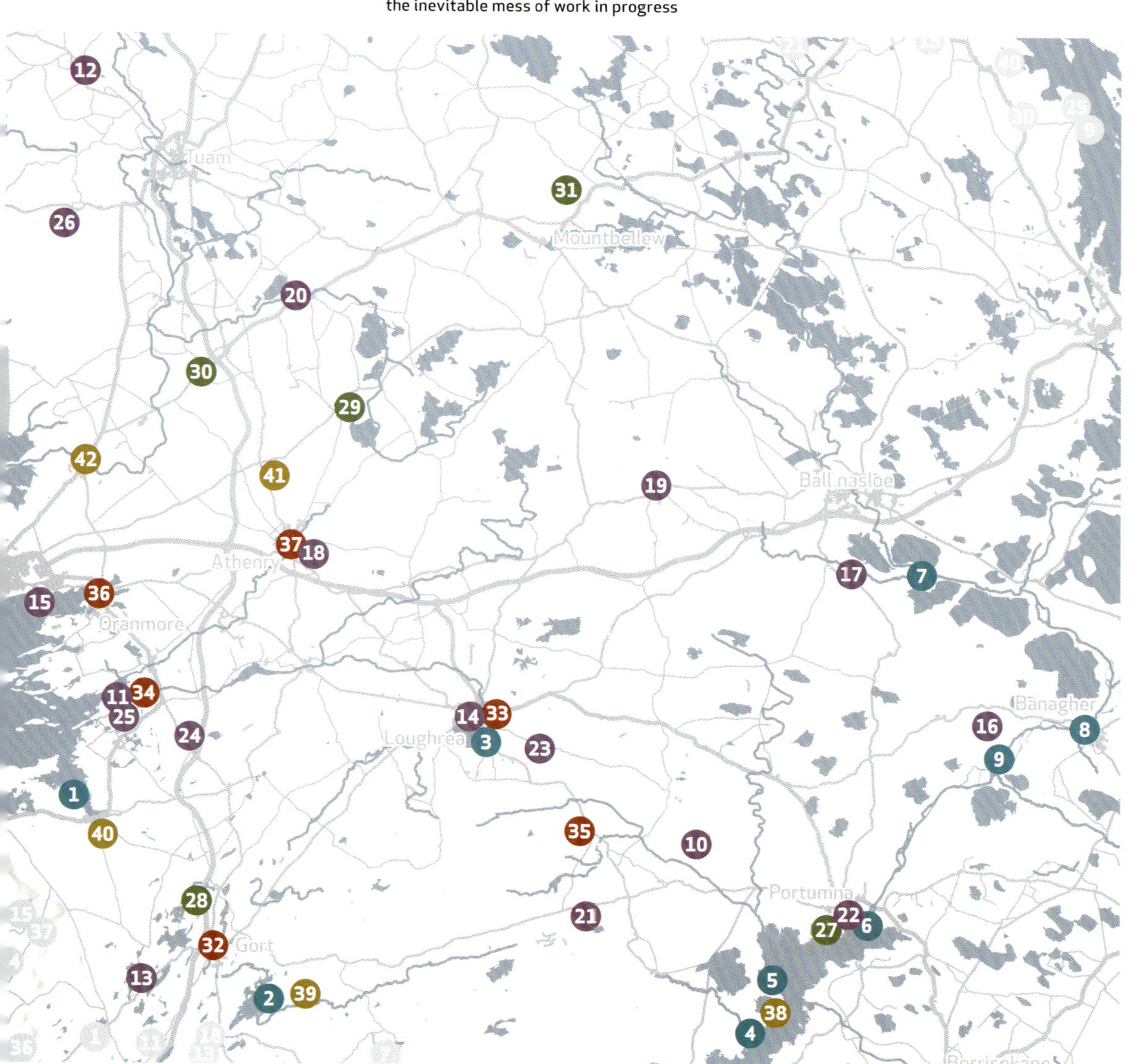

THE ARAN ISLANDS

Our perfect weekend

- **Plunge** from the rocks into the perfect pool of Poll na bPéist or laze on the sands of Cill Mhuirbhighe over the narrow waist of Inis Mór.
- **Climb** the hill to Turmartin Tower, see the Puffing Holes below, then stop for a swim at Port Daibhche on Inis Mór's less-visited east coast.
- **Picnic** with views over Inis Mór at the flower-filled cashel of Dún Eoghanachta, find an EIRE marker and watch the sunset over the sea.
- **Cycle** past the basking seals and sailors' memorial on Inis Oírr's western coast and look for a white eel at lovely Tobar Einne.
- **Pause** for a dip at Poll na gCaorach on the way out to Inis Oírr's iconic shipwreck, the rusty and monumental Plassey.
- **Pitch** in the dunes at Rua Camping nearthe buried Teampail Caomhán church and hilltop of O'Brien's Castle, on Inis Oírr.
- **Dine** on fresh-caught fish and local produce at Tig Congaile, stay the night, then walk up to medieval Dún Fearbhaí to greet the dawn over Inis Meáin.

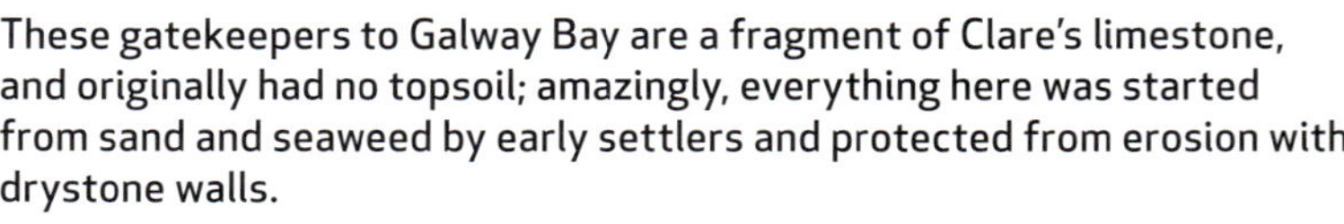
These gatekeepers to Galway Bay are a fragment of Clare's limestone, and originally had no topsoil; amazingly, everything here was started from sand and seaweed by early settlers and protected from erosion with drystone walls.

That determined island spirit is still alive today. This is a proud Gaeltacht area, so entries have the Irish names you will find on the signs. The English names for Inis Mór (Inishmore), Inis Meáin (Inishmaan) and Inis Oírr (Inisheer) give a good pronunciation guide. Visitors are not expected to be competent, but it's fun to practice. We have used just Mór, Meáin and Oírr for brevity in headings.

Inis Mór is the most visited, but those who say it is 'spoiled' have mostly only seen bustling Kilronan harbour and the buses at Dún Aonghasa (stay overnight and visit there early). There is much more here, from ruins the buses can't get near to blowholes and beaches. Inis Meáin is the least visited, with no daytrip possibilities and also no campsite; Inish Oírr is a happy medium. All have lovely beaches, fascinating ruins, dramatic cliffs, and wildlife to watch. You won't be taking a car over, so the walk-in times are given from the harbours – but unless you came to walk with days in hand we recommend hiring bikes or e-bikes, which is easy on arrival.

Beaches are mostly on the northern coasts, and the southern coasts are not recommended for swimming as swells can be deadly. But perhaps Ireland's most iconic swimming spot is on a southern shore: the mighty Poll na bPéist rock pool.

There are many cashels here for a place we consider remote, but once the sea was the transport highway, and the islands are perfectly placed to control the bay. Some were built in prehistory, others are from the early medieval era when this was a renowned centre of learning, and all the islands have churches from this time, two sunk into the sand. Later history did not pass the islands by, and there are castles, signal towers and lighthouses too.

The islands have inspired many writers, from local master of the short story Liam O'Flaherty to Dublin playwright J.M. Synge, who visited often. He noted that clocks were little used; the locals could tell everything they needed from the level of the tide and the movement of the shadows. If you stay awhile, you might begin to feel the same.

BEACHES - INIS MÓR

1 CILL MHUIRBHIGHE

The sheltered white bay of Kilmurvey has the most accessible swimming sands on the island, so it won't be empty on a summer afternoon, but try morning or evening. Cutesy thatched café Teach Nan Phaidi is just up the lane.

90 mins, 53.1310 -9.7502

2 KILRONAN

This huge, flat bay stays shallow, so is best for children and paddling, or a LT walk or picnic in the flowery grass at the top.

8 mins, 53.1176, -9.6735

3 TRÁ NA MBUAILTE

If you seek solitude, try this small and deserted curve of shingle and some sand, with views to the mainland on the horizon, at the end of a long and uneven track, R after passing H91 Y6KR.

23 mins, 53.1311, -9.6711

4 CILL ÉINNE PIER

Plunge straight into deep water from this often-deserted harbour at HT, use the steps when lower. You can swim below the ruins of Caisleán Aircín, a mostly medieval stronghold.

35 mins, 53.1049, -9.6621

5 FRENCHMAN'S BEACH

Facing the morning sun, this long sweep of sand is perfect for an early dip, especially if staying at the campsite. Popular later in the day, but still not really crowded.

12 mins, 53.1253, -9.66083

6 PORT DAIBHCHE

Our favourite beach on the island, a sheltered, shelving cove below dunes, with crystal turquoise water over silver sand. We had sandpipers skimming the water around us as we swam, and no other company.

60 mins, 53.1003, -9.6379

BEACHES - INIS OÍRR

7 TRÁ INIS OÍRR

This wide, dune-backed bay by the village is the main beach, with lifeguards, but is big enough to remain uncrowded and a great place to start or end a visit to the island.

3 mins, 53.0658, -9.51987

8 POLL NA GCAORACH

A quiet, tucked-away sandy cove with upturned curraghs and kayaks on the grassy slope down. About 200m SE is more sand among the rocks (53.0620, -9.5037) depending on the tide.

20 mins, 53.0635, -9.5059

BEACHES - INIS MEÁIN

9 TRÁ LEITREACH & CHURCH

This is the most popular beach for swimming on the island, with silver sand, rocks, and a pier. There are great views, even better from the 9th-century Cill Cheannanach ruin above, with a lifting stone by the perimeter wall to the left as you go in; only three men in memory have lifted it onto a nearby wall (53.0805, -9.5755).

40 mins, 53.0830, -9.5696

14

10

10

12

13

ROCK POOLS & COAST

10 POLL NA BPEIST, MÓR *

You'd swear this famous rectangular pool was cut by human hand, but the 'serpent's hole' is a collapsed sea cave. Most people jump in off the edge, and a few from the cliff ledge; check that the water is high enough to reach the corner climb out! Swim shoes recommended. Signed path to the shore from Gort na gCapall, where a short diversion leads to the glittering pink granite erratic the Mullán, a 171kg lifting stone immortalised in a story by local author Liam O'Flaherty; you could try the smaller practice stones near it (53.1216, -9.7458). Then head W on the middle of the shore platforms, a slippery walk with abrupt drops. Walk beyond the pool to see Dún Aonghasa from below.

20 mins, 53.1215, -9.7548

11 BULLÁIN MHÓRA SHORE, MEÁIN

An extraordinary limestone shore where loose stones have worn holes like bullauns in the platform, many still sitting within them. There are also larger rockpools; this exposed rocky coast is not recommended for swimming. The 13km Lúb Dún Fearbhaí walk takes in this and other Inis Meáin highlights, and is well-signed from the pier.

120 mins, 53.0672, -9.60079

LOST RUINS

12 O'BRIEN'S CASTLE, OÍRR

Visible from almost all the island, this 15th-century castle on the hilltop site of an ancient cashel was slighted by Cromwell's army. Some scramble up at the SE corner and walk around the ledge inside the castellations.

15 mins, 53.0622, -9.51926

13 PLASSEY SHIPWRECK, OÍRR

A freighter driven onto the rocks in 1960, this impressive tawny hulk became famous in the 'Father Ted' credits and is freely explorable. The islanders rescued the entire crew, salvaged the cargo (including the whisky) and upcycled materials from the hulk into local buildings and farm gates.

35 mins, 53.0558, -9.5037

SACRED & ANCIENT

14 DÚN EOGHANACHTA, MÓR *

This smaller, early medieval ringfort was built when there was an active monastic site below. It has an internal terrace and magnificent views, but lies almost completely ignored up a rough track and across fields studded with summer flowers, perfect for a picnic. Signed from the road at Shrawn; where the track

17

15

21

22

bends L look for the footpath R between field walls (53.1395, -9.7725).
120 mins, 53.1398, -9.7768

15 ST CIARAN'S CHURCH & WELL, MÓR

A quiet little ruin with big views and cross-incised slabs, one holed. The well is atmospheric, with a path between stone walls, where some have left offerings like painted pebbles. Below is a cove where you could take a dip, or possibly see a seal colony.
35 mins, 53.1318, -9.6850

16 TEAMPALL BHEANÁIN, MÓR

Spectacular views from reputedly the smallest church in Ireland, its distinctive gable peaks a marker for boats below. Dated to the 7th-century, it may have been an oratory from the now-vanished St Enda's monastic site. It has the remains of a cashel wall and a clochán nearby, and close to the lane up stands the stump of 9th-century Cill Éinne round tower (53.1031, -9.6638).
40 mins, 53.1023, -9.6661

17 TEAGHLACH ÉINNE, MÓR

St Enda is said to lie under the altar of his 'house', a chapel from a 9th-century monastic site. The dunes seem determined to bury him twice, as the building is now shoulder deep in the ground. Carved fragments of a high cross on one wall show one of the horsemen of the apocalypse.
50 mins, 53.1012, -9.6526

18 DÚN CHONCHÚIR, MEÁIN

This vast oval cashel has a second wall outside, three levels of terracing and steps on the massive rampart, and clochans inside. It is one of the oldest on the islands, dating back into pre-history, but still in use in the medieval period.
40 mins, 53.0834, -9.59479

19 LEABA & TOBAR CHINNDEIRGE, MEÁIN

Said to be the grave of a princess-saint, this 7th-century burial is still the site of an annual local pilgrimage on August 15th, also taking in the holy well in the next field (53.0835, -9.5907). The Church of Mary Immaculate on the corner also has stunning Harry Clarke stained glass windows.
35 mins, 53.0837, -9.5902

20 DÚN FEARBHAÍ, MEÁIN

This well preserved cashel, also called Mothar, is an unusual squarish shape and possibly built as late as the 9th-century. Generally overlooked in favour of the larger Dún Chonchúir (see entry), you might get it entirely to yourself.
45 mins, 53.0807, -9.58007

21 TOBAR EINNE, OÍRR

This large pool in a stone enclosure sits remote and serene in fields of grey rock, a beautiful place. The turas here takes three Sundays, but legends say if you then saw an eel, your tongue would be blessed and heal wounds by licking them. Nearby is another small well, Tobar na Bróige (53.0560, -9.5432).
30 mins, 53.0580, -9.5447

22 CILL GHOBNAIT, OÍRR

The pretty and peaceful little church stands where the 6th-century St Gobnait had a vision telling her to go and found a religious

22

23

36

33

37

settlement in Cork, and still has its original altar. There are two bullaun stones by it, and the low remains of a clochán in which she is said to have lived.

11 mins, 53.0659, -9.52921

23 TEAMPALL CAOMHÁN, OÍRR

This beautiful little 10th-century church is sunk almost up to the eaves in the dunes; villagers dug it out annually until a retaining wall was built. Local children believed squeezing through the window above the altar absolved your sins, but visitors joining in is taking a toll on the fabric; we recommend only children try this. The saint's grave is in the corner of the churchyard.

15 mins, 53.0639, -9.514

LOOKOUTS & VIEWS

24 EIRE 50 WEST, MÓR

With the same number as the one on Dun Oghil (see entry), this pilot's marker is on an otherworldly limestone hilltop in the empty far W. Step over the wall at the lowest point (53.1419, -9.8194), and walk about 100m SW – you'll feel triumphant when you spot it. Catch a sunset here or from the road end at the shore below (53.1409, -9.8278).

180 mins, 53.1411, -9.8209

25 DUN OGHIL RUINS, MÓR

This hill has stunning views and ruins from across the ages. Newest is an EIRE pilots' marker (53.1255, -9.7019), then the disused lighthouse and Napoleonic signal tower next to it. Oldest is impressive Dún Eochla Iron Age cashel just E (53.1268, -9.6995) which has steps up the walls inside. Walk up the steep lane off the main road, be careful of walls and livestock crossing to the cashel.

50 mins, 53.1273, -9.7023

26 TURMARTIN TOWER, MÓR

Probably a maritime marker, with mighty views E to Inis Meáin. Cross fields from the bend in the road at 53.0966, -9.6424, follow shore S 400m to a sign to head up a steep climb R and over and flowery fields. SW from the tower across stony fields are the Puffing Holes blowholes (53.0898, -9.6420).

100 mins, 53.0915, -9.6389

27 CATHAOIR SYNGE, MEÁIN

This sheltered stone seat was a lookout over the waters to Inis Mor long before Synge's time, but a favourite place of his to contemplate or write. There's a signed path along the rugged coast, and an engraved tablet facing inland.

50 mins, 53.0841, -9.61245

26

28 LIGHTHOUSE & MEMORIAL, OÍRR

Operational, so not accessible, but an impressive sight with views over to the Cliffs of Moher. Continue W around the coast for the poignant memorial to much-loved journalist Charlie Bird, set where he would gaze out looking for the mythical isle of Hy-Brasil (53.0488, -9.5401).

10 mins, 53.0463, -9.52636

WILDLIFE WONDERS

29 INIS MÓR SEALS

Seals swim in Port Chorrúch bay and haul out onto the shingle; the viewpoint by a ruined iodine works is distant to avoid spooking them. There is a track from 53.1376, -9.7053 around the E of the lake with birdlife to N end of beach, but do not take this if it would bring you nearer to any seals.

60 mins, 53.1375, -9.7135

30 INIS OÍRR SEALS

There is a good chance of seeing this growing colony basking at low tide; do not disturb them. At high tide, if there are no anglers, the long, narrow pier to the N provides a way in over the rocks to sheltered water (53.0674, -9.5352). Further S along the shore, look through the hole in the wave memorial sculpture to those lost at sea (53.0629, -9.5447).

20 mins, 53.0653, -9.54236

CLASSIC PUBS

31 JOE WATTY'S PUB, MÓR

This colourful little pub has a good seafood menu, but is most renowned for the atmosphere and especially the music. H91 N889, +353 86 0494509

53.1239, -9.6708

32 THE BAR, KILRONAN, MÓR

Lively pub with plenty of outdoor tables too, serving hearty dishes; try the Connemara Brewery lager. Kilronan, H91 DP95, +353 99 61130

53.11947, -9.6693

33 TIGH NED, OÍRR

Almost too easy, right near the pier, but perfect for a pint and bowl of soup - or more. Memorabilia on the walls includes old newspaper pages about the island, better than any modern guide, and the lifting stone for the island is just across from the gate. H91 KT63, tighned.com

53.0681, -9.5255

LOCAL PRODUCE

34 ARAN GOAT CHEESE, MÓR

Gabriel Faherty's herd of Nubian and Saanen goats graze on these unique, herb-rich pastures to produce award-winning cheese. You'll find it in many local shops and restaurants, but the farm also has tours in season. Five fields W of H91 TX32, +353 87 2226776

53.1353, -9.6984

35 MAN OF ARAN FUDGE

Now a second generation business offering 20 buttery flavours; if choosing is hard, try the original Tiger Butter, the recipe made by founder Tomás Póil's grandmother. Stalls at the harbour on Inis Mór and Inis Oírr.

53.1192, -9.6690

ORGANIC & GASTRO

36 BAYVIEW RESTAURANT, MÓR *

The food in this seasonal restaurant is based on fresh local produce, including seaweed, cooked in a style influenced by the Guatemalan roots of head chef and owner Byron Godoy. No licence: bring your own, or try their lemonade, made to order. Kilronan, H91 YD9X, +353 86 7929925

53.1193 -9.66879

37 CAFÉ ÚNA, OÍRR

Cheerful little café with excellent home baking right by the harbour and bike hire. Sit indoors or out and try the orange polenta cake; no need to go further. H91 D6D6

53.0672, -9.5232

CAMPING & RETREATS

38 ARAN ISLANDS CAMPING & GLAMPING

The best views over the bay are from the pods (book well in advance), but they shelter the tent field behind them, which has no marked pitches or electricity. Good modern facilities, where everyone goes to charge phones and chat. Frenchman's Beach, Kilronan, H91 F65P, +353 86 189 5823, irelandglamping.ie

53.1246 -9.66196

39 RUA CAMPING INIS OÍRR

You can pitch your own tent, or book one of the bell tents well in advance, and sit by a firepit in the dusk. Set in the dunes just behind the quiet end of the big beach, and very basic: the reception and a small kitchen are in a block with public toilets and showers, which the campsite uses. Near H91 P9P1, +353 83 8633907, inisoirrcamping.ie

53.0646, -9.5207

40 TIG CONGAILE, MEÁIN

Set a short walk above the island's best swimming beach, Vilma's guesthouse and restaurant are perfect for sunrise dips and meals influenced by her Guatemalan background, made using her husband's fishing catches and vegetables from her own garden. H91 N28A, +353 87 2035171

53.0835, -9.5780

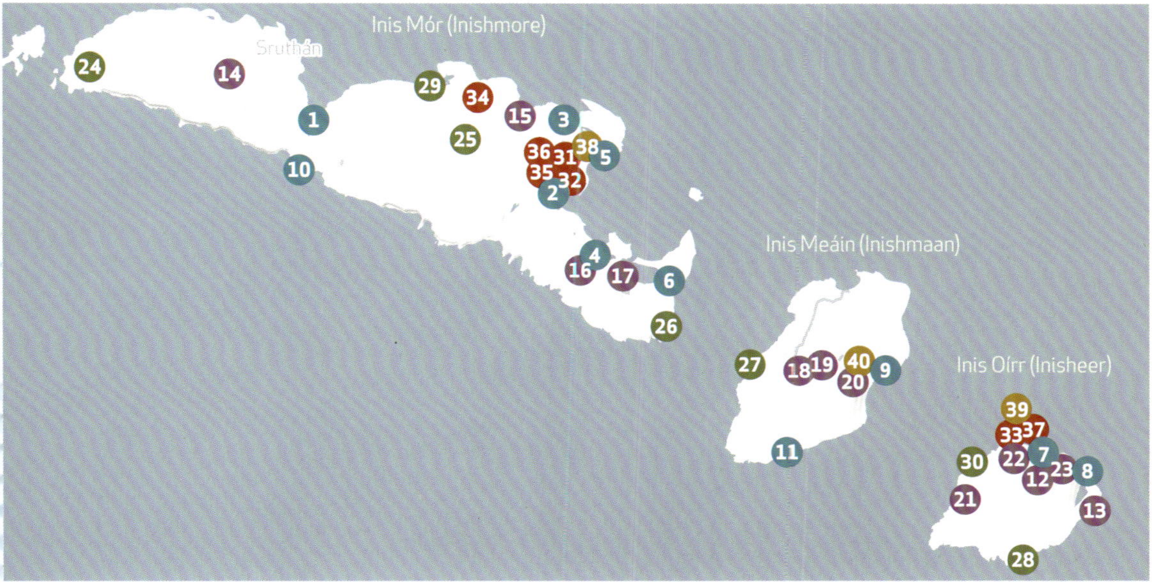

Inis Mór (Inishmore)
Sruthán
Inis Meáin (Inishmaan)
Inis Oírr (Inisheer)

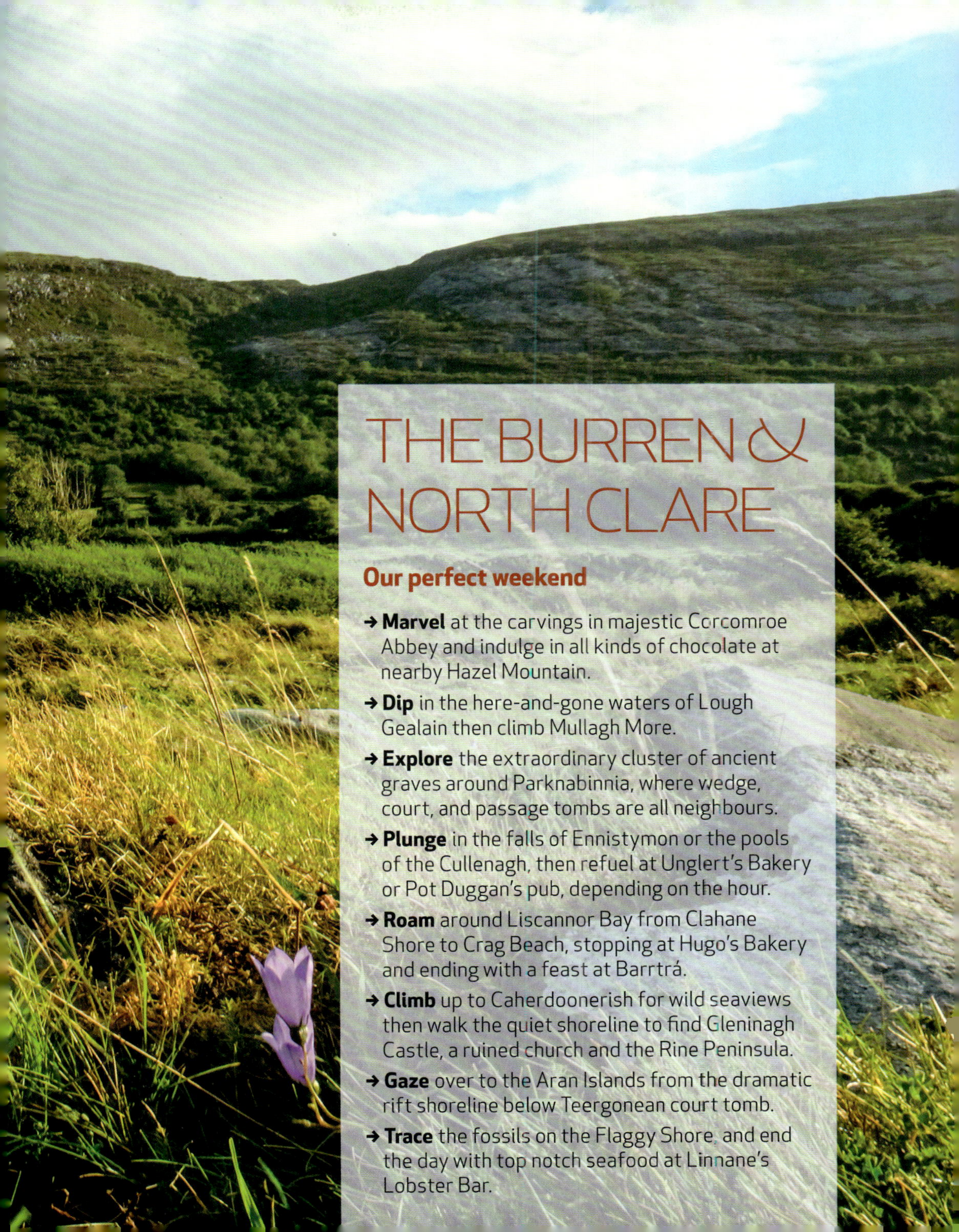

THE BURREN & NORTH CLARE

Our perfect weekend

- → **Marvel** at the carvings in majestic Corcomroe Abbey and indulge in all kinds of chocolate at nearby Hazel Mountain.
- → **Dip** in the here-and-gone waters of Lough Gealain then climb Mullagh More.
- → **Explore** the extraordinary cluster of ancient graves around Parknabinnia, where wedge, court, and passage tombs are all neighbours.
- → **Plunge** in the falls of Ennistymon or the pools of the Cullenagh, then refuel at Unglert's Bakery or Pot Duggan's pub, depending on the hour.
- → **Roam** around Liscannor Bay from Clahane Shore to Crag Beach, stopping at Hugo's Bakery and ending with a feast at Barrtrá.
- → **Climb** up to Caherdoonerish for wild seaviews then walk the quiet shoreline to find Gleninagh Castle, a ruined church and the Rine Peninsula.
- → **Gaze** over to the Aran Islands from the dramatic rift shoreline below Teergonean court tomb.
- → **Trace** the fossils on the Flaggy Shore, and end the day with top notch seafood at Linnane's Lobster Bar.

The first description of the Burren I remember hearing was a brutal historical assessment that 'there is not enough water to drown a man, wood enough to hang one, nor earth enough to bury him'. It was said by a Cromwellian army commander, and is an exaggeration on all counts, but the first and most famous impression of this place is still that it is hundreds of square kilometres of bare limestone paving. First impressions can be deceptive.

A mild coastal climate gives one of the longest growing seasons in Ireland, and the cracks in the paving support extraordinarily diverse plant growth, including more than 20 species of fern and orchid; I saw my first gentian here long ago, and I wish you the same thrill. As well as the pavement, there is limestone heath, some grasslands and bogs, even little scraps of ancient woodland in the valleys. Once there was more green here: early farmers cleared trees at the end of the Neolithic, and when climate change brought more rain, the fragile, shallow soil simply ran off the land.

The porous karst geology determines everything here. Firstly, it means there are no permanent rivers or lakes, but instead turloughs, seasonal lakes that vanish through drainage into underground caves – a rare Irish language word that has made it into international usage. It also means that there are cave systems like famous Aillwee, potholes like Pollnagollum, and almost certainly more that are undiscovered. And in a very practical sense it means that when walking here, you always step on the bare rock; any vegetation is likely growing in one of the ankle-spraining fissures.

But it is worth walking. The views from the top of the big spiralling hills are awe inspiring, and some are even topped with cashels like Caherdoonerish. There are abbeys, churches, oratories and holy wells tucked into the lower slopes, some like Templecronan possibly having pagan roots. And of course there are very ancient tombs like famous Poulnabrone – but also less visited sites that are just as fascinating.

And down at the edge there are some of Ireland's favourite coastal spots, from the geological wonders of the Flaggy Shore to the holiday sands of Lahinch – and of course the Cliffs of Moher between if you can brave the crowds. There are lively pubs and excellent restaurants to visit after a day on the heights, but the shores are still wild places that can, as Seamus Heaney put it 'catch the heart off guard and blow it open'.

SECRET COVES & BEACHES

1 AUGHINISH ISLAND

Created by floods after the 1755 Lisbon earthquake, it still has a cut-off feeling despite a causeway that was built in 1811 to reach the Martello tower (now a home). You could walk right around the island and only meet someone harvesting seaweed. On the N side there are views to Galway – the Galway Bay swim starts from here – and Aughinish Point at the W is great for a sunset. Easy parking at N or S shore.

2 mins, 53.1674, -9.073

2 THE FLAGGY SHORE

A classic swimming spot and geological wonder, the flags marked with vast, beautiful branching coral fossils and grooves gouged eons later by glacier-borne gravel, some of it now visible in the cliffs across the inlet. Poet Seamus Heaney recommended visiting here 'In September or October, when the wind/And the light are working off each other' – and when you could see starling murmurations too. Roadside parking 300m S, where there is a little sand.

10 mins, 53.1589, -9.0922

3 BISHOP'S QUARTER BEACH

A straight run of silver-grey shingle becoming golden sand and dunes, with clear water favoured by local swimmers. Down here by the flat, green coastal fields, you can actually forget that the scraped limestone expanse of Moneen Mountain is just behind you – until you turn around. Medium car park with height restriction.

2 mins, 53.1325, -9.1250

4 THE RINE PENINSULA

A wild and beautiful arm of sand and shells thrown out from the shore around a rocky outcrop. Some come here to see seabirds, choughs, and birds of prey, others to fish or swim in the deep water off the steeply shelving shore. Rough layby parking opp the gated 200m track, 53.1320, -9.1904; the ornate roadside Pinnacle Well is 300m W.

3 mins, 53.1359, -9.1768

5 FANORE BEACH & COVES

Big, golden Fanore can fill up, as it's the only sand for a long way, and often has good surf. For something a little more secret, walk 500m along the shore and drop down to some tiny, sandy inlets in the rock; can also be reached from the gate on the R477 at 53.1145, -9.2878, but no parking there.

2 mins, 53.1190, -9.2892

6 FISHER STREET, DOOLIN

A hidden pebble cove, away from the bustle of Doolin harbour. 300m W from Gus O'Connor's Pub, V95 FY67, people pull off R and take with track to beach field gate opp. The Cliffs of Moher coast walk starts here, but in 2024 sections closed for extensive safety work; check the current status. Along at Doolin pier (for Aran Islands) is small tidal bathing pool.

5 mins, 53.0101, -9.3921

7 CLAHANE SHORE

When the tide goes out this is an otherwordly landscape dotted with rock pools full of life. When the tide is in and the sea is calm, you can snorkel in the shallows among the rock stacks (wear swim shoes). Parking spaces on road.

2 mins, 52.9323, -9.4225

8 KILMACREEHY BEACH

A quiet beach, looking over to the much busier Lahinch, with rock pools at low tide. Can be rip currents by the river mouth. Path down from parking in the cemetery.

2 mins, 52.9421 -9.3746

9 CRAG/CREGG BEACH

This quiet, empty beach with clear water is pebble with sand at LT. Pull onto verge opp caravan park entrance on N67 and walk 150m

S to the shore track with vehicle barrier. S end also accessible from lane end at 52.9147, -9.3599 (tight parking).
2 mins, 52.9205, -9.3509

POOLS & CASCADES

10 CULLENAGH POOLS

Quiet grassy riverbank below a small bridge with small cascades and shallow pools for up to 60m downstream. Just off N85 on L1128 SE of Ennistymon, pull off R before bridge.
2 mins, 52.9087, -9.2338

11 ENNISTYMON CASCADES & GLEN

Impressive series of limestone pavement falls with some deeper pools for the brave – the best at the bottom. From the Falls Hotel & Spa car park (V95 D2PC) follow the river path upstream 100m. Or downstream for a wide, deep river section and then up a fern-lined tributary glen. Make time to visit the 18th-century ruined church (52.9392, -9.2917).
3 mins, 52.9398, -9.2959

12 LOUGH GEALAIN, MULLAGH MORE

Rock hop your way through a stretch of limestone paving nicknamed the Giant's Playground to a pseudo-turlough: it fluctuates depending on the water levels below, but the NE part is deep and permanent. The blue trail continues to the peak of Mullagh More (see entry). Pull off by the path entrance.
3 mins, 52.9958, -9.0212

13 INCHIQUIN LAKE, COROFIN

Serene freshwater glacial lake set within pastoral landscape just out of town. There's a tiny harbour with concrete quays for the fishing boats, a picnic area and easy parking, but it's quiet enough for a swim.
2 mins, 52.9509, -9.0782

LOST RUINS

14 CAPPAGH CASTLE

Remote and secret, the remnants of a tower on the wild foothills of the Burren, a good challenge for adventurers. Follow the private track from 53.0565, -9.0053 and then turn L onto the moor at 53.0588, -9.0097
20 mins, 53.0574, -9.0140

15 ST COLMAN'S HERMITAGE

St. Colman was said to be here in the 7th century; there is a stone oratory, cave (called St MacDuagh's Bed on older maps), and holy well, with beautiful views of Eagle's Rock cliff, and wildlife including birds of prey and feral goats. Parking at 53.0763, -8.9989 and a path through limestone paving and a small area of mature native woodland.

30 mins, 53.0848, -9.0022

16 GLENINAGH CASTLE & CHURCH *

This quiet but well preserved tower with a sunken holy well has a superb position on the shoreline among twisted trees down a driveable track from R477. You can't go inside but you can enjoy the wild beach. The sweet medieval church hidden nearby has its own signed path, opp a bit of layby at 53.1341, -9.2069.

3 mins, 53.1376, -9.2059

17 FINAVARRA MARTELLO TOWER

At the far end of a tiny lane along a cobbled spit stands a tower and ruined barracks. A rope hangs from one of the 4m high windows, and inside a spiral staircase leads up to the roof and a 200-year-old cannon. Great for a sunset over Black Head and an overnight. Ruin hunters might also seek out the shell of 19th-century Finavarra House, next to farm buildings, back in the village (53.1501, -9.0982), ask permission from farmhouse opp.

2 mins, 53.1498, -9.1355

18 LEAMENAH CASTLE

You can't miss this imposing shell, a 17th-century mansion built onto an earlier tower. When Conor O'Brien died in battle, his widow 'Red Mary' offered to marry any Cromwellian officer to keep her home and lands. Some tales say the marriage lasted, others that she did away with the officer. Private land, owners at the farm may give access. Park on the junction and walk up 30m.

2 mins, 52.9877, -9.1399

TOMBS & CASHELS

19 CAHERDOONERISH *

In places 4m high, this impressive oval cashel on high plateau pavement is a pathless ascent whichever way you go, and you will likely get it to yourself. Parking for one at 53.1496, -9.2694 also gives access to an EIRE marker above, to R of field wall (53.1490, -9.2693), then follow wall 750m further, a total of 200m climb. Or follow the Green Road part of the larger Black Head Loop Walk. From the W, there's some parking by farm at Murroogh (53.1301, -9.2724); after about 2.5km head up. There's a longer walk from more parking to E by R477 at 53.1344, -9.2100; ascend from Green Road at 53.1429, -9.2372 and navigate W.

60 mins, 53.1467, -9.2590

20 PARKNABINNIA WEDGE TOMB

A wedge-shaped chamber covered by a large turfed capstone; you can even get inside. This

17

18

tomb type is usually thought to be Bronze Age, but remains here have been dated to the Early Neolithic. It's visible off a quiet lane with a clear sign and some parking opp. There are several more here worth seeking out, with many upright stones 400m W at 52.9878, -9.1018, then a further pair 325 SW, through scrub, at 52.9862, -9.1058 and 52.9856, -9.1057; turn back E from these for more.

2 mins, 52.9881, -9.0955

21 TEERGONEAN COURT TOMB

An unusual example of a court tomb in the southwest. This stretch of coast is the closest to the Aran Islands, so would have been a crossing point in the Neolithic. There is parking at the end of a long straight lane with Killilagh ruined medieval church on the way, and you can (livestock permitting) wander on down to explore the limestone paving by the sea. Dramatic chasm, undulating erosion, and a 'doorway' in the wall around 53.0302, -9.3920.

2 mins, 53.0290, -9.3891

22 CAHERMORE FORT *

At the start of the popular and beautiful R480 uplands road, an easy but easily missed early medieval cashel encloses the whole hilltop in two ramparts, with magnificent views out to sea and foundations of buildings among its wildflowers. Perfect for a summer picnic. In the 14th century a lintelled entrance and guardhouses were added, but no history is recorded. Park at entrance on bend in the R480 (53.0859, -9.1641) Ballyallaban rath (53.0901 -9.1585) is visible from the road but hard to make out.

2 mins, 53.0853, -9.1645

23 POULNABRONE & GLENINSHEEN

The largest and most famous of the Burren dolmens. However the large car park and ring fence do detract a little, and it is crowded in high season. Just 2km back/N on R480 seek out lesser known Gleninsheen – a gorget, one of a handful of iconic Bronze Age gold necklaces and star of the National Museum display, was found near it in 1930. Park on verge at 53.0651, -9.1500 and you'll see it 50m to SE in the corner of the field.

2 mins, 53.0469, -9.1405

24 CATHAIR CHONAILL/CAHERCONNELL

Well signed on the R480, this important and well-preserved cashel has been the centre of an archaeology summer school for many years, and the finds have rewritten much of what was thought about their use. Entry is €10; you will learn a lot, but if you prefer the wilder, lost cashels, there are more than 100 in the wider area. Just 2km back/N on R480 park carefully in the stone gateway splay at 53.0601, -9.1485

25

16

and you can see one up the track; walk track 200m E to field gate.

2 mins, 53.0409, -9.1395

25 CAHERCOMMAUN

A fine walk leads up to a 9th century triple-rampart cashel, perched on the edge of a small gorge with commanding views of the surrounding landscape. The innermost wall, over 3m thick, encloses a small settlement with traces of dwellings and animal enclosures. Park at the trailhead (53.0099, -9.0816) and follow sign through a field gate L of the farm track 1km.

20 mins, 53.0146, -9.0705

SACRED SITES

26 PINNACLE/TOBERCORNAN WELL

This elaborate roadside folly covers a holy well, with steps down from the entrance. Built just after the famine; offerings are still left in a niche inside, where there is also an incongruous council sign. Easy parking, on the R477.

2 mins, 53.1330, -9.1944

27 ST MOGUA'S, NOUGHAVAL

In a quiet hamlet, the ruins of this 14th-century church are overgrown but show beautiful archways and fine stonework. Near the little chapel in the graveyard is a low ringed cross with rounded holes, a design more often seen in Cornwall. The ivy-covered ruins in the NW corner may have been a round tower, and the base of a market cross stands at the gate; marks on it were said to be used to measure cloth and other materials at fairs.

2 mins, 53.0158, -9.1803

28 CARRAN CHURCH

This 13th-century church was fortified in the 15th century with a bartizan and draw bar slot for the door. A cairn in the field S gives it its name; it was traditional for coffins to be carried around this pagan burial on their way to church. In NE corner is a carved helmeted head; there were originally three, the others a king with a leafy crown and a woman with a headdress. Signed gate in, pull off inside or between gateways opp. Just over 1km N on a crag above the road is a painted, shallow-relief scene of three riders (53.0325, -9.1370); it is said to commemorate a hunt in which a man was killed.

2 mins, 53.022 -9.1333

29 KILLINABOY CHURCH

Easily missed on the R476, this medieval church has the stump of a round tower and carvings aplenty. There's a sheelagh na gig above the entrance, a crucifixion scene, effigies of prelates, a grave slab with a Tau cross, and a Lorraine cross in the gable wall (easily missed if the light isn't right), which may mean there was a relic here. Roughan Hill nearby had a Tau cross (52.9778, -9.1148), now in the museum in Corofin and replaced by a replica. Park in layby.

2 mins, 52.9702, -9.0854

30 SAINT MUADHÁN'S WELL

Behind the very ancient Kilmoon Church, with a carved human head and an incised Latin cross slab in the graveyard, lies a 'well' of hollows in limestone rock which collect rain and hold round stones to be turned by pilgrims, but acting as cursing stones if turned 'against the sun'. A local tale goes that a farmer prosecuted for beating a beggar woman claimed that 'she swore to turn the stones of Kilmoon' against him to deform his face, and the equally superstitious magistrate advised him to pay her off. One car space at gate.

3 mins, 53.0441, -9.2700

31 TEMPLECRONAN CHURCH *

A remote 12th-century stone oratory with several carved human and animal heads in the walls, in a tranquil, mossy, magical setting. The cyclopean walls and blocked door appear more ancient, and some even argue that this was a reused pagan shrine. There are two rooflike tomb shrines outside, and 100m S over two stone walls is the holy well, in a cleft with prayer

26

27

28

31

flags and miniatures. Park at the lane end and take the signed path E then S, 200m.

3 mins, 53.0461, -9.0609

32 BISHOP'S QUARTER CHURCH

A picturesque ivy-hung medieval church, also called St Colman's Abbey, with views to bare Moneen Mountain on one side, the sea on the other. Follow the N67 2km E from Ballyvaughan; the nearest good space to pull off the N67 is in front of a house 300m before the church on the R. Cyclists can pull into the church gateway more easily.

3 mins, 53.1230, -9.1248

33 KILFENORA CATHEDRAL

In the 12th century Kilfenora became the 'the City of the Seven Crosses', with one of the greatest concentrations of high crosses in Ireland, including the beautiful pictorial Doorty Cross. A steel and glass roof over part of the cathedral protects the carvings, some with features in common with Corcomroe Abbey (see entry). Famous graves include Neptune Blood, uncle of Thomas Blood who tried to steal the English crown jewels, and Kitty Linnane, leader of the Kilfenora Céilí Band, where musicians still play on St Patrick's Day. Easy parking by Burren Visitor Centre next door.

2 mins, 52.9905, -9.2171

34 CORCOMROE ABBEY

In high season coaches do stop here but the wealth of fine Romanesque carvings inside is worth it, and the ruins got a mention from WB Yeats in 'The Dreaming of Bones', as well as in Eileen Aroon, a romantic song about eloping lovers. The tomb of Conor O'Brien, 13th-century King of Thomond, is one of very few contemporary carvings of an Irish chieftain. The approach signed from Bealaclugga, passes through a discernable rath at 53.1226, -9.0644.

2 mins, 53.1268, -9.0540

35 DYSERT O'DEA CHURCH *

Tranquil, rural 12th-century ruin, with a beautiful Romanesque doorway, part of the earlier St Tola's monastic site which also has an ancient round tower stump. Park on lane just outside. From the back R climb the stone stile and cross the field 100m to the Tola high cross, with a striking high relief Christ and bishop and intricate interlacing on the back. If livestock make this impossible, park opp the Castle and Archaeology Centre gate (52.9101, -9.0645) and walk W to the cross. The shop at the museum (admission €5) sells maps of a history walking trail (3 or 5km options). These include the shell of a lodge near the road by the church (52.9096, -9.0704) and the 1823 'soup school', signed 3km W on lanes (52.9101, -9.0796)

2 mins, 52.9088, -9.0684

35

35

36

HILLTOPS & VIEWS

36 MULLAGH MORE

Distinctive bare limestone terrace curves culminating at a cairned peak showcase the Burren's flora, including rare orchids and Arctic-alpine plants, alongside wild goats. A free bus runs from the Burren National Park Information Point in Corofin to Gortalecky Cross (52.9969, -9.0372) 9.30am–5.15pm Mar–Aug to relieve parking problems. In quieter times you can park near the crossroads or at 52.9958, -9.0212 for blue trail ascent, or on E side at 53.0168, -8.9813 for red trail.

60 mins, 53.0074, -9.0018

37 TURLOUGHMORE HILL

Start at Slievecarran parking (53.0763, -8.9989) and follow yellow trail to 53.0741, -8.9899; you might be able to park at the layby there. Go through the gate opp and up the hill NE. There are climbing crags all over, keep just L of the two big cols in the summit, known as Léim an Phúca Mhóir and Léim an Phúca Bhig (Big and Small Fairy's Leaps). At the top follow a long drystone wall L to the highest summit of the massif, with spectacular views. There's no loop, but committed hikers with plenty of time could follow the wall down L, over the road, and up Slievecarran on a big walk.

60 mins, 53.0746 -8.9827

38 SLIEVE ELVA HOLY WELL & CLOCHÁN

Follow the beautiful green road onto Slieve Elva, the tougher part of the larger Black Head Loop Walk that starts and ends at Fanore beach (see entry). For this part, park at 53.0850, -9.2887 (limited space) and follow track 1.3km, then turn up path R 500m to a sunken, stone-lined well with a stream gurgling below, with big views. Back at the road, walk S and follow track R through farm down into an area with a beehive clochan (53.0817, -9.2976) and five ringforts visible, notably Lios Cúnaire (53.0835, -9.2946) – many more lie hidden beyond.

45 mins, 53.0917, -9.2685

NATURAL WONDERS

39 POLLNAGOLLUM & CAHER BOLG

This sheer, deep cleft, with dripping vegetation and the sound of gushing water below, leads to 16km of stream passages and decorated grottoes, the longest cave system in Ireland. Descent requires a rope, so peer in from a distance, or go with a local guide (try Outdoor Education & Training Centre, +353 87 7414822, burrenoec.com). Walk in NW from a metal pole on the lane by some stone steps in the wall. Space to pull off 270m N on lane; opp is path up to remains of Caher Bolg fort (53.0791, -9.2519).

2 mins, 53.0772, -9.2513

40 LOUGH MURREE SWANS

This is the slate-grey lake lit by the earthed lightning of a flock of swans in 'Postcript', Seamus Heaney's hymn to Clare, and you stand a good chance of seeing swans. Pausing on the gravel at the corner, maybe take a stroll down along the cobble beach on the other side. There are stretches of sand here at lower tides making it easier to swim if you choose, or you could just walk in the wild wind.

2 mins, 53.1522 -9.1192

LOCAL PRODUCE

41 VAUGHAN'S ANCHOR INN

Popular seafood destination with fish landed daily, everything cooked fresh and as much Clare produce as possible. Eco-credentials and rooms too. Main Street, Liscannor, V95 FN5R, +353 65 7081548

52.9388, -9.3910

42 ST. TOLA GOAT CHEESE FARM

Award-winning artisan goat's cheese. Established in the 1980s, the farm specialises in high-quality, organic cheeses made from the milk of Saanen, Toggenburg, and Nubian goats. Visitors can take guided tours to learn about sustainable farming, cheese production, and meet the friendly goats (€15/head)

Gorbofearna, V95 XA9C, +353 65 6836633
52.9031, -9.1783

43 HUGO'S BAKERY, LAHINCH *
Using regeneratively farmed flour to produce sourdough bread, viennoiserie, pastel de nata and fine coffee. Need we say more? Ennistymon Road, Lahinch, V95 XR58, @hugos_lahinch
52.9332, -9.3448

44 UNGLERT'S BAKERY, HEALTH SHOP
This excellent bakery run by a German couple, who use buttermilk to bake and have fabulous apple strudel, has been open for decades and is an institution locally. New Road, Ennistymon, V95 NV08, +353 65 7071217
52.9386, -9.2931

45 BURREN SMOKEHOUSE
Peter and Birgitta Curtin started smoking salmon over 30 years ago, drawing on Irish and Swedish traditions and serving it in the family pub, The Roadside Tavern. Their hot- and cold-smoked fish is now served at state banquets and shipped all over the world. Kincora Rd, Rathbaun, Lisdoonvarna, V95 HD70, +353 65 7074432
53.0280, -9.2920

46 AILLWEE BURREN EXPERIENCE
Burren Gold cheese is made on site with milk from the farm at Caherconnell ringfort (see entry), and still naturally smoked. The shop also makes its own fudge, and sells other local cheese, honey, jam, and seaweed. Café too and, of course, the unique showcaves (€27). Ballyvaughan, H91 F7PE, +353 65 7077036
53.0904 -9.1468

47 HAZEL MOUNTAIN CHOCOLATE
Ireland's only bean-to-bar chocolate factory sits amid great grey Burren slopes and strips of hazel woods. You can watch the work through windows from the shop and buy everything from bars to spreads. The café menu includes several hot chocolates, and indulgent baked goods. Open all year, café hours vary seasonally. Oughtmama, Bellharbour, H91VCF1
53.1262, -9.0480

48 LINNALLA IRISH ICE CREAM CAFÉ
Using the milk of the traditional shorthorn, this dairy farm family has been here since the 1830s. The cows snack on seaweed on the shore (a feed supplement that can reduce their methane production) and sometimes swim to Scanlan's Island for fresh grazing. Outside tables have great sea views. Rine, H91 KP84, +353 87 7857569
53.1494, -9.1194

ORGANIC & GASTRO

49 BARRTRÁ SEAFOOD RESTAURANT *
Ruben is the second generation at the helm, showcasing food from local suppliers and their own kitchen garden and chickens wandering outside. Lahinch, V95 HX5K, +353 65 7081280
52.9112, -9.3582

50 POT DUGGAN'S
Old fashioned pub with modern food being served in the converted barns and covered courtyard: café menu during the day, Melting Pot seasonal menu and pop ups with chefs from around the country in the evenings. Weekly quiz nights, bingo sessions, and music. New Road, Ennistymon, V95 PY82, +353 65 7072212
52.9389, -9.2932

51 VAUGHAN'S PUB, KILFENORA
Traditional style food done well in an upmarket but cosy setting. Trad music Friday and Sunday, and since Kilfenora ceilídh band are nationally famous, you're in a good place for it. Kilfenora, V95 DT8K, +353 65 7088004
52.9900, -9.2197

52 HOMESTEAD COTTAGE, DOOLIN *
Modern cooking using locally sourced produce in a traditional Irish cottage. Sophie and Robbie work with local farmers, growers, and artisan producers to highlight the great food in the area, changing the menu daily to what is fresh, locally available and best in season. Luogh North, Doolin, V95 KH30, +353 65 6794133
52.9927, -9.4029

53 RUSSELL'S BAR, DOOLIN
Seafood chowder is one of the many things Viv Kelly gets right at this totally laid-back restaurant; for something to take away, try fish and hand-cut chips or oysters from the little Fish Shop on the side. Fiddle + Bow Hotel, Teergonean, Doolin, V95 XR0K
53.0168, -9.3752

54 WILD HONEY INN, LISDOONVARNA
Restored and family run 19th-century inn, Ireland's only Michelin starred pub, also wonderful hotel rooms March to October. The food and furnishings are both the very best of local finds. Kincora Road, Lisdoonvarna, V95 P234, +353 65 7074300
53.0284, -9.2958

55 BURREN FINE WINE & FOOD
Meals, wine sales, private tastings, gourmet hampers, May to September. Corkscrewhill Road, Croagh North, Ballyvaughan, H91 WY94, +353 87 7633241
53.0903, -9.1735

56 AN FEAR GORTA TEA ROOMS & GARDEN

Summer café and lovely gardens to sit in, now being run by the second generation, after being restored from derelict in 1981. Lisnanard, Ballyvaughan, H91 HR68, +353 65 7077157

53.1188, -9.1536

57 LINNANE'S LOBSTER BAR, NEW QUAY

Right on the pier, with views to Aughinish. Fresh lobster and crab, directly from the bay, paired with oysters and mussels grown in nearby waters. H91 NWX6, +353 65 7078120

53.1559, -9.0758

RUSTIC RETREATS

58 BURREN GLAMPING

A vintage horse box (truck size, not the coffee shop type!) converted into a wood-lined tiny house that sleeps six, complete with a solid-fuel stove and bathroom. The farm has a productive polytunnel and a range of livestock; you can buy their free-range pork produced from saddleback pigs or eggs from the roaming hens and cook it on the barbecue. Cahirminnaun, Tullagh Lower, Kilfenora, +353 65 7088931

52.9861 -9.1921

59 GREGAN'S CASTLE HOTEL

One the best country house hotels, stylish and a little quirky, with an excellent restaurant and also good bar food. A founding member of The Burren Ecotourism Network, The Burren Food Trail and a member of The Burrenbeo Trust. They will even arrange babysitters and massage treatments if given enough notice. Tesla charger. Ballyvaughan, H91 CF60, +353 65 7077005

53.0768 -9.1843

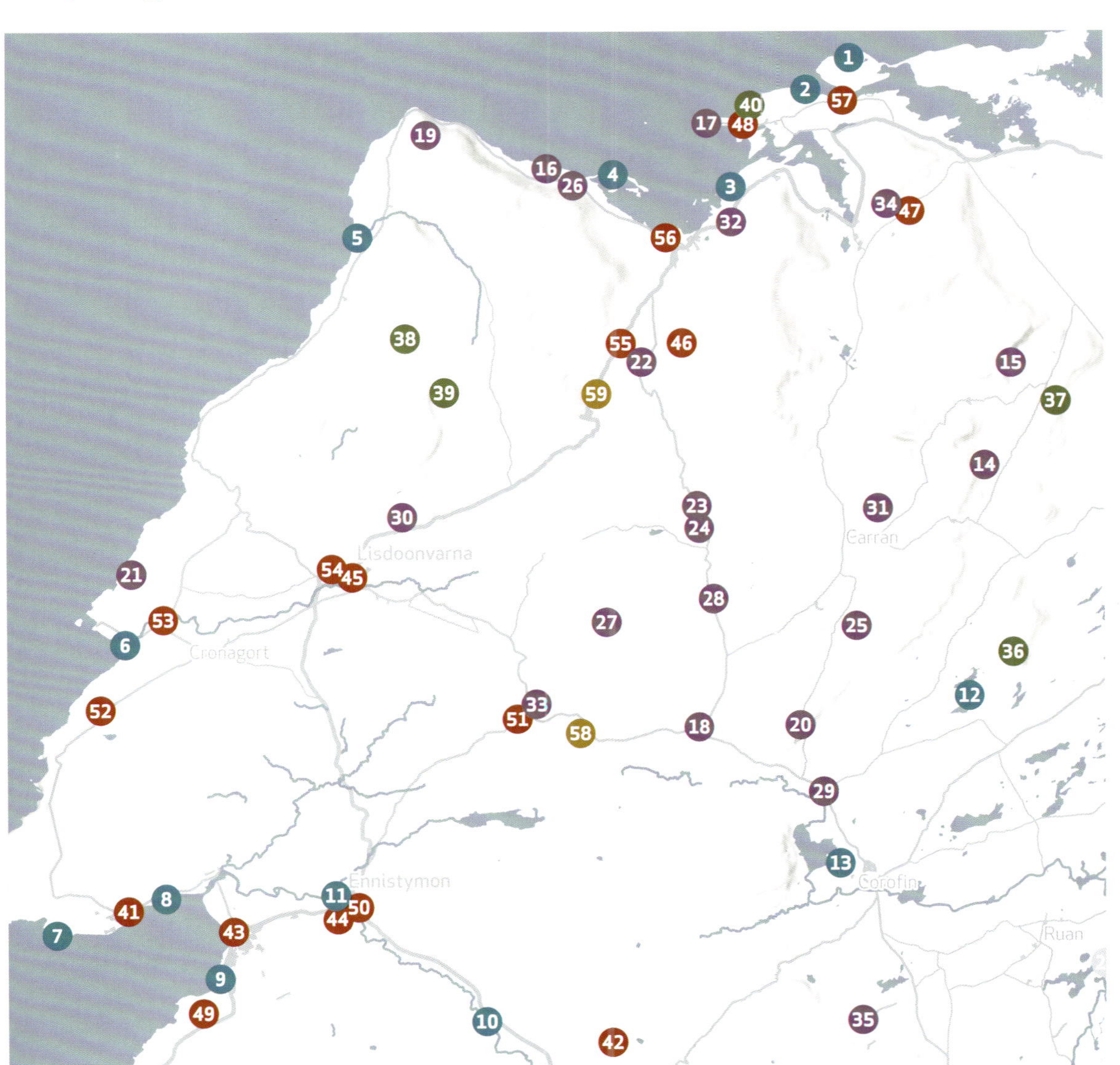

9

SOUTH WEST CLARE

Our perfect weekend

- → **Swim** with the sunset in the Pollock Holes, then warm up with a drink and home-baked treats at the lovely Diamond Rocks café above.
- → **Gaze** from the clifftop ramparts of Foohagh and visit the nearby holy well, then look for the ravens by Bishop's Island along the road.
- → **Descend** from the hilltop church of Killard, swim at the sheltered White Strand below, and pitch up by the sea at Strand Camping.
- → **Jump** in the deep tidal pool of Kerin's Hole, and warm up with a sauna after at nearby Whitestrand Beach.
- → **Peer** into the blowholes on Donegal Point, with views back to the dramatic Baltard Cliffs, and secret Blue Pool.
- → **Feast** on local seafood at the Long Dock, sleep in your campervan by the shore, rise to visit the castle and take a trip with Dolphinwatch.
- → **Find** medieval graves at hidden Killernan, visit ancient Knocknalassa tomb, then swim with a picnic on the wild shores of Doo Lough.

2

3

4

A visit here is like travelling back in time in one very specific way: a generation ago, the Cliffs of Moher were as wild as those at Loop Head lighthouse and Baltard. True, these headland cliffs are not as high, but they share the same dramatic geology, with wave-cut caves and fascinating strata, and here there are choughs and butterflies and far fewer people. Also no fences, so treat the edges with great respect if you want them to remain wild: the winds are gutsy and gusty.

The coast here is dominated by cliffs, often with blowholes and many excellent locations for spotting seabirds and marine life, including dolphins. And of course there are rock pools, some safe and popular swim spots like the Pollock Holes, others remote and risky. These shores have a deadly history, from the Armada burials above the reefs of Spanish Point to the little Grave of the Yellow Men roadside memorial near Kilbaha. Around coastal towns locals have added platforms and ladders at favourite spots, like Byrne's Cove, and of course there are famous sands like Doughmore, but there are wild, shingly coves to find and gentler bays on the southern shore.

That shore runs into the Shannon estuary, with an important commercial and military history that has left defensive ruins, from 15th-century Carrigaholt castle to several Napoleonic-era batteries that could cover the estuary with crossfire. Of course there were domestic conflicts here too, none more dramatic than the story of the Little Ark in Kilbaha, a protracted conflict in the 1850s between local Catholics and a ferociously evangelist landlord's agent – whose hilltop Doondalhen House unsurprisingly fell to ruin after taking serious damage in the War of Independence. There are lovely hilltop church ruins too, many with house-like tombs and grave slabs packed tighter than limestone paving. Often a holy well lies right next to them, marking an ancient association of clear springs and religious sites.

After your adventures, it's easy to find fine seashore pints and local seafood here, from high-end and home-grown produce overlooking the Kilkee cliffs at Lir to Kelly's winkles with a pin on the beach.

For overnights, there are beachside campsites where you can sleep to the sound of the sea, or woodland tent sites for cyclists and off-grid cabins at lovely Pure Space; stay for a few days, this wild corner of Clare deserves more exploration than it often gets.

SECRET BEACHES

1 SEAFIELD BEACH, QUILTY

Take your pick of beaches at this headland and pier: the sheltered and popular Seafield with a Green Coast award E, or the exposed and quieter beach W. In summer, cars are parked all along the road, but it is large enough to absorb a lot of people, especially if you're willing to walk a bit further. You might find a couple of spaces at the E end of the sand (52.8091, -9.4763), or even park on the beach.

2 mins, 52.8079, -9.4883

2 DOUGHMORE BAY

A vast 3km long sandy beach backed by high wild dunes is rare for Clare. There is a right of way across the golf course; the surfers often use it as a shortcut to the middle of the beach. Ignore the main signed WAW car park by the Trump hotel; wilder access is signed L6104 off the main N67, find parking on bends at end. Cross road and bear R before house, 300m across golf course. Can have severe rip currents.

5 mins, 52.7529, -9.4898

3 WHITE STRAND, DOONBEG

Life-guarded but low-key beach of white sand with a promontory in the middle, sheltered between rocky coast on either side, and parking along the road that backs it.

1 min, 52.7479, -9.5501

4 BYRNE'S COVE, GEORGE'S HEAD

Tucked in the cleft of George's Head on the N end of Kilkee Bay is a little shingle and slab cove, with steps down to a concrete walkway and a swimming ladder. This was long a semi-official naturist beach for men, and although it is now reclaimed for more general use you may meet the occasional local in the buff, talking about the old days. Best at mid to HTfor jumps, but great rockpools and sea caves at LT to the L. Car park up East End road past the golf club, walk over footbridge and 200m. Beyond are super views from the headland.

3 mins, 52.6919, -9.6547

5 GLASHEEN BEACH & WHITE STRAND

Sandy cove with rock ledges and good swimming and snorkelling. Down an unsigned lane off the Loop Head circuit, with a small parking area at end. If it's busy, then White Strand is 1.5km W; it's a long, wild sand beach at LT, but about a 500m walk down a farm track (from 52.6189, -9.6775)

1 min, 52.6158, -9.6504

6

POOLS, ARCHES & ISLANDS

6 BLUE POOL, DOONBEG

This legendary, deep tidal rockpool sits below Captain's Hill, in Pulleen Bay. Ledges and pools all along here are famed for sea fishing, but freak waves have claimed several lives, and authorities even tried to dynamite access for safety. At LT in calm seas, park by the farm at Oldchapel (52.7405, -9.5868) and follow track 500m to tricky descents R and 500m W along ledges; keep an eye on the tide and don't go W of pool. You can descend to Ballard Bay SW via the stream gully to explore the cliff ledges and stacks, but this is also a risky shore.

30 mins, 52.7445, -9.6020

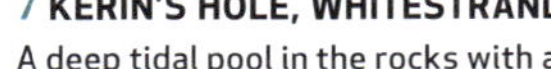

7 KERIN'S HOLE, WHITESTRAND

A deep tidal pool in the rocks with a ladder to climb out, renovated through the efforts of local swimmers in 2013. Follow the clifftop track 400m W from the car park at Whitestrand beach, which has surfing and Suaimhneas sauna, but also a lot of caravans. It's worth exploring the little headland too, all the way around to small pebble coves on the N side (also reached from the lane, park by the old cottage, then 100m to 52.8718, -9.4357).

3 mins, 52.8678, -9.4319

8 DOO LOUGH

Surrounded by rough pasture and old stone walls, this is a quiet spot for a picnic and swim. Take L2116 for Mullagh from the R474 past Carty's Pub (V95 RF38) to sign L at crossroads. There's an access road R to parking by the water treatment works (52.7954, -9.3154). Then walk to the lake shore track E 100m.

5 mins, 52.7949, -9.3118

9 POLLOCK HOLES & KILKEE BEACH

Kilkee is an old-fashioned, classic seaside town vibe with a great family beach. To the W are great slabs of sandstone, officially called the Duggerna Reef, dotted with natural pools popular for swimming at LT; they are warmer than the sea. Once the innermost of the three large pools was reserved for women and the outermost for men. There's also great snorkelling in or around the pools, where you might see the pollock that give them their name. Further W is a good cliff walk path and slabs below popular for bouldering and scrambling. Large car park just above the rocks, by Diamond Rocks Café.

1 min, 52.6829, -9.665

10 GOLEEN BAY & COASTEERING

Narrow, hidden pebble cove; a safe haven for seafarers of past, although lights used be left on Lantern Rock at the entrance as the tiny inlet was difficult to see. There's a huge tidal pool on the slabs (52.6440, -9.7402). For the cove, park on the verge opp gate (52.6417, -9.7324) and cross the field down. For the slabs and pool, take the track from 200m further up the hill (park at 52.6409, -9.7350) then walk 500m. There are more superb pools and gullies around to the L for adventure coasteering in calm seas. Nevsail in Kilkee leads groups (+353 86 3308236, nevsailwatersports.ie).

5 mins, 52.6428, -9.7353

11 BRIDGES OF ROSS & TOURKEAL

Once there were three bridges, within my memory there were two; now just one stunning arch remains over an inlet where golden seaweed swirls in a turquoise pool. On a blowy

11

11

14

day the vast rock slabs W are an exhilarating place to watch waves break. On a rare calm day, the sure-footed can scamble down to sea level (depending on tide) to the E and swim back into the collapsed sea-cave, but any swell makes getting back again difficult. Alternatively head down to the bay from the corner into the car park and try the dramatic inlet on the W edge (52.5910, -9.8692) or the tiny inlet just E of this bay (52.5910, -9.8599). Signed off the L2000 next to V15 Y297, with a car park. There are further dramatic blowholes and caves along the coast, in particular Toorkeal Point 2.5km W on L2000 (or walk along coast): take the farm track 600m N from 52.5938, -9.8285 and explore both sides.

7 mins, 52.5912, -9.8733

12 KNOCKALOUGH LAKE PARK

A neatly-tended lakeshore picnic area for swimming or overnights with the remains of a small castle on a crannóg 300m offshore.

2 mins, 52.7151, -9.2707

13 QUERRIN PIER

A remote little quay and slipway on a tiny tidal harbour lagoon. At HT it's popular for swimming and jumps, at LT you can walk out to the salt marshes. There's also a handball court and picnic tables. Good overnight.

1 min, 52.6277, -9.5880

LOST RUINS

14 FOOHAGH PROMONTORY FORT

Many promontory forts are barely discernable; this one (also called Doonaunroe) has a complete rampart with spectacular cliff views around a flowery interior, and a sea arch beneath it. Park on the coast road at field gate (52.6704, -9.6921) and walk W across field. Over the lane is St Kee's Well, a cute white hut in an earthen circle (52.6700, -9.6915). Walk N 300m to view the monastic ruins on Bishop's Island sea stack and look for ravens. Lovers of wells can also visit Foohagh chalybeate well, in a flowery wet meadow on lanes 1km E (52.6691 -9.6801), recommended for colic or an 'over-moist brain'. SW 3km on the spectacular coast road are Dunlickey or Kilkee Cliffs with a car park, very popular with sea anglers on the slabs below 52.6558, -9.7203.

4 mins, 52.6708, -9.6955

15 CARRIGAHOLT CASTLE

This slender tower is five storeys high but just one room deep; the locked interior is home to colonies of zooming swifts or swallows, and you might see the Shannon dolphins from the cute 19th-century turret in the bawn. Dragoons once drilled on a lawn beyond, long since eroded, and legend says their ghosts appear over the water; in truth, they were part of the first mass

15

15

18

20

21

21

emigration from Clare, when over 20,000 sailed past here into exile in the 1691 Flight of the Wild Geese. Signed car park and path in.

2 mins, 52.5999, -9.6993

16 KILKERIN BATTERY

D-shaped battery from around 1812 with a dry moat and rampart, six gun placements (up a narrow mural staircase) facing the estuary, and musket loops defending the battery. Several of these were built to defend the estuary; the most visited is on Scattery Island in the middle of the estuary. Parking, a sign and a path in at the end of the lane, 6km west from Labasheeda.

4 mins, 52.5998, -9.3377

17 KILCREDAUN POINT RUINS

Two medieval churches and a D-shaped battery, one of several against Napoleon along the Shannon estuary. R of the lane in is Templenaard Oratory (52.5840, -9.6994), and L is Kilcreadaun Church, an ivy-clad single-cell church with an overgrown burial ground. The mausoleum of the owner of Carrigaholt Castle (see entry) is here, and soldiers from the battery who died in a cholera outbreak in 1830. Saint Credaun's Well in the cliff (52.5841, -9.6962) only flows at LT and has a cave where pilgrims stayed. Pull off at the corner and walk the track.

10 mins, 52.5840, -9.6971

18 DOONDALHEN HOUSE & TURRET

Hilltop ruins of a house built in the 1840s, with a cliff-edge octagonal turret folly (52.5652, -9.8623) reputedly a smoking retreat for owner Marcus Keane, the brutal and detested local land agent in the story of the Little Ark (see entry). Park at field gate verge (52.5691, -9.8645) and walk up track 400m. At LT you might spy the tidal pool cut into the platform at the base (52.5644, -9.8636). For those who can find a way down or kayak in 500m from Kilbaha pier, there are vast sea caves to explore beneath.

10 mins, 52.5655, -9.8641

SACRED & ANCIENT

19 KNOCKNALASSA TOMB

On the slopes of Slievecallan, western Clare's highest point, this tomb's massive flat capstone creates a perfect dolmen form; also called Oisín's Dolmen, it's one of several supposed graves for the legendary warrior-poet. Lughnasa was traditionally celebrated here with feasting, games, music and dancing to start the harvest. Just off R474, park in the large layby by the turbine access gates (52.8241, -9.2828) and walk 200m SE parallel to the road.

5 mins, 52.8235, -9.2796

20 KILLERNAN GRAVEYARD & HOLY WELL

This hexagonal hilltop cemetery, also called Kilmurry, is said to be the oldest cemetery in the area, with burials for over a thousand years. Grave slabs, some with early Christian artwork and inscriptions, cover almost every inch between gabled crypts with stone or turf roofs. St Earnan's holy well is just outside the cemetery to the N, tucked under an arch of uncut stone; an obvious and less attractive white well is down the hill.

2 mins, 52.8203, -9.3506

21 KILLARD GRAVEYARD & HOLY WELL

Hilltop graveyard packed with weathered slabs and little house-like mausoleums, plus a cute well right outside it, a flower-filled lane up (open gate and drive) and views down to the sea. Founded by St. Senan in the 6th century, the church ruin is 11th century, and was sacked in 1651 by Cromwellian soldiers, although the graveyard stayed in use. Over a stile is Tobar Chruthnóir an Domhain, the Well of the Creator, venerated with rosaries on Good Friday.

1 min, 52.7447, -9.5560

22 GRAVE OF THE COLLEEN BAWN

The cailín bán or 'fair girl' was Ellen Hanley, a 15-year-old servant seduced by her employer's son, who then paid a servant to kill her and throw her body into the Shannon; both men were hanged, and the tale inspired plays and songs. She lies in Killimer old graveyard in the family grave of the scholar Peter O'Connell, by the stile in. Grave slabs are packed like paving around the medieval church ruin, many beautiful; look for Thomas just outside the door, with smith's tools on it. Car park behind church heading E out of Killimer, L 350m after the ferry terminal.

1 min, 52.6176, -9.3767

23 THE LITTLE ARK

Inside the Church of Our Lady Star of the Sea is a strange covered cart and a stranger tale from the 1850s. Catholic churches were ruined or destroyed in Penal times, and the local land agent (see Doondalhen House entry) even destroyed tents where mass was held. The priest had this 'little ark' built and pulled to Killbaha shore, a legal no-man's land; the legal case became so infamous that eventually the church where the ark now rests was built. N of Kilbaha, 1km from the Lighthouse Inn.

1 min, 52.5787, -9.8676

SUNSET VIEWPOINTS

24 SPANISH POINT

Low headland named after two Spanish Armada ships that were wrecked in 1588: looking out

over the great slanting, wave-cut platforms of rock, it's not hard to imagine. Those who escaped drowning were executed at the shore and are buried on the headland, giving the Irish name Tuama (tomb) Na Spáinneach. At the northern edge is all that remains of an ancient promontory fort (52.8497, -9.4502), and at LT there are fascinating huge rock pools. Medium car park at 52.8475, -9.4458, some pull offs beyond.
5 mins, 52.8490, -9.4503

25 KILMIHIL MASS ROCK

With sweeping vistas south over the landscape, and a flowery grassy area beside it, mass was said here once again in 2012. Many people walked from the village as their ancestors would have, but without the pressure of secrecy. Open the gate and pull in to park (the lane is narrow) and enjoy the views for a while.
2 mins, 52.7388, -9.2883

26 DONEGAL POINT & BALTARD CLIFFS

Spectacular yet little-visited shale cliffs, far better than Moher. From the tiny car park at the lane end at Cloghernagun bear around to the S side of the bay 800m to Donegal Point, pierced by two huge blowholes, one in the remains of the promotory fort. Around from the N side of the bay 600m is the 'Horseshoe' inlet, a collapsed sea cavern with more huge cavern behind it, accessible to sea kayakers. A little to the E the low ruins of Baltard Signal Tower stand at the highest point on the cliffs, 70m. There's also lane access to this N side at 52.7330, -9.6078.
30 mins, 52.7271, -9.6212

27 LOOP HEAD

This is really Leap Head: legendary Cú Chulainn sprang onto the sea stack fleeing a witch. Walk to the pilots' EIRE marker at the tip among bold choughs, hares, and butterflies, above cliffs full of gulls; you might even see dolphins, basking sharks, or humpback whales. NE from the lighthouse are sea caves in the contorted cliff strata below the unfenced edge. The R487 ends at the car park and the light is automated, so you can pay €3 for the great exhibition or stay in the old staff housing (loopheadlighthouse.ie).
15 mins, 52.5599, -9.9371

WILDLIFE WONDERS

28 DOLPHINWATCH CARRIGAHOLT

Daily trips run by a marine biologist around the Shannon estuary to seek peregrine falcons, choughs, gannets, grey seals, and the resident bottlenose dolphins. Or try your luck spotting them from the end of the quay. Adults €50, children up to 14 €35; +353 86 8429505 or book on dolphinwatch.ie
1 min, 52.6039, -9.7088

38

36

36

32

29 RINEVELLA BAY

Two curving bays full of life. Pull off the L2002 coast road at the W bay for oystercatchers, curlews, and rarer migrants, walk to the E one for the stumps of a drowned forest, sea campions and yellow horned poppies, and wintering Brent geese or breeding ringed plovers and the song of the skylark depending on the season.

1 min, 52.5864, -9.7317

SHORESIDE CLASSICS

30 DIAMOND ROCKS CAFÉ

Family-run, child-friendly, with all home-made, locally sourced foods. Right on the rocks for coffee with spectacular views, including of the Richard Harris statue (the Limerick native won swimming and racquets competitions here in his youth). Closed winter. West End, V15 YT10, +353 86 3721063

52.6818, -9.6648

31 KEATING'S OF KILBAHA

The 'nearest pub to New York' is friendly and perfectly placed on the harbourside for a pint in the sun; does bar food, but be prepared to pay cash only. The Pier, Kilbaha, V15 N678, +353 86 8241846

52.5693, -9.8629

32 KELLY'S WINKLES

A summer weekend fixture, this little roadside stand sells bags of locally collected winkles cooked with seaweed, and raw red dillisk, a family business for generations. Sit on the sea wall and eat them in the sun. Strand Line, Kilkee, opposite V15 E659, +353 87 6481721

52.6801, -9.6476

33 BEAG CAFÉ & BAKERY

Exceptional café in a historic Kilrush corner house, serving Calendar coffee, great home-baked cinnamon rolls, sourdough toasties and specials. Quality ingredients perfectly translated into curious and tasty dishes. 9.00am–4.00pm, Wed–Sun, Henry Street, Kilrush, V15 Y966, order cakes on beagfood.com

52.6395, -9.4850

ORGANIC & GASTRO

34 MORRISSEY'S OF DOONBEG

Bright, corner bar-restaurant, with gardens down to the river and views to the castle, and maybe the best fish and chips we've had. Times vary through the year, check and ideally book. Main Street, Doonbeg, Kilrush, V15 W674, +353 65 9055304

52.7309, -9.5243

35 LIR RESTAURANT

Golf isn't always a benign presence in the west of Ireland, but Kilkee Golf Club plays host to this restaurant in the summer months. Great chef, great views, and you can walk up to George's Head or take a dip at Byrne's Cove beforehand (see entry). East End, Kilkee, V15 T634, +353 65 9083000, lirrestaurant@gmail.com

52.6868, -9.6509

36 THE LONG DOCK

Wood-panelled and stone-floored bar, famous for fresh seafood sourced almost at the door and simply served. Lunch and dinner Wed–Sun, breakfast on weekends. West Street, Carrigaholt, V15 NR23, reservations +353 87 4947951

52.6040, -9.7107

BEACH CAMPING

37 STRAND CAMPING, DOONBEG BAY

A small, friendly, family-run campsite with cheerfully painted facilities, right by the sea, with local pubs serving food a 10-minute walk away. Children and dogs are welcome, with exercise areas for both, and you are advised to bring bikes and boots. Barbecues allowed and blocks supplied to raise off the ground. Killard Road, Doonbeg, V15 W659, +353 65 9055345

52.7352, -9.5338

38 GREEN ACRES CARAVAN & CAMPING

Camping right on the wilds of Doonaha Beach, with almost a mile of unvisited pebble and

sand and Doonaha Battery (private, seek permission); the downside is you are also next to static caravans. Closed winter. Doonaha West, Kilkee, V15 YV59, +353 65 9057011, greenacrescamping.ie
52.6187, -9.6420

39 CARRIGAHOLT BEACH CAMPING

The grassy area above this Green Flag beach is operated as a weekend (Fri–Tues morning) camping area by the local Tidy Towns volunteer group. Campervans and tents only, no caravans. No fires, carry out your rubbish, and no amenities, but there are hospitality businesses just over the bridge. Free, but you can leave a donation (€10 suggested) in any of the local shops or pubs.
52.6053, -9.7087

RUSTIC RETREATS

40 KILKEE THALASSOTHERAPY CENTRE

This longstanding centre offers everything from locally harvested seaweed baths to modern spa treatments, with five guest rooms that can be booked whether or not you're having a treatment. 19 Gratten Street, Kilkee, V15 ET92, +353 65 9056742
52.6809, -9.6449

41 PURE SPACE

Only accommodates cycling campers to minimise wear on the woodland site; for others there are wooden lodges, off-grid cabins, and bell tents (2 night stay except unfurnished bell tent). You can book the pizza oven or barrel sauna, take a solar-heated shower using harvested rainwater, or book a yoga class or meditation retreat. There is a canine B&B nearby, pets on site sometimes allowed. Querrin, Kilkee, V15 F602, +353 86 3819216
52.6310, -9.5982

42 BEDS OF SILK

The name is a translation of the village name, and the kingsize beds and divine sheets in these shepherd's huts live up to it – though not actually silk! We recommend booking one with a barrel seaweed bath tucked into the trees behind (pizza oven, sauna and hot tub can also be booked) – or just sit by your firepit with a chilled glass or a hot mug under the stars. No children, no pets. Labasheeda, V15 DE22, +353 87 9765226
52.6252, -9.2458

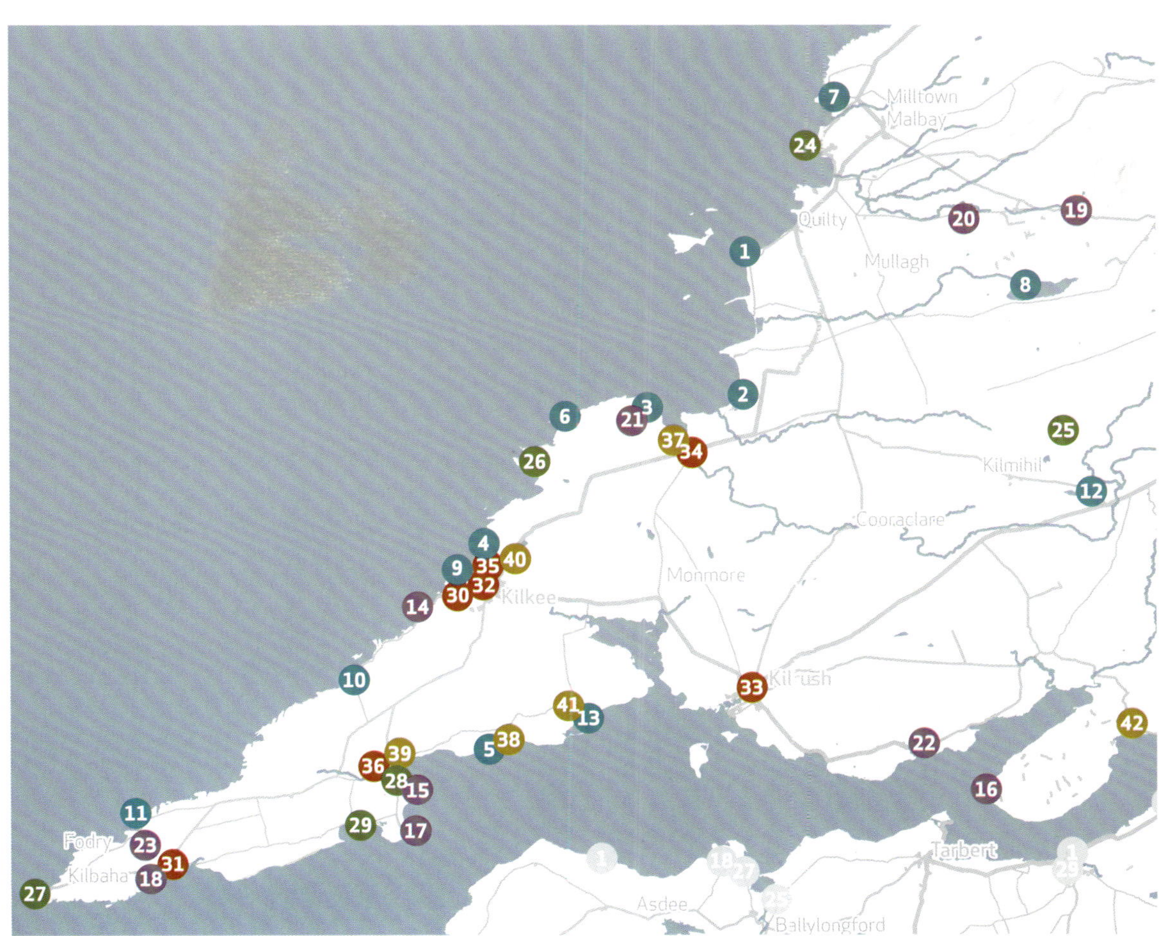

1

EAST CLARE & LOUGH DERG

Our perfect weekend

- → **Climb** to the summit of Moylussa Hill, then descend for a refreshing dip from the wooded jetties at Rinnaman Point.
- → **Picnic** and swim in the woodlands of Cullan House ruins, then cross the shore for the sunset.
- → **Scale** the massive ramparts of ancient, wooded Mooghaun, then find the three faces on the wall of Fenloe Graveyard, and dip in the quiet lake.
- → **Drift** from the limestone shore at Lough Bunny, with a ruined tower on the skyline, then climb to the top of Fiddaun Castle.
- → **Watch** for squirrels and owls in the woods that clothe Ballybeg Crag, or follow the ancient pilgrim track to St John's Well.
- → **Seek** healing at Tobar Mochulla by the grave of two pigs then find the river caves of Kiltannon.
- → **Walk** the friars cloister at impressively intact Quin, and explore the ivy-clad shell of Clooney House with its own churchyard.
- → **Camp** on the shore of Lough Derg at Lakeside and kayak over to the ruins on Holy Island.

This area is the most populated part of the county, with not only Ennis but the 'new town' of Shannon, which grew up around the airport. Between the two rivers of the Shannon and the Fergus lies a landscape of woods and farms, dotted with more than 40 lakes to discover and dip, and of course there's Lough Derg along the Shannon.

There are also woodlands like Ballygar and Dromore to walk in, and hills with vast views, some with marked trails like the 12 O'Clock Hills, others much more wild.

Without a doubt, the most famous site in this region is Bunratty Castle & Folk Park. The imposing castle was an early tourism success, restored from a derelict state and opened to the public in the 1950s, followed by nearby Knappogue. The attached folk park is an entertaining place for a young family, as are the reconstructed roundhouses of Craggaunowen, which leaves the rest of the region a little quieter.

In much older history, this was the homeland of Brian Boru, who began life as one of 12 sons of the regional king and ended it as the high king of all Ireland. You can visit an ancient oak that legend says he planted, and the fort from which he may have taken his name near Killaloe (where there is a Brian Boru festival in early July).

Two local sites tell contrasting tales of how the past has been valued: one of the greatest European hoards of Bronze Age gold jewellery was found near monumental Mooghaun Hillfort in 1854, but most was sold and melted down; 60 years later when Ardnacrusha power station raised the level of the Shannon, workers dismantled little St Lua's oratory and rebuilt it in Killaloe rather than let it drown.

Fortunately a wealth of ancient places has survived here to be explored. Most notable is Inis Cealtra or Holy Island with a host of medieval ruins, but there are many country churches, holy wells and graveyards full of curious features like Fenloe.

And of course there are castles and ruins other than the big honeypots: one of the best is Fiddaun, where if you ask for the key you can see more than at almost any other old tower house. This is the real thing, far better than any reconstruction.

LAKE SWIMMING

1 LOUGH BUNNY

This superb limestone lake has ethereal blue water over a white stone beach and some smooth rock ledge islands, depending on levels; it can dry out in droughts. Popular in summer, but the long shore means there's always room. On the R460 between Gort and Corofin, with a main access area and smaller pull-offs for your own piece of shore. Cloondooan Castle tower stands out on the horizon, close to the roadside at 53.0301, -8.9238. Bring water shoes.

2 mins, 53.0139, -8.9323

2 MUCKANAGH LOUGH *

If Lough Bunny is a little too busy, come here for wilder shores, longer grasses and slightly deeper water, although it still warms quickly in summer. Track to a rough parking area from lane SE of – and parallel to – R460 between Gort and Corofin.

2 mins, 52.9768, -8.9350

3 BALLYALLIA LAKE & RIVER FERGUS

The shore by the parking has tables and a floating platform; in season there's a lifeguard, and kayak and SUP hire/lessons from Clare Water Sports/Clare Kayak Hire (+353 85 1485856). For a quieter stretch, head to the S end of the parking bays (52.8726, -8.9731) and take the woodland path to a small pier. The wider lough is an SAC for birds, with shore waders and a variety of wintering ducks and whooper swans. Can suffer algal blooms in summer; check for warning notices. For something much more remote, try the River Fergus upstream 5km N at 52.9102, -8.9729 and walk E.

4 mins, 52.8748, -8.9704

4 CULLAUN LAKE

Swimming entry point created through local effort, with a car park and a narrow jetty out into deeper water. A good spot to watch the sun go down across the water. On R462 1.5km N of Kilkishen.

2 mins, 52.8222, -8.7531

5 ROSSLARA LOUGH & FONTANE CASTLE

With a pretty offshore island to swim to (50m) this is mainly a fishing lake, but locals swim here in the summer if there is no one fishing and it's usually not busy. Easy access off quiet lanes. Fontane Castle is 1.3km S on R (52.8832, -8.6940), one face remains with chutes, chambers and a creepway.

2 mins, 52.8919, -8.6982

6 LOUGH BRIDGET

A footpath leads down Swan Island, in fact a long, narrow wooded peninsula, with plenty of places for a dip if you wade out past the reeds. This is a fishing lake with wheelchair access, so be discreet and give anglers a very wide berth. This spot right on the R352 is easy; for more peace continue E and take first R (signed Silvergrove Shore) to find layby parking after 2km (52.8666, -8.6522).

5 mins, 52.8801, -8.6492

7 LOUGH GRANEY, CAHERMURPHY

The 'Killarney of Clare' this wooded lake valley is also famed as the setting of the poem 'The Midnight Court' by Brian Mac Giolla Meidhre (Merriman) and the birthplace of Biddy Early, Ireland's best known bean feasa or 'wise woman'. The White Sands shore here is really more orange, but lovely for picnics and overnights, and the well-marked Cahermurphy Loop walk leads through the woods. In Flagmount 2km S is another good access point with concrete piers for fishing boats, signed 'coarse angling' down a tiny lane at 52.9876, -8.6507).

5 mins, 53.0044, -8.6568

8 HOLY ISLAND, LOUGH DERG

Those with a kayak can set off from here to the beautiful Inis Cealtra monastic site with well-

preserved ruins, including a round tower and church, and ancient grave slabs. Even without the island, the jetties here make a lovely spot for a picnic and swim. Signed off the R352. You can take a boat crossing and maybe tour of the island with local historian Gerard Madden (Apr–Oct in good weather, no pre-booking, €) from Mountshannon Pier, where there are more amenities and a stone maze (52.9295, -8.4283).

5 mins, 52.9202, -8.4539

9 RINNAMAN POINT, BALLYCUGGARAN

A well developed lakeside picnic area and aquapark on the R463. Take paths to R for much quieter wooded peninsula and jetties.

2 mins, 52.8359, -8.4640

LOST RUINS

10 OUR LADY'S HOSPITAL, ENNIS

Built in 1868, this vast imposing structure once housed over 1,000 patients; its size alone tells a sombre story about Ireland's attitudes to mental health in even the recent past. The hospital, then called the Ennis Asylum, closed in 2002 and has changed hands several times since, most recently in 2024. It's strictly off limits today, with effective fencing, and earmarked for potential retirement housing and community care, but you can easily walk the 1km perimeter and appreciate the exterior. Parking at the back on Gort Road.

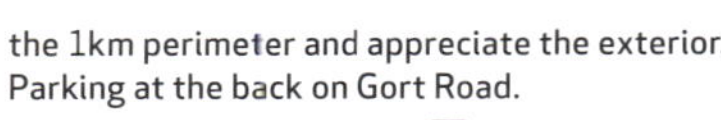

2 mins, 52.8608, -8.9794

11 FIDDAUN CASTLE *

Marvellous six-storey tower with bawns, in extraordinary condition. Get the key at Fiddaun House (53.0021, -8.8876), walk and explore this on your own. A woodland walk will bring you there, and you'll have access to the courtyard and the keep, all the way up the spiral staircase to the views from the top. If no one's home, pop over to Kilmacduagh Abbey or Gort and come back later.

20 mins, 53.0104, -8.8794

12 CLOONEY HOUSE & CHURCH

The 17th-century home of the Bindon family burnt down in the 19th century and is now a romantic ivy-clad shell. The family patriarch wanted a Catholic church, Protestant church, castle, and lake on the estate and govt his wish: he gave the roadside graveyard to the Catholic church, with Protestant church ruins within it. Park on the lane for the graveyard (52.8533, -8.8592). A gatehouse and front drive to the ruins are on R with safety notices. You may also be able to drive in the back entrance from 52.8614, -8.8633.

10 mins, 52.8563, -8.8633

13 ARDAMULLIVAN TOWER

Six-storey tower house with traces of bartizans, a machicolation, murder hole, slit windows, fireplaces, and a slopstone, some outer defences remaining. Re-roofed and lime-rendered in the 1990s to protect late-medieval paintings inside, and sometimes open for events, but usually it's just an atmospheric walk around the impressive exterior. Car park by the road and a walk up through old parkland.

7 mins, 53.0042, -8.8293

14 CULLAN HOUSE & CRAGGAUNOWEN *

Also called Cullane Castle, this romantic 18th-century villa ruin overlooks Lough Cullaunyheeda, with ample opportunities for a quiet picnic or dip. The woods are Coillte; park at the road gate (52.8263, -8.7755) or at the sailing club (52.8235, -8.7759) and walk SW along the forest track. The house was owned by 'Honest Tom' Steele, a friend of Daniel O'Connell, eventually brought to ruin by his campaigning against poverty and disenfranchisement. He also restored Cragganauwen Castle (52.8118, -8.7907), which can be visited along with a living past project (craggaunowen.ie), highly recommended for €10 per adult.

25 mins, 52.8211, -8.7814

15 BRIAN BORU'S FORT

An impressively steep bank and deep ditch lost in woodland today, this was a high-status fort with a stone wall and palisade inside a ditch. It is beautifully sited on a spur where Lough Derg narrows into the Shannon, giving Boru control of the river until it was destroyed in 1116. Park on side of R463 1km N of Killaloe and go through turnstile on R.

5 mins, 52.8186, -8.4512

HOLY WELLS

16 ST JOHN'S WELL & KILLONE ABBEY

Dedicated to St. John the Baptist, this well is still visited for outdoor mass, which started in the 1740s during Penal times. It lies in a chamber under a rock outcrop, with an altar, religious statues, and a shrine, plus a tank just S, possibly a washing area; access is through Ballybeg Woods (see entry). You can look over to the 13th-century abbey, one of only three cloistered nunneries in Ireland, with some lovely features, but it lies on private land and there is often a bull in the field. The signed lane to it, ending at 52.7997, -9.0099, has forbidding signs; we hope this changes.

25 mins, 52.8067, -9.0022

17 FENLOE GRAVEYARD

This quiet ancient graveyard holds a church that may date back over 1,000 years, and storied treasures. A 'curing stone' in the outside of the W graveyard wall (52.7818, -8.8374) has two domes cut with a cross and a ring, said to be boils pulled off a plague victim by founder St Luchtighearn. Three carved heads on the inside of the E wall (52.7819, -8.8365) are three witnesses to the miracle; the one who believed it is the least weathered. There is also a holy well, and a broken partial bullaun by the gate. The name means 'fair lake', and there's a shady slope into the water 150m W of the parking layby where you could picnic and paddle on a sunny day.

2 mins, 52.7819, -8.8370

18 TOBAR NA LÁMH

The 'well of the hand', also called St Collman's, lies in a pretty and peaceful spot among trees. The mossy stones sheltering it look ancient, but were actually part of a restoration scheme in the 1990s that cleansed the raggedy tree and put up a plaque with the history and 'pattern'. It's traditional to leave metal offerings here, especially horseshoes. Park outside the house on the lane at 53.0165, -8.8252 with a signed path opp to the well, 300m.

6 mins, 53.0147, -8.8228

19 TOBAR MOCHULLA & TULLA CEMETERY

Incongruously hidden behind a pre-school is this holy well, with steps down to a stone-walled, round court topped by a Celtic cross. The stone in front of the well is said to be marked by the saint's knees, and there is a medieval cross-inscribed slab in the wall. The graveyard above contains low remains of the 7th-century church and the ruins of an 18th-century Protestant church, a good collection of Celtic crosses, and a very curious tombstone with pigs on it. This is the grave of Michael O'Sullivan, who was eaten by his own pigs; the church decided the only way to give him Christian burial was to bury the pigs.

2 mins, 52.8667, -8.7536

SACRED & ANCIENT

20 CLARE ABBEY, ENNIS

Bearing signs of its use as a home and at times a military encampment after dissolution, this was a ruin by the 18th century. Extensive remains of church with a belfry and domestic buildings around a cloister garth, up a long and circuitous dead-end route signed from the Clare Abbey roundabout on the N85. Local people park near the start of the lane in to walk the off-road walk/cycle path; continue past them up to the abbey.

2 mins, 52.8290, -8.9689

21 MOOGHAUN HILLFORT

Possibly the largest in Ireland, this complex fort occupies an entire hill with three concentric

16

17

17

20

8

28

26

33

limestone ramparts, all built in the late Bronze Age; a modern tower at the centre gives views over the woodlands. It also holds three early medieval cashels, built using stones of the original ramparts, one on the way up at 52.7821, -8.8792. The owners of the Dromoland estate used these as picnic spots. This was clearly an important place, and a major hoard of ancient gold was found nearby. Parking and trailhead 52.7800, -8.8802.

15 mins, 52.7828, -8.8781

22 QUIN FRIARY

These 15th-century Augustinian ruins are well-preserved, with a very impressive, intact cloister at the heart, despite being sacked and burned by Cromwellian troops. On the way in you pass the humbler ruins of 13th-century St Finghin's Church. Easy parking at gate or on streets.

4 mins, 52.8192, -8.863

23 KILCREDAUN BURIAL GROUND

Wild, remote and possibly dating back to the 8th century, this graveyard is full of trees, with some lovely old stones but no trace of any church. There isn't even a gate in the walls, which were circular until the 19th century, just a stile and a substantial coffin rest. The bullaun stone with a small enclosure still gets visits. Park by gatelodge at 52.7731, -8.4916 and walk away from it NW to corner; follow track through field gate R along hedges.

8 mins, 52.7779, -8.4918

24 ST LUA'S ORATORY, KILLALOE

The small church originally stood on Friar's Island in the River Shannon, flooded and submerged when the Shannon hydroelectric scheme was built; the oratory was saved and rebuilt outside St Flannan's Church. The nave is possibly 10th-century, with a cyclopean doorway, and may have had a wooden roof. The chancel is 12th-century and has the steep stone roof seen on several smaller churches across Ireland, including nearby St Flannan's Oratory, outside St Flannan's Cathedral, which is also worth a visit (52.8065, -8.4393). Find on-street parking.

5 mins, 52.8069, -8.4443

CAVES

25 KILTANNON CAVES

In the 1700 and 1800s, these river caves (part of Toomeens of Tulla network) and ornate bridge were a popular tourist attraction. The local gentry brought visitors and sometimes concerts were held; one 1780 travelogue compared the caves to continental natural wonders to be seen on the Grand Tour. They are in private farmland, contact Pat Harrison in advance for tours for up to five +353 86 8662615, kiltannoncaves@gmail.com

10 mins, 52.8785, -8.7935

CRAGS & HILLS

26 MOYLUSSA HILL

The highest point in Clare (532m) has a simple, well-maintained trail about 10km straight up; if you find this too tough, follow the gravel forestry road for most of it. There's a stretch of boardwalk right to the summit. Start from substantial Ballycuggan car park (52.8343, -8.4666). You can cut short with fine views over the lough on the summit of Feenlea if the weather looks poor or the main trail is busier than you like; fewer people visit the lower peak (52.8316, -8.4907).

180 mins, 52.8335, -8.5223

27 BALLYBEG CRAG & WOODS

A limestone crag with erratic boulders, mossy tuffets, ringforts, ruined cottages. and pockets of hazel woodland. It was planted with conifers in the 1950s, but these have been largely removed and replaced with beech, rowan and oak. There are looped paths in the northern part, some of them quite steep. You might spot red squirrels, or at dusk hear a long-eared owl – this is also a great site for lesser horseshoe bats. Part of an ancient pilgrim's road known as the Rocky Road runs south to St John's Well and Killone Abbey (see entries). Car park turning is after V95 W9X4 (52.8161, -8.9973).

5 mins, 52.8163, -8.9971

ANCIENT FOREST

28 DROMORE WOODS, CASTLE & LAKE *

Woods, ruins, lakes, a river; something for everyone. From the trailhead it's a 200m walk to the ruined 17th-century castle with ravens and kestrels. The reed-fringed lough is populated by kingfishers, swans, otters, and ducks, orchids grow in the wetland areas, and the mature woods with bluebells, violets, and wild strawberries are home to foxes, squirrels, and pine martens. Some swim from the rocks on N shore beyond the castle (52.9233, -8.9679); there's also a boat ramp W of the car park and another smaller lake. Well signed off the minor road E of Ruan. The access road follows the River Fergus, with pools in several places, like 52.9374, -8.9531

3 mins, 52.9238, -8.9617

29 BRIAN BORU'S OAK

The last remnant of the ancient 'Suidain' sessile oak forest survives here among forestry, the rest cut for ironworks – without coppicing, to reduce cover for rebels. The 1,000-year-old Brian Boru Oak stands out majestically; at 8m girth, it is one of Ireland's oldest and best-known trees and thousands of its acorns have been planted. Park at 52.8969, -8.5391 to walk up old driveway and through woods 3km, or take a less woodsy 500m walk from the lane into Raheen Community Hospital (52.8937, -8.5057), possible parking there or at salvage yard.

10 mins, 52.8970, -8.5070

ORGANIC & GASTRO

30 TOWN HALL BISTRO

The restaurant of the Old Ground Hotel delivers modern cooking in an imposing building furnished in vintage style with old wooden tables and chairs. O'Connell Street, Ennis, V95 WDX2, +353 65 6828127

52.8425, -8.98311

31 THE WOODEN SPOON

This colourful, boho café has lots of good vegetarian and vegan options, lovely staff, and great coffee. Really great coffee. Main Street, Ballina, V94 A326, +353 61 622415

52.8092, -8.4370

LAKESHORE RETREATS

32 LAKESIDE HOLIDAY PARK

Campsite right on the lakeshore with kayaks for hire, diving boards and jetty. Facilities are a little tired and it's not cheap, but the location makes up for it. +353 85 8552100, lakesideireland.ie

52.9261, -8.4190

33 LOUGH GRANEY COTTAGE

Cute and cheerfully decorated old farm cottage, almost on the shore of the lovely lough, booked on on Airbnb. Mary and Flan are the kind of hosts who give you all sorts of extra information to enjoy the area. Sleeps 8, with a good garden, a great place to gather extended family or friends. Caher, V94 PP30, +353 86 1078699

52.9638 -8.6456

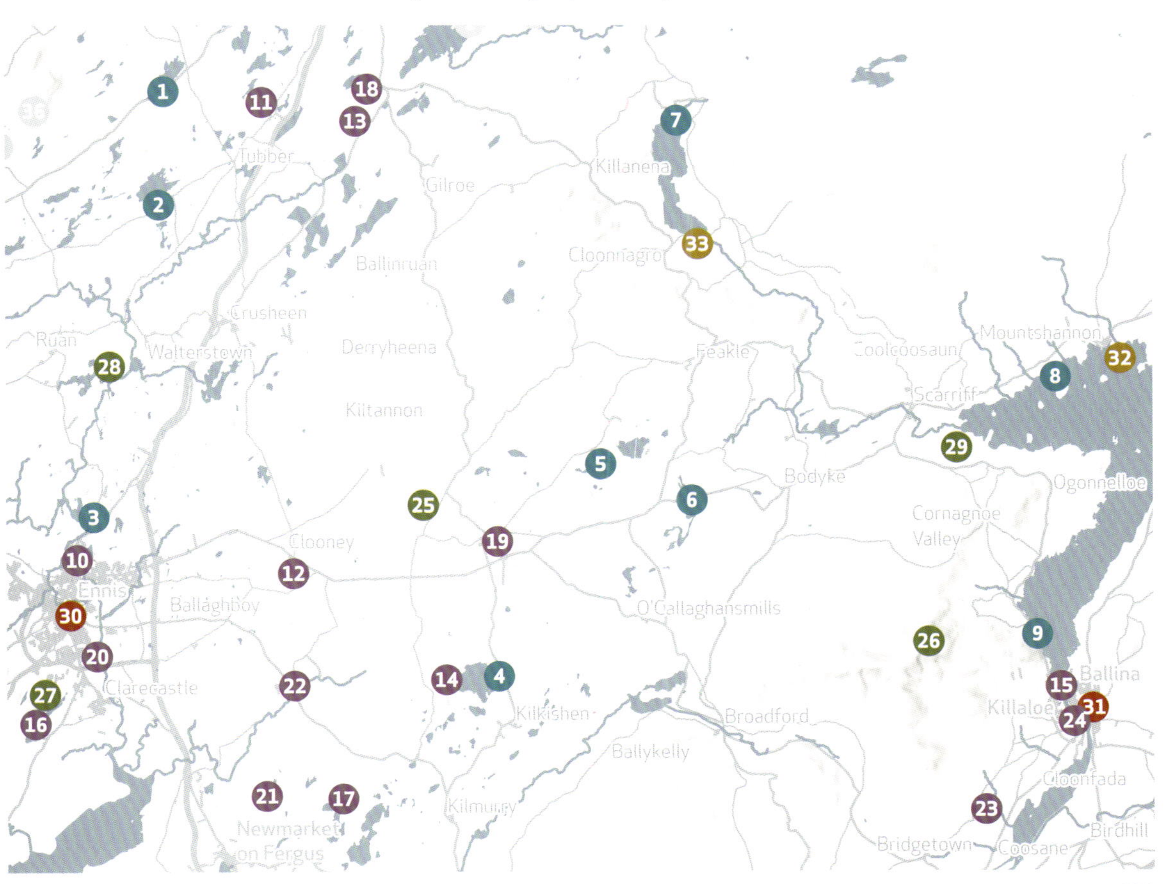

5

LIMERICK

Our perfect weekend

- **Gather** supplies at Limerick's Milk Market, drop in on St Mary's Cathedral, and picnic with cormorants at Caisleán na Coran river island.
- **Scramble** up the little hill at Kilfinane Motte or the round tower stump at Ardpatrick Graveyard on a road made by St Patrick's cow.
- **Cycle** the Greenway through the Barnagh Tunnel to Tullig Wood, or across Ferguson's Viaduct.
- **Jump** from the end of Glin Pier at high tide and warm up in a sauna or by climbing the hill to Cailín Bán viewpoint on the Knight's Walk.
- **Explore** the slopes of Knockfierna, keeping an eye out for fairy women or a phantom horseman, and feast at the Mustard Seed.
- **Climb** the beautifully conserved round tower at Dysert Aenghusa, and swim to a little island from remote and ruined Anhid cemetery.
- **Wander** the woods of Curraghchase spotting veteran trees, maybe stay to see the horseshoe bats, and dine on local produce at 1826 Adare.
- **Contemplate** in rural quiet at Our Lady of the Snows or Kilagholehane Church.

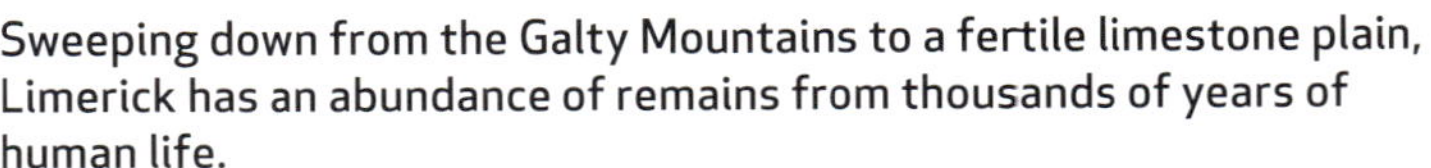
Sweeping down from the Galty Mountains to a fertile limestone plain, Limerick has an abundance of remains from thousands of years of human life.

There are the graves of ancient farming communities, like the superb wedge tomb at Lough Gur, and the ruins of later religious buildings, including some that seem to be the oldest surviving in the country, like tiny Killulta Church or the oratory at Labbamolaga. And given that the northern edge of the county is the Shannon, once a major trading and military highway, there are tower houses and fortifications like the fantastically ruined 'Black Castle' of Castletroy.

Later, railways changed transport utterly, and then even their time passed; a line west out of Limerick into Kerry, long disused, has in recent years been transformed into the Limerick Greenway, a long-distance cycling route with industrial and natural wonders along its course.

Swimming on the Shannon is definitely doable, although it is tidal for much of the length here, so be aware of changing depths and currents. The industrial and trading past of the shore has left some substantial stone piers, and you can even sleep in a cottage right by one and at the foot of ruined Beagh Castle. Above Limerick city are more typical river swimming spots like the weirs at Castleconnell, and there are other rivers like the Annagh, with a lovely tree-lined gorge.

There are woodlands right down to the Shannon banks, and many little wooded glens, perhaps the best on the Greenway at Tullig. The expansive parklands of Curraghchase demesne are enough to lose yourself in for a while. And although the county is largely river plain and the rolling Golden Vale of farmland to the east, there are some peaks.

To the south lie the Ballyhoura Mountains, where you can climb Seefin on part of the long distance Ballyhoura Way. Even in the centre of the county there is Knockfierna or the 'Hill of Truth', where you would be wise not to refuse hospitality when offered: in an unusual local folk tale of a 'fairy woman' bringing bread and milk to workers on the hill from a cave, the one suspicious man who spurned the offering died.

Make some time to visit the city, which has a rich history going back to the Vikings. You can pick up the best of local produce in the Milk Market, visit the local Treaty City brewery and eclectic pubs, and even spot wildlife, from cormorants to otters. The county and its city hold plenty of surprises.

SHANNON SWIMMING

1 GLIN PIER

There are sweeps of shingle here, but the real attraction is a running jump off the end of the stone pier into the Shannon estuary. It's tidal at this point, so do check the depth first, and keep an eye on your position relative to the shore when swimming. There's even a sauna to warm up in on summer weekend high tides, Tide Side Sauna on social media.

2 mins, 52.5753, -9.2833

2 KILTEERY PIER

This stone pier has a bay area sheltered from the currents for summer swimming, a few tables and grass areas for picnic spots, and summer weekend sauna open at higher tides, Tide Side Sauna on social media.

2 mins, 52.5947, -9.2236

3 CAISLEÁN NA CORAN, CORBALLY

Swim or canoe across to the W tip of St Thomas Island, where the 'Castle of the Weir' sits on a rock by the old salmon weir, with gunloops and a (now blocked) entrance above the usual level of the river to allow for tides; it was slighted in the 1690 Siege of Limerick. In winter you might see many cormorants here, feasting on migrating eels. There is also an 18th-century mansion shell, but the island is private and grazed; call Pat Lysaght +353 86 8487042 about going ashore. River access with parking at bottom of Mill Road (52.6885, -8.6209). Upstream 400m on a path are remains of the Corbally river baths (52.6866, -8.6158).

3 mins, 52.6899, -8.6235

4 CASTLETROY CASTLE & RIVERSIDE

In woods by the shore this ruin, also called the Black Castle, stands 'like an old chief with his armour all shatter'd' as the 'Bard of Thomond' Michael Hogan described it, and you can park in the science park on McLaughlan Rd (52.6765, -8.5506) and turn R into the woods. From here explore the long riverside path upstream 1.5km to the rugby club or downstream 2.5km past various islands and beaches behind the university campus (a popular sand beach at 52.6757, -8.5645 but no parking nearby) to the university boat house.

2 mins, 52.6777, -8.5507

5 CASTLECONNELL & FAIRY WOODS *

A delightful stretch of the river with a footbridge, stepping stones and stone weirs creating many pools, and a little 'Fairy Wood' with doors on mature broadleaf trees. The deepest pool is at the car park and playground on the river bend; explore downstream and cross the footbridge into Clare for wooded falls and ruins a further 2km downstream. Upstream 1km, the World's End boat club is a popular locals' swimming location with a sauna (serenitysaunas.ie, 52.7267, -8.5055).

2 mins, 52.7119, -8.5053

WATERFALLS & POOLS

6 CLARE GLENS, R ANNAGH

A sometimes slippery loop path follows the dramatic and popular Annagh River gorge through mossy native woodland, past waterfalls and ravines. The best waterfall is after about 50m downstream of the halfway footbridge, and the left bank path is easier with better access to the water, so go anti-clockwise. The return path on the opp bank is higher level, with steeper river access. Well-signed, big car park, there is even a pool by the road bridge.

10 mins, 52.6897, -8.3998

7 ANHID CEMETERY, R MAIGUE

A charming little church ruin and graveyard with grass-roofed raised tombs, right by the river with an island where the Camoge joins the Maigue. Look out for the wide iron gates, signed on the fast N20, with parking just about for one in the gateway without blocking access 52.5018, -8.7118 (you may be able to park on grass inside). In Croom 2km downstream the Riverside Walk gives access to the banks

and weir from parking at 52.5177, -8.7192. For something more rural, 5km downstream, park in the rough verge by the stone bridge at 52.5431, -8.7677 and follow L bank fishing path 250m downstream for a deep section above the weir.

6 mins, 52.5035, -8.7074

LOST RUINS

8 ASKEATON CASTLE & ABBEY

A perfect defensible spot at a fall (eas) on the river, this island had Anglo-Norman fortifications by 1199, which were increased and remodelled until the Cromwellian wars of the 17th century. As well as a medieval tower and banqueting hall, there's an 18th-century Hellfire Club building to see; site was closed during 2024 for vital work by the OPW, but should re-open even better, though with a charge. Nearby are the ruins of a Franciscan abbey (52.6040, -8.9752), free and open seasonally. Parking on streets.

2 mins, 52.6000 -8.97398

9 CARRIGOGUNNELL CASTLE

Overgrown and precarious but wonderful ruin, blown up in 1698, with views of the Shannon, vaults and various levels to explore – with care! At the end of a tiny lane, there is parking just for one at the house entrance (52.6451, -8.7418) but better to park at St Joseph's Church and walk up 1km (52.6427, -8.7332).

15 mins, 52.6464, -8.7424

10 KING JOHN'S CASTLE , LIMERICK CITY

This sprawling riverside castle complex with activities and exhibits is not wild, but is a great place to learn how medieval people lived, how a great castle and its city functioned, and how their usefulness ended. Our favourite part was the undercroft excavations of the 13th-century structures hidden beneath, which they underplay on their website. It is pricey, so certainly not for everyone (€15 adult), but a useful option if Irish weather lets you down. Nicholas Street, Limerick, V94 FX25 (kingjohnscastle.ie), car park at 52.6712, -8.6251.

3 mins, 52.6697, -8.6255

11 KILFINANE MOTTE

The impressive Norman motte is fun for children to scramble up and down, and the top is perfect for a secluded picnic. It stands on the site of an earlier trivallate ringfort, and you can explore the overgrown lower outer banks and ditches. There's a camper van park opposite the entrance, so you could catch a sunset up here on an overnight (ballyhouracampervanpark.ie). Signs say 'The Moat'; parking on street.

3 mins, 52.3578, -8.4672

12 KILLAGHOLEHANE CHURCH RUINS

This charming rural ruin was Muire Sneachta, 'Our Lady of the Snows', a name still used for the church in Broadford. Legend says locals could not agree on a church site, until after prayers a summer snowfall covered the entire area except for this field. The baptismal font, a 15th-century tomb, a holy water stoup in the outside wall and three soaring windows remain, one with a curious later makeover. Parking by graveyard; from the end of this a short track leads L to a small copse with fairy doors.

2 mins, 52.3314, -8.9768

13 KILLULTA CHURCH & CURRAHEEN

This tiny, simple structure in Kildimo is among the oldest stone churches in Ireland, possibly even from the 5th century, and lies almost forgotten up the end of a track in what looks like an old orchard, now full of ragwort and butterflies. Killulta could mean 'Church of the Ulsterman' or 'Church of Saint Ultan', but neither is local. Lane is signed 'Bleach Lough Angling' off N69, park L before first gates. Walk on 150m to two paths R at 52.6297, -8.8395; we were directed down the first, with the safety notice; overgrown, a stick is helpful. 1km N, the vast gothic ruins of Dromore Castle are near the shore of the lough but well hidden by trees and clearly private, 52.6367, -8.8362. But another 1km NE on lanes there is a track across a field to the overgrown ruin of Shanpallas Castle next to farm buildings. Look for the turret with stairs and the undercroft (52.6425, -8.8416).

5 mins, 52.6290, -8.8359

14 DYSERT AENGHUSA

The late medieval church ruins are handsome, but the draw here is the 20m round tower. Local folklore says it was built in a single night by a witch; more conventional work by the OPW includes a staircase up to the Romanesque tower door and a floor inside so you can enjoy the views. Signed from lane W of Croom.

2 mins, 52.5209, -8.7447

15 KILLMALLOCK FRIARY

These rambling riverside remains are the best-preserved Dominican building in Ireland: it has perhaps the finest tracery window in the country, carved canopies, cloisters, and a mural staircase. Established in 1291, it was immediately the subject of a legal battle when the bishop of Limerick tried and failed to evict the friars. Other medieval remains include a collegiate church (52.4011, -8.5745), tower house (52.4013, -8.5766), and the Blossom Gate, the only remaining gate of its original five (52.3990, -8.5750). On-street parking.

5 mins, 52.4025, -8.5749

13

13

15

15

15

16 MUNGRET MONASTERY

On one side of the road, with parking at the cemetery, is a medieval abbey with a square tower, and further back the low remains of St Nessan's Church; on the other is a curious little pre-Norman church with a lintelled doorway and inclined jambs, a style of the oldest churches. Maybe the oldest building in Limerick is the church of St Mainchán mac Setnai, who cursed the city natives (52.6608, -8.6551); perhaps as revenge, it is marooned in modern housing.

2 mins, 52.6340, -8.6757

17 MONASTERANENAGH ABBEY

These solid Cistercian ruins are also called Manister. The monks here were stubborn; in 1228 they fortified the abbey against Stephen of Lexington, an English abbot sent to bring Irish monasteries to heel, and although the abbey was dissolved in 1540 some stayed here until 1580. Then the English Lord President of Connaught turned his cannon on the abbey and massacred the surviving community. Gate and sign on road W, pull onto verge.

2 mins, 52.5168, -8.6628

18 ST. MARY'S CATHEDRAL LIMERICK CITY

If in Limerick city, this slightly dishevelled but wonderful 12th-century cathedral is worth a visit. The magnificent Romanesque doorway is believed to be from the palace that stood here before, and the stones bear the marks of sword sharpening by the city's defenders in many sieges. Inside are fantastically carved misericords, a lepers' squint, a pre-reformation high altar, and cannonballs that struck in 1691. The €5 charge funds the constant upkeep and restoration work. Car park on Merchants' Quay adjacent (€), Bridge Street, V94 E068.

3 mins, 52.6682, -8.6235

19 GRANGE STONE CIRCLE, LOUGH GUR *

This vast and beautiful Bronze Age stone circle is Ireland's largest, with 113 stones set against an embankment (the Irish name Líos means ringfort). They form a near-perfect circle, and a hole packed with clay and pottery, possibly for the 'foot' of a compass, was found in the centre. Standing at the entrance, the sun sets behind a distinct low stone opposite on Celtic Samhain, now Halloween; other alignments have been suggested. In 2022 specialist photographer Ken WIlliams found unknown rock art on Stone 9, left from the entrance – small wonder that visitors still leave offerings here. Layby parking.

2 mins, 52.5142, -8.5419

20 ARDPATRICK GRAVEYARD

Walk up the ancient trackway, said to have been made by St Patrick's cow, to massive views from a ruined church and round tower stump. A square outline in the grass at 52.3380, -8.5323 is filled-in St Patrick's Well or Robbers' Well; local folklore said that if you cast no reflection in it you would be dead within the year. The earthworks across the track are from a field system and settlement. Park in the car park in Ardpatrick to the E (52.3409, -8.5242); the track, concreted at the start, rises from the end of a lane R of the Spruce and Willow café.

10 mins, 52.3384, -8.5318

21 LABBAMOLAGA CHURCH & STONES

One inside, this place feels very ancient, with the ruin of a 10th-century church aligned towards mountains rather than the E, and an ancient oratory (the 'Molaga's bed' of the name) with a doorway like a trilithon. In the next field stands what looks like a Scottish four-poster stone circle (52.3098, -8.3474), but too large, and it is thought that the uprights of the oratory doorway were robbed from what was a circle of at least six stones. Layby at the entrance.

2 mins, 52.3106, -8.3476

22 MOOR ABBEY

This riverside Franciscan abbey has survived three attempts to destroy it. It was burned almost immediately; in 1570, after Dissolution, the Lord Deputy of Ireland ordered it and three

20

20

23

men trapped in it to be burned; and in the War of Independence the police tried and failed to blow up the long abandoned shell. There is still a cute, niche sedilla, inscribed grave slab, and displaced stone with a carved head. The little River Aherlow runs through the pretty field next to it and the Ballyhoura Way loop walk follows it downstream from the parking 2km before looping back on lanes; perfect for a picnic.

2 mins, 52.4025, -8.2783

TOMBS & TUNNELS

23 LOUGH GUR WEDGE TOMB

This long Neolithic wedge tomb is in such good shape, with four roofstones on the main chamber and an almost intact outer wall on one side, that in the 19th century an old woman was said to have lived in it. It gives a great idea of the type to remember when looking at less lucky survivors. The bones of at least 12 people were excavated from it in the 1930s, along with Neolithic and Beaker pottery; earlier diggers had come before, looking for gold. By the road, with tight parking.

2 mins, 52.5125, -8.5232

24 DUNTRYLEAGUE PASSAGE TOMB

This hilltop Neolithic grave is similar in style to tombs in Brittany and lovely in late afternoon light – despite the rising forestry, last cut in 2006. According to its alternative name, this is Diarmuid and Gráinne's bed, but according to local legend it is the burial place of an ancient king of Munster. A loop around the hill takes in a heather-clad cairn (52.4064, -8.3224) and views to the Galty Mountains to the south. Small parking area and a steady uphill track.

30 mins, 52.4070, -8.3248

25 BARNAGH TUNNEL & GREENWAY HUB

This access point with a car park, cycle hire and café is next to the Barnagh tunnel and the dramatic rock cutting to the W of it, hung with verdant vegetation. In the other direction it's a short ride to cast-iron Ferguson's viaduct (52.4337, -9.1305) for those who love industrial heritage. Entrance from the N21.

5 mins, 52.4197, -9.1332

HILLTOPS & VIEWPOINTS

26 KNOCKFIERNA & FAMINE HOUSE

The name means 'Hill of Truth', and it is steeped in the local folklore of Donn Fírinne, an otherworldly phantom horseman who brought thunder and lightning. There are panoramic views of Limerick and beyond from the cross-topped cairn at the summit, and other monuments on the slopes, including famine cottages and a sweathouse at the

21

24

25

26

35

43

44

bottom, ringforts, and a cave. A determined local heritage society look after the paths and gather in the house at the start of the walk for 'rambling house' music and storytelling.

50 mins, 52.4722, -8.8350

27 SEEFIN, BALLYHOURA TRAILS

Climb up to the cairns at the top of Seefin (528m) with huge views around; you could even continue on the Ballyhoura Way to Carron summit 4km W. There are forestry trails set up for mountain biking from the large car park and visitor centre (52.3187, -8.5067), but also the walker only route, and it is possible to join the summit trail further up by pulling off the lane at 52.3349, -8.5296 and approaching from the N (3km). Otherwise join the fun and hire a bike at the centre.

60 mins, 52.3128, -8.5215

28 CARRAIG AILLE RINGFORTS & LOUGH

On a hilltop above Lough Gur, these two medieval cashels are missed by many. Sit on the wide, low walls, take in the huge views in all directions, maybe bring a picnic. Gate in field corner to NE. Pull onto verge by gate with sign just below. 800m further along the lane is pretty Lough Gur and with lakeside paths and picnic areas, and a wooded island crannog.

2 mins, 52.5166, -8.5115

ANCIENT FOREST

29 THE KNIGHT'S WALK, GLIN

A mostly looped trail through the oaks and beeches of Rook Hall Wood and flower-filled fields to the Cailín Bán viewpoint, with a panoramic view into three counties, before descending under majestic beech, oak, ash, and holly in Furry Hill woodland. Gravelled path, but walking shoes recommended. Map board at car park by the gatelodge to Glin Castle.

120 mins, 52.5688, -9.2865

30 TULLIG WOOD, LIMERICK GREENWAY

The native oak, ash, and elm here are home to willow warblers and chiffchaffs, badgers, and butterflies. Small parking at 52.3865, -9.2181 to the W. This is perhaps the wildest stretch of the old railway line Greenway.

10 mins, 52.3864, -9.2105

31 FOYNES WOOD & FLYING BOAT MUSEUM

Trails through native woodlands, including oak, ash, and hazel above a beautiful pebble beach and rocky foreshore with herons, swans, and cormorants. Layby parking and entrance on N69. This area played a key role in early aviation history as a hub for transatlantic flying boats in the 1930s and 1940s, and the Foynes Flying Boat & Maritime Museum just 1km E has the world's only full-size replica of a B314 flying boat (€14, 52.6115, -9.1098).

2 mins, 52.6138, -9.1259

32 CURRAGHCHASE FOREST PARK

Surrounding the ruins of the grand house where poet Aubrey de Vere lived until his death in 1902, this old country estate is now public. Sweeping parklands, old oaks, a pet cemetery, an arboretum of venerable specimen trees, plus hawfinches, horseshoe bats, and waterfowl.

5 mins, 52.5897, -8.8710

WILDLIFE WONDERS

33 COONAGH NATURE RESERVE

This estuary wetland is a fine place for waterfowl, winter starling murmurations and flocks of swans, and birds of prey like merlins, kestrels, and sparrowhawks. It is an old settlement pond, so bits of infrastructure lie in the undergrowth. Take Coonagh Road from the R445 to Coonagh Upper and follow the track between the houses, L of V94 P6WA, to a sliding steel gate and an intercom system; buzz to be let through and pass under motorway.

5 mins, 52.6597, -8.6978

LOCAL BARS & TREATS

34 THE THATCH BAR

Picture-perfect old fashioned thatched bar by the roadside, with a good chance of music. Castleroberts, Adare, V94 H298,+353 87 2942926

52.5466, -8.7516

35 TREATY CITY BREWERY

As well as eye-catching specials, this craft brewery has a core range honed to perfection; they might just make the best red ale in Ireland. This is their showhouse, with a cosy, eclectic taproom and brewing tours. Toasties from the bar for soakage. 24/25 Nicholas Street, V94 EH57, +353 87 1405560. The other great place for local brews is Mother Mac's, 9 High Street, V94 W8XF.

52.6694, -8.6240

36 THE MILK MARKET

Go to this Saturday morning market hungry, there will be plenty of savoury and sweet options as well as great produce to stock up on. Try the Turkish coffee made in a hot-sand brazier, it's always a wait, but fun to watch. Cornmarket Row, coffee is by V94 T6X0. On a Friday, Castletroy has a farmers' market 10.00am–2.00pm near V94 H029, +353 85 1319437.

52.6636, -8.6220

ORGANIC & GASTRO

37 1826 ADARE

Top notch modern cooking in an old thatched cottage. Church View, Blackabbey, Adare, V94 R672, +353 61 396004

52.5646, -8.7875

38 THE OAK ROOM AT ADARE MANOR

As it says, an imposing oak-panelled room in the even more impressive architecture of Adare Manor. The Michelin-starred menu celebrates Irish produce; one to consider for a special occasion. Adare, V94 W8WR, +353 61 605200

52.5637, -8.7779

WOODLAND CAMPING

39 CURRAGHCHASE CARAVAN & CAMPING

Summer campsite with gravelled pitches under the trees for vans and an open lawned area. Should reopen in 2025 under new management with better facilities and the same relaxed atmosphere, café, and quirky playground. Check for updates. Kilcornan, V94 KP8H, coillte.ie

52.5925, -8.8782

40 CROKERS FARM

This small, secluded woodland site is on a working farm and only takes campervans/tourers. It offers seasonal produce, fresh eggs and honey for sale, cricket at weekends, and a quiet rural experience. Ballinagarde, V94 Y793, +353 86 3698918

52.5844, -8.5705

RUSTIC RETREATS

41 BEAGH CASTLE COTTAGES

A terrace of five 300-year-old cottages, recently restored from dereliction. Originally soldiers' houses, they lie below a castle on the Shannon estuary by a pier to swim from and a tiny coffee shop. V94 6X06, +353 12 018440

52.6606, -8.9492

42 THE MUSTARD SEED

Quirky and elegant country house hotel, with fine gardens including their own working kitchen garden to supply the restaurant. Ballingarry, V94 EHN8, +353 69 68508

52.4753, -8.8669

43 ADARE IRISH COTTAGES

Two restored old cottages, one thatched, offering a peaceful retreat on a farm. Sleeping 4 or 5 and listed on Airbnb, they have fires as well as modern heating and outside spaces. Knockanes, V94 WK0Y, adareirishcottages.com

52.5628, -8.7575

44 NEW THATCH FARM

Cosy, romantic restored cottage with whitewashed walls, vintage furniture and real fires. Knocklong, V35 ET28, +353 86 8352998

52.4263, -8.3689

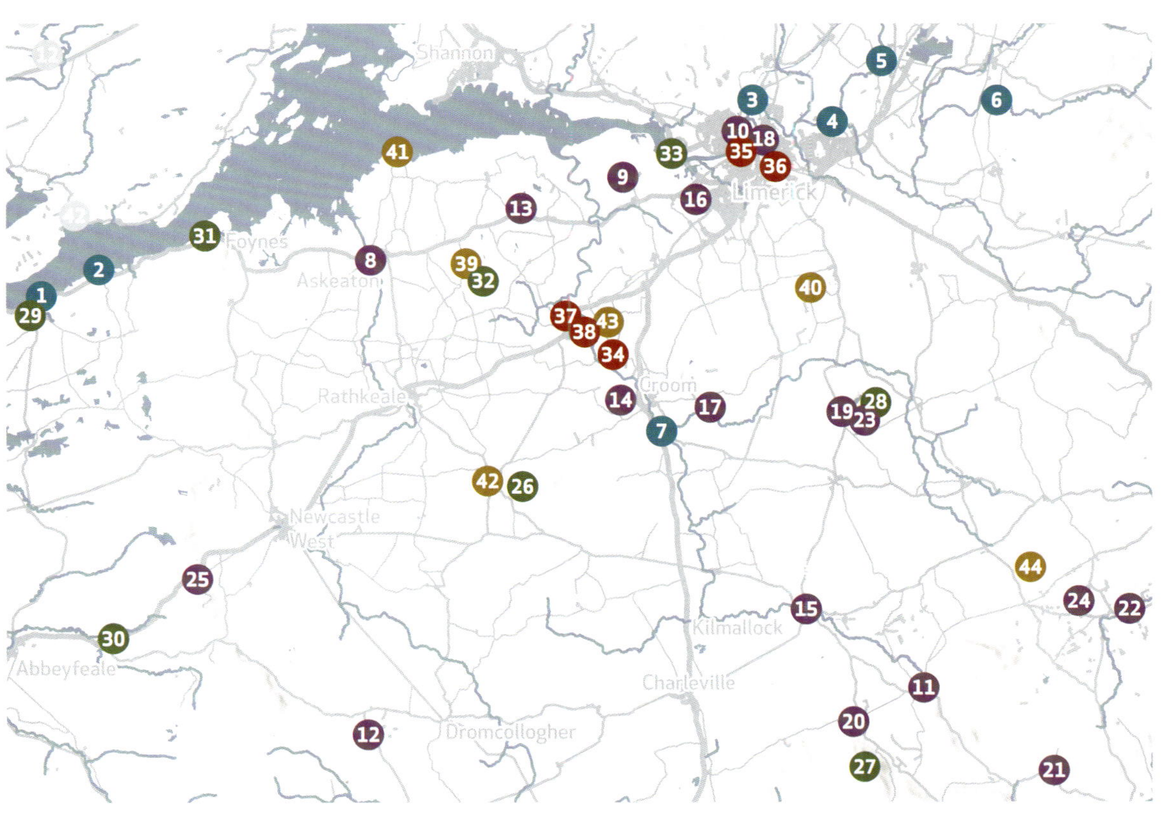

NORTH KERRY & DINGLE

Our perfect weekend

- → **Hike** up to Loch an Mhónáin to bathe beneath the peaks of Mount Brandon then dip in the torrents of the wild Owenmore river in the valley below.
- → **Choose** any one of the many dune-backed north coast beaches on which to park for the night, after wood-fired pizza at Gregory's Garden.
- → **Enter** the vast sea caverns of Nun's Bay then wild camp at remote Cashen or Kilmore beaches.
- → **Gaze** out where Luke Skywalker saw his last sunset, swim at Béal Bán and wild camp at dramatic Sybil Head.
- → **Raise** a glass to Antarctic hero Tom Crean at his own South Pole Inn in Annascaul, and pick up excellent black pudding at Ashe's.
- → **Explore** the many curiosities of Kilmalkedar, from a vast bullaun boulder to a medieval sundial at the beautiful church.
- → **Jump** from Meenogahane Pier at high tide and explore the cliffs for caves and a blowhole.
- → **Marvel** at coastal Carrigafoyle Castle, ripped open by cannon fire, then head to Lislaughtin Abbey, sacked by the same troops.

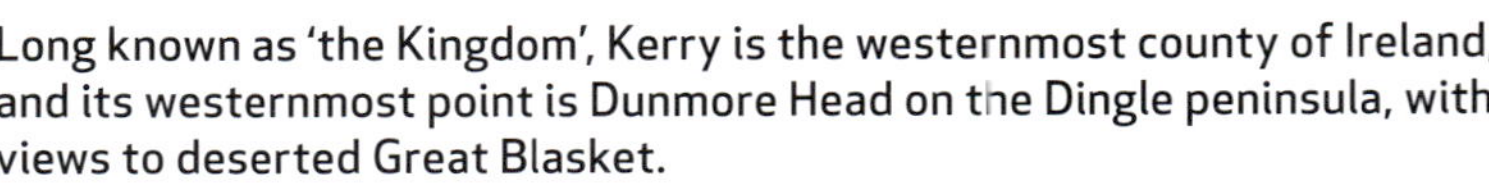

Long known as 'the Kingdom', Kerry is the westernmost county of Ireland, and its westernmost point is Dunmore Head on the Dingle peninsula, with views to deserted Great Blasket.

This is perhaps where modern Irish tourism started: when a movie production team arrived in 1969 to film Ryan's Daughter they put millions into the local economy, employing everyone from masons who built a new village to child extras who sat in its schoolhouse. The locals never looked back, and still welcome film crews like those for Star Wars Episode VIII.

The sandy beaches and coastal villages of the peninsula are popular with families, and everyone drives the high, twisting Conor Pass (go early or late to avoid meeting buses), now part of one of Ireland's newest national parks. Colourful Dingle town, in the Gaeltacht west, has great food and there is no better place to experience traditional festivals.

But there are still wilder, emptier locations. You can climb to the summit of Brandon and look down on the 'paternoster' lakes, linked by braided streams like the beads of a rosary, or look down on Caherconree scenic pass from the promontory fort above. There are oratories other than Gallarus, remote rock art panels, and even some hidden beaches.

The eastern region is sometimes overlooked, and perhaps best known for the Rose of Tralee festival and Listowel Writers' Week. It lies between the two meandering estuaries of the Shannon and the Lee, which have given the coast the bird-rich sands of Beale Point and the beautiful but fragile Fenit Island tombolo. Between these two are long west-facing strands that are perfect for sunsets but often popular, like Ballybunion and Ballyheigue. Banna Strand, famous in Ireland for its place in the 1916 Rising, has some deserted stretches.

Away from the coast the land is flat, with farmland and bog rising to the Mullaghareirk Mountains, an area protected for birdlife. This landscape is where Kerry produces over 12% of Ireland's wind energy, and historically has less to draw visitors. But you can still find rivers to swim, and ruined castles and old abbeys, sometimes with entwined histories. There are plans to link the Tralee to Fenit Greenway to the Listowel to Abbeyfeale (in full the Listowel to Limerick) Greenway, opening up new options for green travellers through a green landscape.

6

SECRET BEACHES

1 LITTOR & BEALE STRANDS

Vast, empty golden sands with shallow pools at low tide. The resident population of bottlenose dolphins will swim by if you're lucky, and there are oystercatchers, sandpipers, curlews, dunlins and migrating Brent geese. Signed opp shop from the WAW L1000 Beale road, ending in narrow lane parking, or park on beach. Beale Strand is easier, and best for birds and overnights, signed 2km further W up a rough track (52.5770, -9.6031). Another 2km along is Beale Point with a medium, free car park (52.5740, -9.6312), but with less sand and dangerous swimming.

2 mins, 52.5734, -9.5798

2 CASHEN BEACH

Vast sands and dunes, with a small tidal pool at the river mouth. Park at River Feale car park (52.4868, -9.6762) and walk along the foreshore W. Watch out for currents and rips at the river mouth.

15 mins, 52.4835, -9.6877

3 KILMORE BEACH

Lovely sands below low cliffs, but currents from river outflow and a shallow rocky shelf are dangerous, so caution is needed. Also the small road gets busy in season; come down in the evening to enjoy a sunset after others leave.

2 mins, 52.4794, -9.6960

4 MEENOGAHANE PIER

Beautiful little harbour with massive sea stack in the middle, known locally as the Horricles. At HT you can jump from the wall. Even with wild offshore wind, the surface of the water is fairly protected. On calm days, kayak or paddle board to explore the coastline with sea arches, blowhole and caves, and you can walk E to Poll a' Taraibh blowhole.

2 mins, 52.4486, -9.7705

5 BANNA & CARRAHANE STRAND

Vast sandy beach, backed by dunes with views across Tralee Bay to Dingle's peaks. Sir Roger Casement landed here in 1916 in a failed attempt to bring German arms for the Irish rebellion (the ringfort where he was arrested is inland, 52.3199, -9.8019). There's a main car park, but this rough parking in the dunes is much quieter. Or 500m S is rough parking for Carrahane strand and lagoon, even wilder (52.3236, -9.8419). Height barriers on both.

2 mins, 52.3306, -9.8372

6 CAMP BEACH & KILGOBBIN

The far W end of more popular Derrymore Strand, this is properly Trá Bhun Abha. There's a small rough parking area just beyond the farm, lots of sand and a little stream. It's relatively sheltered so good for swimming. There's also access and some parking at Kilgobbin Church, 1km W, although the beach is rockier there (52.2306, -9.9171). The Junction Bar on the N86 has great food and good views (V92 D277, +353 66 7130120).

2 mins, 52.2288, -9.9016

7 CARRIGAHA BEACH, AUGHACASLA

There are several tiny unsigned lanes ending with a little parking on the remote sandy shores E of Aughacasla Strand. This is good for overnight, as is another at 52.2358, -9.9646. Further along, Castlegregory has an unsigned secret section to the E of the main sands where people overnight in the dunes down a short sandy track (52.2492, -9.9986).

2 mins, 52.2315, -9.9543

8 MAHAREES BEACH & FAHAMORE

This whole side of the peninsula is another long sweep of beach popular with surfers, with several access points down sandy lanes. There's naomhóg racing (a local type of currach) on most summer evenings. The far

N end has a barrel sauna near the car park (brandonbaysauna.com) and Spillane's Bar with good food and often music (Fahamore, V92 PX93, +353 66 7139125).

2 mins, 52.2892, -10.0313

9 BRANDON BAY BEACHES

Vast golden sands with a wild feel, perfect for swimming, surfing, horse riding and camping, and several named stretches. You can drive onto the beach here, or park behind the dunes, signed Fermoyle. There are other even quieter access tracks E along the road: park on the beach signed Kilcummin Strand (52.2447, -10.1018), or our favourite Ballinknockane, signed simply Trá (52.2479, -10.0855), or beyond the golf club signed Stradbally Strand (52.2549, -10.0701).

2 mins, 52.2435, -10.1246

10 CAPPAGH BEACH & BALLYQUIN

Perfect little cove, E facing so sheltered from swell, but on the estuary mouth so watch for currents. Signed off R550; park on corner or drive onto beach. Good for overnights. Another option, with good parking for overnights in the dunes, is down tiny unsigned lanes 2km N at Ballyquin (52.2628, -10.1582).

2 mins, 52.2494, -10.1613

11 WINE STRAND & BÉAL BÁN

The lane ends on a low grassy headland, the remnant of an ancient graveyard exposed by a storm in the 18th century, with an ogham stone (52.1789, -10.3816) – seven more, including two cigar-shaped river boulders, were taken to a country house (now Coláiste Íde boarding school) and can be visited (52.1268, -10.3063). There's some parking and a slipway, and a lovely popular sheltered cove on the E side. We prefer the beach to the W: ignore Wine Strand turn, continuing straight for rough parking behind the dunes (52.1780, -10.3886) and a 1km sweep called Béal Bán. This has a small car park at 52.1793, -10.4054, good for overnights. Beyond this is another slipway below Dún an Óir, carrying low remains of a bastion hastily built in 1580, where 600 died in a rebellion (52.1901, -10.4149).

2 mins, 52.1791, -10.3864

12 VENTRY BAY

Vast, sheltered and very quiet sands; Cuan Fionntra in Irish, with rough parking behind the dunes or the tarmac car park 700m S at 52.1217, -10.3773, signed burial ground from the R559.

2 mins, 52.1271, -10.3747

13 TRABEG, DOONSHEAN BEACH

Lovely remote beach down a honeysuckle and blackberry-filled lane. At LT walk R around the headland and you can swim off the white sand facing the open bay, but don't try to swim from the sand facing the far bank in the estuary at HT, there is a strong sideways rip. Look up to the right to see a substantial fosse cutting off the further Doonshean headland, a promontory fort.

2 mins, 52.1253, -10.2169

14 MINARD BEACH

This short, sheltered cove, with cobble at the top and sand below at lower tides, is missed by many. Lovely with the sun in the west sinking behind 16th-century Minard Castle, rendered a ruin by Cromwellian attack; visit pretty stone-lined Tóbar Eoin holy well signed off the lane just W (52.1258, -10.1116). Parking at E end and along verge.

2 mins, 52.1265, -10.1092

SEA CAVES & COASTEERING

15 NUN'S BEACH, BALLYBUNION

Dramatic LT sands with a sensational sea cavern to explore, enclosed by a horseshoe of striated cliffs and a stack with an arch, known as the Virgin Rock (there was once a convent above the bay). Park at end of Nun's Beach Road (52.5195, -9.6746). Follow path S 400 beyond the buildings and climb fence to find a rough path down ending with a short, steep, slippery mudstone section, with rope. You can explore the headland with ruined Ballybunion Castle and Nine Daughters blowhole above this as part of the short Ballybunion Cliff Walk from the main Ballybunion beach 200m S, which has seaweed baths and cliff caves.

20 mins, 52.5170, -9.6777

16 FENIT DIVING BOARDS & TOMBOLO

There's a plan to reinstate diving boards at this high-tide bathing quay, on a headland with views to the lighthouse and Slieve Mish. Walk 800m W from parking at the pier, along Fenit beach (with barrel sauna, fenitlighthousesauna.ie). Just N on the through road is Fenit Island tombolo (52.2806, -9.8725), a fragile thread of dune with double white beaches, for a circular walk (or overnight). Stay on the sand and respect the fencing, as it protects vital new plantings. Go dolphin spotting with Tralee Bay Experience (+353 86 3048650) or coasteering/sea kayaking with Wild Water Adventures (+353 87 9101290, wildwateradventures.ie). Recharge with excellent coffee at Mike's Beach Shop (V92 NX58) or local seafood at the West End (V92 X8EK, +353 66 7136246). A new Greenway from Tralee leads to all this (try traleebikerental.ie).

8 mins, 52.2741, -9.8741

TINY ISLANDS

17 GREAT BLASKET

The deserted village looking across the sound is the main focus of day trips to the island; although this lies just 1km from the mainland, it might as well have been in the mid-Atlantic in some winters. Ferries leave from tiny Dunquin Pier (buy tickets at blasketislandferry.com €50). OPW guides lead free tours. There is also a beach to the N along this shore (52.1077, -10.5142) where seals haul out; stay well back if they are there. If the beach is empty, you can walk on it, but the OPW bans swimming anywhere from the island; the currents are treacherous. If you have a long day, you could walk W to the An Cró Mór summit (52.0868, -10.5601) with spectacular views and a trig point; see if you can find any trace of the EIRE pilot's marker on the lower summit on the way (52.0977, -10.5240). But the boats don't wait, so keep an eye on the time; the hike takes about four hours. Even the trip over is an adventure, starting from a harbour down a twisting path (52.1242, -10.4605) and landing in inflatables because there is no harbour on the island. There are no facilities of any kind there – the summer café does not always open – so bring everything you will need. Before going, it's worth visiting the excellent Blasket Centre / Ionad an Bhlascaoid Mhor to learn about island life (V92 TH73, +353 66 9156444).

10 mins, 52.1044, -10.5118

18 CARRIG ISLAND

Walk over the beach causeway to this estuarine island of neat fields. At the far W tip is a Napoleonic battery fortress which can be entered, more beach and low rock ledges to jump from (52.5790, -9.5100). Follow sign to Carrig Island East (perhaps from the higher paved causeway at 52.5708, -9.4968) to reach a pebble beach with rough parking, perfect for swimming and overnights.

2 mins, 52.5720, -9.5025

RIVER & LAKE SWIMS

19 RIVER FEALE RAILWAY BRIDGE

You can swim in the Feale almost anywhere you can get access. There might be anglers: it is famed as a sea trout and salmon river, but only fished in spate. This is a good corner pool, upstream of the old railway bridge. Park on the verge just SE, at the stone bridge on R557 (52.4201, -9.5626), and take the bankside track 100m. Another option is the ruined Dysert church nearby at 52.4355, -9.5985.

2 mins, 52.4215, -9.5673

20 ANNASCAUL LAKE

Beautifully set in a scoop of glacial valley, this lake at the end of a narrow road has a small parking area and lone picnic table. There may be anglers, but there is plenty of shore. Walk on up the valley (the road gives out) 1.5km for falls tumbling down the end; the hills themselves are a moderately serious scramble.

2 mins, 52.1799, -10.0731

21 LOCH AN DÚIN/ADOON

Follow the new waymarked path across streams and stepping stones to reach this beautiful lough, below mountains and waterfalls. It's 2.5km and very boggy in places, wellies advised. Layby parking opp kissing gate on R560 at 52.2126, -10.1621.

30 mins, 52.1937, -10.1480

22 RIVER OWENMORE, CLOGHANE

Find sandy river beaches with meanders and deep pools on an exquisite wild river; this and the Conor Pass above are included in the new Kerry Marine National Park. Take unsigned lane off R550 at Cloghane, take first L to park at 52.2203, -10.1857; follow the track 350m E to the river and upstream over a footbridge. Afterwards, refresh at O'Connors in Cloghane (V92 PV48, +35 66 7138113), a properly old-school pub and inn, brightly coloured outside and woody inside with a real fire and pieces of the Luftwaffe plane that crashed on Brandon Mountain (see entry).

7 mins, 52.2190, -10.1814

22

27

29

30

31

23 LOUGH DOON/PEDLAR & CONOR PASS

This glacial tarn in a spectacular cliff bowl is highly popular with tourists, but it is a rather amazing swim if you are driving the famed Conor Pass and don't mind company. Also called Loch an Pheidleara or Pedlar's Lake, it is sunniest in the afternoon. Parking area directly below, by a small waterfall.

5 mins, 52.1860, -10.1890

24 LOCH AN MHÓNÁIN & SOUTH BRANDON

This dramatic lake, anglicised as Lough Avoonane, is sheltered by sheer mountains with a waterfall tumbling down. It's one of the most accessible of the Brandon lakes and well worth the short hike up. Park sensibly on the verge near the junction to the farm (52.2075, -10.2083). Walk up through the farmyard – the brothers are very friendly, so you could ask as a courtesy. A good track leads up 700m. Serious mountain walkers do the whole horseshoe around the lake, taking in Gearhane (803m) and Brandon Peak (840m).

25 mins, 52.2098, -10.2212

LOST RUINS

25 LISLAUGHTIN ABBEY & PIER

This ruined Franciscan house was built at the same time as Carrigafoyle Castle (see entry), funded by the same family, and sacked by the same soldiers who destroyed the castle; a lovely tracery window remains. Parking by gate. Just 500m away is quiet Saleen Pier, once a commercial port, now good for jumps at HT or birdlife at LT (52.5607, -9.4671), and a 1.3km track over the mudflats to empty Kilcolgan Lower beach (52.5698, -9.4667); both have views to the castle.

2 mins, 52.5573, -9.4698

26 LARTIGUE MONORAIL

The only small railway in the county of Kerry – and the only train at all, save the one line into Tralee – is this French-designed raised monorail, with carriages balanced like panniers either side of the rail. The only one of its kind in the world, it ran between Listowel and Ballybunion 1888–1924, despite being intended for desert sands. The shortest and maybe strangest train ride you'll ever take, plus a small museum of memorabilia and equipment in an old goods shed; volunteer run, with parking. Open daily 1.00–4.30pm (last train 4.00pm) May to Sept. €8/€4 adult/child. John B Keane Road, Listowel, V31 HX00, +353 68 24393.

1 min, 52.4496, -9.4904

27 CARRIGAFOYLE CASTLE

Once the 'Guardian of the Shannon' for its position on the shipping lanes into Limerick city, this robust 24m tower from 1490 is almost in the water, but stable, with daily access. Built around 1490, it met its end in 1580 when possibly the first use of cannon in Kerry collapsed the west wall, crushing many inside. Today it is like looking into a cutaway illustration of a castle. The square tower on the end of the remaining outer wall was used as a dovecote, and there is a ruined church of about the same date in a field over the road, accessible (52.5698, -9.4961), and a battery on Carrig Island (see entry).

2 mins, 52.5698, -9.4941

28 RAHINNANE CASTLE

Rugged walls of a 15th-century tower house built on a bivallate ringfort and souterrain, with commanding views of Ventry Harbour. Once a stronghold of the powerful FitzGeralds, who also built the tower house at Minard Beach (see entry), it was destroyed by Cromwell's forces around 1650. Reached through the farm S, owners allow access and ask for €2 in the honesty bucket for parking by the stone barns.

2 mins, 52.1413, -10.3823

29 RYAN'S DAUGHTER SCHOOLHOUSE

The ruined schoolhouse at this Blasket viewpoint feels historical, but is a leftover movie set built in 1969 for Ryan's Daughter, like the whole village seen in the film. Only this building was left standing after. Park at the track entrance (52.1371, -10.4625, just room for one), and continue up track 700m, or park at the Blasket Centre (€2, see Great Blasket entry) and walk 700m N.

15 mins, 52.1365, -10.4680

SACRED & ANCIENT

30 RATTOO CHURCH & ROUND TOWER

Recently conserved, amid rural fields under a vast sky. The 27m round tower is one of the finest, built of yellow sandstone on a limestone plinth, with a cap restored in the 1880s, when a sheela na gig was discovered on the inner face of the north window. It is the only sheela known in a round tower. The medieval church is believed to have used stones from an earlier church; it has strange levels inside because of a huge tomb vault. Above this is a superb double ogee window, and an old stone font is cemented into the S window. Another church building can be seen to the E, but inaccessible on private land.

2 mins, 52.4426, -9.6501

31 TOBAR NA MOLT/WETHERS WELL

Beautiful holy well with steps down to a large, deep 2m pool, a wellhouse, an ancient altar used in Penal times, and an inscribed tomb. The water is said to cure all ailments, whether drunk, bathed in or taken away. Signed path

in from lane to S, 500m, but very narrow parking (52.3209, -9.7322).
10 mins, 52.3234, -9.7329

32 ARDFERT FRIARY

Plenty of detail is left here including a tower and lovely covered section of cloister, lancet and tracery windows, and ornate tomb niches. Workmen reported a sheela na gig 'fairly high' on the W wall of the tower in 1980; try your eye. After its religious life it was fortified as barracks and then preserved as an 'eyecatcher' for the country estate of Ardfert House. Car park by cemetery to NW. Ardfert Cathedral in the village (52.3287, -9.7817) has some similar features, plus a smaller church with carved griffins and a grotesque head.
2 mins, 52.3301, -9.7739

33 BALLINVOHER BURIAL GROUND

Set in a lovely valley on little lanes, this peaceful old graveyard has a lonely feel. It is packed with raised tombs; the medieval church that once stood in it was demolished two centuries ago and its stone used to build the vaults. Among them, seek out two cross-marked ogham stones: one about 1m high standing against the side of a modern tomb near the E wall, the other about 1.3m long lying flat beside one about 14m from the W wall. Space for a car at the gate.
2 mins, 52.1685, -10.0281

34 AGHACARRIBLE ROCK ART *

This large boulder has at least 40 cups plus some cup-and-ring marks. Once obscured in a field wall, it is now by a farmyard drive. It should be OK to pull up in the yard for the short time you will be there; if in doubt ask at farm across road. Nearby at Ardamore is a row of three flat stones aligned with the winter solstice sunset (52.1326, -10.1587) and a rounded, cup-marked outlier. A track in from 52.1303, -10.1561 with 'beware of the bull' sign passes the row without entering fields, but ask at the farm to the W if they are in (52.1308, -10.1628).
2 mins, 52.1292, -10.1734

35 TEAMPALL GEAL

This dry stone boat-shaped oratory on the SE side of Lateevemore Hill overlooks Dingle Harbour, and the Skelligs to the W. It has various names: Temple Geal means bright church, and it was also dedicated to St Mancháin or Managhan; the cross pillar with an ogham inscription is traditionally believed to mark his grave (fenced to protect from livestock); there are several other cross-inscribed slabs and boulders. Other recorded features nearby, now invisible, are a holy well and a souterrain. Park by farm at end of road (52.1528, -10.3293), walk up track and through gate L.
8 mins, 52.1545, -10.3312

36 KILMALKEDAR COMPLEX

There is an incredible cluster of sacred and ancient sites in this valley bottom, all along a bend in the country lane that is on the Cosán na Naomh pilgrim path. The 12th-century church is thought to be modelled on Cormac's Chapel at Cashel, with high-quality Romanesque stonework doorways. Look for the alphabet stone inside, with the Latin alphabet in 6th-century script, and scrolled crosses. There is also a holed ogham stone outside, and a vertical sundial with a hole for a separate gnomon, and the grave markers include two rare Tau crosses. The church sits between two holy wells, one marked by a cross slab in a field across the road (52.1842, -10.3375), the other a spring in front of the medieval house ruin up the track (52.1855, -10.3363). In a field just around the bend is the more ancient Keelers, a vast boulder with seven large bullauns in the upper surface, like big salad bowls; keelers were cooking vessels (52.1855, -10.33823). There's another bullaun stone in the hedge opposite the gate. And a short walk further on the lane is a path to St. Brendan's Oratory (Teampaillín Breanainn, 52.1867, -10.3410), a corbelled drystone oratory like the famous Gallarus. It isn't in such good shape, being open at the top, but still the feeling of retreat within is powerful. If all this isn't enough, on the road down you pass the ruins of the medieval diocesan chancellor's house (52.1818, -10.33819) and Caherdorgan

cashel (see entry). Park in the lane by the church or easier outside the cemetery L before the oratory.
2 mins, 52.1847, -10.3362

37 CAHERDORGAN STONE FORT

If you drive the Ring of Kerry, you will find several clochán or beehive hut sites signed near Slea Head along the S coast; they all have their merits, and they also all have charges and plenty of other people exploring. But this great example is a National Monument that you can wander around for free and often alone, an impressive circular cashel in a sloping field with broad views down to Smerwick Harbour. Inside

36

36

37

39

the rampart are the substantial remains of five corbelled clocháns, and a souterrain entrance at the base of the wall. There is no car park, just pull in tight at the field gate.

2 mins, 52.1792, -10.3395

38 KILCOLMAN CROSS OR MAUMANORIG

Not just one but two crosses, the larger one very striking, and a line of ogham, all inscribed on a boulder. An unusual combination, but even more peculiar, the ogham inscription curves around the large cross, rather than following the usual straight line or corner. It reads ANM COLMAN AILITHER, meaning 'name of Colman the pilgrim'. It lies in a circular early Christian enclosure, inside livestock fencing within a field. The gate is at the N (52.1450, -10.3588), with no forbidding signs, but sometimes livestock.

2 mins, 52.1438, -10.3586

39 RIASC MONASTIC SETTLEMENT

We have no written history for this early Christian site, but the remains are extensive, if low. Inside an oval cashel rampart around 2.2m thick are the remains of a stone oratory, a rectangular building, several clochán, and two other round huts. Excavations found a cemetery with over 42 stone-lined graves and many later cillín graves. Scattered around are cross slabs and pillars, one 1.6m high inscribed with a fine Greek cross in a circle with spiral designs down the shaft. Easy parking.

2 mins, 52.1675, -10.3875

40 AN RAINGILÉIS

The lane clips the edge of this very early Christian burial site, also called Calluragh, with sweeping views; in the recent past it was used as a cillín. There is a ruined building, thought to be an oratory like Gallarus, a mound of stones that marks the location of two leachts or altars, and the top of a cross slab, decorated on both sides but mostly embedded in earth. On the S side of the road to the E of the enclosure is a 1.23m-high plain stone cross, pull off opp.

2 mins, 52.1587, -10.4069

ANCIENT WOODS

41 GLANAGEENTY FOREST

Streamside paths lined with old, twisty, moss-covered hazel, beech and birch, waterfalls and tunnels contrast with tree swings and 'fairy houses' in this Coillte woodland. You might spot ravens, hen harriers, kestrels, pheasants and cranes, or bats at dusk, and wild goats are often seen. The woods were used for refuge in both the Desmond Rebellion and the Irish Civil War; the main loop walk takes you by the site of the Desmond Castle and on via the Raven's Glen waterfall to the ruins of Sean Thaigh Og's cabin.

20 mins, 52.2693, -9.5447

41

42 SCOTIA GRAVE & BALLYSEEDY WOODS

A pretty riverside walk in a wild wooded glen, leading to the grave of the Egyptian princess Scota or Scotia, who gave her name to Scotland – or to a misleading group of rocks, depending on who's telling the story. Take the trail from the lane at 52.2301, -9.7009. Walk SW, then up along the river to the third bridge, about 500m; the stones are within sight of the bridge. For a much larger and more accessible old estate wood, 3km NE are Ballyseedy Woods with ruined house and watermill (car park at 52.2515, -9.6584).

10 mins, 52.2283, -9.7041

HEADLANDS & VIEWPOINTS

43 CAHERCONREE PROMONTORY FORT

This high spur (683m) has steep cliffs for defence, and impressive remains of Iron Age stone ramparts. Said to have been the stronghold of a legendary warrior, Cú Roí mac Daire. From here you can climb the full peak of Caherconree (835m) for even more sensational views, and continue around on the horseshoe to the summit of Baurtregaum peak. There's some parking about halfway up the narrow 'scenic route' mountain lane (52.1881, -9.8773) and a rough trail up the R side of the stream valley, crossing N to the spur. Or simply enjoy the drive through the top of the pass.

100 mins, 52.1975, -9.8621

44 AN SÁIS COAST

Spectacular views down on the 'snare' of An Sáis bay (or Sauce Creek) are 4km cliff walk W from the clifftop Súilóid a tSáis path car park (52.2878, -10.1605), passing bird-rich cliffs and a lookout post. Too steep for casual descent; the last inhabitants left the horseshoe bay after a midwife fell and died on her way to a delivery. The path returns as a loop inland via part of the Dingle Way. Back down the lane are the more accessible red sands of Ballymore Point (pictured), visible from R550; park on

road at 52.2735, -10.1631 and take track 700m, crossing field at end.
120 mins, 52.2724, -10.2104

45 BRANDON MOUNTAIN

You can take the Saint's or the Pilgrim's Path to the Cnoc Breanáinn summit cross, ruined Brendan's Oratory, trig point and spectacular views. The easier path is from the W, some 8km up the smoother side; the end of the medieval Cosán na Naomh or Saint's Path, it's marked with crosses (car park at 52.2146, -10.2914). The 9km Pilgrim's Path up the glacier-scoured E side has views over deep corries and lakes (car park 52.2392, -10.2056). It also passes the site of a 1940 Luftwaffe reconnaissance plane crash (52.2346, -10.2328). Allow a good half day for the 700m ascent, and be aware of rapidly changeable weather here.
180 mins, 52.2345, -10.2542

46 EASK TOWER

Solid stone 19th-century navigation marker, built during famine as work scheme, set above 100m cliffs with super sea views. It's worth paying €2 parking at the little hut on lane (52.1217, -10.2816) just to meet the charming gentleman who even provides water and a brush to clean your shoes on your return.
15 mins, 52.1155, -10.2816

47 SYBIL HEAD & LUKE'S SUNSET

The land at Sybil Head (Ceann Sibéal) rears up dramatically to pointy knife-edge cliffs with views to the Blaskets. There's a derelict lookout here, precarious on the edge and possibly incorporating the original 1804 signal tower, a superb spot for sunsets or campouts. Park on verge before last house (52.1797, -10.4491) at Ballyoughteragh South, just beyond Ferriter's Cove. Walk 1km up on farm track through fields. A more famous sunset point is 2km NE along the coast, where Luke Skywalker watched his last binary sunset in Star Wars Episode VIII. Walk up the coast and back on lanes in a loop, or park in the car park at 52.1870, -10.4292 and walk 700m (well signed, donations).
30 mins, 52.1834, -10.4650

48 DEVIL'S HORNS & DUNQUIN PIER

Walk out to a dramatic view of conical rocks from the westernmost mainland point of Europe. On the way you can pass Coumeenoole ogham stone (52.1101, -10.4738) and a lookout post (52.1101, -10.4736). Park at the large car park (Slea Head, 52.1098, -10.4656) above Coumeenoole Beach, a beautiful, popular strand with views to the islands. Also, 2km N on coast road, is Dunquin Pier (52.1255, -10.4599) for Great Blasket (see entry). Its steep track down is well worth walking for the views (pictured).
20 mins, 52.1093, -10.4787

WILDLIFE WONDERS

49 LOUGH GILL, CASTLEGREGORY

This shallow lake is a vital habitat for Ireland's only native toad, the natterjack, with about two thirds of the breeding population. It is also a great place to watch birds, the E end in particular. From late autumn to early spring look for swans (this is one of the few places where you can see whooper, mute and Bewick swans), and ducks like scaup, teal and wigeon; in summer, there are reed buntings and sedge warblers. Small parking area, big serene waters.
2 mins, 52.2617, -10.0309

43

45

47

50 DINGLE HORSE RIDING

There are few better ways to see the sweeping landscapes of Dingle than from the saddle on a half-day ride over the hills. This family-run stable also offers beach rides, and can even arrange multi-day treks with overnight stays. Ballinaboula, Dingle, V92 YW94, +353 86 8211225

60 mins, 52.1518, -10.2812

TRADITIONAL PUBS

51 ROUNDY'S BAR, TRALEE

Quirky retro bar, great for cocktails and dog friendly. Now part of The Ashe Hotel, which does vintage afternoon teas. 5 Broguemaker's Lane, Tralee V92 NA46, +353 66 7106300

52.2706, -9.7054

52 SOUTH POLE INN, ANNASCAUL

Drink in a little history with your pint; not many pubs get school trips, but not many were run by Antarctic expedition heroes. Local Tom Crean joined the navy and went on three expeditions with Scott and Shackleton, accomplishing several feats of astounding endurance. In 1920 he came home to renovate this riverside cottage and open it as an inn, rarely talking of his endeavours. Now restored to something like its original look, and with Crean's story in photographs on the walls. Work up a thirst or appetite with a stroll up the hill to his grave (52.1598, -10.0754), and maybe have a beer from the Crean brewery, which you can visit in Kenmare (tomcreanbrewerykenmare.ie). Lower Main St, Annascaul, V92 N220, +353 66 9157388

52.1513, -10.0565

53 MURPHY'S BAR, BRANDON

Right on the seafront with pier, the stone front conceals a cosy, colourful interior with open fire and excellent quality seafood on daily changing menus. Lisnakealwee, Brandon, V92 T680, +353 87 1875635

52.2685, -10.1599

LOCAL PRODUCE

54 THE LITTLE CHEESE SHOP *

Mostly Irish cheeses with a few special continentals. Also charcuterie, condiments, everything that goes with cheese. Grey's Lane, Dingle, V92 X07X, +353 87 7578672

52.1405, -10.2711

55 SPA SEAFOODS

Handy shop for fish, oysters, deli and takeaway. Ballygarron, Spa, Tralee, V92 HC81, +353 66 7136901

52.2753, -9.7826

56 ASHE'S, ANNASCAUL

Three generations have built the reputation of Annascaul Black Pudding here since 1916, using the same traditional cake-baked recipe and fresh local ingredients. Over the years white pudding, dry-cured bacon and excellent pork sausages have joined the range. Since 2021 they've had Báinin café as a neighbour, serving great coffee, locally baked cakes and toasties – including the iconic black pudding. Main Street, Annascaul, V92 FP5P, +353 85 1194749

52.1524, -10.0523

57 MURPHYS ICE CREAM

Local all-natural ice cream with adventurous flavours: brown bread is an Irish classic, but whiskey chocolate, or Dingle gin and pink peppercorn sorbet are pleasant surprises. Strand Street, Dingle, V92 H982, +353 87 1330610

52.1395, -10.2717

58 DINGLE DISTILLERY

Small distillery run by an eclectic and free-spirited crew making whiskey, vodka and gin. The tour of the copper stills and cask maturing process is up-close and entertaining (€24). Dingle, V92 E7YD, +353 21 4355582

52.1418, -10.2891

59 TIG BHRIC TAP BREWERY *

The house pub for West Kerry Brewery is a firm favourite with those looking for something locally made and good. The excellent dark mild is a best seller. Does food to keep you fuelled, and has rooms and a self-catering lodge. Reask, V92 F681

52.1704, -10.3863

ORGANIC & BISTRO

60 LIZZY'S LITTLE KITCHEN

Delicious and healthy dishes, plant-based and all home-cooked from fresh, additive-free ingredients. 40 Church St, Listowel, Co. Kerry, V31 EEOO, +353 87 3907133

52.4467, -9.4843

61 GREGORY'S GARDEN

Top-notch chef who's cooked in some much bigger places, closes in winter. There's also a shipping container with Forge wood-fired pizzas in the garden. 4 Main St, Martramane, Castlegregory, Co. Kerry, V92 N2F7, +353 87 2130866. If in Castlegregory on a summer Sunday, you can find local food and crafts from 10.00am–1.30pm at the market, Community Hall, West Main Street, V92 YT72, +353 87 2984717

52.25489, -10.0224

62 ASHE'S RESTAURANT, DINGLE

A family-run pub, serving pints since it was a drapery and general store in 1849, Ashe's has a homely traditional interior and real fires in winter. The menu is based on local seafood and farm produce, and there are local beers to accompany it. Also has rooms. Main Street, Dingle, V92 X0D7, +353 66 9150989

52.1415, -10.268

63 LAND TO SEA, DINGLE

Fine European style with local provenance, and a particularly well-regarded tasting menu. John St, Farran, Dingle, V92 ET22, +353 66 9152609

52.1415, -10.2681

64 MY BOY BLUE

Very popular modern coffee shop, a great place to go for breakfast burritos and everything on sourdough. Holyground, Dingle, V92 F40F, +353 85 7597156

52.1396, -10.2707

65 BEAN IN DINGLE

Serves and sells locally roasted blends and baked goods, including local specialities like Ashe's black pudding sausage rolls. Also on Plunkett Street in Killarney. Green Street, Dingle, V92 K593, no phone.

52.1409, -10.2709

66 FENTON'S, DINGLE

Bright, modern restaurant with a seafood-based menu and local Dexter beef. Closes in winter. Green Street, Dingle, V92 YA72, +353 66 9152172

52.1400, -10.2715

67 OUT OF THE BLUE, DINGLE

The Blue was a well-kept secret, until it started winning awards. This is a place for true pescatarians, with no chips, nothing deep fried, and fish from local boats landed just over the road: if nothing is landed, the restaurant doesn't open, and it closes in winter. Colourful interior harks back to its seafood shack origins. Waterside, Dingle, V92 T181, +353 66 9150811

52.1393, -10.2754

68 ÉALÚ AT THE STONEHOUSE

This entirely stone house, like an overgrown oratory, is home to a visitor centre and this restaurant showcasing local and artisan producers in modern dishes. Kallam and Clíona started as chocolatiers, but this newer venture has been winning admirers. Fahan, Ceann Trá, V92 YKP5, +353 86 4590071

52.1052, -10.4099

HOSTELS & CAMPSITES

69 SANDY BAY 2, STRADBALLY BEACH

Superbly located beach campsite, perfect for surfers, swimmers and sunset watchers, although more space could be given to those with tents. Magherabeg, Maharees, V92 ED99, +353 876791692 (phone booking only)

52.2827, -10.0284

70 RAINBOW HOSTEL & CAMPING

Very homely – the hostel here is a typical rural bungalow, and the camping field is simply the lawn. No large groups, caravans or electric hook-ups, just all the usual basic kitchen, shower and laundry facilities, and a great family-friendly atmosphere, about 20 minutes walk from Dingle. Ballinaboula, V92 HE95, +353 66 9151044, rainbowhosteldingle.com

52.1474, -10.2891

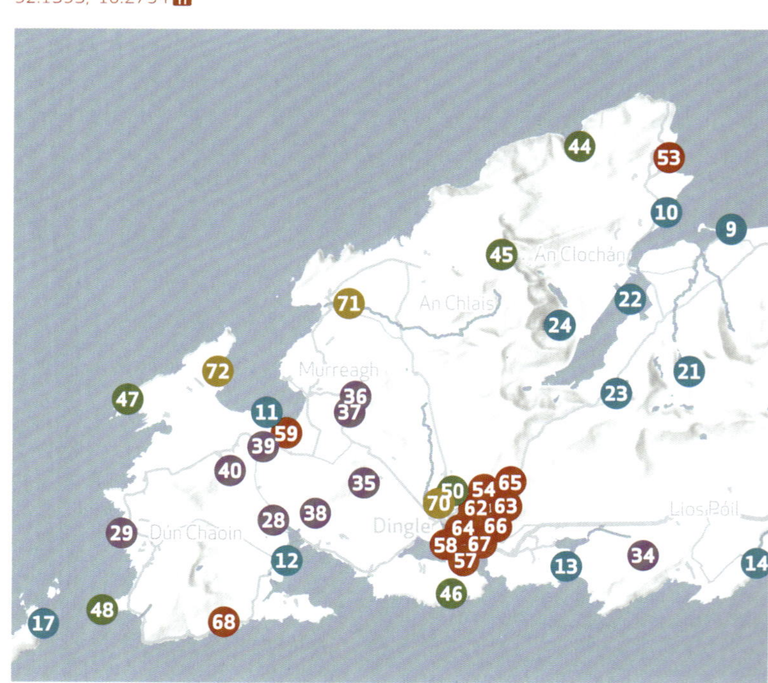

71 AN RIASC BOUTIQUE B&B

This stone-fronted farmhouse was recently built, but looks like it has been in the landscape forever, tucked up a short grassy lane below Mount Brandon just a few hundred metres from the sea. Host Denise Begley keeps four rooms to a high standard, with local artists' work on the walls, eco-friendly products, great showers, and pared-back but cosy furnishings. Breakfasts and light suppers use home-made and local ingredients. Moorestown, Ballydavid, Dingle, V92 Y562, +353 66 9155446

52.2172, -10.3402

72 ATLANTIC BAY REST *

This is a special, family-owned place, with Peter who lovingly renovated it from derelict still living on site. The Bungalow sleeps eight, and there are smaller lodges too, with direct access onto shore rocks and private beach with kayaks, plus sauna, Swedish hot tubs and seaweed baths. Smerwick, V92 RX30, +353 87 1037031, atlanticbayrest.com

52.1933, -10.4141

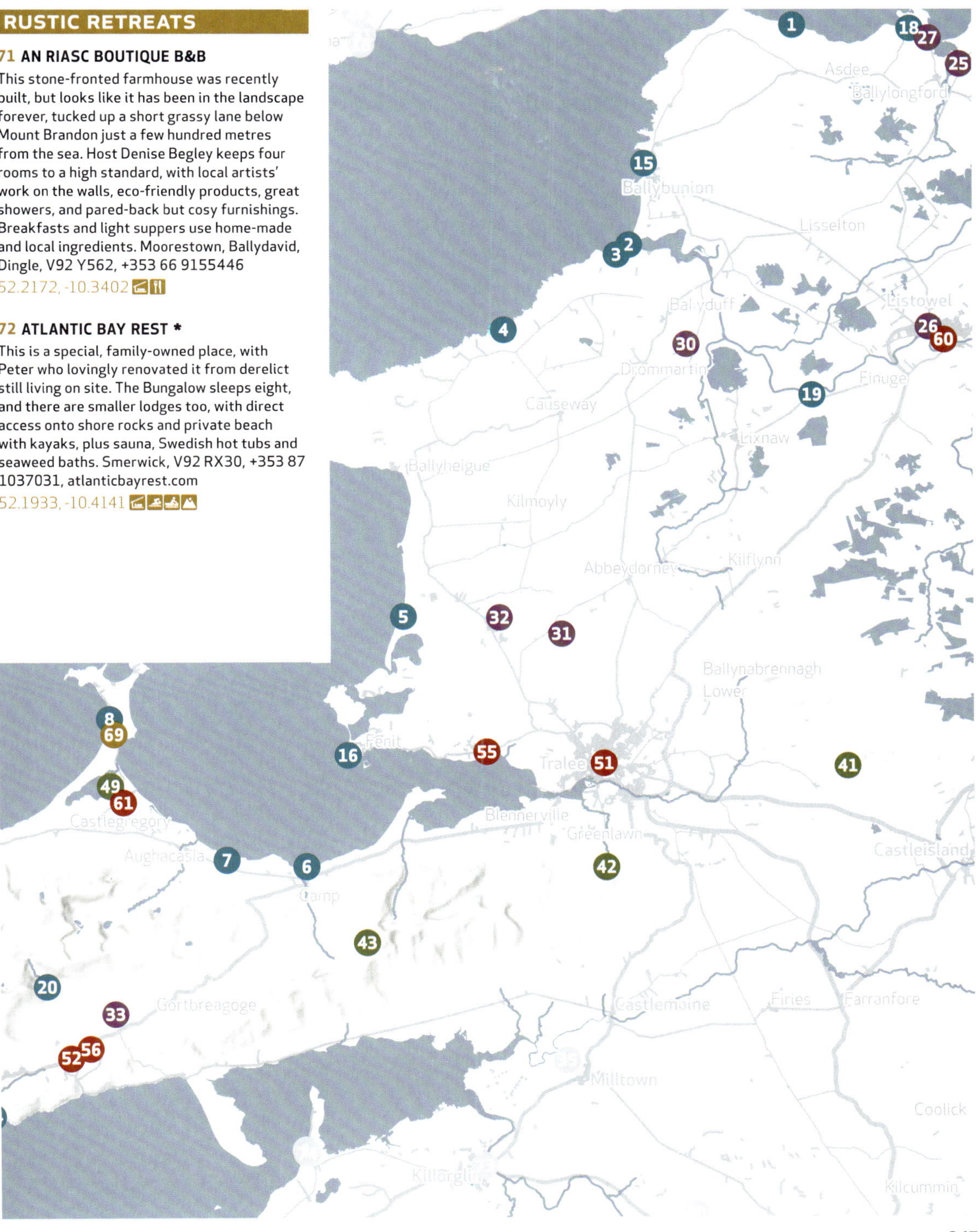

RING OF KERRY & KILLARNEY

Our perfect weekend

- **Camp** at Cronin's Yard for the scramble up Knocknapeasta, with a dip in wild Lough Callee.
- **Climb** the old oaks in Derrycunnihy Woods, and continue on to swim in the lake by Dinis Cottage café or ride the rapids under Old Weir Bridge.
- **Make** a pilgrimage to possibly the oldest surviving Christian shrine in Ireland at Caherlehillan, with an ancient cashel above.
- **Dine** in a church at the Oratory in Caherciveen and spend the night at the legendary local campsite Mannix Point.
- **Visit** Ballinskelligs, the abbey where the Skellig monks settled after leaving the islands, with a seaside castle and sweeping sands.
- **Climb** the stairs inside Staigue cashel's massive walls and peer into the low creepway chambers.
- **Look** out for deer and strawberry trees on the walk to Tower Waterfall, and take a dip in the waters of the Long Range.
- **Explore** the mature woodlands and wetland habitats of Reenagross Woodland Park and feast on local fare at No 35 in Kenmare.

1

3

6

Killarney was perhaps Ireland's first 'tourist' destination, made famous by a visit of Queen Victoria and her family to Muckross House in 1861. It's unlikely that she completed the route around the Iveragh Peninsula now famous as the 'Ring of Kerry', but she and her ladies in waiting stopped at Ladies' View.

The Muckross demesne parkland became the heart of Ireland's first national park, and is worth a pause, with champion trees, ancient yews and the first copper mine beyond the European mainland. There are dippable shores, but the famous lakes are not ideal for swimming, and better explored by boat; to use your own kit, get it power-washed and obtain a free permit in advance (+353 64 6635215). The smaller Long Range and Upper Lake are better, but there is so much lovely coast from wild Reenroe to little coves like Cuas Crom that you're spoiled for choice.

The Ring and the Gap of Dunloe 'scenic drive' give the impression this is a place to stay in the car, and too many people do just that, pausing only for crowded 'highlights'. Even Ballaghbeama Gap is known as a scenic drive; almost nobody ascends the Derrynablaha hillside to the richest collection of rock art in the country.

Those on foot see so much more – literally, from the summit of Carrauntoohil, Ireland's highest mountain, or neighbouring peaks of the MacGillycuddy's Reeks with lakes like Gouragh nestled below them. Everybody visits dramatic Torc Waterfall, but longer walks into lovely Tomies Wood or past the rare strawberry trees of the Killarney forest lead to more solitary cascades.

There are many cashels and clochány here, and those away from the Ring like Leacanabuaile or Cahergal are less visited than those along Slea Head; of course trips to the most famous monastic clochány or the remote Skelligs need to be booked well in advance and can be disrupted by sea swells.

There are other islands much closer: Valentia has a Napoleonic signal tower and cavernous slate quarry, and from its harbour you can get a boat to empty Beginish, with seals and the remnants of a Viking village. You can even walk to a tidal island at Derrynane with a beautiful abbey ruin, offshore from the home of Kerry's most famous son, the Liberator Daniel O'Connell. Inland or island, there are many treasures hidden in plain sight off the main route, even on this most famous peninsula.

SECRET BEACHES

1 CROMANE STRAND

Quiet shingle and sand beach with fine mountain views, good for overnights, with the bonus of a barrel sauna to warm up with a view of the sea (€10, samhradhssauna.com)

2 mins, 52.1126, -9.9029

2 DOOKS BEACH

Fine, sheltered, sandy beach on the Caragh Creek estuary, with views to mountains on both Dingle and the Iveragh peninsulas. Watch out for tidal flows. Verge parking along a little lane that backs the sands; the turning into this looks like a large private gate with a postbox in the pillar (52.0809, -9.9209).

2 mins, 52.0778, -9.9296

3 ROSSBEIGH STRAND

This sensational peninsula of white sand and dunes can get busy in summer, but with almost 4km to explore there's plenty of room. People drive out onto the beach and along the sand tracks to find remote places to camp.

2 mins, 52.0602, -9.9739 

4 CUAS CROM BEACH

Small, sheltered, undeveloped beach with quay, sand and trailer sauna (skelligsauna.ie). 1.5km NE on the hill above is Kimego tower, which looks like a very slender signal tower but is in fact the last remains of a peat processing works from 1847 (51.9759, -10.2504).

2 mins, 51.9648, -10.2648

5 BEGINISH ISLAND

From the scant remains of an ancient Viking settlement on the E side to the 19th-century pilot's lookout on top of its solitary volcanic tor in the W (51.9380, -10.3117), Beginish is worth a boat trip. Between these lie two back-to-back beaches, a seal colony (51.9353, -10.3076), and on the NW coast high hexagonal basalt columns (51.9393, -10.3131). The usual way over is to find a boat trip from the harbour at Knight's Town on Valentia, from where it's a 1km crossing. Experienced sea kayakers can find shorter routes, perhaps from 51.9450, -10.2760 and including little Church Island, with its beehive clochán and burial shrine mound (51.9376, -10.2831).

20 mins, 51.9390, -10.2899

6 ST FINIAN'S BAY & GLEN PIER

White sand cove with sunset views over the Skelligs, a holy well above W end, and easy roadside parking. Exposed, so watch for rips. Just W is Glen Pier, a narrow inlet with more views onto the Skelligs, perfect for swimming, coasteering and kayaking in calm seas, or overnights (51.8468, -10.3568); you could take a boat trip around the islands on the Skellig Falcon (+353 87 2229797).

2 mins, 51.8455, -10.3365

7 INNY STRAND, REENROE

Large, wild sandy beach with views to Scariff island, overlooked by the eerie remains of the 1960s Reenroe Hotel complex, derelict for 30 years, with recent redevelopment schemes stalled in planning (51.8440, -10.2364). Park at end of lane (signed Trá off R567) – or book a beach ride with ROK Equestrian (+353 87 6353999, rokequestrian.wordpress.com). The wild sandy river estuary/tidal lagoon is at lane end, 51.8468, -10.2076. 3km E towards Waterville is the Smuggler's Inn gourmet restaurant (51.8371, -10.1947).

2 mins, 51.8452, -10.2314

8 TOOR BEACH

A quiet sunset-facing bay of LT sand (pebble at high) hidden below earth cliffs. Park in the little layby, cross bridge and follow the stream path down through the gate.

3 mins, 51.7928, -10.1760

9 WHITESTRAND BEACH, KILLEEN *

Superb silver-sand cove with islands and stacks to explore, hidden just below the N70. It is

11

10

10

13

13

signed, with some parking at top of lane, or park in large layby directly above it and follow paths down.

5 mins, 51.7737, -10.0210

10 SNEEM RIVER QUAY & ROSSDOHAN

The river quay on the edge of this lively waterside village gives easy access to the tidal waters and a quiet parking place for overnights, with a barbecue area in the riverside park next to it. You could walk up the river shore to the pool below the town falls, also accessible from beside the road bridge (51.8379, -9.9002), and there are deep river pools behind the GAA ground (51.8421, -9.9005, with car park). For warmer water, try Sneem Seaweed hot barrel baths behind Sneem Hotel (€48, V93 XV44, sneemseaweed.ie). For a more remote pier, continue on 5km E on N79 for signs to Rossdohan (51.8113, -9.8585).

5 mins, 51.8342, -9.9033

RIVER, LAKE & WATERFALL

11 LOUGH CARAGH & UPPER CARAGH

With a backdrop of soaring mountains, this vast lake is beautiful and this is the only public access. Signed 100m down a dead-end lane is a wooded shore with a small concrete pontoon and S-facing pebble beach. Park on lane. To explore the dark waters of the Upper Carragh river, along fishing paths, head 15km S to Blackstones Bridge and take the riverside path upstream on the river's L bank (52.0147, -9.8801). It crosses via footbridge/island after 1km. Or start from further S, at the little Bealalaw Bridge, where a river L path heads downstream, along the deep narrow gorge-like pools (51.9861, -9.8718). Obey signs.

12 mins, 52.0747, -9.8581

12 CHURCH ISLAND & LOUGH CURRANE

Only 100m across, yet home to the remains of a 12th-century monastery with the remains of an oratory, a graveyard and several beehive huts. If you have your own paddle board it's 700m from the fishing parking and shore area at 51.8429, -10.1308 (signed off lane, go through field gate). Michael O'Sullivan also hires fishing boats from here (+353 87 2202355). A more public launch point is signed off N78 in Waterville, a nice spot for a swim with mountain views, but a 2.5km paddle (at 51.8234, -10.1612). We also had a lovely wild swim from the lane that hugs the rocky S shore (park in layby at 51.8193, -10.1047).

15 mins, 51.8351, -10.1303

13 GLACIER LAKE & SECRET BAY

An unexpected roadside lake on the N70. Rock walls for jumping on the opp shore. Easy parking on the passing shoulder. 4km further E

on N70 is 'Helen's Secret Bay', a rugged, sunny shore on Kenmare Bay with a tidal island and a fire-pit, backed by pines. A steep scramble below a small wooded layby (51.8464, -9.7518).
2 mins, 51.8339, -9.8048

14 BLACKWATER PIER, RIVER, WOODLAND

A quiet pier for a swim or picnic, down an unsigned lane off the N70 800m W of Blackwater Bridge. Or turn R at the bridge for an unsigned lane signed Maulcallee and fishery office. After 3.2km a small stile in the fence R (51.8656, -9.7520) leads to an enchanting riverside woodland path and island with cascades; there are laybys before and after. This is a prime fishing river, so please be discreet and obey signs (locals do walk here).
2 mins, 51.8501, -9.7464

15 LOUGH GLANNAFREAGHAUN

This remote mountain lake, also called Shrone, is reached by the dramatic Slyggudal Pass, an ancient route beneath The Paps of Anu (see entry) that linked Shrone City to Clonkeen. The far side reputedly has a cave used as a hideout in the War of Independence. You can try your luck driving up – it's paved until about 1km before, at 52.0297, -9.2430, but verge parking becomes boggy and difficult. Maybe best on a bike, or on a hike up the East Pap of Anú.
30 mins, 52.0197, -9.2499

REEKS & KILLARNEY SWIMS

16 COOMLOUGHRA LOUGH

High lake on the W approach to Carrauntoohil via Caher peak. Follow Hydro Track from car park at 52.0230, -9.7895 (donation box). The Coomloughra Horseshoe above is a stunning but serious all-day hike, with plenty of pathless scrambling.
90 mins, 52.0063, -9.7704

17 HAG'S GLEN & DEVIL'S LADDER

Two cold and glimmering loughs, Callee and Gourtragh, lie under the sheer wall of Ireland's highest mountains, up a popular but beautiful 3km trail following the Gaddagh River. There's a large, well-signed free car park (Carrauntoohil/ Lisleibane, 52.0259, -9.7098, or park at Cronin's Yard campsite, €2). From the lake, experienced hillwalkers continue up to the ridge and Carrauntoohil (1040m) for the classic horseshoe. The Devil's Ladder heads directly up from the ridge between the two lakes, or the Zig Zags path ascends up to the L. These peaks can be dangerous, with rapidly changeable weather. Ideally go with a guide, like Mór Active (moractivetours.com).
60 mins, 52.0045, -9.7196

14

14

18 CUMMEENDUFF & CURRAGHMORE LAKES

A tiny lane winds along the Cummeenduff Glen to reach this lough. The Macgillycuddy's Reeks tower over. It's a quiet spot to pull over for a swim or overnight. For a far more remote option, continue 2km to some parking on bend at 51.9744, -9.7129. Just beyond is the ruined farmstead among twisted trees and tumble-down walls photographers call the 'slate house', on a 2km walk to the final farm and 1km to remote Curraghmore (51.9862, -9.7422). From here an off-trail ascent is possible to Carrauntoohil on SW-facing slopes; you are unlikely to meet anyone until the ridge.

2 mins, 51.9686, -9.6982

19 R OWENREAGH CASCADE

Beautiful hidden pool below a little waterfall on the Owenreagh, with good riverside access and space to pull off the lane. There are more roadside waterfalls and pools to explore 700m upstream; walk along the lane and get in from 51.9609, -9.6351 upwards.

2 mins, 51.9665, -9.6353

20 R OWENREAGH & LORD BRANDON

An elegant stone bridge over the Owenreagh sits at the entrance to Lord Brandon's Cottage and has a deep, wide pool for a dip. There are grassy banks, mossy oaks and parking. Legend says that Lord Brandon imprisoned his wife here in the 1820s, suspecting her of an affair with prime minister Lord Melbourne, and built the tower for her to take the air without being able to leave (in fact his wife had sensibly left the marital home, and the country). Now a cash-only café, it's often reached by a two-hour boat trip from Ross Castle through the lakes. From the café you can follow a riverside path down to the lake, or walk upstream another 1km via tiny lanes, passing wooded banks to join the River Gearhameen on the Black Valley road, to find a track leading to a more secret pool (51.9803, -9.6356).

2 mins, 51.9805 -9.6248

21 LAUNE BRIDGE

Follow the R bank of the river Laune upstream and explore the wooded shore of Lough Leane for up to 2km to the boathouse pontoons, finding a place to dip or paddle board (if you have obtained a permit for your kit, +353 64 6635215) along the way. There's a parking layby and path sign opp. You can also explore the fisher path downstream. Those keen for more Laune riverbank might also get in at Ballymalis Castle downstream (52.0845, -9.6924).

10 mins, 52.0617, -9.6161 

23

22 O'SULLIVAN'S CASCADE, TOMIES

The stream plunges down a mossy gorge, with Lamb's Fall higher up, into several deep pools near the shores of Lough Leane. It's an enchanting walk through Tomies, one of Ireland's oldest oak woodlands; take the longer uphill side of the looped route in for breathtaking views and look out for red deer, red squirrels, and white-tailed sea eagles above. There's a medium car park at 52.0449, -9.6033 signed on the corner, off the lane 1.5km E of Dunloe Castle hotel. Trail to falls about 1.6km.

25 mins, 52.0378, -9.5822

23 TOWER WATERFALL

A beautiful waterfall, though without a pool. Layby parking heading W (51.9884, -9.5573) 120m before an ivy-covered tower that gives the woods their name. Descend SE to the Crinnagh River and follow it upstream about 600m; you have to cross a small stream. You walk among old oaks and could visit the strawberry trees, including the tallest one surviving (51.9806, -9.57381); look out for red deer. You can walk on above the falls, it's all beautiful. Much further up this river is the Cores Cascade (see entry).

15 mins, 51.9872, -9.5519

24 LONG RANGE & UPPER LAKE

There are some superb spots for swimming just off the N71. The easiest is a gravel beach with parking, easy to spot R as the road first approaches the lake heading SW from Killarney. Another 1.7km SW the road joins Upper Lake, with a small layby (51.9852, -9.5633) and two much smaller pull-offs for one car (51.9839, -9.5688 and 51.9826, -9.5708) all on the lake side, with slab rocks for jumps once you've checked the depth.

2 mins, 51.9976, -9.5507

25 DINIS COTTAGE, MUCKROSS LAKE

Upper Lake and Muckross Lake converge at 'Meeting of the Waters' before flowing into Lough Leane. Here stands Dinis Cottage, an 18th-century hunting lodge that's now a simple café. Behind are stone slabs leading into a huge river pool. Walk 300m upstream to the Old Weir Bridge, also dating back at least two centuries. It spans the fast-flowing waters of the Long Range, where the waters narrow into rapids or the 'shoots', fun on a kayak, paddle board or rubber ring. Some boat trips ascend to or descend from Lord Brandon's Cottage (see entry) 7km to SW, below the Gap of Dunloe. There's a large well-signed layby car park on N71 (52.0049, -9.5303) and walk W on the good woodland road for 1.4km.

30 mins, 52.0091, -9.5493

26 CORES & TORC WATERFALLS

This remote waterfall on the Crinnagh River upstream of Tower Falls (see entry) has a deep pool, shingle beach and more pools above, all in the wild foothills of Mangerton Mountain; perfect for a wild camp or skinny dip. Walk or cycle 3.8km along the good forest track – boggy at end – from the car park above Torc Waterfall (52.0002, -9.5053), signed Old Kenmare Road off N71. Detour up to Torc Mountain (good boardwalk path from 51.9901, -9.5185) about 1km with 200m ascent for superb Muckross views. This top car park is also the best option for Torc in season, as most people park at the lake and never make it this high; a short way down is a series of accessible deep pools below the old stone bridge (only in low flow, take care).

160 mins, 51.9765, -9.5438

LOST RUINS

27 ARDTULLY CASTLE & ROUGHTY RIVER

This dramatic turreted mansion was burned in the War of Independence, and has stood as a ruin since. Beyond is a stone bridge, once part of the original driveway, over the beautiful River Roughty. This is private land but access allowed on the track L of the new house, around the ruin and over the bridge (and beyond, following the river upstream), so be respectful. There's room for one car on verge at the end of the lane by the entrance gate (51.9001, -9.4745), then go through the squeeze gate/stile.

5 mins, 51.8996, -9.47393

28 ROSS ISLAND COPPER MINE

Standing here, you can be fairly sure you are on the exact spot where the Neolithic period ended in Ireland: this was the source of all worked copper from before 2200BCE, used in artefacts found even in the Netherlands and Brittany, and Bell Beaker pottery found here implies the skill arrived from the continent. Extraction continued into the 19th century, and there are walls from this era, including the dam of the green holding pool by the shore. Lead was mined too, and there's another 18th-century mine in the Muckross House demesne (see entry). Park at Ross Castle and walk in through lovely woods (52.0415, -9.5293).

15 mins, 52.0353, -9.5368

29 AGHADOE RUINS

There are house ruins hidden in woods in Aghadoe, next to the Abode flats (park there temporarily) at the junction of the R563. Through the trellis gates opp the flats' entrance (52.0735, -9.5760) lie two houses, one single-storey from the 1870s, the other Arts & Crafts from 1943. Across the R563 is a path to the ruins of the old coach house of Aghadoe House at 52.0732, -9.5779. These are leased, and the main house S was put on the market in 2024 after the youth hostel closed, so visiting may be impossible in the future. Both are private but accessed by locals.

2 mins, 52.0732, -9.5749

30 DERRYCUNIHY BARRACKS

With two gothic towers this looks more akin to a castle but it's actually a Royal Irish Constabulary barracks, built in the 1830s and burned in the War of Independence. It's right on the N71, but there are small laybys just downhill to the E by the bridge, and parking further uphill; take care on this twisting road.

3 mins, 51.9651, -9.5912

31 BALLYCARBERY CASTLE, WHITESTRAND

Ivy-clad and somewhat precarious ruin near the shore, once home to the McCarthy Clan and built sometime in the 15th century. You can partly walk around it on the LT shore. Do not ignore the 'keep out' signs, but those who do find vaults, passages and staircase inside the rear face. Whitestrand beach is a further 3km, a simple, sandy family beach with lifeguards and medium car park and toilets (51.9450, -10.2760), with views to nearby Beginish Island (see entry).

5 mins, 51.9488, -10.2586

32 VALENTIA SLATE QUARRY & GROTTO

The oldest quarry in Ireland, this ran from 1816 until a rock fall closed it in 1910, supplying high-quality slate used as far afield as St Paul's in London and the Paris opera house. It remained abandoned until the 1954 Marian Year, when statues were installed high above the quarry and a yearly community mass has been said ever since. The old quarry is fenced, but a new area opened in 1991, where tours can be booked (€5, +353 66 9476922). For another geological wonder, visit the nearby 'Tetrapod Trackway', some of the earliest footprints on the planet fossilised on the shore. They are believed to be over 350 million years old, when aquatic animals started to occupy the land. Car park at 51.9294, -10.3457 and a 300m walk down.

2 mins, 51.9251, -10.3427

SACRED & ANCIENT

33 THE CITY OF SHRONE

Properly named Cathair Crobh Dearg, this cashel may be one of the oldest Christian pilgrimage sites in Ireland, although some rituals – like bringing cattle on May Day – feel more pagan. Inside are possible remains of a tomb, a primitive stone altar and cross-scratched slabs, a Marian statue and the ruins of a cottage, while a holy well lies outside it. Entrance on W side. Also the start of the Dunhallow Way, with an information board. Park considerately – there's only rough verge.

2 mins, 52.0403, -9.2567

34 PARKAVONEAR CASTLE & AGHADOE

This 13th-century ruin, known locally as the Bishop's Pulpit, is one of very few circular Norman keeps. The mural staircase goes up only one floor; it may only ever have been two storeys high. The original entrance was probably on the upper floor, with external stairs. Across the lane E is a round tower stump and 12th-century cathedral ruin with a Romanesque doorway, a 7th-century ogham stone in the chancel, and a 17th-century crucifixion plaque near it. The Aghadoe Crozier, of walrus ivory carved in a Viking style, came from here. Views from this area of the lakes are stunning, and there is parking for a viewpoint, from where people walk E to the castle (52.0770, -9.5570).

2 mins, 52.0759, -9.555

35 KILLAGHA ABBEY

If you can, go for a sunrise at this 13th-century abbey in a serene broad valley setting, also called Kilcolman It was once rich and powerful, and the fine tracery window stonework has been restored by a local community group. After dissolution it became a fortified home, but then suffered greatly in Cromwellian attacks and stone was robbed out for other buildings. Now only the church with a single long nave remains. Park at gate. Nearby, another site of religious strife is the mass rock where mass is still said every October, in Killaclohane Wood (52.1552, -9.6825). Local legends say that ten minutes lying on the rock is as refreshing as a full night of sleep.

2 mins, 52.1496, -9.73057

36 DERRYNABLAHA ROCK ART

The stunning Ballaghbeama Gap valley has some 50 panels of ancient rock art, widely spread across the NE of the valley. The most heavily decorated, sometimes called the Rosette stone (51.9291, -9.8002), has five other examples near it, all overlooking Lough Brin across the valley. There's a gate on the bend (51.9315, -9.7957) and a wider gate splay 100m N on opp side; or there's a longer layby back almost opp the 'only house in the valley' ruin (51.911883, -9.7510). Follow the stream up; this is sheep farming land, so no dogs.

20 mins, 51.9291, -9.8002

37 COOM WEDGE TOMB

Good example of a S Irish wedge tomb, with on-end shale slabs. Near the WAW but a wild location on a tiny lane, 50m into field.

3 mins, 51.8235, -10.3136

38 BALLINSKELLIGS ABBEY, CASTLE, BEACH

This shoreside abbey ruin is where the monks came when they abandoned Skellig Michael in the 12th century. It's off the road to the Skelligs' pier. Pull aside carefully on the lane, don't block the turning space at the abbey end. It is flanked by a wild pebble beaches and a spit leading 500m N to a 16th-century tower house castle with a mural staircase you can climb, more recently used as 'fish palace' for curing pilchards (51.8200, -10.2704). 300m beyond is popular, sandy Ballinskellig Beach (car park at 51.8209, -10.2732).

2 mins, 51.8156, -10.2714

39 STAIGUE CASHEL *

There are great views from this imposing late Iron Age cashel, probably from the 4th century, with fascinating features. The entrance is a long lintelled passage, the massive walls are up to 5.5m high with a network of staircases and walkways below the now undulating top, and there are two low creepway chambers in them. Vertical joints in the wall show it was built in sections, which were joined together after.

2 mins, 51.8050, -10.0154

40 CAHERLEHILLAN SHRINE & CASHEL

This may be the oldest Christian site identified in Ireland, with post holes of a wooden church and a stone shrine. There are two cross slabs, one with a typical early Christian bird above the cross, and two other stone fragments with partial birds. In the field above is a ruined once-fine cashel, now collapsed, but with the remains of circular huts inside and stunning views of valley hutdotted with hut site. Ask to park and visit at the farm.

2 mins, 51.9872, -10.0786

41 DERRYNANE ABBEY & BEACH

One of the most beautifully sited ancient monastic sites in Ireland, with Romanesque church ruins and ancient burial ground on an island. Walk over at low tide from a bay of famously golden sands and clear waters. It lies below Derrynane House and gardens, the home of statesman and barrister Daniel O'Connell (1775–1847), the Great Emancipator. When quiet, the W beach car park is closest (51.7603, -10.1422). A gorgeous walk 500m NW from this along the stone garden wall leads to a tiny secret cove (51.7636, -10.1459) and then Bealtra Bay (51.7655, -10.1508), part of the 6.3km Derrynane Mass Path loop. In summer both beach car parks may be full; try the free parking for Derrynane House (51.7632, -10.1285) or, for the seashore trail down lane L before this (51.7620, -10.1243), about 1.5km along the beach to the abbey island.

10 mins, 51.7574, -10.1427

42 LOHER CASHEL

This impressive drystone cashel from the 9th century was a defended farmstead, with stairways up the ramparts and the remains of a large round house and a smaller rectangular one. It is somewhat reconstructed and tidy. For a totally wild fort on a rock outcrop, very much left to nature, try Caherdaniel 12km S near Derrynane on N70 (51.7704, -10.1107). Park in layby on N70 by lane entrance (51.7711, -10.1092) and walk down lane 60m to find route in on R; access may not be possible.

2 mins, 51.7861, -10.1656

43 CAHERGAL & LEACANABUAILE FORTS

Two neighbouring forts here. Impressive 7th-century Cahergal has an inner ring and one very high wall section, with staircases up to the top and wide views over the sea. It was

a metalworking site at some time; bronze, iron and forging tools have been found. Leacanabuaile was a 9th-century defended farmstead, containing three round clochán-style buildings, with a later square building added (51.9582, -10.2618). Parking at corner (51.9555, -10.2614).

5 mins, 51.9559, -10.2577

44 INNISFALLEN ABBEY ISLAND

Small boats and guided kayak tours from Ross Castle cross to a substantial island with an abbey and Romanesque church and oratory from the 12th century; this was once a centre of learning that produced the Annals

45

47

52

52

of Innisfallen, a vast chronicle of Irish history going back to the 5th century now held by the Bodleian in Oxford, England. You can kayak solo on the lakes, as long as you have a permit for your kit (+353 64 6635215).

20 mins, 52.0466, -9.5541

SCRAMBLES & HILLTOPS

45 WEST PAP OF ANÚ

These iconic twin peaks (690m, 694m) have panoramic views and large cairns and were named after the Celtic mother goddess Anú. A line of stones, known as Na Fiacla, connects the two tops and is believed to have been a processional route. West Pap is perhaps the easiest, as you can follow the ridge line straight up, although there are still wet and boggy sections. The trailhead is on the steep forest road, with some parking on the bends (e.g. 51.9963, -9.2701), then 3km and 400m ascent.

100 mins, 52.0152, -9.2750

46 MANGERTON & DEVIL'S PUNCHBOWL

This 843m summit has incredible views, and below are several beautiful high lakes, such as the photogenic Devil's Punchbowl, with infinity-pool views NW to Muckross. After a 5km walk with about 700m elevation gain, on any warm day it would be madness not to take a dip before you descend. Signed from Colgans/spa hotel on N71 to small car park on the lane at 52.0067, -9.4803.

180 mins, 51.9761, -9.4881

47 KNOCKNAPEASTA SCRAMBLES

Originally Cnoc na Péiste, this is on the less-trodden E ridge of the Reeks, with less clear or non-existent paths up; a serious and potentially dangerous high-level ridge walk just 52m lower than Carrauntoohil. The NE spur is a classic Grade 1 scramble. Start as for Lough Callee (see entry), but bear L at the footbridges (52.0194, -9.7044) and ascend to the R of Lough Cummeenapeasta. For a less-remote Grade 1 gully scramble, follow path to near Lough Callee, but bear R of adjacent Lough Gouragh, and then L of tiny Lough Cummeenoughter (52.0029, -9.7446), to ascend Brother O'Shea's Gully. At the top ridge, turn R for more scrambling R along the knife-edge to The Bones/Beenkeragh Ridge, or L for Carrauntoohil.

120 mins, 51.9981, -9.6954

CLIFFS & HEADLANDS

48 BOLUS HEAD SIGNAL TOWER

The ruins of a Napoleonic signal tower and the shell of a Second World War lookout post stand on the summit of this headland, with superb sea views over to the Skelligs and the chance of seeing white-tailed sea eagles. For the best views, walk the 7.5km Bolus Loop or Barracks Loop clockwise, heading up to the ridge and signal tower, then descending to the cliffs and back to the start. This is a moderately tough climb; for a shorter and easier walk, follow the cliffs to the tip and then retrace your steps. Parking is at 51.8139, -10.3370; follow the coast road and choose low or high at the first fork.

60 mins, 51.7926, -10.3361

49 REENCAHERAGH BEACH & CLIFFS

The far end of Iveragh has impressive cliffs, but there's limited access so the pretty shale beach is a good route in. Park at the end of lane and follow pathless clifftops L around headland. After 1km you pass a blowhole and cove (51.8822, -10.3950) and after another 750m a medieval gatehouse with arrow slots and drawbar, built into the much older promontory fort defence across the headland (51.8782, -10.3968). Another (shorter) option where the cliffs are higher is from a farm track end by shed at 51.8772, -10.3843. A further 1km S on the R566 is the Kerry Cliffs development (€5 entry); it is gravelled and fenced, but the highest point and handy for campervans to overnight (€20).

30 mins, 51.8837, -10.3876

50 BRAY HEAD SIGNAL TOWER

The signal tower here is Napoleonic, but looks much more modern; it was refurbished and used during the First World War as a signal station, and even briefly re-occupied by coast watchers during the Second (51.8856, -10.42489). It commands terrific views to the Skelligs, and you can even go inside and view them framed. The EIRE 35 pilots' marker has fared less well, barely visible now at 51.8845, -10.4258. Paid parking.

25 mins, 51.8913, -10.3979

ANCIENT TREES & WILDLIFE

51 MUCKROSS ABBEY & YEW

The well-preserved ruins include a church with a tower and fine windows and a vaulted cloister arcade around a square courtyard. The star of the show is the yew that fills this, said to have been planted when the abbey was founded in 1448, but possibly older. Whatever its age, it would be hard to match the atmospheric setting and rippled beauty of this tree. Small car park off N71 (52.0259, -9.4899) or much more at Muckross House and walk through the parkland.

10 mins, 52.0261, -9.4947

52 MUCKROSS HOUSE DEMESNE

Given to the state in 1932, these lands were the basis of Ireland's first national park, with some of its finest ancient trees. Following the

5km loop path N of Doo Lough look for caves off R (52.0204, -9.5144, perhaps copper mines), on the way to Reenadinna or Mossy Wood, the largest yew woodland in Europe (52.0190, -9.5188). After this you pass a vast oak (52.0189, -9.5248). The return along the Muckross N shore passes a 18th-century copper mine (52.0160, -9.5324) and a good dipping cove, Rosie's beach – see if you can find the limestone caves and pillars under the little peninsula (52.0154, -9.5305). Near the boathouses there's also a magnificent Monterey cypress with a girth of over 10.5m. Free parking at Muckross House.

90 mins, 52.0171, -9.5071

53 REENAGROSS WOODLAND PARK

This wooded island was an ornamental parkland, planted in the 19th century. The now-mature woodland is home to abundant wildlife, with eight species of bat including the lesser horseshoe, and the shore areas add even more – picnic at Lover's Point at the E tip, with views across the estuary, and if the tide is out, watch the oystercatchers foraging. It is reached through an inconspicuous gate (51.8752, -9.5837) that leads between mossy stone walls. Parking on streets tricky, try Pier Road (51.8748, -9.5844).

5 mins, 51.8765, -9.5791

54 DERRYCUNNIHY WOODS & FALLS *

This nature reserve has some of Killarney's easiest and most idyllic mossy ancient oak woodlands, where you might see red or sika deer drinking from the stream, or spot the distinctive Killarney strawberry tree. The easiest parking is by the old church, now an important bat roost (51.9644, -9.5809), walking in down the river, which has pretty falls. There's also a tiny pull-off by another entrance 1km on towards Killarney (51.9723, -9.5813), or you could walk in from Lord Brandon's Lodge (51.9800, -9.6220); the forest is particularly twisty on this path.

5 mins, 51.9685, -9.5833

55 WATERFALL WOODS, DERRYNANE

The Kerry Way passes through this enchanting twisted woodland, reaching a waterfall with small plunge pools and a miniature stone bridge. There is a pretty wild woodland path that follows the stream up from Derrynane House, about 800m, or for just the waterfall, park considerately on small verge on narrow lane just below the Kerry Way signs (51.7691, -10.1343) and continue E through woods 200m. In opp direction on Kerry Way are more woodland and super views down to the coast.

5 mins, 51.7703, -10.1305

51

54

56 THE EAGLE'S NEST

This impressive peak was used as an echo feature in the early days of tourism here in the 19th century, with guns fired on the lakes below. Now it is peaceful again, and you may see white-tailed sea eagles, which were re-introduced in 2007; numbers have been expanding gradually since, with several pairs in the national park. They are often seen flying above Dinis, so start from there (see entry). From the Old Weir bridge above the Meeting of the Waters, make your way SW up the slope as far as you like – perhaps to the little lake (52.0029, -9.5600). From here you could also walk to the summit views (no paths), a three-hour trip.

20 mins, 51.9951, -9.5718

CLASSIC CAFES

57 KILLING TIME CAFÉ & OWENREAGH

This very home-made café is based in David's shed, with a friendly sheepdog and fresh bakes; 450m E down the road a field gate leads to a series of river pools and cascades (51.9492, -9.6771). Crossderry, Blackwater, Co. Kerry, V93 KV29, +353 87 6074405

51.9497, -9.6822

58 THE STRAWBERRY FIELD

Cheerfully coloured cottage, with Dutch-style pancakes savoury and sweet, local beers and organic wines, and home-made apple pie with local ice cream. Has its own well with sweet water, so great coffee and tea. Yosta and Mayra, daughters of founders Peter & Margaret Kerssens, took over in 2021. Blackwater, Moll's Gap, V93 K099, +353 64 6682977

51.9145, -9.6856

59 THE VILLAGE KITCHEN, SNEEM

Café/pub food with fresh local fish, widely praised veggie options, and an open fire in winter. Closes in January until summer season starts. 3 Bridge Street, Sneem, V93 C578, +353 64 6645281

51.8384, -9.9001

60 THE ORATORY, CAHERSIVEEN

Pizzas made with fresh local ingredients, in a funky converted church or at the tables out on the grass; takeaway too. Evenings all week Apr–Oct and Fri–Sun in winter. Main Street, Caherciveen, V23 YC03, +353 66 9481670

51.9450, -10.2289

61 CILL RIALAIG ARTS CENTRE *

Art gallery, workshops and café with freshly prepared local foods and bread; stone-baked pizzas are great too. Ballinskelligs, V23 RK57, +353 66 9479277

51.8325, -10.2664

LOCAL PRODUCE

62 O'NEILLS THE POINT SEAFOOD BAR

Right by the quay, very popular, leans heavily into seafood, great place for a swim, a pint and a seafood platter. Walk-ins only. Renard Point, Cahersiveen, V23HK06, +353 66 9472165

51.9292, -10.2773

63 SKELLIGS CHOCOLATE

Café and factory shop of an innovative chocolate maker, where you can try before you buy. Closed in winter, but you will still be able to buy them locally, and we recommend it. The Glen, Ballinskelligs, V23 HP64, +353 66 9479119

51.8460, -10.3301

64 KILLARNEY BREWING COMPANY

If you're looking to sample locally made beers, this is the place to come. A comfortable, lively taproom serving up great pints, great pizzas and a great atmosphere. Muckross Road, Killarney, V93 RC95, +353 64 6636505

52.0543, -9.5071

65 PETIT DELICE

Terrific patisserie – buy a jar of their salted caramel spread. 11 Main Street, Caherciveen, V23 H5K8, +353 87 9903572. They are also in Killarney at 41–42 High Street, V93 T8K7

51.9461, -10.2263

66 SKELLIG SIX18 DISTILLERY

Named for the number of steps in the famous monastic islands, this little distillery is doing great things. €19–25 for an award-winning fully guided tour including local history and samplings. Valentia Rd, Garranearagh, Cahersiveen, V23 YD89, +353 66 9400618

51.9355, -10.2395

ORGANIC & GASTRO

67 CELTIC WHISKEY BAR, KILLARNEY

Local and other craft beer and a terrifyingly large whiskey selection, with bar staff who can give good recommendations for both. Good pub menu lunchtime, much more considered restaurant menu in the evening. 93 New St, V93 KXD4, +353 64 6635700

52.0588, -9.5111

68 QUINLAN'S MAD MONK, KILLARNEY

Taking a 'tide to table' approach to its menu this seafood restaurant in Killarney sources its fish from local Kerry fishermen. Fans of a traditional fish supper won't be disappointed with the beer-battered fish and chips (the latter freshly peeled and sliced each day) but the menu also stretches to crab arancini, homemade seafood

chowder, Cromane mussels with a cider velouté and pan-fried seabass with pickled carrots. 21-22 Plunkett St, V93 Y796, +353 646623597
52.0585, -9.5080

69 NUMBER 35

Serious food, strong on local produce, with local craft beers on offer as well as wine, in a cosy wood and stone interior. 35 Main Street, Kenmare, V93 Y038, +353 64 6641559
51.8795, -9.5821

70 THE GRILL, THE DUNLOE HOTEL

Expensive but superb, with a wealth of local produce including from its own herd of Irish Angus cattle. The gardens have a 13th-century tower that guests can visit (52.0625, -9.6281) and access to the beautiful river Lourne. Dunloe Lower, V93 E029, +353 64 6644111
52.0597, -9.6274

71 MULCAHYS, KENMARE

Long-established chef-owned restaurant serving classic dishes with a local and individual slant in a smart but cosy atmosphere. Main Street, Kenmare, V93 W35F, +353 64 6642383
51.8796, -9.5823

72 BOATHOUSE, DROMQUINNA MANOR

For a luxurious treat, this seafood bistro restaurant is on the shores of a country house hotel. Focused on local producers and its own kitchen garden produce in season. Sneem Road, Kenmare, V93 PK83, +353 64 6642888
51.8711, -9.6436

73 10 BRIDGE STREET, KILLORGLIN *

In its former guise as Sol Y Sombra, it was a local legend for Spanish food. After 16 years, the same team under Cliodhna Foley changed the focus to the range of excellent local produce now available, and so the name changed too. Housed in an old church, great ambience. Lower Bridge Street, V93 K858, +353 66 9762347
52.1061, -9.7853

74 JACKS' COASTGUARD & STATION BAR

Award-winning seafood, with trad sessions in the bar on Sunday afternoon; restaurant closed Tues. The back of the pub, which is in an old coastguard cottage, overlooks the sea. The rest of the terrace of cottages are available as self-catering lets. Cromane Lower, Cromane, V93 Y42F, +353 66 9769102
52.1113, -9.9023

COOL CAMPING

75 CRONIN'S YARD

Real hikers' campsite with backdrop of the mountains and plenty of space for tents, great shop and cosy café, three pods and a bothy. Perfect start for several walks. Mealis, Beaufort, V93 HK71, +353 64 6624044
52.0262, -9.6962

76 WAVE CREST CARAVAN & CAMPING

Family-friendly highly rated campsite overlooking Kenmare Bay. Although it is mostly caravans, it is informal and the sea views are magnificent, and there's even a path down to a small cove that's essentially private. Shop and pizzas, closed in winter. Caherdaniel, V93V2YP, +353 66 9475188
51.7578, -10.0937

77 MANNIX POINT, CAHERCIVEEN

This site and owner Mortimer Moriarty are local legends. What started as a very small and basic site in 1984 has won over a dozen awards. Well-equipped communal areas with a turf fire and even musical instruments on hand, so impromptu musical evenings are not a rarity. But it remains an outdoorsy site with its own rugged foreshore. Garranbane, Caherciveen, V23 PA07, +353 66 9472806
51.9427, -10.2434

RUSTIC RETREATS

78 KILLARNEY GLAMPING

This couples-only site has a range of heated wood and canvas lodges with covered private decks, kitchens and your own bathroom, and a communal fire area above the shore of the river. Ballycasheen, Killarney, V93 YT32, +353 87 9750110
52.054, -9.4842

79 THE HAPPY PIG, KENMARE

This cosy B&B has six simple and bright rooms and views over rolling fields. For cyclists and bike tourers, it has secure and dry shelter for your wheels overnight, hose and air to keep them on the road, and a drying room for biking or hiking gear. Irma makes great Irish breakfasts, taken in the dining room or in the garden on a fine day. Sneem Road, Kenmare, V93 P52K, +353 64 6640704
51.8823, -9.5956

80 FARMYARD LANE GLAMPING

Two locally made glamping pods, set among the apple trees of a working farm. Breakfast basket is included, filled with locally sourced ingredients, including eggs and honey from over the fence. Lahard, Beaufort, Killarney, V93 W2T0, +353 86 1019503, farmyard-lane.ie
52.0860, -9.6462

81 BLACK VALLEY YOUTH HOSTEL

Bunk dorms and two tiny self-contained family lodges each sleeping four, in a great location. Gap of Dunloe, Black Valley, V93 ENN8, +353 64 6634712, blackvalleyhostel.com
51.9866, -9.6524

82 ANAM VALLEY COTTAGE

Traditional stone cottage under the slopes of Carrauntoohil, near the shores of Lough Curraghmore. It has a double bed up in the eaves on a mezzanine and a wood-burning stove, perfect for romantic getaways. The farmhouse next to it is also available. Black Valley, V93 TR77, anamvalley.com
51.9805, -9.7301

83 PIER COTTAGE, WESTCOVE HOUSE

Two attached coastguard cottages, right on the water's edge by a slipway and small pier (public) for swimming and boating. Sheltered in Westcove natural harbour and estate, you can also rent the waterside Georgian manor house, crammed with gorgeous antiques, six bedrooms and a waterside garden. V93 N7Y8, westcove.ie
51.7701, -10.0552

84 HIDDEN HILLS WATERVILLE FARM

Stay in a farmhouse in a remote valley (sleeps seven, on Airbnb) on a working sheep farm where they also do farm experiences. Oughtive, V23 VN24, +353 87 6416041
51.8602, -10.0720

76

77

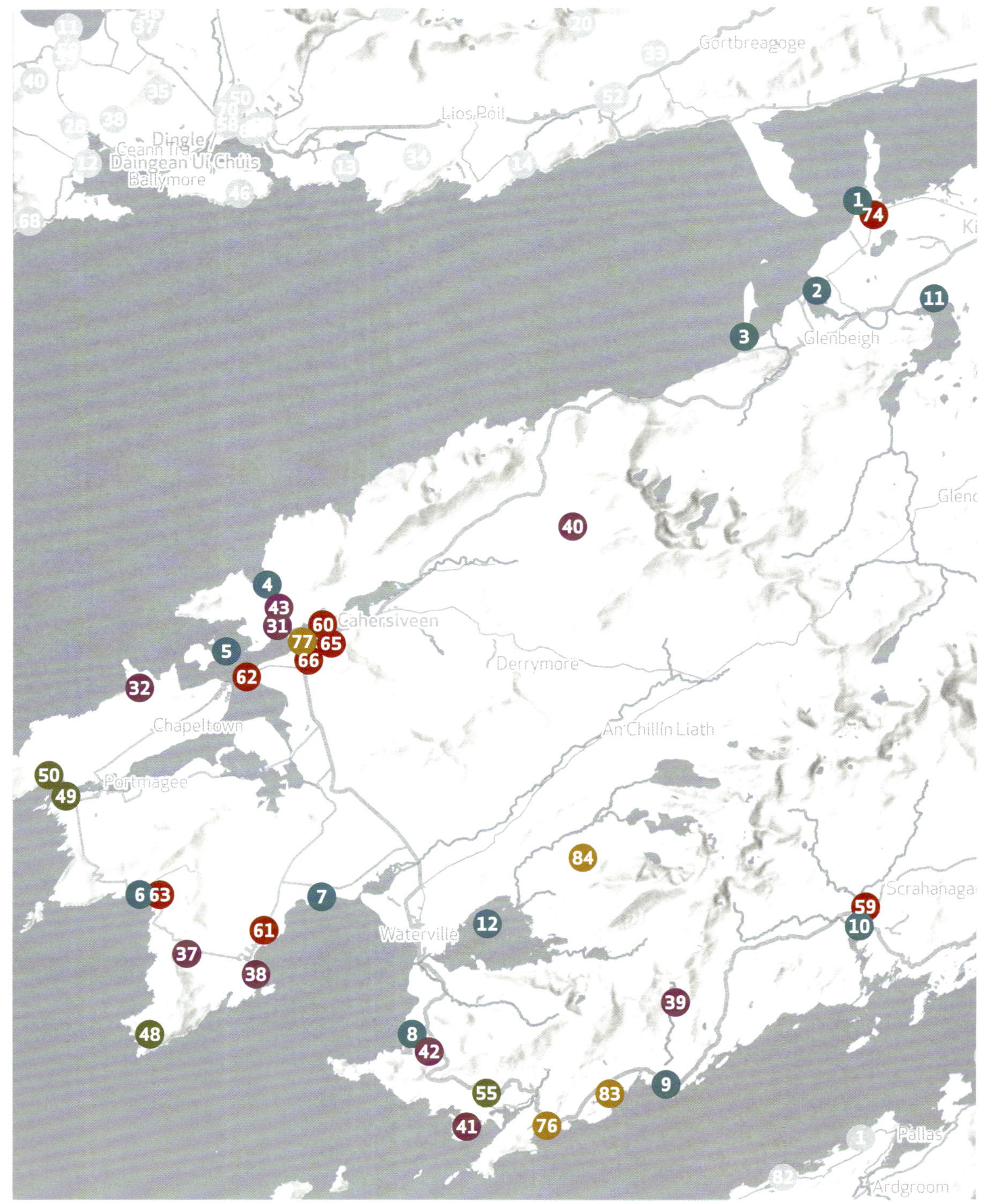
Gortbreagoge
Lios Póil
Dingle
Ceann Trá
Daingean Uí Chúis
Ballymore
Glenbeigh
Cahersiveen
Derrymore
Chapeltown
An Chillín Liath
Portmagee
Waterville
Scrahanagal
Pallas
Ardgroom

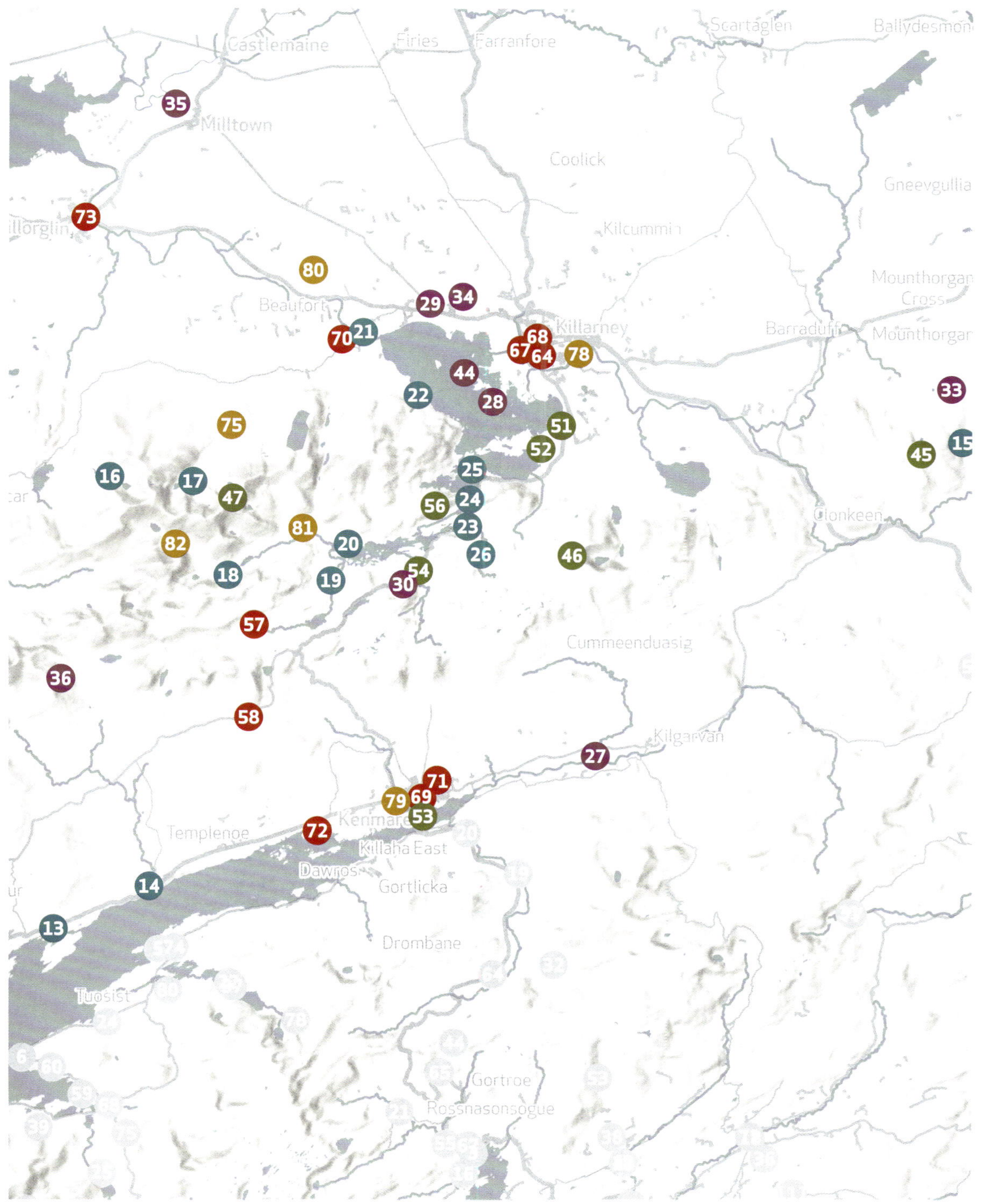
Castlemaine
Firies
Farranfore
Scartaglen
Ballydesmon
Milltown
Coolick
Gneevgullia
Killorglin
Kilcummin
Mounthorgan Cross
Beaufort
Killarney
Barraduff
Mounthorgan
Clonkeen
Cummeenduasig
Kilgarvan
Kenmare
Templenoe
Killaha East
Dawros
Gortlicka
Drombane
Tuosist
Gortroe
Rossnasonsogue

21

THE BEARA PENINSULA

Our perfect weekend

- → **Wander** in Glengarriff woods looking for squirrels and strawberry trees, and end with a swim in the beautiful Pooleen.
- → **Swim** into the booming sea caves at Cuas and walk along the heathery clifftops.
- → **Make** river dams on Ballydonegan Beach, enjoy local music and the sunset at O'Neill's Bar.
- → **Climb** up to remote Rabach's Glen to find the lost village, dipping and jumping in the waterfalls as you go, to arrive at the glacial tarn.
- → **Retreat** with the Buddhist monks at Dzogchen Beara, or alone at remote Pulleen Harbour.
- → **Sunset** sauna at Coornagillagh with bio-luminescence, near Beara woodland campsite.
- → **Camp** on a sunset beach and headland at Eagle Point, with supplies from Manning's Emporium
- → **Fuel** up with a hearty breakfast at Helen's Bar and walk through the woods to the twin stone circles of Cashelkeelty.
- → **Seek** ancient rocks in Cooleenlemane valley and look for alignments at Little Mills below.

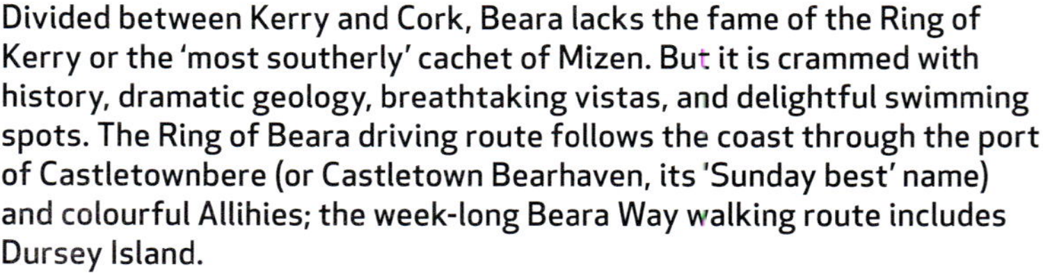

Divided between Kerry and Cork, Beara lacks the fame of the Ring of Kerry or the 'most southerly' cachet of Mizen. But it is crammed with history, dramatic geology, breathtaking vistas, and delightful swimming spots. The Ring of Beara driving route follows the coast through the port of Castletownbere (or Castletown Bearhaven, its 'Sunday best' name) and colourful Allihies; the week-long Beara Way walking route includes Dursey Island.

The coast here is rocky, with hidden coves and quays rather than broad sands – perfect if you like to jump, snorkel or drift without crowds. A few classic locations, like the Blue Pool in Glengarriff or Zetland Pier have become famous and busy; instead head to Pooleen Wood waterfall or remote Pulleen Harbour.

Three sandstone mountain ranges dominate this area with their sheer bulk. In the east the peninsula meets the Shehy Mountains, a wild landscape of bog and glacial valley lakes. On the peninsula the craggy Caha Mountains include famous Hungry Hill; the Healy Pass winds through them, built as famine relief work and now one of Ireland's best scenic drives. To the west is the almost alien landscape of the ribbed Slieve Miskish Mountains. Their name means 'mountains of malice', and this unforgiving landscape offered little wealth save for the copper beneath; a ruined 19th-century mine stands at the coast. Woodlands are tucked in the valleys, mostly to the east, homes to pine martens and red squirrels, barn owls and bats. Glengarriff Woods contains many species unique to south-west Ireland and northern Spain and Portugal, while self-seeded tree ferns have made an exotic wilderness in the old plantings of Derreen Garden.

The megalithic monuments here include a concentration of stone circles, typically with a recumbent 'axial' stone similar to circles far off in Scotland. Almost uninhabited Dursey Island offers deserted villages and markers on its windswept hills, reached via Ireland's only cable car; larger Bere Island has fortifications from its long history as the sentinel of a deep-water port.

This wild place is where Dave Grohl of the Foo Fighters retreated incognito after the death of Kurt Cobain, and where a teenager in a Nirvana t-shirt hitching a lift home from a beach jolted him back to his life. Whether you explore the rugged coast, walk the windswept uplands or hunt out the echoes of past lives, Beara can deliver experiences that linger long after the journey ends.

SEA CAVES & POOLS

1 CUAS CAVES, PULLEEN LOOP WALK *

The start of a coast path from Cuas Quay (parking and HT jumps) leads to an inland beach linked to the sea via a large double sea cave tunnel. The stones are very slippery, but you can wade in (easiest on the R) and swim through in calm conditions, or just admire from dry land. The path continues to Dog's Point (51.7604, -9.8824) where there is a long cobble beach and spit. There are sea caves all along this shore, great for coasteering.

5 mins, 51.7528, -9.9020

2 BEARA BOWL

No part of Beara's breathtaking geology is quite as dramatic as this shoreline amphitheatre. Swimming is a venture for a flat day (better at Trawnfearla, see entry), but good for coasteering and glorious at sunset. Space for a few cars on gravel at bend just to N, much more at WAW discovery point 350m S.

2 mins, 51.6513, -10.0564

3 THE POINT, BLUE POOL, GLENGARRIFF *

Where the Glengarriff river and waterfalls meet the sea there's a rocky natural harbour called the Blue Pool with stone quays and a ferry pontoon. Cross the bridge into the woods beyond for the Point, a rocky headland with steep steps into the deep blue water where people jump from the old diving board platform. Park in town and walk down the well-signed path at the R side of Quills, 200m.

3 mins, 51.7473, -9.5484

4 TRAWNFEARLA COVE & SEA CAVE

The pebble cove and quay here sit in a bay of dramatic rock features from the nearby Beara Bowl (see entry), the Reenroe headland visible across the water behind the Blue Islands where a land bridge crosses a blowhole and sea cave (51.6524, -10.0708). A layby on lane and gate (51.6547, -10.0676) lead onto the headland (300m, some bushwhacking), or down a gully to the waterline.

10 mins, 51.6539, -10.0577

SECRET BEACHES

5 COORNAGILLAGH BEACH

The waters at this little bay are noted for bioluminescence, a good reason to linger after enjoying a sunset or jumping from the pier at HT. There is parking at the pier, and the mobile Sunset Sauna (+353 87 2238211).

2 mins, 51.8259, -9.7409

11

8

12

9

15

6 LOUGHAUNACREEN BEACH

This headland has a secluded cobble beach sheltered by a little reef on N side, or views across Kilmakilloge Harbour S; I was scolded by a pair of stonechats for breaking their solitude. Neighbouring Kilmakilloge just to the S is a WAW discovery point with a cobble beach good for sunsets and kayaking on the N side (51.7830, -9.8209). Both good for overnights.

2 mins, 51.7844, -9.82425

7 EYERIES POINT & CREHA QUAY

The remote estuarine beach on this low headland has fine sunset views. Rough parking at the lane end, good for a picnic or overnight. Follow Trá signs down tiny lanes from Sullivan's Food Store in colourful Eyeries. From here the lovely Creha Quay Loop heads 2km NE on the coast (dogs turn back on lane at 51.6927, -9.9662) to the quay with its tiny shingle cove, good for swimming and jumping (also called Drinagh Pier, 51.6991, -9.9645); you can drive here, but very limited parking. The loop turns inland back to Eyeries and lanes to the start.

2 mins, 51.6895, -9.9729

8 TRAVAUD BEACH

Sheltered, tranquil and remote shingle beach by a pier with easy access.

2 mins, 51.6721, -10.0169

9 BALLYDONEGAN BEACH

Just outside Allihies, the Ballydonegan river meanders around a huge dune of coarse golden sand before reaching the sea. For the quietest area and finest sand, ignore the car park by the campsite and head for the lane by the river at the other end (51.6319, -10.0566) where you can pull off onto the gravel and grass.

2 mins, 51.6322 -10.0582

10 TRAMORE, LOUGHANE BEG

From lane end walk S past pier (jumps possible from steps at HT) to the second, larger cove. The rocky cliffs of White Ball Head to S are dramatic and visited by climbers; at sea level there is a slot to a blowhole known as Thunderbolt Hole (51.5976, -10.0500), and further around the Arch Cave (51.5966, -10.0511). Or more quickly accessed from quay on S side of headland and walk up farm track 500m, P75 YC83, 51.5964, -10.0410.

5 mins, 51.6021, -10.0420

11 PULLEEN HARBOUR *

Remote harbour in a steep, rocky inlet, with a jumpable quay, a shingle beach and a river cascading through fun cisterns. Very limited parking outside harbour gates, where vehicles must stop. Despite memorials to two drownings, on a typical day it is sheltered and idyllic. Several boats, but quiet on our weekend visit.

2 mins, 51.6210, -9.9664

12 CLOUGHLAND STRAND, BERE

The best swimming at this lovely little shingle beach and slipway is at HT and facing the morning sun. You can scramble, swim or kayak around to two hidden coves to the right; the furthest one has caves (51.6275, -9.8197). Limited parking.

2 mins, 51.6287, -9.8212

13 SCAIRT BEACH, BERE

There are very few beaches on Bere Island; this E-facing slice of white sand in a rocky inlet is the most secluded, although a locals' favourite. It lies beside a firing range (only occasionally in use) where you can usually park. If the range is in use, head to Cloughland Strand (see entry).

5 mins, 51.6345, -9.8019

14 AGHABEG PIER

Remote pier and slipway for small boats with rocks and a cobbled beach. Boher Bank pier is also quiet and has a lovely natural harbour for swimming at HT (51.6603, -9.7922).

2 mins, 51.6617, -9.7739

15 REENABULLIGA PIER

Secluded shingle and cobble bay with rocky fingers reaching into the sea and a pier for HT jumps. Several stretches of beach L and R. Off R572 on tiny lane L95723-13.

2 mins, 51.6710, -9.7450

16 ELLEN'S ROCK & ZETLAND PIER

This tidal creek and quay is right by the R572 but it's a popular and beautifully clear and sheltered spot for a swim or kayak, with very easy parking and access. Another 6km W is the turning for Zetland Pier. This has white sand and an island but has become very popular and crowded (51.6953 -9.5981).

2 mins, 51.7392, -9.5544

17 SNAVE PIER, CÉ SNAVE

Perfect place for an evening swim or to put in a kayak, with jumps possible at HT. Pick up supplies from Mannings (see entry) and picnic at the tables or further out on the rocks as the sun goes down.

2 mins, 51.7277, -9.4523

RIVER, LAKE & WATERFALL

18 RIVER OUVANE & KEALKILL

At Carriganass Castle bridge there's easy access to pools and waterfalls for a dip. Two good looped walks start here, Póc an Tairbh and Srón na Gaoithe; both are about 10km and half a day and have great views over Bantry

19

Bay at the end of the walk on quiet lanes and to the crossroads by Maughanasilly stone row (51.7704, -9.3867).

5 mins, 51.7531, -9.3789

19 DROMANASSIG WATERFALL *

A series of cascades just below the bridge with three huge infinity pools big enough for a good swim. Avoid if anglers present. Pebble beaches 100m upstream. Just off the N71 on L4066, signed Waterfall Farmhouse; park carefully R before the bridge. Scramble down on the L near side of bridge.

2 mins, 51.8545, -9.5208

20 SHEEN FALLS

An exciting series of cascades with a beach and large pool behind low weir. Next to the fast N71 and no easy parking so follow the fishery riverside path 1km upstream from gate at 51.8731, -9.5635 (patrons of Stables Brasserie & Bar park within the hotel complex opposite).

5 mins, 51.8699, -9.5524

21 POOLEEN WOOD WATERFALL *

The 'little pool' on the Glengariff/Kerry River that gives the woods its name is actually pretty bg. There's a lovely waterfall, a shingle beach and large slabs for jumping and sunbathing, plus woodland path. Heading N on N71, pass

18

20

24

22

21

the main turn for the Nature Reserve and take next L signed Barley Lake L4927. It's 2.6km to the free car park on L with pool adjacent. After 400m you'll also cross the Canrooska tributary and stone bridge with a short, mossy 'Waterfall Walk' to Esknamucky falls, 200m upstream (51.7608, -9.5645). There's a three-part waterfall and small pool and a woodland loop back. There are also pools along the 'River Walk' from the main Glengarriff Woods Nature Reserve car park.

5 mins, 51.7630, -9.5933

22 AMEEN RIVER & CLOONEE LOUGH

Below the little footbridge from the Uragh stone circle (see entry) parking is a deep pool where the Ameen enters Cloonee Lough Upper. The lough can also be reached at a pretty stone boathouse and pier 600m back along the lane (51.8176, -9.7012). Alternatively follow the wild wooded shores of Lough Inchiquin SW from below the circle (51.8092, -9.6970). 5km further SE on up the lane lies private Gleninchaquin Park, with good managed trails, waterfall and lake; access is €7 cash per person (51.802, -9.6605).

2 mins, 51.8131, -9.6979

23 ADRIGOLE WATERFALL & HEALY PASS

Two large, deep river pools await you below the bridge, linked by cascades. It's a scramble down, but great for the adventurous. Look out for a narrow, unsigned lane descending to the R off the R574, 1km N of Adrigole Bridge. This is also the start of the dramatic and famous Healy Pass over the Caha Mountains on winding roads.

2 mins, 51.7009, -9.7157

24 LEHID BRIDGE SECRET WATERFALL

A tiny stream creates a particularly impressive waterfall and plunge pool, hidden just below the R573. Park in the layby at 51.7979, -9.7718 and walk 50m W, past the junction, to find the pool L below stone bridge parapet, through the undergrowth.

2 mins, 51.7976, -9.7720

25 GLANMORE LOUGH & CROANSHAGH

These are 'the swimming rocks' where locals get in to swim in the serene lake with little islets and forested slopes opposite. There's a small stone boathouse too. Pull over to the side carefully, it's a quiet road. There's also a rather special private set of pools, islands and bridges downstream on the Croanshagh River (51.7507, -9.7805).

2 mins, 51.7398, -9.7752

26 GLENBEG LOUGH

A secluded lough in a steep mountain valley, signed up a dead-end lane. A shingle beach and steps make an easy entry, and there are picnic tables and adjacent parking. If there are anglers, just walk on along the lane for other spots. Easy for overnights.

2 mins, 51.7221, -9.8806

27 KEALINCHA CASCADES, EYERIES

The Kealincha river tumbles down a rock face into a picturesque pool, with more whitewater rapids (grade 5) downstream. Pull off on the R571 on the Eyeries side of the R575 junction, walk down R575 for Allihies to a field gate R (51.6846, -9.9550) and follow track to river.

8 mins, 51.6844, -9.9570

28 RIVER COOMHOLA BRIDGE

A gate in the stone wall below the bridge leads down to deep, rocky pools. Some parking on W side of bridge, as this is the start of the Coorycommane Loop walk to W, with views over Bantry Bay. Another secret spot is upstream, accessed 150m N from the roadside (51.7525, -9.4407) on fishing path.

2 mins, 51.7433, -9.4567

LOST RUINS

29 DUNBOY CASTLE

Climb the grassy walls of this 15th-century castle, built to overlook the harbour and destroyed after a two-week siege in 1602. The remains of a 17th-century bastion fort built around it are also still clear, and on the way in you pass Puxley Manor, a 19th-century Gothic confection burned in 1921 and twice in recent years on the brink of a new life as a luxury hotel. Daphne Du Maurier was a friend of the family and used their story for her novel Hungry Hill. You can also walk S along the coast for Dunboy Woods (see entry).

2 mins, 51.6332, -9.9246

30 ALLIHIES COPPER MINES

Dating back to 1812, this was once among the larger copper mines in Ireland, employing 1,600 men. Today the ruins of the (fenced-off) engine house are a picturesque marker, but there are other ruins on the site, fantastic sea views, fun scrambling and a little swimming lake below. The Copper Mine Museum in the village provides more detailed history. There's a small layby here and the track ascends 200m.

2 mins, 51.6478, -10.0398

SACRED SITES

31 ST FINBARR'S ORATORY

At the source of the Lee lies the beautiful Gougane Barra lake and the island hermitage of Cork city's founding saint. A causeway leads out to low 6th-century ruins, a substantial 17th-century hermitage with cell-like recesses in the walls, and a Celtic Revival oratory from 1903. Used for secret masses in penal times, this is

29

30

31

34

35

36

36

still an active pilgrimage site, with a crowded mass at the end of September. There is also an organised swim in the lake at the start of the month, and a dip here when the hills turn russet in autumn is a wonderful thing, as are the walks through the surrounding mixed woodland.

2 mins, 51.8396, -9.3185

32 DROM FEAGHNA GRAVEYARD

Dating back possibly to the 6th century, this graveyard has two concentric walls: the inner one is very old, the outer one was a Famine relief project in the 1840s, and between them lay a cillín. Now there is a platform for viewing the Rolls of Butter or Petrified Dairy to the S, a boulder with several bullauns holding stones, which has no public access (Bonane Heritage Park arranges occasional visits). The folklore says that St Feaghna turned to stone both a woman who stole milk and the butter she made. Over the road through a gate lies a holy well by a holly (51.8196, -9.4994). The lane leads on 1.3km S to a stone bridge over waterfall pools on the Coomeelan (51.8127, -9.4887) and then on tiny lanes up to the Priest's Leap mountain pass (51.7934, -9.4711).

2 mins, 51.8196, -9.4994

33 KILMACKOWEN & ST FINNIAN'S WELL

A little-known standing-stone and wedge tomb on the W slope of Eagle Hill, with a farm track in from road W to the stone, and a stile giving access to the little tomb at the far side of the next field (51.6817, -9.9084). Curiously, the two are linked by a line of stones that is not a field boundary. For more hidden antiquity, only 2km S find twin holy wells, surrounded by hexagonal paving slabs in a wild heathland setting atop a small raised enclosure. Track at 51.6672, -9.9218, then 100m W.

10 mins, 51.6827, -9.9094

34 GLEBE GRAVEYARD, KILLACONENAGH

Although the ivy-covered church ruins and several costly looking stones are 19th century, this quite ancient graveyard is now abandoned, overgrown and quite chaotic. Stones lean at all angles and the ground is riddled with dips and holes. Folklore says a monster from the nearby stream broke open the graves. Behind the church is a famine plot, and over a wall if you can find the stile in (easiest in winter) are four huge hollows cut into a rockface – the largest a metre wide – that are classed as a holy well (51.6461, -9.9308).

2 mins, 51.6460, -9.9313

35 KILCATHERINE CHURCH & HAG OF BEARA

Glorious views cut to sea from the medieval church of the obscure local St Chaitighern, anglicised and sex-changed in the modern name. An early antiquarian fancifully identified the odd carved head on a long neck over the door as a feline to explain the name as 'Cill-cait-iairn' or 'church of the iron cat'. At the E of the flowery graveyard stands a simple cross thought to be 1,500 years old, among Ireland's oldest. Just east along the road (51.7157, -9.9628) is the Hag of Beara, a winter goddess, turned to rock by the saint for stealing his prayer book; if you look charitably from the right angle, you may see her.

2 mins, 51.7156, -9.9692

STONES CIRCLES

36 KEALKILL & BREENY MORE CIRCLES

Kealkill has a five-stone circle, two taller outliers, and a flat cairn with a few remaining kerbstones, all on one hilltop. Park at gate at the bend in the steep lane. The superb views W to Bantry Bay take in Breeny More circle on a similar summit (51.7422, -9.3751), with 'boulder burials' inside it. Take the next lane L driving down the hill from Kealkill and park by the gate and ringfort at the last bend before the farm; the family were happy for us to visit.

2 mins, 51.7451, -9.3705

37 URAGH STONE CIRCLES & SUMMIT *

Bronze Age five-stone axial circle in a stunning valley setting with breathtaking views over

37

37

37

37

39

40

42

42

42

the lake – almost better viewed from the huge boulder on the rise above, a perfect spot for a picnic. It lies at the end of a scenic drive along a narrow lane, well signed from Coornagillagh R571, with rough parking for a few cars beyond the gate after the River Ameen (see entry) then walk L 300m. Along the farm track SW is a ruined 'famine house' off the track 50m R (51.8108, -9.7057) and Uragh West stone circle and 'boulder burial', tricky to find by a tiny stream 400m SE in beautiful woodland along the lough shore hillside (no clear path, 51.8078, -9.7039). We then followed the stream up through fields SW, then on rocky spurs, to the summit of Knockagarrane (404m) for sensational views.

5 mins, 51.8115, -9.6954

38 LITTLE MILLS COMPLEX

A five-stone circle, three 'boulder burials' and a standing stone pair, all 3,000–4,000 years old, with other stones piled around. It may have been a large observational arena, with alignment possibilities for solar and lunar events, but there is no certainty. Pull off near corner and go through field gate L before bridge. About 1km N on lane (51.7642, -9.4686) is the start of a walk to Cooleenlemane Bealick (see entry).

3 mins, 51.7533, -9.4636

39 CASHELKEELTY STONE CIRCLES

Bring a picnic to these two circles and their neighbouring stone row and sit with Beara's rocks (and incongruous electricity lines) at your back and views out to sea in front. There were offerings on one recumbent stone. Ignore the sign indicating the route starts in the car park (R571 at 51.7594, -9.8035); go back to the road and walk E 100m to a stile. Head up through the woods with the stream on your right to meet a remnant of the medieval Old Green Road at the top. Follow it R to the circles. If you have a map and sturdy gear, there is a ruined cottage and old walls in the forestry (51.7589, -9.8131).

30 mins, 51.7571, -9.8138

40 DERREENATAGGART STONE CIRCLE

This hilltop circle is very atmospheric when the cattle amble out of it. There may have been 15 stones originally, but a few have gone and three have fallen. Room for two cars in broad gateway almost opposite. Continue W along the road for Teernahillane Ringfort, which may be a fort or just a strange natural feature; see what you think, and look for the holes of solitary bees nesting in the sunny vertical side v(51.6508, -9.9616).

2 mins, 51.6538, -9.9289

41 LOUGHANE MORE RINGFORT

Superb sea views from this cliff-top fort, which has stone facing to the inside of its earthen bank and the entrance to a blocked souterrain in the middle. The rugged headland to the SE is thought to be a promontory fort. Pull over on the R572 above the sign and stile (51.6021, -10.1071).

3 mins, 51.6005, -10.1051

VIEWPOINTS & HEADLANDS

42 RABACH'S GLEN *

A long grassy lane leads down a dramatic valley to two remote farms and Shronebirrane, a Bronze Age axial circle of eight stones, in a field next to a house where you can park, sometimes for a €4 fee (51.7377, -9.8040). Up the remote river valley are the ruins of pre-famine cottages nestled in a glen below a pyramind rock (The Pocket on OS maps); you might spot a cashel on the way (51.7325, -9.8157). Scramble on up the slabs further for a glorious glacial corrie with jumps at the far end (51.7281, -9.8293) and standing stones on the W shore. Follow the stream down to explore the waterfalls – some have deep pools (51.7270, -9.8211).

30 mins, 51.7255, -9.8211

43 COORYCOMMANE HILL

Sublime views over Bantry Bay and Glengarriff Harbour are the reward for an occasionally steep and mucky looped walk route through mixed woodland, fields, bogs and quiet lanes from parking by Coomhola bridge for a dip (see entry).

90 mins, 51.7437, -9.4566

44 ESK MOUNTAIN RIDGE & MINE

The bracing and occasionally muddy Cailleach Beara route, named for the winter hag, is a good half-day introduction to hiking in the Caha Mountains, well marked from the Bonane Loops trailhead next to Molly Gallivans. There are stunning views N over the Macgillicuddy's Reeks and Kenmare Bay, and from the W end down to Bantry Bay. Shortly before this, divert over a stile L for a Neolithic copper mine, an opening in a low cliff that holds two shafts, and a third tucked in a crevice above them (51.7858, -9.5741).

130 mins, 51.7896, -9.5603

45 BERE ISLAND SIGNAL TOWER

Bere Haven was historically a vital deep-water port, and Bere Island guarded it. Park at 51.6333, -9.9044 and follow trail up to the hilltop ruins of the Napoleonic signal tower via 19th-century Ardnakinna lighthouse (51.6184, -9.9180) with views over to the Sheep's Head peninsula. You can descend on the lanes after this, or continue E to the summit of Knockanallig with equally fine views and a

41

45

47

47

Holy Year cross (51.6308, -9.8690), and then 3m tall Greenane Standing Stone or Gallán (51.6311, -9.8608), There is also Ardagh Martello Tower, which can be entered (51.6340, -9.8475). Lonehort battery at the E end is open in summer (at other times call Barry Hanley on +353 86 8845709 or Teresa Hall on +353 86 1981541 about access).

90 mins, 51.6268, -9.8947

46 KILCATHERINE POINT

A wonderful wild headland for sunset over the sea. A couple of parking spaces at the end of a rough gravel road; go carefully in a normal car. Good for overnights – those with tents could walk N for a sheltered spot between the ridges. There is a small wedge tomb (51.7192, -9.9997), best approached on the green track snaking around the hill from 51.7181, -9.9962; the inner headland is boggy.

2 mins, 51.7160, -10.0053

47 CAHIRKEEM MASS ROCK

A short walk up to magnificent sea views in splendid isolation with a simple stone cross. Parking just to the E (51.6702, -10.0414) opp the sign; this points straight inland, but the route – just a trodden trail – slopes up R through bracken. Enough people visit to keep the path mostly visible, but we still had it to ourselves for a summer sunset.

5 mins, 51.6694, -10.0443

48 MASS ROCK, COPPER MINE TRAIL

Follow this track up past the copper mine with chimney (51.6482, -10.0374) to the rugged spine of the peninsula and a mass rock in a sheltered scoop known as Cúm an Aifrinn, mass valley. Walk up and back from parking at W end (51.6449, -10.0382) or have a lift arranged for the E end where there is only a gate and stile at 51.6640, -10.0035.

50 mins, 51.6530, -10.0298

49 BLACK BALL HEAD SIGNAL TOWER

A beautifully remote and dramatic 19th-century signal tower shell with some of its original slating. From gate at 51.5977, -10.0345, pass the old quay then 1km across heathland with old field walls. Trick parking; you could ask at the final farm.

20 mins, 51.5900, -10.0379

50 GARINISH POINT

A well-marked loop trail heads up the dramatic cliffs to a 150m high point with views as far as the Skelligs. There are a couple of popular sandy coves below, then return along little lanes in a 5km loop. Park as for cable car to Dursey Island (see entry).

40 mins, 51.6131, -10.1472

51 CROW HEAD

As you walk out on this wild headland fields give way to gorse and heather. The cliffs are full of dramatic fissures and the end, with its unreachable island, is a good spot to watch dolphins and whales, or a summer sunset before a twilight walk back or a night of stargazing. The path starts at the end of the road, 51.6027, -10.1420; there is also a short inland loop walk.

90 mins, 51.5823, -10.1602

52 DURSEY ISLAND CABLE CAR

Make an early start to avoid queues on the unique cable car to Dursey, and follow the trail along the spine of the island to the impressively intact signal tower on the summit. Nearby is an EIRE pilots' marker, cleared in 2024 (51.5956, -10.2069). The loop walk route returns along the lane, passing the graveyard with a ruined church (51.6042, -10.1593) and the low, sod-covered remains of a 17th-century castle on a little island beyond. If you have the time, an extra 6km out and back reaches the W tip with views to the lighthouse stump on Bull Rock which has a huge sea cave tunnel through the middle of it (boat trips go there).

2 mins, 51.5957, -10.2052

CAVES & SCRAMBLES

53 COOLEENLEMANE BEALICK & PRIEST'S LEAP

From 'an bhéillic' (cavern), three chambers between mighty leaning boulders by a stream. Two are decorated with ancient motifs cut in the stone, as well as modern initials and crosses. The outcrop was used as a mass rock in Penal times, and one 1841 travelogue even recorded a family living here in summer. Some just admire this beautiful valley from the Priest's Leap viewpoint (51.7935, -9.4712), but a walk up it is a walk through time. Park by bridge at end of the road after Little Mills megaliths (51.7642, -9.4686, see entry) and head upriver. You pass a collapsed tomb by a ford (51.7648, -9.4674), ruined cottages, abandoned potato ridges and a low cashel (51.7747, -9.4721) to reach the bealick. Or park on Priest's Leap road and head down over stream (51.7770, -9.4643).

15 mins, 51.7763, -9.4723

54 HUNGRY HILL SCRAMBLING

The steep, rugged quartzite flanks of the highest peak in the Caha Mountains (682m) offer fine scrambling and spectacular views. Take the L95723-16 off the R572 and after 1.6km (through a farm gate) park at 51.6736, -9.8088. Follow the track past the lake and then take a line up the SW ridge. (The track continues onto a stream and waterfalls, a good return route, 51.6831, -9.8131). The steeper SE flanks can be reached from the lane at

37

51.6830, -9.7656 for a hike to the dramatic and deep Lough Coomadayallig (51.6905, -9.7783).
60 mins, 51.6822, -9.7985

WOODS & WILDLIFE

55 LADY BANTRY LOOKOUT, GLENGARRIFF

From the main Glengarriff Woods Nature Reserve car park (signed off N71) a 600m trail leads up on stone steps through ancient woods to a craggy lookout over the forest. There are other walking trails (Esknamucky, Big Meadow etc) through the wider forest, largely old oak with some recent regenerative planting.
10 mins, 51.7509, -9.5654

56 DUNBOY FOREST

Old mixed forest with oak, birch, Scots pine and western hemlock. From the central car park (51.6301, -9.9327) head E to the coastline trail along Bullig Bay, running S past Traneen/Dunboy beach to a picnic bench at the point (51.6237, -9.9249) or N to Dunboy Castle (see entry) where there is also parking.
10 mins, 51.6302, -9.9276

57 ADRIGOLE PIER SEALS *

Swim from the pier or kayak out across the bay to where the seals are calm and curious. You can hire from Kayak with Seals on the pier or or even take a skippered sailing trip with Gail and Niall McAllister (P75 YY86, +353 83 1156672, westcorksailing.com). Signed off the R572, blink and you'll miss it.
10 mins, 51.6827, -9.71635

58 DURSEY CLIFFS TRIP, GARINISH

A boat trip from Garnish Pier is the best way to really see the dramatic cliffs of Dursey Island, and the only way to see Bull, Cow and Calf Rocks, home to an extraordinary sea arch and the mighty stump of a cast-iron lighthouse. There's plenty of history to hear, and you will see puffins and Ireland's largest gannet colony, with a chance of whales, dolphins, basking sharks and seals. Parking at the pier. +353 83 8989999, durseyboattrips.com. Arrive early to enjoy a dip at beautiful White Strand just before the quay.
2 mins, 51.6188, -10.1344

CLASSIC CAFES & BARS

59 DERREEN GARDEN & CAFÉ

The café here uses produce from the kitchen garden and is famous for the home-baked cakes, drawing people who never even enter the rambling woodland estate. Café 11.00am–5.00pm Mar–Nov. Lauragh, Kenmare, V93 D792, +353 83 1662160
51.7701, -9.7873

60 HELEN'S BAR & CAFÉ

This second-generation local institution by the harbour is legendary for its seafood and great prices equally, and the tables along the pier fill quickly in fine weather. Helen is a mine of information and it's a great place to get breakfast and tips on your plans, although her B&B guests get priority. Kilmakilloge, Lauragh, V93 NF70, +353 64 6683104
51.7805, -9.80567

61 MACCARTHY'S BAR

This fourth-generation pub is alive with culture and history, with live music regularly and everything from books to a fin whale vertebra on the wood-panelled walls. Most dramatic is the family story of Dr Aidan MacCarthy, an RAF medic who was in a Japanese prisoner of war camp and became a humanitarian hero in the Nagasaki atomic strike. Sit at the long bar or in a high-backed settle and try the excellent seafood. Main Street, Castletownbere, P75 NX52, +353 27 70014
51.6517, -9.9102

62 O'NEILL'S BAR & RESTAURANT

On the main street of colourful Allihies, this buzzing local serves excellent food, especially seafood, and local musicians congregate up to play tunes from trad to modern together.

61

62

63

68

70

In summer the tables outside and even across the street are full, get there early. Main Street, Allihies, P75 PE80, +353 27 73008
51.6416, -10.0440

LOCAL PRODUCE

63 MANNING'S EMPORIUM

Selling the best local and European artisan produce for five decades – the cheese counter alone deserves multiple visits. Also a café and restaurant, and wood-fired pizzas to take away; often busy, so book if you can. Ballylickey, Bantry, P75 CX86, +353 27 50456
51.7195, -9.4382

64 LORGE CHOCOLATIER

Superb chocolate from this roadside factory shop (there's another outlet in Kenmare town). You can't see behind the scenes from the shop, but you can book a one- or two-day making course and learn it all. Bonane, Kenmare, V93 F344, +353 64 6679994
51.8160, -9.5366

65 TWO GREEN SHOOTS FORAGING

In summer, book a foraging tour or one of their other garden and wild food experiences, most with a meal using foraged plants and local ingredients from salted caramel spread to farmhouse cheeses. Keep an eye on the website. Glamping may be available. Tooreen, Glengarriff, P75 AW26,+353 89 7081099
51.7784, -9.5687

66 MILLEENS CHEESE

This superb semi-soft cheese has been made by the Steele family since 1974. Ideally buy in local shops, as the farm has no shop and isn't suitable for dogs or boisterous children, but Quinlan is a passionate champion of his product and area who will accommodate people if he can – and a keen kayaker. Eyeries, Béara, P75 FN52, +353 86 2105267
51.6766, -9.9565

ORGANIC & GASTRO

67 SUGARLOAF CAFÉ, GLENGARRIFF

A little café with extra tables outside that fill up rapidly, serving excellent coffee and great cooked breakfasts, waffles and pancakes, all made in a tiny kitchen area in full view. Main Street, Glengarriff, P75 AK71
51.7501, -9.5514

68 AN SIBIN WINE BAR, RESTAURANT, B&B

One end of this long, low building is still styled like the traditional illicit pub of the name, with a stove and memorabilia; the rest is a more elegant dining room with rooms above, serving simply superb food and wine. Hours vary through the year; usually at least weekends in winter. Lauragh Lower, Lauragh, V93 T4C2, +353 64 6683004. Josie's Lakeview House is also nearby (+353 646683155, 51.7416, -9.7740)
51.7656, -9.7708

69 SUGRUE'S ON THE SQUARE

This bright café is the perfect place for a hearty breakfast before taking the ferry to Bere Island for the day, to set you up for walking the hills. The Square, Castletownbere, P75 HX47 +353 83 0060815
51.6509, -9.9106

70 BREEN'S LOBSTER BAR

With a strong menu featuring excellent seafood, this is the place the locals all recommend, and booking ahead is advisable, not least because hours are variable. Cash only; ATM opposite. 2 Bank Place, Castletownbere, P75 T862, +353 27 70031
51.6511, -9.9108

COOL CAMPING

71 CASTLE FIELD MOTORHOME PARK

A small, basic paid parking area for touring vans, looking on the ruins of Carriganass Castle and scenic hills beyond. The Ouvane river is adjacent with small pools and waterfalls. Fresh water, disposal, and a toilet all at the back of a cabin with tourist information and fresh eggs (honesty box); phone number to ring on arrival in the window, +353 86 3653637
51.7536, -9.3794

72 EAGLE POINT CAMPING, BALLYLICKEY*

Occupying a whole peninsula with its own beaches and slipway to kayak or paddle board from, this site can find a pitch to suit almost everyone (sadly no pets), from family spaces with power near the facilities to little shoreline hollows at the furthest rocky tip with its little island and perfect sunset views; tell them what you're looking for when you book. Reendesert, Ballylickey, P75 WP58, +353 2750630
51.7203, -9.4491

73 HUNGRY HILL LODGE & CAMPSITE

Camping and van pitches among the trees and a few lodges, with excellent facilities, open Mar–Dec. Dogs on leads accepted on pitches. Just along the (quite fast) road is a HT swimming spot with a little parking and a wooden jetty among rocks where cormorants sun themselves (51.6895, -9.7315). Adrigole, P75 CY62, +353 83 1196659
51.6940, -9.7254

74 BEARA CAMPING

A good woodland camping area and some simple, affordable old-school wooden cabins with bunk beds. Well placed for Uragh stone circle and Coornagillagh beach. Coornagillagh, V93 YP29, +353 64 6684287

51.8264, -9.7310

75 CREVEEN LODGE CAMPING *

Tent and van pitches scattered up a hillside (climb higher to see sunset over the lakes) among trees in a friendly, quiet and slightly ramshackle site with a home-built feel. Fire-pits allowed, bring your own fuel. There are also three very traditional farmhouses that can be rented by the week. Lauragh, V93 YHY9, +353 64 6683131, creveenlodge.com

51.7548, -9.7604

76 ALLIHIES CAMPING

A bit exposed, right on the beach and cliffside, and can be a bit of a party site, but a good summer option if the weather holds. +353 86 8121582, anthonybattos@gmail.com

51.6340, -10.0618

RUSTIC RETREATS

77 GOUGANE BARRA HOTEL

This cosy family-run hotel is right on the lake by St Finbarr's Oratory (see entry) with the woods behind. Great home cooking, partly supplied from their own organic kitchen garden. Closed in winter. Derreenacusha, Gougane Barra, P12 PP27, +353 26 47069

51.8389, -9.3168

78 SECRET GARDEN GLAMPING

Three pods in the spectacular remote settings of Gleninchaquin Park with its cascade, waterfall pools, walking trails, mountain lake and views (usual entrance fee €7/€5). Gleninchaquin, Coomacaragh, V93 D5X2, +353 89 2486935

51.7984, -9.6567

79 THE BOATHOUSE, ADRIGOLE PIER *

Rooms with a communal kitchen in this eco-upgraded sister project to Kayak with the Seals. Simple modern rooms, geothermal underfloor heating, views and a balcony over the sea. Adrigole Pier, P75 YY86, +353 86 2214724 (or Airbnb or booking.com)

51.6826, -9.7161

80 THE NAKED SHEEP

Two stone cottages with lovely views, with alpaca trekking, and occasional wool spinning and knitting courses on hand. Derrylough, Tuosist, V93 W2R6, +353 876272183, thenakedsheep.ie

51.8100, -9.7349

81 WILD ATLANTIC GLAMPING, BERE

Ten bell tents by a sunrise beach; kayaking trips including night kayaking depart right from the shore and the welcome pack includes fresh home-made scones, Bere Island honey, local blackberry jam and marshmallows for toasting in the fire-pit on the covered terrace. Two-night minimum. Ardagh, P75 RF68, +353 86 6027819

51.6392, -9.82805

82 PIGEON HOUSE

Secluded stone cottage just 200m from the sea surrounded by its own land with coves, cliffs, lakes and ruins galore. +353 646641126, pigeonhouse.org

51.7377, -9.9495

83 DZOGCHEN BEARA

Go on a meditation retreat at this wonderful cliff-top Buddhist centre, or just book accommodation: there is a hostel and three cottages. Also an excellent café open 9:30am–5.00pm. Strict no alcohol and no pets policy. Garranes, Allihies, P75 C670, dzogchenbeara.org

51.6153, -9.9793

17

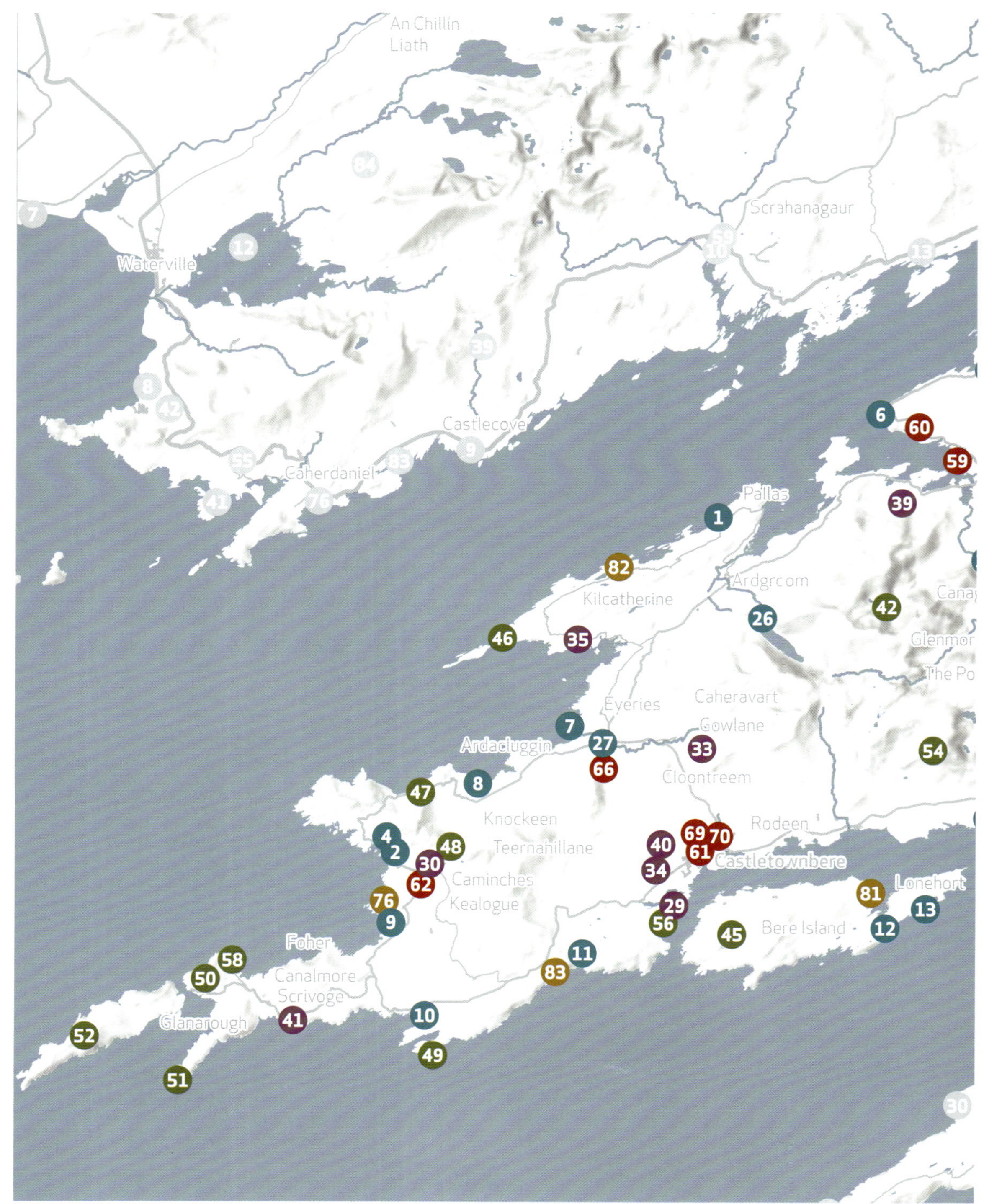
An Chillín Liath
Scrahanagaur
Waterville
Castlecove
Caherdaniel
Pallas
Ardgroom
Kilcatherine
Eyeries
Caheravart
Gowlane
Ardacluggin
Cloontreem
Knockeen
Teernahillane
Rodeen
Castletownbere
Caminches
Kealogue
Lonehort
Bere Island
Foher
Canalmore
Scrivoge
Glanarough

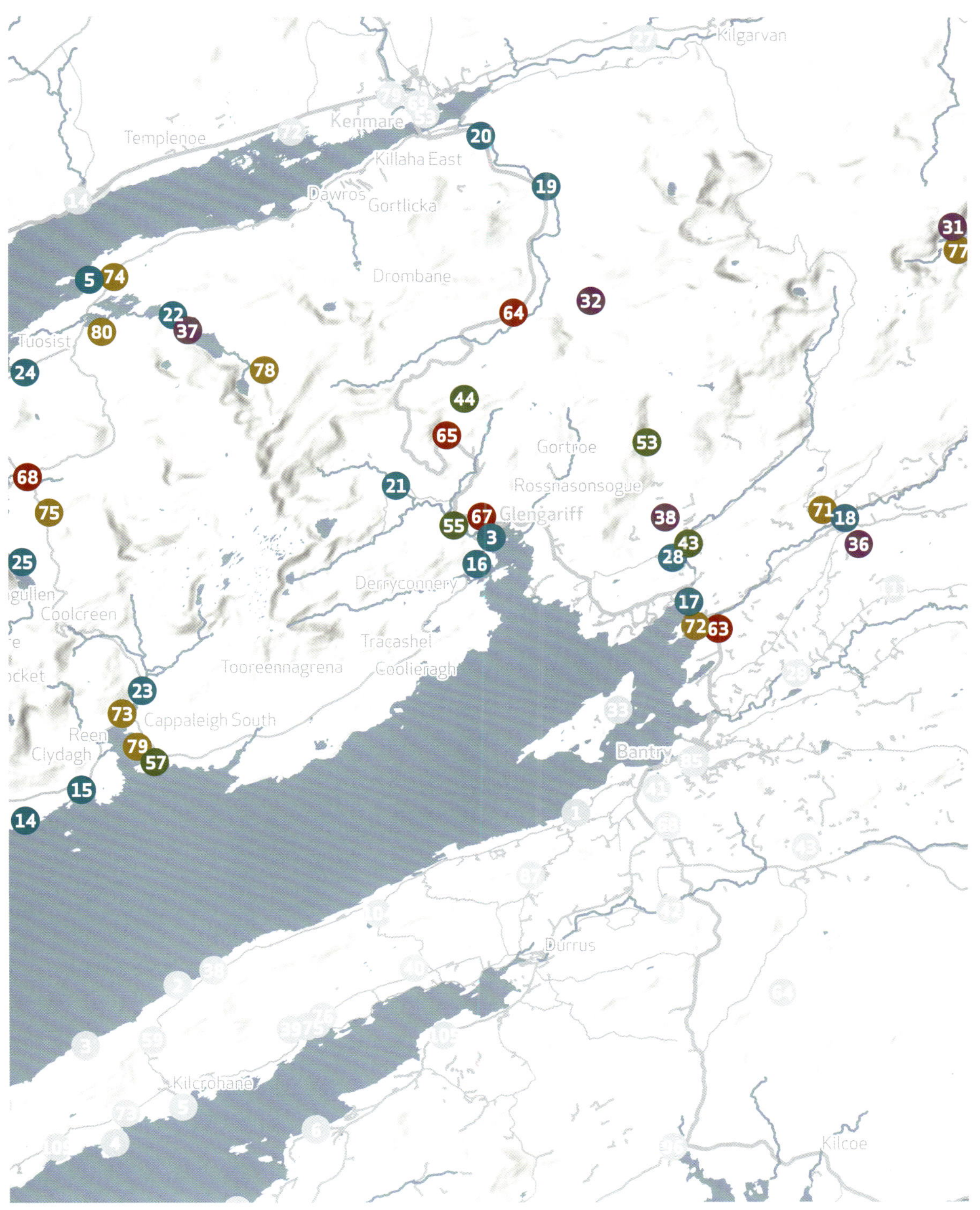
Kilgarvan
Kenmare
Templenoe
Killaha East
Dawros
Gortlicka
Drombane
Tuosist
Gortroe
Rossnasonsogue
Glengariff
Derryconnery
Coolcreen
Tracashel
Tooreennagrena
Coolieragh
Cappaleigh South
Reen
Clydagh
Bantry
Durrus
Kilcrohane
Kilcoe

SOUTH WEST CORK

Our perfect weekend

- → **Peer** into blowholes at Galley Head and relax at Long Strand with dinner from The Fish Basket right on the shore.
- → **Explore** ruined Coppinger's Court or imagine ancient ceremonies at Drombeg Stone Circle, and end the day with dinner on the seafront at Hayes' Bar in Glandore.
- → **Cycle** round Sherkin Island to pick your favourite beach and then have dinner on the mainland at one of Dede's restaurants.
- → **Camp** and kayak at Goleen Harbour, or use it as a base to explore Rock Island and Crookhaven.
- → **Jump** from Kilcrohane Pier with the rising sun, walk to remote Gortavallig Mine, and end the day in the garden of the Ahakista 'Tin Pub'.
- → **Ascend** to the ancient stones of Reenascreena and the ringfort churchyard of Castleventry, then settle in for an evening of trad at DeBarra's in Clonakilty.
- → **Learn** to smoke fish or forage wild foods at Up There The Last or Woodcock Smokery – or just indulge in one of their marvellous meal events.

1

2

5

The shorthand for travelling the length of the west coast is 'Malin to Mizen', and the dramatic peninsula with its signal station, buzzing Schull town and famous sites such as Altar wedge tomb does justifiably take a lot of the limelight – but the supporting cast flanking it have plenty that's worth notice.

The narrow Sheep's Head peninsula to the north is home to some of Ireland's most inviting walking paths, leading to stunning views, as well as a remote little lighthouse and a failed copper mine. A lack of big, sandy beaches keeps things quiet, but there are lovely coves and harbours, and almost all the entries for these could begin 'at the end of a flower-filled lane'. Every so often one is 'discovered' and overrun – at time of writing, it was Canty's Cove – but novelty-hungry media sites move on and peace returns.

The southernmost point of Ireland is Brow Head on the south of the Mizen, a high walk past a historic Marconi signal station and Napoleonic tower. South of this lies Roaringwater Bay, an SAC that's home to whales, dolphins, sharks and 'Carbery's hundred isles' as recorded in poetry – in truth no more than 50, but some of the most species-rich land in Ireland. They include the large islands of Cléire, Sherkin and Heir, and a host of smaller outposts.

From here the coast runs east with broader white sands; some are crowded in summer or dubiously developed, but there are smaller bays and quays to discover. Inland, this area is home to the densest concentration of stone circles in Ireland, from tiny five-stone sites such as Lettergorman to broad rings such as Reenascreena.

The local 'axial' type has a recumbent stone opposite two tall portal stones; strangely, no accurate seasonal alignment has been found. Many also have 'boulder burials', with small stones supporting a large boulder; these were originally taken as graves but none has yielded remains.

West Cork is renowned as a foodie hotspot, with plenty of superb restaurants to be found from colourful Clonakilty to double-Michelin-starred Dede in Baltimore. Great cheeses and preserved foods have been produced here since the 1970s, with Durrus Cheese on the Sheep's Head an early exemplar. Whether you pack a gourmet picnic for your adventures or book a table for the end of the day, you won't be short of choices here.

3

3

4

SHEEP'S HEAD SECRET COAST

1 SHANVALLYBEG BEACH

A shingle and shale cove, with interesting rock formations and a friendly labrador called Bolt. Park carefully on the verge and follow the stream path down 50m.

2 mins, 51.6640, -9.5069

2 GORTNAKILLA PIER

A wild little harbour in a natural inlet. Not the most sheltered but perfect for a sundowner dip, with deep water full of swirling, golden seaweed strands. Signed down a tiny winding lane with limited rough parking at the end.

2 mins, 51.6120, -9.6988

3 GLANROON ROCK QUAY *

A pretty stroll to a secret stone-cut quay and slipway in a dramatic bay. Good for coasteering and jumps, but bring rock shoes as there are no steps out! Signed off the tiny coast lane, with a small parking area at the end and a pretty path.

3 mins, 51.5936, -9.7433

4 DOONEEN PIER, KILCROHANE *

A deep, sheltered harbour with a large quay, great jumping at many states of tide, a little islet and regular summer bioluminescence. There are fascinating caves in the cliffs, especially L, and Darren's in Durrus rent kayaks (P75 RP26, darrenskayaks.com). Popular for fishing in mackerel season and for picnicking; try breakfast with the rising sun. The fishing path S from the last turn in the lane may yield sandy coves depending on the last storm; find the large rock pool at 51.5599, -9.7319.

2 mins, 51.5640, -9.7294

5 KILCROHANE PIER & FARRANAMANAGH

This shingle and cobble bay and pier are usually sheltered, and HT swimming is good. Pretty Farranamanagh Bay is 800m N along the foreshore, backed by a large lake (51.5801, -9.6910) reached by lane, but no parking.

2 mins, 51.5749, -9.6966

MIZEN HEAD HIDDEN COAST

6 KILCOMANE COVE

Sheltered cobble beach and quay, good for jumps at HT, with offshore reefs that are lovely to snorkel; look for spider crabs and dogfish. Space for up to five cars. A little back up the lane is a track R to a cillín on the wood edge L, with lovely sea views and a few markers discernable (51.5666, -9.6327). Or walk the track W 1km for more coastline and views to Oileáin an bPaorach.

2 mins, 51.5679, -9.6325

6

6

7

11

7 DUNMANUS POINT ARCH

A headland with hidden coves and amazing rock bridge, overlooked by a medieval castle by an inland lagoon. Park by the stone barns (51.5398, -9.6650) and find gate 30m opposite to follow E side of headland, then over to the arch bridge/blowhole. Castle is E along the lane from parking. All above are fenced/gated so you may need to ask at the farm.

15 mins, 51.5432, -9.6706

8 CANTY'S COVE QUAY *

A tiny quay in a beautiful sheltered N-facing inlet, perfect for swimming and coasteering, a famous secret on social media. Reached on unsigned lanes from Dunkelly West (51.5209, -9.7137). There's another small quay 2km E at Dooneen Coos, Gortduff (51.5250, -9.7303).

2 mins, 51.5254, -9.7098

9 TOOR PIER & SEA ARCH

At the end of tiny lanes, remote harbour and quay accessed by path and stone ramp carved into the cliffs with steps. It's all unforgiving rock here, so only venture in when calm, but it leads to a huge sea arch. Small parking and turning area at the end of the lane.

2 mins, 51.4942, -9.8027

10 O'SULLIVAN'S PIER, MIZEN

Anglers have made a path to this remote old pier on E facing coast for its deep waters, though it's over private land. Park in layby at 51.46344, -9.7863 and walk down drive, following R at first houses and the trodden path L before the last to zig-zag down.

12 mins, 51.4582, -9.786

11 BARLEY COVE & WALKWAY

Wide, golden sands and stream estuary, reached by a walk through dunes and over a fun 200m floating pontoon. Houses and a hotel at one end, but plenty of room to escape crowds, and the area around the car park is popular for wild camping (be respectful). You can also park 600m further up the lane at 51.4687, -9.7691 for little Chimney Cove, or continue another 1km or to pull over and picnic at quieter Lackenakea Bay among the sea holly and wildflowers; it has rips, no car park and only cobbles at HT (51.4636, -9.7623).

15 mins, 51.4680, -9.7764

12 TRAWNABIRREA *

This hidden cove is a magical place to launch yourself off the rock steps into deep, clear turquoise water at HT, even better if it's sunrise. Park after the bridge (51.4775, -9.7112), walk on the private road back to the stile (51.4784,

11

12

21

-9.7094) and follow the boggy path.
5 mins, 51.4789, -9.7086

13 BALLYRISODE BEACHES
Popular family cove with small car park and no facilities, signed off R591. Walk back up lane 200m for the larger beach. For a much more secret cove, kayak 600m NE across the bay. By land it's accessed through the field gate at 51.5183, -9.6534, then a 400m track, but there's no parking. Best for cyclists.
2 mins, 51.5113, -9.6622

14 ALTAR COVE & CAMPING
Follow the roadside edge of the field next to parking for Altar wedge tomb (51.5140, -9.6439) to the end and then L down to a short path to a very sheltered narrow cove. Despite a sign, this is generally deserted. As a bonus, trails lead south through bracken from the tomb to little spaces popular with wild campers who arrive at the end of the day when visitors leave the car park empty. Idyllic until the next visitors arrive in the morning. You can clamber down over the rocks for a swim if the sea is calm.
2 mins, 51.5154, -9.6446

15 LEAMCON CASTLE & QUAY
A promontory linked to the mainland by a bridge upon which stands a partly restored 16th-century tower. Park in the farmyard and ask permission from the kindly farmer (51.4947, -9.6158) for 1km walk across fields. On lanes 1km N is a tiny inlet with quay, perfect for a swim/jump afterwards, 51.4984, -9.6189.
15 mins, 51.4924, -9.6289

16 DREENATRA PIER
Perfect out of the way pier and rocky cove for a HT swim or jump into crystal-clear water.
2 mins, 51.5217, -9.4989

ROARINGWATER ISLANDS

17 SHERKIN ISLAND
Just 5km long and a ten-minute ferry ride from Baltimore, Inisherkin is perfect for a day trip – or weekend, with a camping and glamping site (sherkinnorthshore.com). There's a ruined abbey right where you land and signed trails. Walk or hire a bike from Siopa Ui Neill near the harbour (+353 87 3825883), then choose from several lovely beaches on the W side, from Silver Strand (51.4743 -9.4239) round to Trá Bán (51.4661, -9.4242). You can even go on a kayak tour (h2oseakayaking.com).
30 mins, 51.4766, -9.3992

18 HEIR ISLAND
The island is rich in wildlife, from seabirds and seals to field birds and summer butterflies. Some claim Trá Bán, a fine, sandy beach sheltered from W winds, is the best beach; it's certainly a lovely spot, but there are others to choose from: little coves on the other side of this peninsula and a meandering estuary on the north shore. Many visitors instead head to the W cliffs and an almost cut-off promontory, where they find kestrels, ravens, rock pipits and choughs, and have a good chance of seeing dolphins or whales in an important breeding ground. Heir Island House is the only B&B, recently refurbished and using toiletries from local producers. They may be able to help with boat hire enquiries. (P81 X590, +353 86 8070715). Ferries from Baltimore and Cunnamore.
30 mins, 51.5001, -9.4237

19 CLÉIRE/CAPE CLEAR ISLAND
This Gaeltacht island is most famous for watching seabirds, migratory songbirds and the few unusual strays each year, and whales, leatherback turtles, dolphins and sharks are spotted regularly. The observatory has information and hostel rooms (P81 H306, birdwatchireland.ie); you can also camp at Chléire Haven cliff-top campsite (chleire-haven.ie) above a swimmable bay. Long habitation has left the holed Marriage Stone for sealing vows (51.4507 -9.4734), a passage tomb (51.4429 -9.4787),medieval ruins like a 14th-century castle (51.4385, -9.5136), and a lighthouse and signal tower (51.4345 -9.4844), with signed walks between them. Regular ferries from Baltimore and Schull.
30 mins, 51.4393, -9.5045

SOUTH CORK COAST

20 LOUGH HYNE & BULLOCK ISLAND
Barloge pier is a good spot to swim in the beautiful natural harbour, or launch for Lough Hyne or Bullock Island. Lough Hyne sometimes has bioluminescence, and joins the sea via narrow Barloge Creek and 'The Rapids', which can be pretty ferocious but fun on a kayak. You could paddle there and back on the tidal currents, or launch from the laneside on the lough and just travel with the ebb. Across the bay, Dromadoon pier is also good (51.4982, -9.2858), and 500m W along the cliffs is an LT causeway to Bullock Island (51.4955, -9.2923) – but don't get cut off!
2 mins, 51.4940, -9.2965

21 TRALISPEAN COVE & TRAGUMNA POOL
A perfect little cove with easy parking and swimming but can fill-up in summer. The R shore leads to a rock arch and sea cave. The L foreshore/scramble leads 600m to a brilliant long, deep pool, well-known on social media (51.4994, -9.2707), but better reached by kayak or bushwhack/path from Tragumna Beach.
2 mins, 51.4981, -9.2789

13

14

15

17

25 LONG STRAND & OWENAHINCHA

Despite the big car park, the many no-swimming signs keep this long beach uncrowded even in summer. There's a steep drop off and rips form easily, as well as clusters of large breakers, so it's renowned for surfing; the W-facing sands are a lovely place to watch the sun set. Alternatively, swim 500m NW at vast Owenahincha Beach: the surroundings aren't pretty, but once over the dunes you wouldn't know it. Park on the road by the bridge at the W end or in car park at the E end (51.5656, -8.9910).

2 mins, 51.5607, -8.9757

22 TRALIGAGH

Sand and shingle beach in a deep bay, a perfect place to hide away for a day. Parking for no more than ten cars at the end of the lane from the coastguard station, signed Trá keeps it quiet. Nearby Trá na nDabhcha (51.4921, -9.2316) is also good but often windy; a path from the bend in the road N leads to a smaller section.

2 mins, 51.4965, -9.2360

23 PRISON COVE

Narrow cobble cove, between dramatic cliffs, with a ruined 'prison' house. Long established as clothes-optional. The lane in is very narrow, with space for about four cars at the end; if you aren't lucky there, people do walk in from as far as Glandore (51.5506, -9.0965) or there's the Drombeg stone circle parking (see entry).

2 mins, 51.5506, -9.0965

24 ROSSCARBERY PIER *

Much quieter than The Warren beach on the opp shore, and with jumps too. The adventurous can simply kayak/swim across the 10m of water at LT from the secondary quay (51.5648, -9.0193), but watch the current: it can be fun being swept upstream in flood, but more scary being swept out in ebb.

2 mins, 51.5617, -9.0131

26 GALLEY HEAD BLOWHOLE & CLIFFS

Rock-cut steps lead down to a tiny harbour slipway below a stone crane dock. Explore N for sea caverns and blowholes (viewable from top), and great coasteering. There's some parking on the corner on the little lane. Across the bay E is Red Strand, a sheltered, easy family beach with facilities and good snorkeling, rock pools, and sea caves to the W for coasteering (51.5478 -8.9259).

2 mins, 51.5350 -8.9517

27 DUNEEN BAY & INCHIDONEY

A good alternative to the white sands of Inchydoney if you don't fancy its giant car park and hotel. East-facing, so great for morning swims especially. Park carefully along the road.

2 mins, 51.5795, -8.8727

WATERFALLS

28 MEALAGH RIVER WATERFALL *

This deep, secret pool below a high waterfall is a rite of passage among local teens, who dare each other to leap. It's very well hidden and you should be discreet. The field gate is recessed on the corner at 51.7054, -9.4019 and then down across the field (private land) to the stone and fence line where the river is hidden below.

15 mins, 51.7061, -9.4006

29

28

28

29 DEELISH CASCADES

Riverside path follows the Ilen from just below the imposing tower house of Castle Donovan down to Top of the Rock campsite (see entry). The upper section has a series of cascades with some deep plunge pools. 100m from car park (51.6921, -9.2827) it's 500m downstream to the first waterfall.

10 mins, 51.6868, -9.2793

LOST RUINS

30 GORTAVALLIG MINE & THE COVE

Isolated on the high, flower studded headland a row of stone cottages and a small reservoir with illies are all that remains of a short-lived copper mine. The path from the designated parking (51.5811, -9.7673) passes the abandoned clachán of Crimea (51.5791, -9.7775), nicknamed for a feud among the residents over grazing rights. Near the mine it is a precipitous cable handhold above crashing waves where the ore was shipped out from a long-gone pier – look down to see the vestige of a crumbled slipway. Continue along the spectacular coast down to The Cove slipway for a dip if calm; there's also some parking here (51.5696, -9.7866).

60 mins, 51.5754, -9.7860

31 MARCONI STATION, BROW HEAD*

The summit here has a Napoleonic signal tower and one of Marconi's early wireless telegraphy stations from 1901. This received the first over-the-horizon messages, from Poldhu in Cornwall. Descend to the field gate (51.4547, -9.7606), which has a sign for insurance, and follow trodden path to the narrow headland, the southernmost mainland point of Ireland. The track, long overgrown, led to a still-impressive ruined copper mine. The R591 approach into Crookhaven is beautiful, passing White Strand beach on L; turn R (signed, L8403), pass Galley Cove on L, to a small gravel area after 1.2km (51.4556, -9.7587), which may be full – go early. A short path L leads up to the ruins. Ruin hunters can admire the vast roadside Crookhaven quarry across the bay, built in 1928 in one of the first uses of reinforced concrete in Ireland (51.4722, -9.7308).

3 mins, 51.4544, -9.7594

32 ROCK ISLAND TOWER

Perfect secret picnic spot by a 19th-century tower with panoramic views over Crook Haven; taller and more slender than a signal tower, this was possibly to spot smugglers. Its eastern twin is visible but private. Park as for Trawnabirrea cove (see entry), walk W to 51.4743 -9.7158 and look for a bare rock in the hedge L. Scramble up – the trickiest bit – and follow the

30

30

thin, winding trail 100m up to the tower.

10 mins, 51.4740, -9.7154

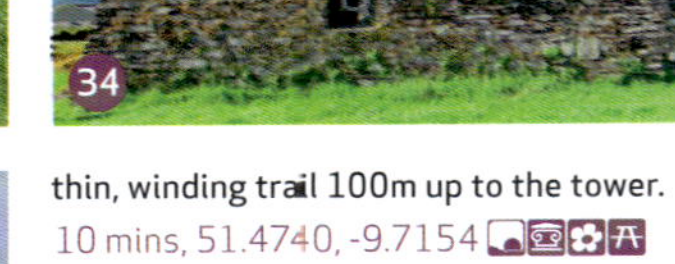

33 WHIDDY ISLAND BATTERIES

There are three large circular Napoleonic batteries on the island, each with a large moat and bridge leading to a defended interior. The 'Middle' Battery is the most interesting, with barracks, magazine rooms and cast-iron water pumps. All are very overgrown and sometimes fenced; be very careful and obey any warning signs. The other two are at the N and S end of the island (51.7046, -9.4810 and 51.6820, -9.5200), and there's a ruined house in the woods on the way to the N battery (51.7016, -9.4827). Take a walking tour with Tim O'Leary (+353 86 8626734), the ferryman who also runs the Bank Bar and Old School House hostel. There's a loop of the Sheeps Head Way on the island, too, if you'd rather do it solo. Five return ferries a day, €8 return from Bantry.

10 mins, 51.6952, -9.4865

34 TOGHER CASTLE

An impressively defensive late-16th-century tower house with a batter and bartizans, on a spur of rock by the River Bandon (a tóchar is a wooden causeway.) Confiscated in 1641, by 1666 it was unroofed. In the late 19th century, it was reroofed, with plans to use it as a school;

today, it's derelict with no internal floors, but if the ladder is there you can go up the ancient staircase at your own risk. Park on the lane, the friendly farmer was happy for us to visit.
2 mins, 51.7616, -9.1650

35 COPPINGER'S COURT

Eerie and surprisingly little-known remains of perhaps the most magnificent fortified house in Ireland, built about 1616 by wealthy merchant Sir Walter Coppinger. He intended it to be the start of a self-sufficient town, but the Cromwellian wars put paid to it. Park carefully on the quiet lane and go through the field gate.
2 mins, 51.5715, -9.0668

36 BALLINACARRIGA CASTLE

This massive tower at the 'Passage of the Rock' was built on a high rocky outcrop in about 1585; a small circular tower is all that remains of the outer fortification. Look for the sheela na gig carving above the second window to the right of the door. You can't go inside but there's a picnic area by the river and a path to the sparkling little lough if you fancy a rushy dip.
2 mins, 51.7055, -9.0316

37 DOWNEEN CASTLE

Perched upon a rock stack, this was once reached over what must have been a very dramatic wooden drawbridge; now it's only reachable by precarious scrambling. Worth seeking out for the sheer drama of the location. From Rosscarbery pier (see entry) follow the cliff line 1km through various fields and gates.
15 mins, 51.5600, -9.0245

SACRED & ANCIENT

38 GOULADOO HOLY WELL & FORT

The water below the tiered stone structure with a Marian statuette is said to cure rheumatic ailments, and young women would look for the face of their future husband in the pool. Below across the field is a promontory fort, which slopes towards the sea for sweeping views and crashing waves. A good picnic spot on a sunny day. Pull on to the verge carefully at 51.6154, -9.6824, opposite the stile.
2 mins, 51.6165, -9.6816

39 AHAKISTA STONE CIRCLE

Also called Gorteanish, this circle of 11 stones was discovered in 1995 during clearance to create a Sheep's Head Way path. Most had fallen; in 2023, they were re-erected by an archaeology team from University College Cork as part of a site study. There are two 'boulder burials', one in the circle, one just outside, and wonderful views. Park on the corner (51.5973, -9.6446), and walk W to a sign and memorial to

35

36

creator of the Way, Tom Whitty, where the path climbs past noisy cascades.

4 mins, 51.5985, -9.6444

40 BRAHALISH RINGFORT

This impressive fort with wide views is on an official looped walk, with access up the track from the road, but it's not easy to park. A broad turn 400m E is probably best (51.6163, -9.5759).

5 mins, 51.6172, -9.5850

41 KILNARUANE PILLAR STONE

This 9th-century cross shaft is among the last remnants of a 6th-century hilltop monastery founded by St Brendan. Also called St Brendan's stone, it has the earliest known image of a currach, probably meant to be the ship of the church, but often taken for Brendan's voyage to America. The stones around it include two bullauns and grooved panels of a shrine. Park at the fingerboard opp the gate (51.6725, -9.4688).

2 mins, 51.6713, -9.4680

42 MAULINWARD GRAVEYARD

Ancient-feeling triangular graveyard inside a stone-faced earthen bank, with the ruins of medieval Durrus Church. There's a bullaun stone with offerings and possibly a skull fragment of renowned healer Father Denis Barnane. His grave was a place of pilgrimage and cures for over a century after his death in 1834, and it was traditional to leave a bottle of whiskey every year. Near the coffin platform, used as a mass rock during Penal times, is an 8th-century slab with a delicately carved ringed cross and grooves probably made by blade sharpening. Signed, parking at gate.

2 mins, 51.6347, -9.4615

43 CULLOMANE EAST COMPLEX

This cluster of monuments was once an important site for Bealtain and St Colman. Follow the lane up to the farm and ask permission to follow the track. Pilgrims completed rounds of the holy well (51.6538, -9.3964) and several small, flattened cairns, and rubbed butter on the massive, white quartz boulder burial, known locally as the Butter Stone; all are in the same enclosure, with a standing stone. Off the track is a five-stone circle L (51.6533, -9.3932), and a hilltop ringfort that was used as a cillín R (51.6540, -9.3943).

5 mins, 51.65357, -9.3963

44 AUGHADOWN CHURCH & GRAVEYARD

This short-lived 19th-century church, rapidly outgrown by its congregation, is a picture-perfect ivy-engulfed ruin on the shore of the Ilen estuary, a lovely place for a picnic or a dip, and to contemplate the vagaries of history. The non-denominational graveyard makes strange companions, like an IRA soldier and Williamite gentry, or a notoriously brutal Famine landlord and a heroic doctor from the same years.

2 mins, 51.5283, -9.3596

45 ABBEYSTOWRY CEMETERY

First you just see old headstones and a ruined chapel, on a site dating back to a 13th-century abbey. But the large, bare, green plot with sunken areas and a single memorial stone ultimately sets the atmosphere: some 9,000 dead lie here, put in pits with no coffins, ceremony or markers in the Famine years, when the local population fell by a third. The history is well told in the Heritage Centre in the town but its reality soaks into you here.

2 mins, 51.5517, -9.2881

46 FARRANAHINEENY STONE ROW

Four standing stones, the tallest about 3m, and one lying, in a beautiful hilltop setting. Thought to date from the late Bronze Age when the uplands here were intensively occupied, their purpose is not known; they seem to point at Nowen Hill, some 11km SW. Park by the gate at the bottom of the field (51.7948, -9.1417) or walk down to there from Carrigdangan wind farm gate (see entry), and follow the

41

45

50

edge R up and around to the enclosure.
5 mins, 51.7946, -9.1381

47 KILBARRY GRAVEYARD, DUNMANWAY

A quiet rural graveyard with many low, uncut markers and some 19th- and 20th-century headstones. A striking one that feels very personal has a cross cut out of its centre and the simple legend, 'Crowley, Castle St, RIP'. The very old ruined church is said to have been used by Cork's patron saint, St Finbar, and a stone-lined well across the field is known as St Finbar's well; it still has a raggedy tree, and rounds on his saint's day (51.7172, -9.1319). Park at corner.
2 mins, 51.7163, -9.1328

48 INCHINCURKA WEDGE TOMB 'CAVERN'

Narrow tomb with at least eight highly visible cup marks on the roof, many more less distinct. This is an unusual feature on tombs, but found on a few regional examples and suggests that this kind of tomb was meant to be visible, not covered with a cairn. It lies in an open field, with bracken around it in summer but still accessible. Park and ask the friendly farmer for permission. His family have always called it the 'bealick', from the Irish an bhéillic, meaning a cavern.
2 mins, 51.7837, -9.1113

49 DROMBEG STONE CIRCLE

One of Ireland's most famous and well-preserved stone circles, with broad views to the sea. It has 13 of the original 17 standing stones in the typical local axial form with a recumbent stone (with two cup marks) aligned on the winter solstice sunset. There are markings, hard to see and harder to interpret, on some stones. The circle dates to the Bronze Age, although cremated remains have been dated to the Iron Age, so it was in long use. Nearby are the remains of ancient stone huts and a fulacht fiadh. Small car park, signed from the R597.
5 mins, 51.5645, -9.0870

50 LETTERGORMAN SOUTH STONE CIRCLE

A hilltop five-stone circle with panoramic views, possibly aligned with the midwinter sunset, especially where it would have been 3,000 years ago. There is a large quartz monolith: an outlier that has been here since at least the mid-19th century. Pull in at the gate to the N at 51.6590, -9.0670,
2 mins, 51.6585, -9.0670

51 REENASCREENA STONE CIRCLE *

This truly magical hilltop circle of 13 stones is almost 10m across and, unusually, there's a shallow ditch around it, evident even in summer as a marshy ring of sedges. People still leave

51

52

56

offerings in the centre; cremated bone was found in a pit here. Park at houses 70m R of gate or a wide splay 750m L and walk up R side of the fields (there were curious heifers, but we were assured it was fine for people, just not dogs), then bear left over the hilltop, which glows yellow and gold with tall wild flowers in summer.

12 mins, 51.6178, -9.0633

52 CASTLEVENTRY GRAVEYARD & WELL *

The sign says graveyard but has the name Caislean na Gaoithe or 'castle of the wind', and it's immediately obvious that a hilltop fort has been reused. It's easy to see why: ringed with thorn bushes and commanding views on all sides, this is a compelling site that has drawn people for well over a thousand years. The medieval parish church is now reduced to turf-covered banks. Behind a neat gate at the bend in the road below is Trinity Holy well (51.6292, -9.0133), where people leave smooth, white pebbles; park by this.

2 mins, 51.6296, -9.0144

53 KNOCKS SOUTH STONE CIRCLE

Five stones in a 7m circle – there were originally at least nine – with a sixth split stone in the centre. Park carefully by the barn – once a linen mill, the curious iron column at the gate is the steam engine chimney – and walk up the track over the hill, ducking under or stepping over any electric fences. The friendly farmer told us that the standing stone by the track (51.6473 , -9.0075) had been taken from the circle long ago. Nearby is Knocks North circle in a field; no keep-out sign but you can check at the farm opp (51.6594 -9.0132).

5 mins, 51.6475, -9.0084

54 CAHERVAGLIAR RINGFORT

This substantial grassed ringfort, 73m across, is named Chathair Mhac Laoghaire for local 12th-century kings, but the fort is much older than that. The impressive double bank fortifications and stone-lined entrance passage hint that it was built by someone of great importance and wealth, and local lore claims that Brian Boru was held hostage here as a child. Car park above.

2 mins, 51.7930, -8.9969

55 KINNEIGH ROUND TOWER

This striking 26m round tower stands on a rock outcrop, giving it the feel of a lighthouse. It's quite late, probably 12th century, and unique in Ireland for its hexagonal base, expertly built in a style typical of the towers of Rhineland cathedrals. Continental stonemasons may even have played a part in this. The last surviving remnant of an early monastic settlement and one of only two round towers in Cork

58

58

58

(the other is in Cloyne, 51.8620, -8.1202). Parking outside graveyard.
2 mins, 51.7641, -8.9755

HEADLANDS & LOOKOUTS

56 SHEEP'S HEAD LIGHTHOUSE

Rugged, wild and always windy, with a tiny beacon built in the 1960s to support the oil terminal on Whiddy Island; everything was brought in on more than 250 helicopter trips. Automated long ago, it's now visited only by walkers, sheep, hares and noisy choughs. An easy 1.5km of cliff views from the car park and Bernie's Cupán Tae at the road end, 51.5459, -9.8265. Lough Akeen is near the route for the brave; the loop section back N of it is tougher.
40 mins, 51.5425, -9.8478

57 DUNLOUGH CASTLE *

One of Ireland's oldest castles, this stands as three towers along a defensive wall from the dramatic 100m cliff tops into Dun Lough; you can climb the staircase of the middle tower. The lough is a nature reserve with no swimming, but a good picnic spot, and the head is popular for wildlife watching, with choughs and ravens, and a chance of spotting whales, seals and sharks. Walk in about 1.5km from small parking S at 51.4787, -9.8150, towards the house then fork L, this is private land with an honesty box (€3) and farmland, so strictly no dogs.
25 mins, 51.4827, -9.8291

58 MIZEN HEAD & SIGNAL TOWER

It's worth the €7.50 entry fee to walk from the visitor centre: the bridge is extraordinary, the ravine it crosses stupendous. The signal station island has different railed routes to vantage points on to the tormented strata of cliffs, sea arches and caves; it'll take longer than you think. For a much wilder approach, the Cloghane Napoleonic era signal tower is 400m N of the car park on top of the hill but no path (51.4545, -9.8129). The gate and layby 200m back on lane (51.4538, -9.8065) is a possible start point.
20 mins, 51.4511, -9.8166

59 SEEFIN

Take the wild, rocky path E 2km and 150m up to the summit, also reached on the massive Seefin Loop from Ahakista. Even the WAW parking has fine views, as well as a Pieta statue and cross, and a line of Heaney poetry carved on a bench (Suí Finn means Finn's Seat). To the W, the 11km Peakeen Ridge loop takes in Caher Mountain.
50 mins, 51.5954, -9.7112

60 SAILORS HILL BELVEDERE

A memorial to those lost at sea, built by local Connie Griffin – although the door is less than child sized, a true folly flourish of false perspective. Park at the cemetery, and walk 1km up the tiny lane to sweeping views over Schull Harbour and the wider Roaringwater Bay to Fastnet. Honesty box at entrance.
15 mins, 51.5138, -9.5508

61

61 SPAIN TOWER *

Walk up a while before a summer sunset, explore the butterfly-filled slopes above booming cliffs below (fenced for livestock), and seek the overgrown EIRE 29 pilots' marker (51.4735, -9.3521). Toe Head Tower can be seen to the east. Then head back to the summit for otherworldly sunset views over all the inlets

65

and islands of Roaringwater Bay from this ruinous signal tower. When we visited there was a fresh fall of masonry inside the tower and we recommend just admiring this one from the outside. Strictly no dogs or bikes.

7 mins, 51.4745, -9.3538

62 DÚINÍN DHIARMUID MHOR, TOE HEAD

The coast of this headland is a wonder, waves crashing into striped cliffs and caves below. Above on the flowery clifftops to the SE is this gradually eroding promontory fort with a narrow neck, and an EIRE pilots' marker to the SW (51.4821, -9.2272). Inland on the summit is a signal tower, less fortified than many, with a later coastguard station (51.4893, -9.2205). You could walk solo on the loop path, but for a deeper dive into local lore and wildlife, book a guided walk with Conor Ó Buachalla of Gormú Tours (+353 83 0153545), ending with drinks and bakes on Tráigh Liceach.

170 mins, 51.4820, -9.2326

63 CARRIGDANGAN WIND FARM WALK

A heathery ridge with majestic views, including down to Farranahineeny stone row (see entry), hosts five towering 76m turbines. You can stand right under the hypnotic blades and watch their racing shadows. Walk a 6.5km loop through the farm and on the extremely quiet, remote lane, parking on the splay at the E gate, or room for one car at the W end (51.7961, -9.1403) – for just a 450m walk to the nearest turbine, go W.

100 mins, 51.8007, -9.1207

ANCIENT FOREST

64 MAGIC FOREST BALLYBANE

Inspire before you expire is the motto of artist and musician Thomas Weigandt, who's created this unique woodland walk art project, with musical instruments improvised out of found objects, seats, a literal frame for the view and floods of bluebells in spring. It's free to wander around, although donations are welcome.

2 mins, 51.6096, -9.4077

65 KNOCKOMAGH WOODS & SUMMIT

Stone steps lead up from the road into the deciduous forest. After 2km the path reaches the summit for fine views over Lough Hyne. Park by steps at 51.5053, -9.3080. 150m S long the lakeshore lane is a quay you can swim by, opp tin house; a much bigger putting-in point for kayaks is along the N shore.

40 mins, 51.5079, -9.3126

66 RINEEN FOREST WALKS

Coillte woodlands with shady walks along the estuary edge. Historical features on the site include the stone Famine wall deer barrier and a lime kiln on the S seashore to climb inside (51.5497, -9.1694). There are numerous fairy house doors.

10 mins, 51.5518, -9.17024

67 MYROSS WOOD

This old parkland has become a public wood with wonderful walks, looked after by an eco organisation at the old seminary in the grounds; park there (CECAS). It's also home to Up There The Last food project (see entry).

2 mins, 51.5714, -9.1505

WILDLIFE WONDERS

68 BANTRY BAY PONY TREKKING

Trek to a ruined cottage via their extensive private farm tracks through woodlands of Scots pines, oaks, alder and holly trees up to hilltops of heather, gorse and fuschia, with views down over Bantry Bay. You may spot deer, kestrel, wild goats and other wildlife. Treks €35/hour. Hollyhill, Bantry, P75 H019, +353 87 7765539

60 mins, 51.6603, -9.4629

69 ROARINGWATER WILDLIFE

Roaringwater Bay is an internationally important whale breeding ground. You can spot the sealife from cliff-tops, but several companies take you closer to dolphins and porpoises, seals on islands, with basking sharks, minke, and humpback whales in summer and fin whales in autumn. A few are Cork Whale Watch from Reen Pier (+353 86 3273226, corkwhalewatch.com), Fastnet Rock Tours out of Baltimore and Schull pier (+353 28 39159, capeclearferries.com), Whale Watch West Cork (+353 86 1200027, whalewatchwestcork.com), and Aquaventures from Baltimore (+353 87 7961456, aquaventures.ie).

5 mins, 51.4738, -9.4593

70 REEN PIER BIOLUMINESCENCE

Kayak N up into the Narrows with woods all around, and sometimes bioluminescence at

69

dusk/night; you can go from here or the spit of shingle 400m E. Atlantic Sea Kayaking runs night trips (+353 28 21058).
2 mins, 51.5282, -9.1665

CLASSIC BARS

71 NOTTAGE BAR & RESTAURANT

Classic European menu with an emphasis on local seafood in the restaurant and Basque influence pintxos in the bar next door, plus wood-fired pizzas you can take away. Crookhaven, P81 T883, +353 28 35963
51.4690, -9.7246

72 O'SULLIVANS, CROOKHAVEN

In the heart of Crookhaven: sit outside by the pier in the summer or inside by the fire inside in the winter. Stone floors, wooden benches, award-winning seafood. Rock Street, Crookhaven, P81 CF78, +353 28 35319
51.4693, -9.7245

73 THE WHITE HOUSE GALLERY & CAFÉ

There's been a shop and bar on this site for longer than anyone remembers. Today it's open April-Sept,and a steady stream of cyclists stop here to refuel. Delicious food, decadent cake, and local knowledge at tables inside or out. Kilcrohane, P75 WV96, +353 85 2725548
51.5730, -9.7240

74 THE AHAKISTA BAR

Known as The Tin Pub for its corrugated roof, this summer-only local has a lovely beer garden out back with trees and views over Dunmanus Bay, and a Tin Shack food truck on Friday evenings. Central in the village festival in late July, when Graham Norton hosts the pub quiz. P75 HX60, +353 86 8450175
51.5994, -9.6366

75 ARUNDELS BY THE PIER

Popular pub restaurant with its own shoreside beach and garden. Once also a shop, with framed bills from the 1980s for pints of beer and pints of milk. Great food, quieter restaurant seating upstairs, lively bar downstairs; booking advisable. P75 XH93, +353 27 67033
51.600, -9.6323

76 HERON GALLERY CAFÉ & GARDENS

Lovely wholefood café with gardens and gallery/shop. Closed in winter. Rushnachara, Durrus, P75 TW89, +353 27 67278
51.6025, -9.6291

77 HACKETTS BAR, SCHULL

The interior of this award-winning bar is an eclectic mix of original and modern, with an old bar and a full mural of a local crowd on the wall. Good food, great pints and frequent live music, with the buskers often coming in after the Sunday Country Market (see entry). Main Street, P81 RX34, +353 28 28625
51.5267, -9.5456

78 D'ALTON'S PUB

Old-fashioned bar on the corner with no food, but a lively atmosphere and a couple of local beers on the pumps. Open all week from 2.00pm in summer, only Fri-Sat from 5.00pm out of season. Market Street Kinsale, P17 E068, +353 86 0834700
51.5267, -9.5452

79 SKIBBEREEN EAGLE BAR, TRAGUMNA

Conveniently close to two beaches in Tragumna Bay for a swim before dinner and a pint: the lifeguarded main beach and a cove right below, where the kayak club puts in. The pub was once run by Colonel Albert Bachmann, a colourful Swiss military intelligence figure who thought the area perfect for surviving a nuclear holocaust. But most people visit for the food and the location. Tragumna, P81 C935, +353 28 22148
51.5006, -9.2629

80 HAYES' BAR GLANDORE

Award-winning restaurant right on the seafront, closed in winter. Modern, funky interior and food, one emphasising wood, the other emphasising local fish. Glandore, P81 WE16, +353 28 33214
51.5653, -9.1180

81 YELLOW HOUSE COFFEE BAR

Wooden cabin pitstop café by the road with tables inside and outside. Serves great coffee with organic milk and freshly baked cakes, and sells homemade jam. Gloun North, P47 K378, +353 86 3693991. Almost next door, Gloun Cross Dairy sells its own milk in glass return bottles, and local eggs, honey and marmalade in an honesty-box shop (51.7937, -9.0561).
51.7921, -9.0591

82 THE FISH BASKET

Right by Long Strand, with outdoor tables, this black shack is a quirky casual café and restaurant, obviously devoted to fish but with something for everyone including GF options. Check socials for opening times or call. Long Strand Beach, Castlefreke, P85 KV48, +353 23 8851716
51.5603, -8.9776

83 DEBARRA'S, CLONAKILTY

This is a pitch-perfect traditional pub and serves hearty home-made food. But it's four

81

82

decades and three generations as a folk venue that made DeBarra's legendary, with regular sessions and gigs. As folk titan Christy Moore said: 'There's Carnegie Hall, The Royal Albert, Sydney Opera House and then there's De Barra's.' 55 Pearse Street, Clonakilty, P85 RH95, +353 23 8833381
51.6229, -8.8890

LOCAL PRODUCE

84 SCHULL COUNTRY MARKET

Street food and a range of produce, including Gubbeen cheeses and cured meats from a couple of miles up the road, fresh, baked goods, preserves, and local honey. Local crafters too, and often music. 10am–2pm Sun, Easter–Sep. Pier Road car park, opposite P81 TD71, schullmarket.ie
51.5261, -9.5449

85 FISH KITCHEN

A seafood deli downstairs, serving oysters, crab claws, fish and chips, local condiments, and a colourful restaurant upstairs doing hearty food with an emphasis on fresh, local fish. 10.00am–5.00pm Tue–Sat. New Street, Bantry, P75 RX70, +353 27 56651
51.6797, -9.4511

86 ORGANICO

Bakery, deli and health store, with coffee and baked goods to go. 2 Glengarriff Road, Bantry, P75 CC80, +353 27 51391
51.6802, -9.4494

87 DURRUS CHEESE

Award-winning semi-soft, rind ripened cheeses. Made on the same farm by the same family since 1970. Fairly widely available, but 10.00am–1.00 pm weekdays only to visit and buy it directly. If you're in luck you might see the cheese being made. Coomkeen, Durrus, Bantry, P75 PN81, +353 27 61100

51.6451, -9.5288

88 WHARTON'S FISH & CHIP RESTAURANT

Sometimes you just can't beat takeaway fish and chips eaten looking out at harbour lights. New St, Bantry, P75 HD27, +353 87 1269655

51.6793, -9.4507

89 THE STUFFED OLIVE

Family-run food and wine store, bakery and café, very popular. Excellent flavoured focaccias and fruited soda bread, and food to go, too. Bridge Street, Bantry, P75 P270, +353 27 55883

51.6790, -9.4502

90 WEST CORK BREWING, CASEY'S HOTEL

Nano-brewery in Casey's Hotel. Try a tasting flight in the bar, at a table on the terrace looking out over the sea, and stroll down the lane to the graveyard with its little church ruin and views out. The Atlantic Mariner wreck from 1996 lies in the bay and is sometimes decorated with flags. Baltimore, P81 YW66, + 353 28 20197

51.4849, -9.3624

91 UP THERE THE LAST *

A deeply visionary slow food project that offers feasts on the beach, and day- or week-long beautiful, immersive workshops in everything from foraging to traditional processes such as cheesemaking and fish smoking. From €75, P81 Y192, uptherethelast.com

51.4987, -9.2777

92 SKIBBEREEN FARMER'S MARKET

Fresh, organic produce, plants and flowers, fermented foods, honey and preserves, baked goods, and crafts. 9.00am–2.00pm, Sat. The Fairfield, Bridge Street, Skibbereen, P81 TH68

51.5487, -9.2691

93 WOODCOCK SMOKERY

Artisan smokery of solely wild Irish salmon. Pricey but renowned half- or full-day smokery course, mushroom or coastal foraging, as well as set menu tasting suppers. Gortbrack, Skibbereen, P81 FA03, +353 28 36232

51.5264, -9.1982

94 CLONAKILTY FRIDAY MARKET

Hot food stalls, fresh local produce, home-baking, and craft directly from the growers, farmers and producers. 9.00am–2.00pm, Sun. Pearse Street, Clonakilty

51.6220, -8.8918

95 THE NEW HAVEN

Justly renowned restaurant that is almost always busy – no advance bookings, so be prepared to leave your phone number and wait for a table. It's worth it and they run the waiting list well. Known for fish dishes and steak, but good vegetarian options, and very family friendly. Main Street, Schull, P81 X052, +353 28 28642

51.5267, -9.5447

96 RESTAURANT CHESTNUT, BALLYDEHOB

Rob Krawczyk opened this intimate restaurant in a former pub in 2018 and won a Michelin star within months. The menu is influenced by his father Frank, a pioneer west-Cork producer of charcuterie and smoked meat. Two menus; reservations (essential) open a couple of months in advance online; four nights a week Mar–Dec. Staball Hill, Ballydehob, P81 X681, +353 282 5766

51.5625, -9.4606

97 DEDE AT THE CUSTOMS HOUSE, *

Ankhara-born and internationally trained chef Ahmet Dede has two Michelin stars for his fusion cuisine here. Meat, fish, produce and honey are sourced locally, including from Cape Clear Island, but expect a Turkish influence with preserved lemons and marinades. Booking essential; hours vary seasonally. Customs House, Baltimore, P81 K291, +353 28 48248; or try the sister venture, Baba'de, The Mews, P81 TC64, babade.ie

51.4834, -9.3723

98 AN CHISTIN BEAG

The 'little kitchen' is a friendly café serving fresh, local food, a great place for breakfast on the road. 46 Bridge St, Skibbereen, Co. Cork, P81 KW57, +353 28 22019

51.5496, -9.2701

ORGANIC & GASTRO

99 O'NEILL COFFEE

Locally roasted coffee, sweet and savoury fresh bakes, in an old sweet shop with the original name over the door and queues on the pavement. Squish into a sofa in the moody blue room downstairs, or head up the worn, wooden stairs for more tables. Closed Sundays outside of high summer. 64 Townshend St, Skibbereen, P81 Y330, oneillscoffee@gmail.com

51.5486, -9.2677

100 KALBOS CAFÉ
Ingredients grown and produced on their own organic farm, plus other local suppliers, free-range, high welfare. Café, food to go, and shop selling both fresh produce and baked goods. 26 North Street, Skibbereen, P81 FX43, +353 28 21515
51.5499, -9.2656

101 O'CALLAGHAN WALSHE
Near-legendary restaurant, highly rated for their seafood especially, year after year. North Square, Rosscarbery, P85 RF34, +353 23 8848125
51.5777, -9.0324

102 CAMUS FARM FIELD KITCHEN *
Authentic farm-to-table experience with much of the produce grown on the organic farm. Set menu determined by what is in season locally. Reservations are essential as ingredients are harvested daily to order. Ardfield, Clonakilty, P85 PX57+353 86 8263429, fieldkitchen.ie
51.5702, -8.9312

COOL CAMPING

103 GOLEEN HARBOUR *
An expansive site set above the sheltered little bay with swimming, kayaking, bike hire, an activity centre and foraging workshops. There are options for every budget, from discounted camping for those arriving by bike to char-clad eco-cabins with sheltered decks. Solar electricity and a small permaculture farm with ponies and newly planted woodland complete the picture. P81 CX98, +353 28 63133, goleenharbour.ie
51.4964, -9.7078

104 GOAT'S PATH POD PARK
Opened in 2020, not just a high row of hillside pods, but generous grass tent areas on the sheltered valley floor below. Fire-pit lit in the evenings, pizzas available and coffee in reception. Woodland fairy trail and playground for children. Chris leads tours of historical sites on the farm and is a mine of local information. EV charging can be arranged, call ahead. Glenlough, P75 DY95, +353 86 8570186
51.6338, -9.6024

105 DUNBEACON CAMPING & GLAMPING *
Paddy and Natasha resurrected a derelict campsite into a very individual experience: when you arrive, ring the doorbell on the TARDIS toy cupboard. No online booking for pitches, as they're tucked among mature trees and shrubs: email or ring with your details and they'll matchmake your ideal spot. Glamping options include teepees and a bell tent, but we loved the hidden Land Rover safari tent. No wifi, take an offline break. Dunbeacon, Durrus, P75 NN88, +353 87 6506059
51.5966, -9.5707

106 TOP OF THE ROCK, DRIMOLEAGUE
The name is no lie: the views are wonderful, from a range of tent pitches, a cute caravan, and some of the first pods in Ireland, locally built and inspired by the Gallarus oratory in Kerry. David always has walkers in mind, with transport to the start and end of routes available, and there's a communal fire in the evenings in summer. Kids get a playground and there are hands-on tours of the farm in summer; some pets by arrangement but, as a working farm, no larger dogs. Rockmount, Drimoleague, P47 KF66, +353 86 1735134, topoftherock.ie
51.6687, -9.2608

107 BILBERRY BOREEN CAMPSITE
Barely-there eco-campsite for tents in re-wilding meadows on a secluded hillside. Timber homebuilt washrooms and a covered dining area, plus a couple of cabins. Quiet site: no music, dog-friendly. L4607, Carrigdangan, L4607, Carrigdangan, Macroom, Co. Cork, P12 P281, +353 86 2183364, pitchup.com
51.8005, -9.1160

RUSTIC RETREATS

108 THREE CASTLE HEAD
The farm at Three Castle Head has three places to let: The Loft and the Tack Room are conversions in farm buildings, and the Hideaway is exactly what it says, a cabin, only sheep for neighbours and big coastal views. Dunlough, +353 87 7419412, threecastlehead.ie
51.4803, -9.8193

109 TRÁ RUAIM LOFT *
Cute little converted farm building, with a living loft upstairs and drying room downstairs. The owner, Finn, is involved in maintaining the many Sheep's Head Way trails. Perfectly sited for walks and just above the beach it's named after, a sunset cove with a slipway and sand at low tide. Lowerletter, Kilcrohane, +353 86 2837453, sheepsheadaccommodation.com
51.5627, -9.7574

110 RINCOLISKY CASTLE
Restored 16th-century tower house on the shore, originally built by a powerful seafaring family. Medieval stone walls and real fires below and a modern glass penthouse with superb sea views above, listed on Vrbo and Airbnb. P81 XK65.
51.5178, -9.4162

111 WILD HIDEAWAYS
Very dog-friendly cabins with great views and spa packages (sauna and cold pool for the brave), and a rewilding pond. The site avoids single-use plastics, and has full recycling, using organic and eco-friendly products, and local products and services wherever possible. Laharanshermeen, Bantry, P75 P599, +353 87 2121675, wildhideaways.ie
51.7317, -9.3535

112 LONG STRAND LODGES
On a slope overlooking Long Strand (see entry), two snug, funky, utilitarian studios, each with two elevated double-bed platforms and woodburners, sharing a verandah in a cedar cabin. Booked through the Fish Basket café down the road (see entry) or on Airbnb. Duneside and Castleside, Long Strand, Castlefreke, P85 TX63
51.5605, -8.9790

91

91

91

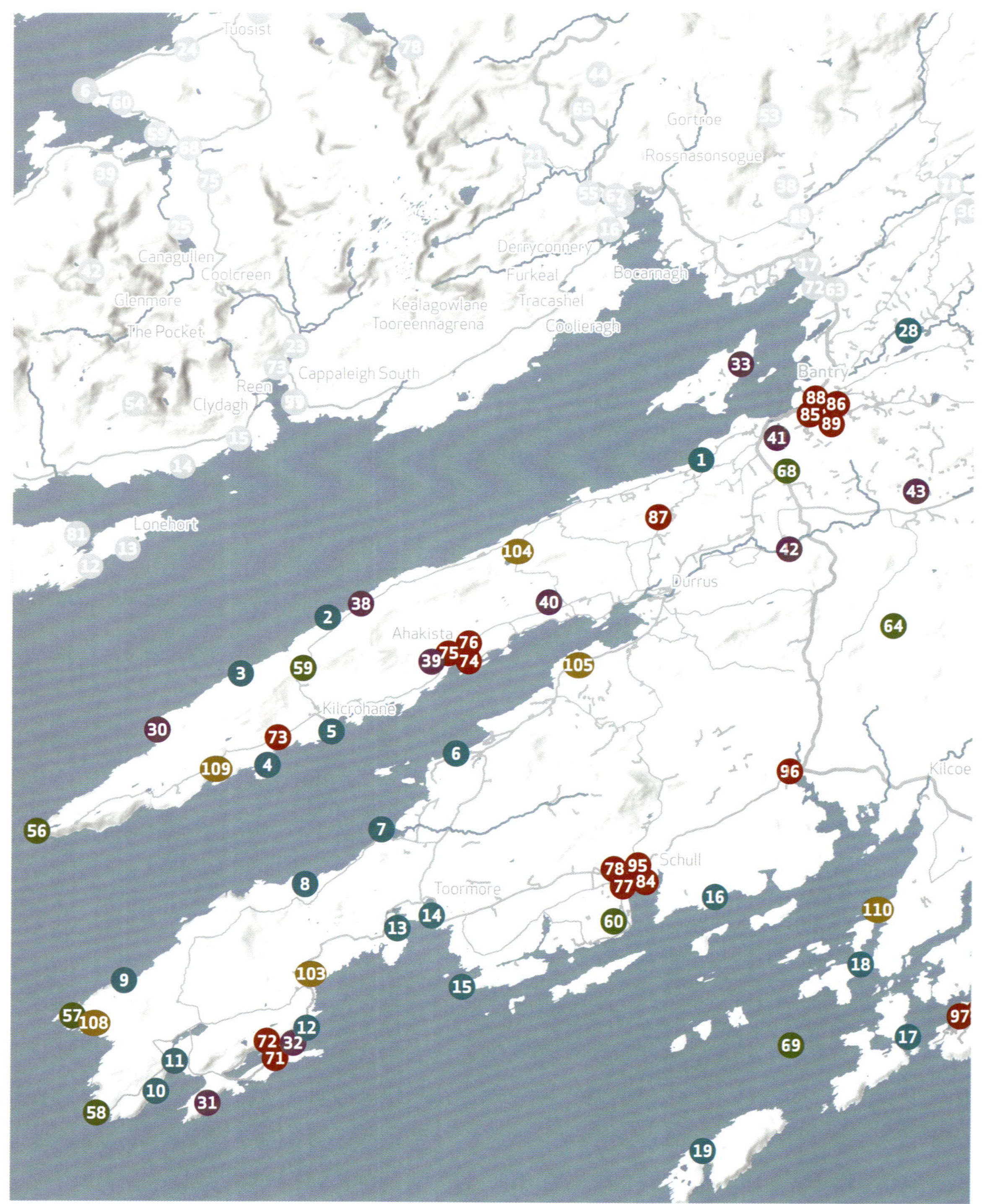
Tuosist
Gortroe
Rossnasonsogue
Derryconnery
Furkeal
Bocarnagh
Tracashel
Kealagowlane
Tooreennagrena
Coolieragh
Canagullen
Coolcreen
Glenmore
The Pocket
Cappaleigh South
Reen
Clydagh
Lonehort
Bantry
Durrus
Ahakista
Kilcrohane
Kilcoe
Schull
Toormore

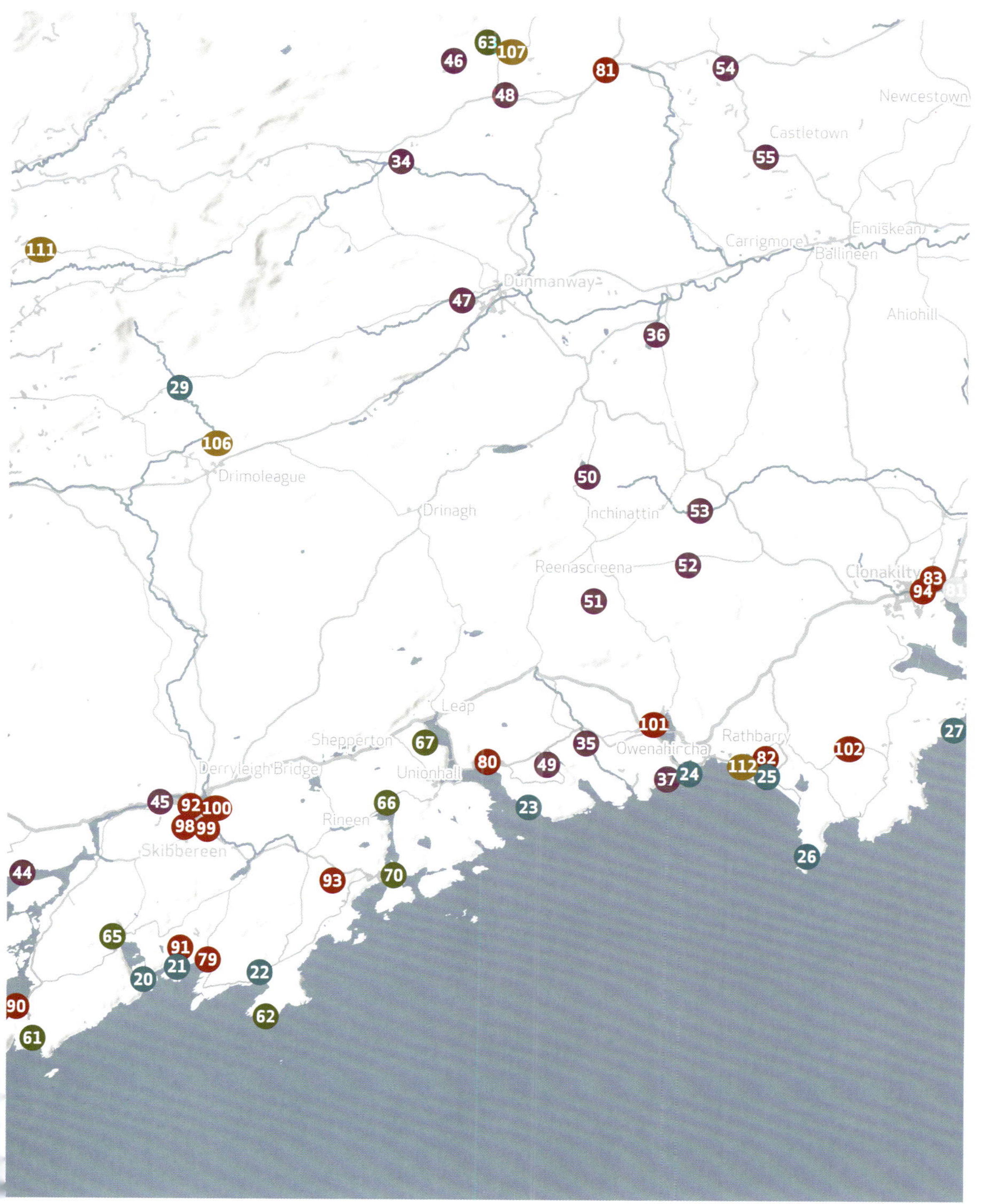

Newcestown
Castletown
Enniskean
Carrigmore
Ballineen
Dunmanway
Ahiohill
Drimoleague
Drinagh
Inchinattin
Reenascreena
Clonakilty
Leap
Shepperton
Rathbarry
Owenahincha
Derryleigh Bridge
Unionhall
Rineen
Skibbereen

17

SOUTH EAST CORK

Our perfect weekend

→ **Coasteer** and snorkel in azure waters among pyramid rocks and ruins at Nohoval Cove.

→ **Follow** the coast path from Ballycotton to see what's left of the Alta ghost ship, and return to a pint in the Blackbird bar or dinner at Cush.

→ **Laze** on the sands of Inch Beach, take a sauna and sleep the night in a colourful yurt at quirky Inch Hideaway Eco Campsite.

→ **Paddle** in the harbour below the lighthouse at Roche's Point and walk to the cliff-top folly that the government rented as a signal tower.

→ **Seek** the strange dolmen on the shore in Rostellan Woods, and try to decide if it's one of the estate follies or a true ancient relic.

→ **Kayak** from beautiful Dunworley Beach or sit on the quieter sands of Moloney's Strand, and book a table at Monk's Lane for the end of the day.

→ **Explore** Glenbower Wood seeking ruins, or take pastries from The Grumpy Bakers in Midleton and drift among the bluebells of Ballyannan.

→ **Enjoy** vast views on the Capel Way to the signal tower and Second World War remains.

2

4

6

This is the least wild part of the Wild Atlantic Way, with calmer seas along a coast of low cliffs and dunes, and this gentler shore and inland wealth gave both Cork city and the eastern harbour at Youghal a rich maritime and mercantile history.

A cruise terminal at Cobh in Cork Harbour brings tourists to visit sites such as Spike Island prison and of course the Titanic Experience, this being the last port of the doomed ship in 1912. Far fewer will visit its last anchorage at Roche's Point, where the lighthouse also received the SOS from the torpedoed Lusitania just three years later. Local fishing boats went to the rescue then, but almost 1,200 still died, with a memorial on the harbour in Courtmacsherry. This is a pretty village for a summer weekend, with beaches, woodland and headland walks, and even a derelict grand house. It sits on Coolmain Bay, one of several smaller estuaries such as Crosshaven, Oysterhaven and Pilmore. All are worth exploring for their bird life and safe, broad waters, but there are also fun little coves, from famous Nohoval to hidden Simon's Cove with its view to tempting caves.

Cork has over one-tenth of Ireland's woodland, some of which is down to historical wealth; those with money to spare maintained or planted woods, from little Dromkeen above Inishannon to the wider shade of Garrettstown. Many hide treasures like old bridges, follies, wells or lime kilns.

Other remnants of the past are more easily found: there are Napoleonic signal towers on headland walks with sweeping views, including one restored example with a Lusitania Museum alongside it, and forts either side of Kinsale Harbour built after a decisive battle there in 1601 cemented English rule.

The other legacy of great land and wealth is great food. Kinsale is well known for top-notch restaurants and even has an award-winning meadery, Ireland's first for several centuries. But the heavy traffic and car parks on the seafront mean these are mostly tucked away from the water; if you want a sea view with your refreshments, you're better off heading down to The Bulman in Summercove. Ballinspittle has more than its fair share of foodie outlets, and this region saw the first farmer's market in Ireland at Midleton, instigated by the legendary Darina Allen of Ballymaloe Hotel and cookery school. From morning pastries after an early swim to dinner after a long coastal walk, it's hard to go wrong in this wonderful part of Cork.

SECRET COVES

1 SHEEP COVE *

Spectacular vertical strata and rocks jutting up from beach and bay; head L for a more secluded section. Parking for four or five cars keeps it peaceful. A beautiful 1km walk leads to a cobble cove on South Ring head where you can forage seakale; beyond this, views are of the megahotel on Inchydoney, but you can return on the lanes in a loop.

2 mins, 51.5942, -8.8351

2 SIMON'S COVE

The beach you want is not the cove at the end of the road (though that has a hidden narrow sea arch and possible coasteering to caves L), but a hidden, perfect arc of shingle between wave-sculpted rocks, reached along the path W below the house, down a V cleft, and across a rock platform. Space for two cars carefully beyond the last house R, which is allowed; don't block in the house L.

5 mins, 51.5937, -8.8260

3 DUNWORLEY & MOLONEY'S STRAND

Well known as one of the most beautiful wild beaches on Seven Heads, there's a grassy cliff top for parking, picnics, views and wild camping. A slipway leads down, and at LT sand, caves and coves are revealed. Popular for swimmers and body boarders, if it's too busy for you head NW 1km to the estuarine beach at Moloney. There's freestyle parking along the road (51.5933, -8.7598), loads of LT sand with little coves along the E shore.

2 mins, 51.5926, -8.7597

4 BROADSTRAND BAY BEACH

Huge, empty beach. This lane ends provides access to the quitest middle section. There's also a small car park at N end, good for overnights (51.6213, -8.7016).

2 mins, 51.6188, -8.7027

5 BLIND STRAND

The best swimming here is at higher tides – when there's the slipway/pier at the end of the road to jump from, too. The best light is in the morning, but the sheltered sands are lovely at any time. Parking along the shoreside road.

2 mins, 51.6116, -8.6921

6 HOWE STRAND BEACH

Explore the ruins of a large 19th-century coastguard station above this beautiful secluded cove, climbing up on the rocks at LT or walking around. Park on the road at the end of the lane; quite popular for wild camping, too.

5 mins, 51.6399, -8.6430

1

5

7 ROCKY BAY, BALLYFOYLE

A quiet little cove of golden sand between rocks, with a curving stream down the middle and a fringe of cobbles at the top. There's a bit of space to pull over on the road and a small car park just above the beach, where some park overnight to catch the morning sun over the waves.

2 mins, 51.7339, -8.3306

8 CUAN BÁN / WHITE BAY BEACH

Small and secluded beach, a short walk from the roadside car park. Sheltered, safe, and you can watch the traffic in and out of Cork harbour. Caves and rock pools when the tide is out.

8 mins, 51.8084, -8.2513

9 INCH BEACH, POWERHEAD BAY

This sandy bay is bigger than it looks when you arrive, extending around the corner L at LT. There's a dead-end lane down to parking each side; Tarmac to the W less formal to the E, and there's a sauna at this end (thesweatysanctuarysauna.as.me). On the way down is old Inch Church hidden up a grassy track (51.8018, -8.1753).

2 mins, 51.7953, -8.1785

10 BALLYBRANAGAN & BALLYCRONEEN

Reopened in 2020 after four years of stabilising the land around the slipway. This is a

1km stretch of sand and rock, with rock pools at low tide and a header of cobbles. Over the rocks at the far end is Ballycroneen beach (51.8081, -8.1126), which is often overlooked.

2 mins, 51.8046, -8.1354

11 BALLYNATRASNA BEACH

This hidden little cove on the Ballycotton Cliff walk is probably different with each storm, but LT only in any case. A good place to break a walk with a dip if the waves aren't crashing on the rocks.

30 mins, 51.8201, -8.0307

12 BALLYNAMONA STRAND

Huge sand beach and flowery dunes, with sheltered, shallow waters at the shore and good views to Ballycotton Island. Internationally renowned for birds, including many rare visitors. Good views over to Ballycotton Lighthouse. Large, rough car park.

2 mins, 51.8443, -8.0220

13 BALLINWILLING BEACH

Big, wild, sandy beach for swimming, rock pooling, shell hunting. Popular with anglers as evening sets in, but walk L from the car park for more seclusion at Ballycrenane end.

2 mins, 51.8661, -7.9795

14 RING BEACH & KNOCKADOON PIER

Small, golden-sand beach with rocks buttressing the ends and a little row of cottages above. Car park at 51.8935, -7.8880. There's also Knockadoon Pier 2km further along the coast (51.8854, -7.8676) at the start of a coastal trail passing Knockadoon signal tower (see entry).

2 mins, 51.8929, -7.8871

15 BARRY'S COVE

A slipway runs down into the sand of this sheltered haven. To the L and R 150m are further sandy inlets – walk, scramble or swim around to them. Park on the verge at the top of the lane (51.5915, -8.7874) and walk down 100m. There's also a large beach 2km W in Ballinglanna (room for a few at 51.5955, -8.8065)

5 mins, 51.5898, -8.7885

16 SANDYCOVE ISLAND & CREEK

At HT, swimmers enter the clear waters from the slipway and steps, at LT there's sand. It's 150m out to the island, or a full circumnavigation is 1km; alternatively swim down the shallow, warm creek from the lane 1km N (51.6863, -8.5282), ideally as HT ebbs to give some assistance.

2 mins, 51.6769, -8.5239

17 NOHOVAL COVE

Crumbling, waterside ruins and dramatic geology of sugar-loaf rock peaks, ledges, caves and arches make this cleft in the cliffs a popular yet remote 'hidden' cove, with good swimming and coasteering in the clear, turquoise waters, especially to the E. Walk up to the L for the classic view. Only a few car spaces at the end of the long, narrow lane, and nothing further back.

2 mins, 51.7148, -8.3850

18 MV ALTA & BALLYTRASNA COVE

Abandoned in Bermuda, this true 'ghost ship' washed up on the Irish coast in early 2020; the oil cargo was removed and it was left to decay. 800m W of Ballyandreen beach car park (51.8178, -8.0484): turn R and take the path above/R of the first cottage on L. 2km E of Ballyandreen is tiny Ballytrasna cove (51.8201, -8.0307). This is the Ballycotton Cliff Walk and can be followed all the way to Ballycotton, with a chance of seeing warblers, swifts, shearwaters and even basking sharks.

15 mins, 51.8114, -8.0565

LOST RUINS

19 DUNDANIEL CASTLE & IRONWORKS

Riverside tower house (a.k.a Downdaniel), strategically positioned on the banks of the Bandon. Built in 1476 on the site of an early Danish fortress ('Dun Danier'). Park on the corner by the gate 50m W, the site of a 1620s East India Company smelting works (51.7661, -8.6800) and the woods once used to feed the furnaces, with remnants of ancient walls and badger dens. Slag is still found in the riverside field which leads to the little stream, with small pool below bridge and riverside path to explore.

2 mins, 51.7671, -8.6789

20 BALLINOROHER CASTLE

This roadside 16th-century tower house probably defended a ford on the Argideen River. Today it is engulfed by ivy – in flower when we visited and alive with wild bees – and a tree

19

19

is slowly filling the interior. Legend says that when Cromwellian forces arrived, the family hid their gold in a secret hollow in the walls; hopeful treasure hunters may have caused some visible collapses. Pull in at gate L.
2 mins, 51.6492, -8.8310

21 KINCRAIGIE HOUSE, COURTMACSHERRY

Once a magnificent country house, first called Woodview, this is in ruins and consumed by its own woodland garden. You'll find one of the largest cypress trees in the country near the entrance. Sometimes off limits or squatted in, but the wall by the path along W side (from 51.6321, -8.7036) is broken in places; the old gateway is on E side (51.6324, -8.6990).
5 mins, 51.6310, -8.7011

22 OLD HEAD CASTLE & SIGNAL TOWER

Built about 1220, this may be the last promontory fortification still serving a defensive purpose; now for a golf club, with no public access. But the sweeping sea and cliff vistas either side are impressive, and you can roam the wildflower-studded clifftops on the W looking for puffins and guillemots below, kittiwakes, peregrines, and choughs above. Park at the Lusitania Museum and restored Napoleonic signal tower (also worth a visit, café, views from the top of the tower, +353 21 4191285), and stroll down on the road to the ancient ditch and wall.
4 mins, 51.6180, -8.5416

23 COURTAPARTEEN CHURCH & BEACH *

This ruin is precariously situated on an eroding cliff edge, beside the remains of a Famine village in the woods to the R. Nearby are holy wells (51.6698, -8 5294) dedicated to St Ruadhán, and a steep scramble leads down to a wild beach with a rocky reef; one of the higher platforms was used as a LT mass rock. Rough parking and steps down at the end of L7321, from 51.6634, -8.5556.
2 mins, 51.6700, -8.5281

24 JAMES FORT & BLOCKHOUSE

Built in 1602 directly opposite the more famous Charles Fort, this much smaller star-shaped fortress is open access and fun to explore. You can ascend through heath on a path to the L from the beach. The E side of the peninsula has rocky inlets and coves, and the water-level blockhouse ruin beyond has views across the harbour. The Dock bar (P17 H529) by the marina is a nice spot for a sundowner. There's a small car park and parking R on one-way road to Castlepark, which can all fill up on weekends or in summer.
10 mins, 51.6985, -8.5122

25 CHARLES FORT & BEACH

Vast star-shaped 17th-century fort with panoramic views from ramparts and an array of ruined buildings. Book online heritageireland.ie, €5 per person. Or you're free to walk down the dry moat below the mighty walls to the quiet, sheltered, sandy cove below (51.6951, -8.4970) and return outside the outermost walls, passing two old graveyards or heading E to Trinity Well (51.6971, -8.4954). Real adventurers could coasteer around the base at LT. Has car park, or take the Scilly Walk from Kinsale to Summercourt and then village lanes.

2 mins, 51.6977, -8.4988

26 ROBERT'S HEAD SIGNAL TOWER

A lovely coastal path leads to this Napoleonic era shell with panoramic views – you can walk on to the Second World War lookout post at the very end (51.7322, -8.3125). Wonderful flowery cliff-tops, bring a picnic. The path starts between two walls behind the first house overlooking Robert's Cove, a sheltered inlet that is almost entirely sand at LT, shallow water at HT.

15 mins, 51.7386, -8.3172

27 ROCHE'S POINT LIGHTHOUSE & TOWER

An array of coastal defensive buildings at the last anchorage of the Titanic (you can swim

28

30

29

31

35

or kayak in the rocky harbour). The 1835 lighthouse received the Lusitania SOS in 1915 and is still active, but you can stay in some of the buildings, listed on Vrbo. Behind the terraced homes leading to the lighthouse are the ruins of square and octagonal signal towers from the 1870s, and a round one from c.1940. But the best is back up the lane to the corner and a track around the edge of fields, a Gothic tower on the hill. Built about 1790 as a folly, it has such commanding views that Lord Fermoy rented it to the government as a watch tower.

15 mins, 51.7931, -8.2548

28 KNOCKADOON SIGNAL TOWER

There's a lovely coastal path to this remarkably intact Napoleonic tower, the machicolation, bartizans and slates still in place. Nearby, as so often, is a Second World War lookout post and there's an EIRE pilots' marker just W (51.8787, -7.8739). The cliff-top headland is full of flowers and birdsong – a wonderful place to picnic. Follow the Capel Way from Knockadoon Pier (51.8857, -7.8692, good for jumps at HT) and loop back on little lanes. Or you can follow a lane signed Residential Area to a car park at the dead end by the tower.

20 mins, 51.8789, -7.8729

SACRED & ANCIENT

29 TEMPLEQUINLAN GRAVEYARD

The ivy-clad ruins of a small medieval church lie in the middle, but it's the grave markers that are striking. Almost all are uncut stones so two lonely memorials stand out all the more. One is the grave of a local IRA quartermaster from the War of Independence, the other a 1997 memorial to those in the unmarked Famine pits here, who 'left their souls to God, their bodies to nature and their names to oblivion', as the plaque at the gate puts it. Pull in across the gate.

2 mins, 51.6327, -8.8150

30 KILSHINAHAN MASS ROCK

Hidden in a little woodland above a stream. Many of the parishioners would have walked here in the stream, to avoid leaving tracks that would lead the authorities to the site. The font is from a ruined church nearby (51.6671, -8.7629); the path in was impassable when we visited. Space to pull off by the sign.

2 mins, 51.6675, -8.7668

31 KILMONOGUE CEMETERY

The gate of this little graveyard claims a date of 1783, but it's much older; the parish church is mostly one picturesque arch. Emigration here

was high after the Famine, and some graves have been recently restored by descendants overseas who have traced their ancestry. Park carefully at the shore beyond, where two disintegrating boats give an abandoned feeling. Mudflats at LT, but a HT paddle upriver reveals ivy-hung ruins of Mountlong fortified house on private land above (51.7121, -8.4696). Nearby, just above popular Oysterhaven Beach, Kinure Graveyard also has one medieval church wall standing and tells a story of the Famine with an area of unmarked pit burials; the local population fell from 374 to just 96 in the 1840s (51.7039, -8.4372).

2 mins, 51.7092, -8.4602

32 GARRANEKINNEFEAKE CEMETERY

This wild and ancient-feeling site is completely circular and within an earthen bank, possibly an older ringfort. There are low ruins of the parish church with the possible remains of an ancient font. There's an old pictorial gravestone with crossed hurleys on it here but we think it was in the most nettled areas; a winter visit might find it. Pull off at the corner; access is allowed but be careful of any livestock.

2 mins, 51.8655, -8.1862

33 BALLYNACORRA CHURCHYARD & WALK

Quiet churchyard on the shore with graves back to the 1740s (still occasional burials) and the ruined parish church. From the far corner opposite the gate a couple of steps lead down to a hidden shoreline walk L along the estuary, 600m along to a green headland with estuary vistas, a lovely spot for a picnic and paddle. Signed Ballinacurra down Grotto View; park outside houses at far end (51.8972, -8.1716) and follow path R of big gates ahead.

2 mins, 51.8979, -8.1735

34 TOBER MUIRE & KILTESKIN CHURCH *

Beneath a mighty ash (and mightier pylon) is a lovely whitewashed holy well, sometimes called Whitewell and still venerated. A nearby slab has a crucified Christ on one side, and the instructions 'Seven Pater Nosters and Seven Ave Marias. The Honour 1731' on the other, with pilgrim crosses on both. Further along the muddy track in a field R is the graveyard and remains of Kilteskin Church, a ruin by the 17th century. Take ladder-like steps by the gate between houses (51.8343, -8.1656, park carefully by corner) but best ask at the farm for the graveyard if there is livestock.

2 mins, 51.8348, -8.1672

35 BALLYMACODA CEMETERY *

Gem of a hilltop cemetery, round and remote amid fields (which were full of fragrant, flowering broad beans), with wonderful views to the sea. The church is long vanished. Take a blink-and-you-miss-it narrow grassy lane (51.8911, -7.9178) up to a space by old buildings where you can turn and park, walk on old track about 250m.

5 mins, 51.8890, -7.9208

ANCIENT FOREST

36 BANDON WOODS

The old Castlebernard estate woodlands run along the Bandon here, an important habitat with mature oak and some ash. Within about 400m you can be at the river, good for a paddle or a picnic, where you might spot cormorants, herons or even resident otters. Winter floods bring lapwing and curlew, as well as ducks. Rooms for several cars to park in the layby by the gate.

7 mins, 51.7393, -8.8007

37 COURTMACSHERRY WOODS

The woods E of 'Courtmac' village are over 200 years old, and sweep down to the shore and shelter several tiny swimming spots. Just keep your eye open for trodden paths. The floor is carpeted with bluebells in late spring. Longer looped walks pass through here: most popular is the short Fuschia Walk, especially when the hedges are alight with the flower. This coast is on the 42km Seven Heads loop around the whole peninsula – with plenty of places to turn back on

37

43

42

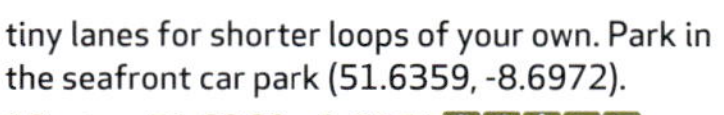

tiny lanes for shorter loops of your own. Park in the seafront car park (51.6359, -8.6972).

10 mins, 51.6369, -8.6874

38 KILBRITTAIN WOODS & WATERFALL

Walk in the mixed Coillte woodlands along the river, where the ground is awash with bluebells in late spring and you can paddle in the waterfall in summer. Or take one of the longer walks on quiet lands marked on the signboard; Rathclaren trail takes in Trinity Well (51.6578, -8.7016), and a pretty old church and graveyard with a lich gate (51.6568, -8.7009). Car park at entrance.

2 mins, 51.6713, -8.6766

39 DROMKEEN BLUEBELLS

Planted about 1740 by colourful local entrepreneur Thomas Adderley, these trees once showed his name across the valley in contrasting foliage. There's a stream and, in May, bluebells flood the slopes; children can count the fairy doors on a short loop walk. Car park at junction or park carefully on forest track splay at 51.7626, -8.6697 for a quieter way in. Opp car park you can go over the wall to see the 1755 bridge arches, built after a Lisbon earthquake tsunami destroyed the old one.

2 mins, 51.7640, -8.6653

40 SHIP-POOL WOODS & BANDON RIVER

A large mixed woodland including beech, oak and ash along the shores of the tidal Bandon River, where otters are regularly seen. Park at the lane end, by the forest gate. River paths also lead N to waterfall (51.7415, -8.6267) and riverside castle ruins (on R605).

2 mins, 51.7384, -8.6291

41 GARRETTSTOWN WOODS

High points in the N give views S to the Old Head of Kinsale and N to Ballycatten ringfort (51.6647, -8.6047, park by houses on Ballycatten Terrace and walk up). Off the waymarked trails are an old deer wall, a holy well (51.6629, -8.6062) and, to S, a Chalybeate Well (51.6537, -8.6027). No woodland car parks: try Ballinspittle GAA on non-match days (51.6620, -8.5941), Templetrine Church to the N (51.6628, -8.6147), or track splays on E side (51.6544, -8.6122 and 51.6579, -8.6167).

2 mins, 51.6623, -8.5970

42 TRACTON WOODS

From a picturesque pool and cascade by the Overdraught pub (P17 A529), walking and mountain biking paths lead up the shallow river through mixed woodland; popular in summer with families who come to paddle. Parking at the wood entrance, with a few more spaces across the road.

2 mins, 51.7615, -8.3924

43 MARLOGUE WOODS & CUSKINNY

Coastal Coillte woodland including oak, beech, Scots pine and eucalyptus, creating a diverse habitat for birds, red squirrels and foxes. There are ruins of a lime kiln and summerhouse. Car park with height barrier. A secluded, pebble beach at the edge of the woods is a peaceful spot for picnics; you could swim here at HT or join locals at Cuskinny Beach to the W (51.8588, -8.2628).

2 mins, 51.8597, -8.2203

44 ROSTELLAN WOODS & RUINS *

This old demesne has long, shady paths and strange ruins. Even locals miss the seaweed-draped 'dolmen' we've marked below HT level on the quiet estuary shore (possibly a folly); the car park map is poor and there's no proper path. Further W by the GAA pitch lie a battery (51.8514, -8.1935) and stump of the 1727 Siddons Tower, named for a visit by actress Sarah Siddons (51.8496, -8.1933). Across the road from here is an ice house (51.8479, -8.1880) and an overgrown, walled garden. Park in Coillte car park (51.8502, -8.1832) or GAA ground for a loop or sections.

20 mins, 51.8572, -8.1826

44

44

44

45 BALLYANNAN WOOD BLUEBELLS

This mixed woodland is at least 400 years old, hiding relics of cobbled paths, stone walls, gate pillars, a ruined cottage and a boathouse. On the perimeter path, you might see foraging seabirds, including little egrets; or walk inwards for forest bathing, especially when bluebells flood the floor. Small parking at the dead end of L3620 from roundabout at 51.9150, -8.1796, passing Midleton Hotel (P25 AX67) L. For a 1.5km riverside walk in, from car park on Bailick Road (51.9047, -8.1738) walk upriver and over footbridge to join dead-end lane.

3 mins, 51.9024, -8.1795

46 GLENBOWER WOOD

Nature reserve in old estate woodlands with many paths to explore along its 2.5km up the tumbling little Dissour River, which once powered a mill. Look out for exotic giant redwoods or forage wild garlic in spring. There are odd ruins along the way, such as a bridge over the path (51.9508, -8.0010) and a bullaun (51.9519, -8.0026). Turn off N25 up the side of the Old Thatch pub (P36 KX25) to car park at dead end with playground (51.9470, -7.9981).

2 mins, 51.9470, -7.9981

WILDLIFE WONDERS

47 INCHY BRIDGE

Admire the damselflies, dragonflies, kingfishers, dippers and even nightjars along the banks of one of the best trout rivers in Ireland. Access is accepted if you aren't inconveniencing the anglers. Pull off considerately on N side of bridge.

2 mins, 51.6620, -8.7742

48 ATLANTIC WHALE & WILDLIFE TOURS

Take a trip from Courtmacsherry for a chance of seeing dolphins and porpoises, basking sharks, sunfish, and fin, minke and humpback whales (regularly seen around here in recent years). Woodpoint House, Courtmacsherry, P72 VF84, +353 87 7744401, trips leave from the pier by P72 XY48.

2 mins, 51.6354, -8.7107

49 HARBOUR VIEW & COOLMAIN BEACHES

Connected to Garranefeen Strand, this large expanse of LT sand is wonderful for evening bird watching and overnight camping, with a large area of accessible wild land behind the sand. For swimming, continue on 3km around to the opposite E side of the estuary via the causeway to Coolmain Beach (51.6454, -8.6658). The water can be very warm when the tides come in across the warm, dark sand.

5 mins, 51.6507, -8.6778

50 PILMORE STRAND

Vast estuarine sands of the Womanagh River estuary at LT are an important winter habitat for wading birds. You'll see flocks of golden plovers, joined by little stints, curlew, sandpipers, pipits and terns – plus occasional farmers ploughing the beach, a low-tech way to sharpen a plough. Shallow HT is ideal for families and paddling. Wildest to the W and the spit of land, with car park near the GAA ground, at 51.9093, -7.8951.

2 mins, 51.9067, -7.8991

CLASSIC PUBS

51 THE ANCHOR BAR, COURTMACSHERRY

Courtmac has been described as a 'quiet drinking village with a fishing problem', a reputation earned by places such as this simple local, with a chatty atmosphere and live music late at the weekends. Main Street, Courtmacsherry, P72 DX30, +353 23 8846180

51.6342, -8.7077

52 THE LIFEBOAT INN, COURTMACSHERRY

This village pub has a relatively small but high-quality menu of local foods, with tables right

on the waterfront in a garden over the road from the pub proper. Given the location, there's an emphasis on fish and it's not one for the vegetarians. Main Street, Courtmacsherry, P72 EA89, +353 23 8864656
51.6337, -8.7062

53 DIVA BOUTIQUE BAKERY & DELI

Covers all your café and picnic and cake needs to go, with artisan bread, pastries and cakes, and sandwiches with vegetarian and vegan options. Open Thur–Sun. Main Street, Ballinspittle, P17 P597, +353 21 4778465
51.6664, -8.5958

54 THE TAP TAVERN, KINSALE

Said to be Kinsale's oldest pub, run by the same family since 1886, and still with a feeling of the 1950s or so. 'Queen Mary' O'Neill has ceded to her son, Brian, who also leads Kinsale ghost tours (an irreverent history tour with guaranteed 'ghosts') from here at 9pm. Music in the backyard in summer. 9 Guardwell, Kinsale, P17 AF50, +353 87 9480910
51.7060, -8.5251

55 THE BULMAN, SUMMERCOVE

Brightly coloured quayside classic – there may have been a pub here since the 16th century. There could be someone in a wetsuit ordering a pint next to you, so do join in. Lunch in the bar, walk-ins only, also an excellent bookings-only restaurant upstairs; no wetsuits or dogs there. Food Wed–Sun (lunch only Sun). Summercove, Kinsale, P17 KF57, +353 21 4772131
51.7000, -8.4997

56 CRONIN'S, CROSSHAVEN

This classic and cosy family-run pub with walls crammed with old photographs is a renowned destination for a seafood lunch. Now has a second string, the Mad Fish restaurant, adjoining the pub. 1 Point Road, Crosshaven, P43 XD43, +353 21 4831829
51.8019, -8.2946

57 GYLEEN ARMS BAR & BEACH

Traditional pub with outside tables looking down to the beach and slipway in this little, pretty village with a coastguard post and distinctive thatched houses. P25 R966
51.7959, -8.1959

58 BLACKBIRD BAR, BALLYCOTTON

Cosy vibes in a dog-friendly, laid-back modern bar with music in the back room and the Trawler Boys Field Kitchen food on weekends. Main Street, Ballycotton, P25 D580, +353 21 4647884. Those looking for a more retro atmosphere might also visit wood-lined Sean McGrath's a few doors along for a hot port and the best Murphy's (P25 P6D3).
51.8306, -8.0142

LOCAL PRODUCE

59 THE WORKSHOP *

Colourful country café: stop in for freshly baked scones piled on vintage-style cake stands, or sandwiches made with local, fresh produce, GF dishes, and coffee freshly roasted in east Cork. There are records playing or you might catch one of the live music performances. They also sell vintage, antique, and restored or up-cycled items. 11.00am–4.00pm most days. Lios Cross, Ballygarvan, next door to T12 CA3C, +353 21 2373033
51.8303, -8.4883

60 LOBSTER'S TALE, COURTMACSHERRY

Summer weekends seafood takeaway. Take your lobster cakes and chips with aioli and eat them right by the water. Sea Road, Courtmacsherry, P72 T652, +353 83 1934020
51.6351, -8.7103

61 WILDFLOUR BAKERY *

Seriously good artisanal bread, backed up by sinful pastries and great coffee. Takeaway, with a bench or two out on the pavement. Main Street, Inishannon, T12 DD27, +353 86 2173266
51.7645, -8.6559

62 GATHER COMMUNITY GROCERY

Lovely, friendly refill and grocery shop with deli products, local produce delivered through the week, and higher-welfare meat and dairy. 4 Main Street, Balinspittle, P17 KC89, +353 21 4708593
51.6665, -8.5957

63 KOKO KINSALE

Frank Keane has been making small-batch artisan chocolates using local flavourings for a decade; his seaweed truffle is a local classic and our favourite. This is where to come for truffles, bars, a palm-oil free chocolate and high-quality hazelnut spread; there's even a vegan range. Main Street, Kinsale, P17 YX22, +353 87 6110209
51.7051, -8.5221

64 KINSALE FOOD TOURS

Returned native Suzanne Burns switched from working as a marine zoologist to running local tours, but sea life remains close to her heart. Take a family-friendly coastal foraging and picnic tour (€75); there's also a high-end tasting tour of the town and a full-day yacht trip. Start point given when booking. +353 85 1076113, suzanne@kinsalefoodtours.com
51.7024, -8.5188

65 ROSTELLAN FARM *

Busy little farm shop café, family friendly, sandwiches, local ice cream in summer. Knockanemorney, Rostellan, P25 KOF3, +353 87 4737636

51.8423, -8.1815

66 MIDLETON & FARMER'S MARKETS

Farmers markets in Ireland started with Midleton, still one of the most varied markets in Ireland, notable for fantastic cheeses. 9.30am–1.30pm Sat, Market Square car park, next to P25 FR64. Also on the weekend, Bandon has local fish and produce with street food, coffee and bakes. 9.30am–1.30pm Sat, 3 Market Street, P72 TX36. Kinsale has some 30 stalls at a midweek market, 9am–2.30pm, Wed, Market Quay, next to P17 FD66

51.9174, -8.1743

67 THE GRUMPY BAKERS

Organic Irish flours, and as many local and organic ingredients as possible are used for breads and pastries that slow ferment for 24 to 48 hours. It's said that grumpy bakers make the best bread due to the small-hours start to produce fresh morning loaves; appropriately, they also sell great coffee to go. Broderick St, Midleton, P25 YR58, +353 83 2078696

51.9123, -8.1736

68 BALLYCOTTON SEAFOOD

One of three outlets for the family-run business – others are in Glanmire and the English Market in Cork city – this is a great place to pick up fresh fish and shellfish, smoked fish, and oven-ready dishes. Local art for sale in the front window. 46 Main Street, Midleton, P25 E6D6, +353 21 4613122

51.9136, -8.1720

69 BALLYMALOE HOTEL & RESTAURANT

It says something that this elegant, wisteria-hung country house and castle hotel is best known for its food. To get the most out of it, stay and eat in, but the restaurant has limited spaces for non-residents in the evenings. This was an eco-conscious fork-to-fork venue before anyone had invented those terms, with as much produce as possible locally sourced or grown on the estate. Serious foodies can try a short course at the famous cookery school down the road. Ballymaloe More, Shanagarry, P25 Y070, +353 21 4652531

51.8652, -8.0733

ORGANIC & BISTRO

70 MONK'S LANE, TIMOLEAGUE

Highly rated restaurant using seasonal local produce, with Irish craft beers, and a good selection of gins and whiskeys on the bar, recommended to book ahead. Mill Street, Timoleague, P72 D798, +353 23 8846348

51.6437, -8.7659

71 O'REILLY'S FOOD TRUCK

Not an average chipper van, more like the food truck culture of the USA: order ahead or be prepared to wait at this highly popular pair of trucks, offering excellent fish and burger options from local suppliers, cooked to order. There's a covered picnic table area if you're breaking a journey, though the urban surroundings are incongruous. Clonakilty Road, Bandon, P72 H337, oreillysfoodcourt.ie

51.7349, -8.7570

72 CRACKED... BANDON

Bistro in Bandon. Funky, bustling, great burrito with the best of west Cork produce and choice of waffles at breakfast. St Finbarr's Place, Bandon, P72 YR53, +353 89 9866467

51.7457, -8.7351

73 WILD RESTAURANT, BALLINSPITTLE *

Chef Rob Platten offers a frequently changing menu that reflects the region's rich agricultural and fishing heritage. His West Cork bouillabaisse has a following all of its own, or try the croquettes stuffed with local Gubbeen cheese, smoked Knockandore and chorizo. From 5.30pm Thur-Sat, from 1.00pm Sun. Main St, Ballinspittle, Co. Cork, P17 YH95, +353 831829303

51.6667, -8.5957

81

81

63

75

78

79

80

74 PINK ELEPHANT RESTAURANT

There's been a restaurant enjoying the panoramic views over Courtmacsherry Bay for over 60 years. Focused on local produce, especially seafood, with local brews; most dishes can be GF on request. If the weather is fine, aim for a table on the patio. Harbour View, Kilbrittain, P72 HC79, +353 23 8849608

51.6456, -8.6831

75 BLACK PIG, KINSALE

As stylish as it is sustainable, this softly lit wine bar celebrates regional, organic, and seasonal ingredients like smoked duck from Skeaghanore and leaves from Horizon Farm, while also keeping an eye on global flavours. For those who want to delve deeper, the website lists many of their suppliers. Opening varies seasonally. 66 Lower O'Connell Street, P17 FX54, +353 21 4774101, theblackpigwinebar.com

51.7028, -8.5209

76 SEEDS BAKERY

A relatively recent arrival in town that's landed well. French baker Benjamin Le Bon was a wholesale baker for years before, and partner Ingrid Kelly sources local and organic products such as raw honey and natural wines. Sold alongside their 48-hour sourdough bread and gorgeous pastries in a bright, rustic, eco-renovated café. 4 Market Quay, Kinsale, P17 XT81

51.7060, -8.5236

77 MAX'S KINSALE *

Anne-Marie and Olivier have run this excellent bistro since 1999. The menus lean into fish in the summer, game in the winter, marrying local ingredients with French culinary traditions and an upmarket wine list with organic options. No gimmicks, no trendy decor, just calm quality with regular returning customers. Booking is advisable, especially for the great-value early bird prices. 48 Main Street, Kinsale, P17 XY07, +353 21 4772443

51.7045, -8.5222

78 THE FLYING POET

Café and book exchange with the odd aeroplane photo on the walls. Feels like having (very good) coffee and bakes in your most boho friend's sitting room. 44 Main Street, Kinsale, P17 H042, +353 85 2635431

51.7043, -8.5219

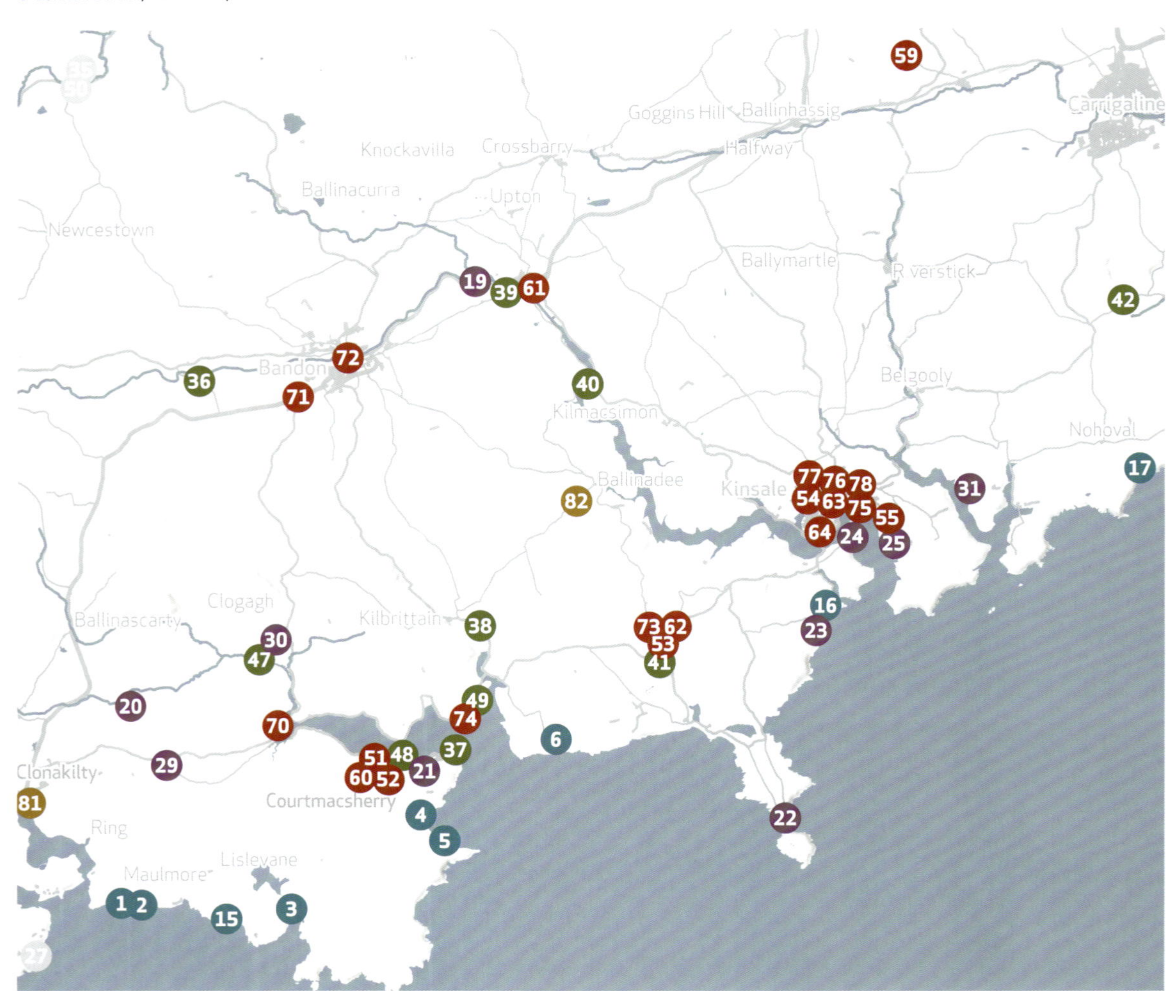

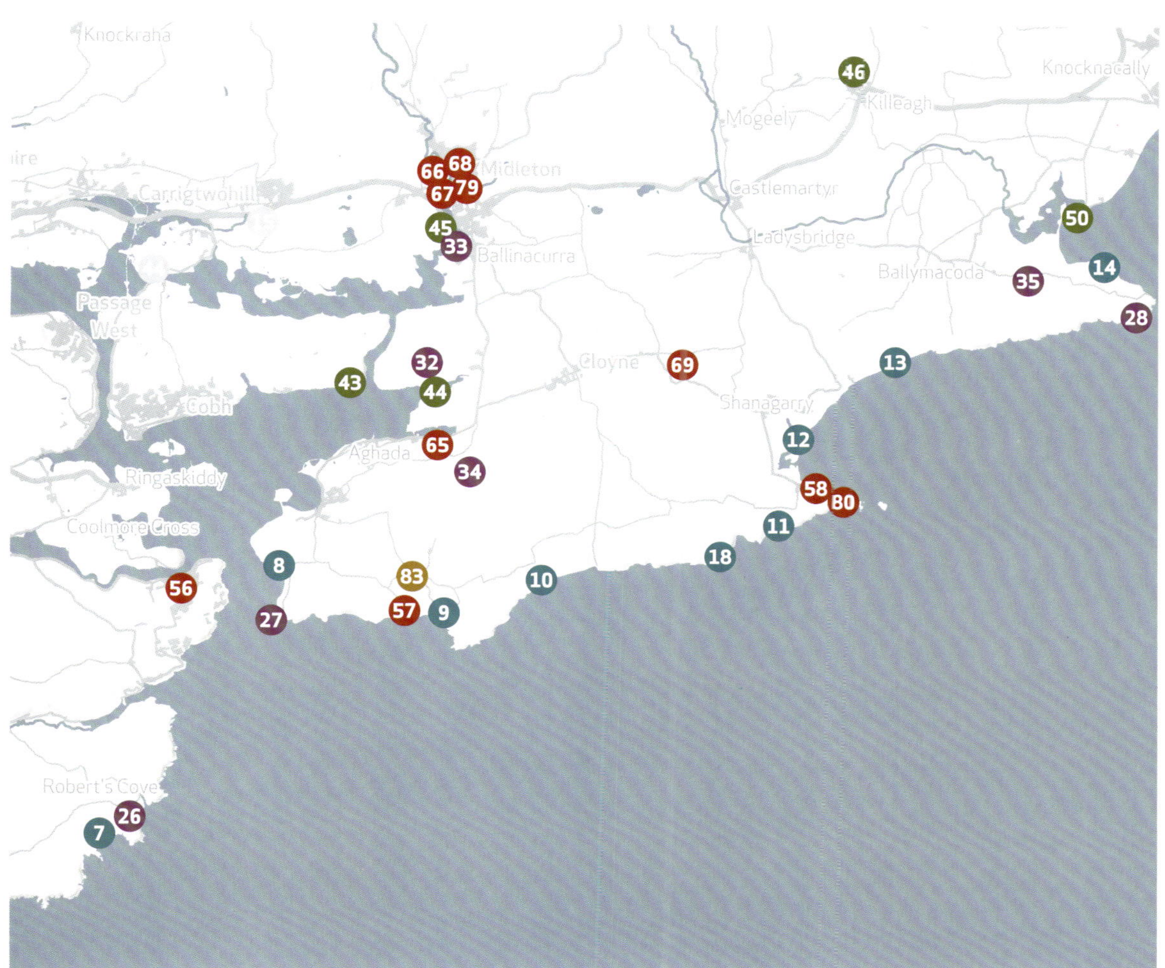

79 FERRIT & LEE, MIDLETON

Modern Irish, strong on fish, but not exclusive, local craft beers, sustainable wine list. Excellently placed if you want to do the distillery tour almost next door. Distillery Walk, Midleton, P25 D259, +353 21 4635235

51.9127, -8.1704

80 CUSH & SEA CHURCH, BALLYCOTTON

Renowned restaurant and chef, with strong focus on local produce and seasonality, and a super tasting menu. The Pier, Ballycotton, P25 FY94, +353 21 4646768. For something more informal and funky, in a converted schoolhouse by the repurposed church, Sea Church is also excellent, owned by the same management (P25 XP03, +353 21 2340525).

51.8268, -8.0021

COOL CAMPING

81 DESERT HOUSING CAMPING

Fine westerly views from a green field, estuarine campsite within walking distance of Clonakilty, although facilities are basic and need upgrading. Desert, P85 XE29, +353 23 8833331. For better facilities, but an inland site with more caravans, try Sextons 6km E on R600 (P72 WY61, +353 87 2208088).

51.6222, -8.8753

82 BALLINADEE BUS & RESCUE FARM *

Stay in a converted bus with a wood-fired hot tub, or bring your own tent and camp with a bus as your communal chill-out space. Or just stop in to buy a coffee and locally baked cakes – for children, the pumpkin patch and a haunted bus (€) are open in October. Conclouse, Ballinadee, P72 CV67, +353 86 4513961, ballinadeebus.com

51.7059, -8.6340

83 INCH HIDEAWAY ECO CAMPSITE

A wonderfully eclectic site, with five colourfully furnished yurts and a converted school bus, a communal barn space and cob house kitchen – also polytunnels and a surprisingly speedy three-legged lurcher, all with an alternative, cosy vibe. Massages, yoga classes and foraging walks can be booked. Glanturkin, Whitegate, P25 ND37, +353 87 0613370, yurtecocamping.ie

51.8055, -8.1925

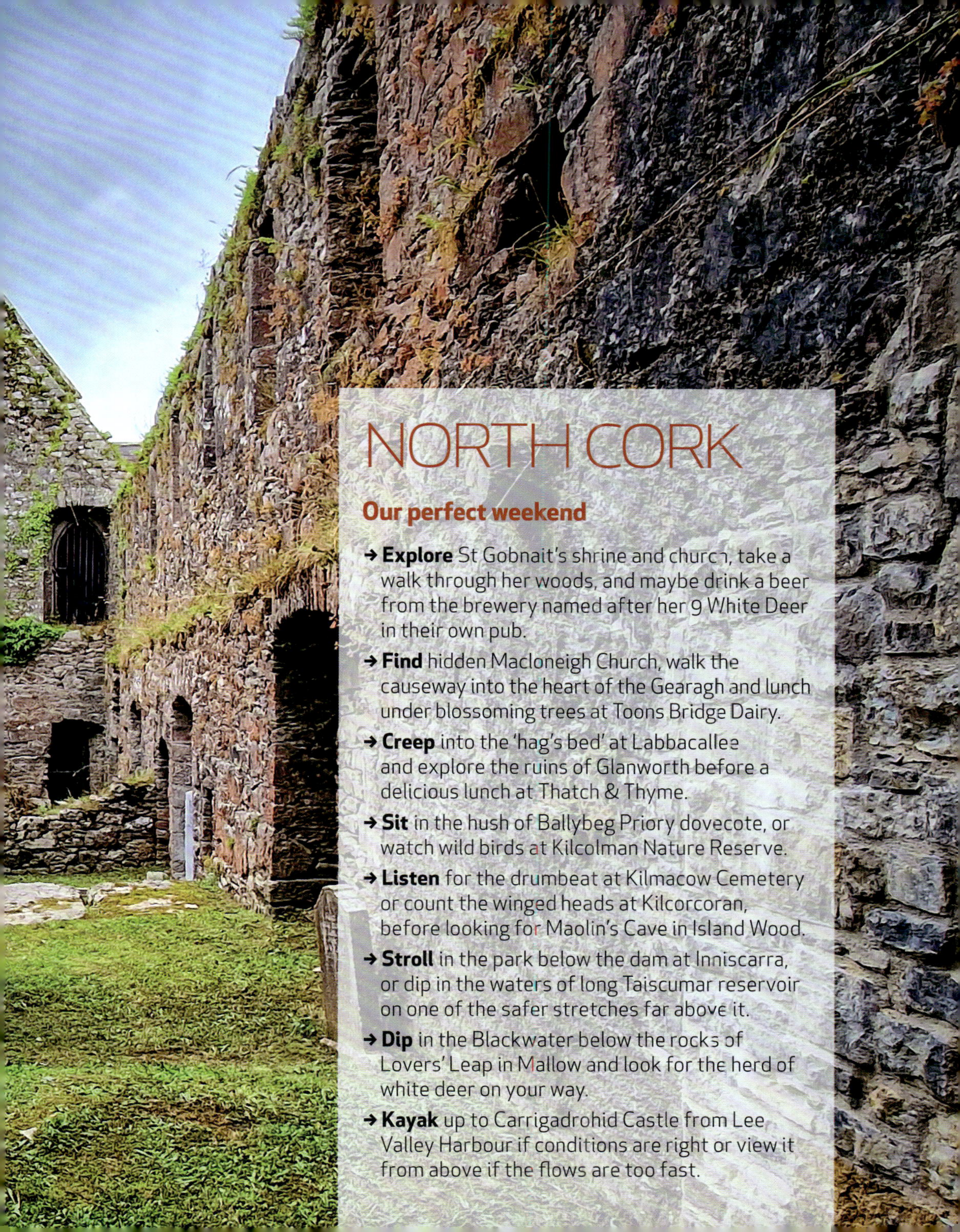

NORTH CORK

Our perfect weekend

- **Explore** St Gobnait's shrine and church, take a walk through her woods, and maybe drink a beer from the brewery named after her 9 White Deer in their own pub.
- **Find** hidden Macloneigh Church, walk the causeway into the heart of the Gearagh and lunch under blossoming trees at Toons Bridge Dairy.
- **Creep** into the 'hag's bed' at Labbacallee and explore the ruins of Glanworth before a delicious lunch at Thatch & Thyme.
- **Sit** in the hush of Ballybeg Priory dovecote, or watch wild birds at Kilcolman Nature Reserve.
- **Listen** for the drumbeat at Kilmacow Cemetery or count the winged heads at Kilcorcoran, before looking for Maolin's Cave in Island Wood.
- **Stroll** in the park below the dam at Inniscarra, or dip in the waters of long Taiscumar reservoir on one of the safer stretches far above it.
- **Dip** in the Blackwater below the rocks of Lovers' Leap in Mallow and look for the herd of white deer on your way.
- **Kayak** up to Carrigadrohid Castle from Lee Valley Harbour if conditions are right or view it from above if the flows are too fast.

Cork is Ireland's largest county and, according to Corkonians, its city is the true capital of the country. Bolstering this self-belief, the earliest evidence of humans in Ireland is a cut mark on a 33,000-year-old bone from Castlepook Cave near Doneraile. That cave is off limits, but there are plenty of more recent and accessible sites to keep you entertained.

Blarney Castle draws huge numbers, with long queues to the famous stone. For ruin hunters, the striking machicolation that holds the stone is a feature almost unique in Britain and Ireland, but apparently a local specialty; incomplete and intriguing Kanturk has supports for one, and lovely, lonely Lohort has an almost complete run.

This inland region has the 'Golden Vale' rolling west from Kanturk, some of the most productive dairy farmland in Ireland. It supported market towns such as Buttevant, where Lombard merchants settled, and powerful estates such as Doneraile, home to the St Leger family of horse-racing fame. The main rivers are the Blackwater and Lee, the latter heavily managed for electricity. Water released from Inniscarra and other dams can change levels abruptly in some places but other stretches are quite safe, with the National Rowing Centre in Farran Forest Park, and the floodplains support species-rich wetlands such as the Gearagh.

There are woods aplenty to walk in, some natives in river valleys like Mullinhassig, others large old parklands such as Fota Arboretum with champion trees and rare exotics. You can hope to see red squirrels and deer – the old demesne of Mallow Castle even has a famous herd of white deer descended from some sent as a gift by Elizabeth I of England; their genes have outlasted their owners' home, now a picturesque ruin. There are summits to conquer, too: Knockboy (706m) in the west is the highest, but there are others in the Ballyhoura range bordering Limerick and the Mullaghareirks.

Cork has been called the Rebel County since the 15th century, a name enthusiastically embraced locally, pointing to natives like rebel leader Michael Collins and legendary United States' labour organiser Mother Jones. Cork city was prominent in the War of Independence, with mayors assassinated and imprisoned, and the city centre gutted by arson; today, it's happier to be known for great food and craft brewers such as Franciscan Well and Rising Sons. It's worth some time in the city to experience these and maybe walk over the famous, bouncing Daly's Bridge, especially during the summer arts festival or autumn jazz festival.

RIVER, LAKE & WATERFALL

1 MALLOW RIVERSIDE & LOVERS' LEAP *

Pretty wooded river beaches downstream from the castle and town. Make sure to continue all the way to Lovers' Leap, white rocky cliffs with little caverns at the base and a slope into the river. The lovers were said to be a private and an officer's daughter, who leapt to their deaths when confronted by her father. White deer live here, descended from two given by Elizabeth I to her godchild at the castle. Walk in from the town and castle upstream (limited parking) or park on Riverside Walk behind the housing estates (52.1344, -8.6280) to find the best beach 250m upstream and the caves 400m downstream.

20 mins, 52.1345, -8.6210

2 MULLINHASSIG WOOD & WATERFALLS

This mossy river and waterfall glen was once home to a series of water-powered mills. At the end of the rock-hewn trail, part of which follows an old carved leat, is a double waterfall with a deep plunge pool below. It's about 500m from the car park (51.9273, -8.8295).

15 mins, 51.9298, -8.8366

3 LEE VALLEY HARBOUR, COACHFORD

Ballyhass aqua park with pontoons, kayak trips up to Carrigadrohid Castle (flow permitting). Waterside sauna with river dipping. Or there's riverside access from the small car park 1km W on R618 at 51.9079, -8.8389.

2 mins, 51.9104, -8.8273

4 COACHFORD QUAY & GREENWAY

A large, stone beach with deep water on the snaking Taiscumar reservoir of the River Lee, with an old concrete quay and wildflower meadows. There are no-swimming signs but it's a very popular spot for a dip. Park carefully at the lane end by the big metal security gates with pedestrian shore access. Down an unsigned lane off the R619 S of Coachford. 500m downstream, another option is the Coachford Greenway, a 3km length of shoreline trackway accessible from lane at 51.8968, -8.7839.

2 mins, 51.9023, -8.7954

5 FARRAN FOREST PARK

This remnant of estate woodland has easy walks and a herd of fallow deer, and treetop walkways (Zipit, €), but it also has an accessible stretch of shoreline below the National Rowing Centre, with secluded spots. €5 car park entry, bring a picnic and take your time. Large entrance and signs on L2202.

20 mins, 51.8949, -8.7408

6 INNISCARRA, LEE VALLEY

Popular informal picnic lakeshore beach area for swimming, kayaking and sailing; anglers use this stretch too, so you may have to walk to find a spot away from them. Small car park off R618.

2 mins, 51.9067, -8.6990

RUINED CASTLES

7 KANTURK CASTLE *

Very little is known for sure about this extraordinary unfinished castle from the early 17th century. Some records say that English settlers complained it was too large and defensible for an Irish lord to own, and no documentation about the construction itself survives. The main door is a fascinating example of classical motifs carved by a medieval hand, with Ionic scrolls cut as flat spirals and pediments halfway up the columns. The roofline shows that a highly unusual machicolation all the way around was intended, like Blarney Castle. Signed, with a car park, and surprisingly few visitors.

2 mins, 52.1643, -8.9027

8 LOHORT CASTLE *

At the end of a grassy avenue, behind Gothic gatehouses and over a moat, is this fairytale

8

8

9

7

7

castle with the rounded corners, machicolation and proportions of a graceful folly – but this is a real 15th-century stronghold, site of one of the bloodiest Cromwellian battles. Much later, it was owned by a famously irascible baronet and burned in the War of Independence. Drive down to the farm gate, climb over and walk in, and hope you're lucky enough to meet the owner, who lives nearby and aims to conserve or restore it.

10 mins, 52.1622, -8.7822

9 GLANWORTH CASTLE, ABBEY, BRIDGE *

This village on the Funcheon was once much more important, judging by its ruins, starting with extensive remains of a 12th-century castle, in use until the mid-17th century. It stands above an 18th-century mill (now a home, walk around it to reach the castle) and a 17th-century bridge with 13 arches, one of the oldest and narrowest still in use. There are views to the ruins of Glanworth Abbey (52.1909, -8.3564), a 15th-century friary with a lovely tracery window – once removed to the local Protestant church and only restored to the abbey in the 1990s. Park by the bridge (52.1874, -8.3544) for the castle and on the lane for the abbey. Farahy mass rock, capped with ferns, lies 8km N, unsigned on little lanes off R512: mass has been held annually here since 2000 (52.2340 -8.4358).

2 mins, 52.1882, -8.3544

10 DUNMAHON CASTLE

Hidden in dense, private woodland, this tower house castle is completely overgrown but still possible to get inside. Ask permission at the adjacent farm. Parking on bend (52.1956, -8.3368).

5 mins, 52.1958, -8.3382

11 CONNA CASTLE

This mid-16th-century tower withstood even Cromwell's cannon, the demise of many castles. It was eventually willed to the state in 1915, still in impressive shape. Access inside is only occasionally possible through guided tours, such as during Heritage Week, but it's a lovely place to admire the views and surrounding trees for a while.

2 mins, 52.0945, -8.1016

12 DÚN DEA-RADHAIRC

This scrap of a building high in a rolling field originally had 70 stone steps to the battlements but much of it fell in the 19th century. It's a lovely setting to explore, from a foot gate on the lane (51.8937, -9.0184, sometimes livestock restrictions); the nearest easy parking is at Dundarirke graveyard near the crossroads below (51.8907, -9.0188) where a large bullaun leans against the E wall.

2 mins, 51.8936, -9.0173

13 CARRIGADROHID CASTLE & TOWER

This 'rock of the bridge' castle is one of only two castles in Europe on a mid-river rock. It's also very cracked, with no access. Originally on one bank, it was marooned when the river level was raised by the hydroelectric scheme in the 1950s. Park on N side and picnic in the little, sloping park looking over to it and note the no-swimming signs: the Lee is fast and furious in this narrow, and the level rises quickly if water is released from the dam not far upstream. A pretty village, the Carrig Inn is a no-nonsense, old-fashioned, Irish pub. Over the river and through the gate to the R of the shrine is the Apple Tower, a pretty belvedere on the corner of an old, walled garden (51.8996, -8.8505).

2 mins, 51.9008, -8.8521

14 BALLINCOLLIG CASTLE

The original, 14th-century tower house still remains, with a moat and most of the bawn with two towers, very ruinous and ivy covered. Beneath the castle a natural cavern runs into the rock. Disused for centuries although renovated in 1857, still privately owned, it has a gate on to a track past it and people do explore, but with constant crumbling and new housing nearby, access may be closed. Park in The Willows (entrance at 51.8798, -8.5911) and walk W to track.

8 mins, 51.8793, -8.5996

15 BARRYSCOURT CASTLE

Restored, 14th-century tower house (with a drop-in dungeon), and outer bawn wall and largely intact corner towers, set in a knot garden and orchard on original designs. A free OPW site and an excellent small castle to see the working type. There's a café in the cottage, and occasional re-enactments and other events. T45 Y290, with car park.

2 mins, 51.9045, -8.2590

SACRED & ANCIENT SITES

16 KILMACOW CEMETERY & WELL *

Atmospheric graveyard inside a larger ringfort, with a nearby holy well. Look for the railed grave of landlord Richard Sankey, who sold his lands cheap to his tenants and asked to be buried here with them. We met a man who swore he and his wife had heard a drumbeat that rolls out from the grave when a local dies. For the holy well, head R at graveyard gate and N across the field, through the ringfort and down the field to a clump of trees R (52.2398, -8.9167).

2 mins, 52.2379, -8.9158

17 KILCORCORAN GRAVEYARD

Every age and place has its own burial style, and this little rural graveyard has a very local

12

18

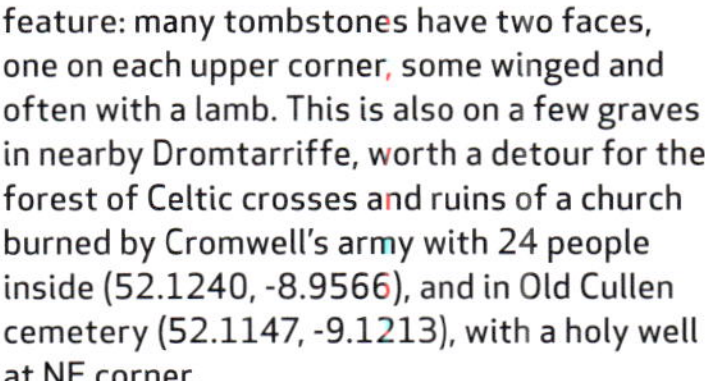

feature: many tombstones have two faces, one on each upper corner, some winged and often with a lamb. This is also on a few graves in nearby Dromtarriffe, worth a detour for the forest of Celtic crosses and ruins of a church burned by Cromwell's army with 24 people inside (52.1240, -8.9566), and in Old Cullen cemetery (52.1147, -9.1213), with a holy well at NE corner.

2 mins, 52.2154, -8.9384

18 BUTTEVANT FRIARY & LOMBARD'S CASTLE

This 13th-century church is all that remains of the friary: the rest is under the graveyard, but carved fragments have been fixed to the walls here, creating a fascinating historical patchwork. Beside the gable a small section of the medieval town wall still stands. About 200m S on the road is the 15th-century Lombard's Castle, built by one of the Italian merchant families who followed the Normans here.

2 mins, 52.2316, -8.6692

19 ST JOHN'S CHURCH *

Hidden up a grassy drive is an elegant Gothic church in an atmospheric graveyard with mature parkland trees (peer through for a glimpse of off-limits Barry's Castle to the N) and picturesque tombs. The soaring spire gives a nod

13

17

19

to the site's fame as the starting point for the original steeplechase in 1752, which ran over all obstacles – including the River Awbeg – to Doneraile, home of the famed St Leger family. Buttevant was famed for horses; Napoleon's mount Marengo came from Buttevant. Park on the drive before the field gate.

2 mins, 52.227, -8.6701

20 BALLYBEG PRIORY & DOVECOTE *

This ruinous priory has fascinating signs of repeated remodelling, with reshaped arches, towers partly blocking windows and two high, carved heads looking on. But don't miss the dovecote in the field behind, with niches from

the floor up to a beautifully corbelled roof hole. Swallows nest here, and you can watch them flying in and out of the hushed space. A tower that may have been in a curtain wall stands across the lane; no internal access. Signed off the N20 1km S of Buttevant, pull off at gate.

2 mins, 52.2195, -8.6698

21 LABBACALLEE WEDGE TOMB *

Ireland's largest wedge tomb is said to be the bed (leaba) of the legendary Cailleach, goddess of winter. You can squeeze under the three massive sloping capstones at the larger end. Local folklore tells of four men who went to find treasure there being chased away by a cat with a fiery tail. Beautiful in late-afternoon sun, by the road with space for a couple of cars.

2 mins, 52.1742, -8.3344

22 MOCOLLOP CHURCH

Two ruined churches in a field, the low remains of the medieval parish church and the later Board of First Fruits Church, with a tower, Gothic styling and remnants of the colourful tile floor. Park in the R666 layby by the bungalow SW and enter through the old iron gate (52.1487, -8.0952).

2 mins, 52.1495, -8.0941

23 BRIDGETOWN PRIORY

These rambling, well-preserved, 13th-century ruins are thoroughly but unobtrusively labelled, a great starting place for those who don't know a cloister from a calefactory (both are here). Abandoned before dissolution, due to local strife or the plague; the oldest gravestone, with an ornate inscribed cross, stands in a small, walled enclosure near a tomb recess where a woman and her two cats lived in the 1830s, given food by locals. Signed from N72 with parking.

2 mins, 52.1495, -8.4503

24 COOLE HOLY WELL

Water flows from an oval clochán-like cover through a stone channel to join a stream with pretty little falls; pull off by sign and stile. To N is a graveyard with ruins of a church with a Romanesque nave and 13th-century chancel, and second medieval church ruin is to the SW (52.1074, -8.2046), stile in from the road.

2 mins, 52.1085, -8.2034

25 MOURNE ABBEY

Ruined 12th-century 'abbey of the great bog'. Most of the original church stands in a rough state in an overgrown enclosure that was much larger before the railway was built. Sections of enclosure walls survive, the large square tower at one corner is believed to have been a mill. Pull

23

23

27

aside on the road into GAA ground. The land was donated by the Cogans of nearby Castle Barrett, almost equally ruinous (52.0842, -8.6415). There's also a holy well and Penal mass site at Analeentha (52.0685, -8.6366) with easy parking at church almost opp.
2 mins, 52.0811, -8.6262

26 CARRAIG AN AIFRINN & FAMINE WALK

This riverbank Mass Rock platform below a cliff among trees made a perfect natural stage. Pull off road to E over bridge, signed path. Opposite is a 2.5km walk to Glenville that was followed in Penal times. It starts on a Famine relief road, then through meadows and a riverside hazel wood with cascades, to ancient Doonpeter graveyard and holy well (52.0583, -8.4464). The path ends at 52.0534, -8.4378 with more space to park.
2 mins, 52.0636, -8.4616

27 KILQUANE MEDIEVAL CHURCH *

Locally known as Templín, this site has an ancient feel; it was used as a cillín into the 20th century and flowers are sometimes left on the altar. Opposite W in an enclosure is the Sinner's Stone: a suspected criminal had to put their hand through the hole: if it came out, they were innocent, but if it stuck, they were guilty. There's a standing stone in the SE corner of the graveyard, and a recumbent stone with a cup by the altar end of the church.
2 mins, 52.0472, -8.6612

28 SING SING & ST CUAIN'S WELL

Kilquane Cemetery is most noted for 'Sing Sing', a crypt that was Cork No. 1 Brigade's cell for military prisoners in the War of Independence, named after the American prison. Pull off by gates, or 300m S on road is parking for a 150m walk into the woods to a picnic spot by a shallow river, steps up to a holy well and more paths to explore in pretty little woods.
2 mins, 51.9675, -8.3422

29 BALLYLUCRA CEMETERY

Fairly crisp gates lead to a fairly ramshackle cemetery hidden in the trees. The medieval church is low ruins, and First Fruits protestant church was demolished in 1923 for its stone – but its lovely hexagonal tower topped by a very elegant, elongated spire remains. It's not hard to see why one would be moved to leave it in place. Pull off at the gate.
2 mins, 51.9385, -8.3773

30 ST GOBNAIT'S CHURCH & SHRINE

People still walk 'rounds' of the features at this large site. One is St Gobnait's House, the early medieval 'mini-cashel' above the shrine – actually an Iron Age forge, containing remains of 137

27

27

smelting pits. Two more stops, a bullaun stone and a large slab, sit on a mound R inside the church gate that likely covers a prehistoric cist, but is known as St Gobnait's Grave. The sheela na gig over the south window of the ruined church is not one! Park outside or walk in via St Gobnet's wood (see entry); nobody can say why two different spellings are used so close together.

2 mins, 51.9384, -9.1664

31 BEALICK WEDGE TOMB

A well-preserved tomb, with the classic dolmen chamber form. It's quite common for a tomb to be called a bealick, from the irish an bhéillic for a shelter; this one seems to have given the name to the whole townland it sits in. Path from 51.9122, -8.9258, a pretty walk in when bluebells are out; if no parking at end of lane, pull off carefully by last houses.

7 mins, 51.9155, -8.9283

32 AGHINA OR CAUM CHURCHYARD

An ivy-hung church shell with a handsome tower from the 17th century; you can ascend one floor of this. The graveyard is lovely but the most interesting resident is actually just over the perimeter wall: Sir Adrian Carton de Wiart, who won a VC on the Somme, lost an eye and an arm, but still tunnelled out of a Nazi prison camp aged 62.

2 mins, 51.8923, -8.8959

33 MACLONEIGH CHURCH

Enchanting little wooded church and graveyard with access up a farm track. Reputed to be the baptism place of St Finbar, patron saint and founder of Cork city, this is also called St Finbar's or Cill na Cluaine, church of the meadow. Mass has been celebrated here again recently, for the first time since the Reformation. Anglers fish near the bridge and the track below runs on through woods to a field by the river: pretty, though deep and can be fast, use discretion. Pull to L on the road by the gate.

3 mins, 51.8895, -8.9546

34 KILCREA FRIARY AND CASTLE

Both of these were built for a MacCarthy, Lord of Muskerry, in the 15th century, probably with a settlement between them. The friary ruins at the end of an avenue of lime and ash are quite complete, and state owned, with a small car park. The tower house shell, with a wildly overgrown interior, lies on private land, with access allowed on the straight line path across the field of barley. The tower stairs are intact but there is a bar across.

2 mins, 51.8651, -8.7113

35 CURRABEHA STONE CIRCLE

This circle with a quartz boulder in the centre lies by a farm track in a field with panoramic

34

34

views around rich, rolling land. Drive to farm at N (P14 CY50) park in the farmyard at the end and knock if they're in; access on farm track is allowed (no dogs), they even offered to let us drive up. Another in a neighbour's field (51.8283, -8.8557) is accessible when there are no livestock or standing crops.

15 mins, 51.8256, -8.8538

HILLTOPS & VIEWPOINTS

36 CLARAGH MOUNTAIN

One of the easiest peaks of the Derrynasaggart Mountains. The heather-covered slopes arrive at a level (clárach) place with panoramic vistas to Kerry and on clear days even the Atlantic. Pick up the signed Duhallow Way from lane at 52.0432, -9.1149 (further up the lane is wide, but leave room for a tractor to pass). Or approach on the Claragh Loop, more forested, and still on the Duhallow Way; nearest parking on dead end in Millstreet Industrial Estate (52.0520, -9.0658), walk back to brown signs on road.

80 mins, 52.0495, -9.0926

37 MUSHERAMORE & KNOCKNAKILLA

Muisire Mór (644m) is the highest peak in the Boggeragh Mountains, with super views over to Kerry and the sea on a clear day and a chance of seeing red deer and peregrine falcons. Small car park at 52.0116, -8.9952 then over stile and about 1km straight up, 250m ascent. St John's Well is also worth stopping at, on road about 1km N of parking (52.0194, -8.9895). Knocknakilla with a stone circle, standing stones and a radial cairn is just off lane 2km to the W (52.0062, -9.0239).

50 mins, 52.0139, -8.9784

38 CAIRNTIERNA/CAIRN THIERNA

This much-abused Bronze Age cairn held two burial cists, but now has only a British army bunker at its heart; we never walk on cairns, but this one is effectively a rebuild. Legend says it holds an ancient King of Munster and that it was built by the Cailleach, of Labbacallee Wedge Tomb (see entry). In 1933 a crucifix was erected next to it and the stations of the cross mark a route up; follow these, turning right where Christ is taken down from the cross. Coillte Corrin Wood car park (52.1105, -8.2876).

20 mins, 52.1149, -8.2827

WOODLAND & WILDLIFE

39 CANON SHEEHAN MASS ROCK

Forestry trails and a riverside path lead on a loop walk through mixed woods with bluebells in late spring and bright rowans in autumn. The mass rock was named for the parish priest of Doneraile, a writer, and great ecumenical and agricultural campaigner; in turn, this woodland gave its name to his most famous novel, Glenanaar, based on a case of Daniel O'Connell's in 1829. The rest of the Ballyhoura walking and cycling trails are in Limerick.

60 mins, 52.2738, -8.5396

40 DONERAILE WILDLIFE PARK, MALLOW

A rare Capability Brown landscape in Ireland. Near the entrance is tame and busy, but beyond are 400 acres of parkland with ornamental lakes off the river, mighty redwoods and a cork oak, as well as natives including cherry and yew in the woods, with sheets of bluebells beneath in late spring. Sika and fallow deer graze in the meadows. Parkland is free, tea rooms in one wing of the house, which can be visited on a guided tour (€). Very family friendly.

5 mins, 52.2190, -8.5807

41 ISLAND WOOD, NEWMARKET

The River Dalua is the main feature of this old estate woodland, snaking through the middle of it. The other is Maolin's Cave, where Lughnasa was celebrated every year in the past. Maolin is an obscure mythological figure, thought to be a fertility goddess. On tiny lanes, but medium Coillte car park with boards.

5 mins, 52.1898, -8.9891

42 ST GOBNET'S WOOD

A hillside SAC wood of sessile oak, and holly, full of ferns. There are some gravel paths and you can follow a rocky trail as an alternative approach to St Gobnait's Church ruins and holy well (see entry) on the far side of the hill. Parking area with a couple of picnic tables, turn S off R618 in Ballyvourney (51.9455, -9.1702) over the river, then L.

5 mins, 51.9444, -9.1693

43 INNISCARRA HYDRO STATION PARK

Park near the dam and walk down steps to the river for an impressive view up to the 1950s buttress dam. The bank downstream is a woody park with a lovely riverside walk that loops around to return above the wood. Particularly beautiful and dramatic in autumn. Entrance from R618, easy to miss.

2 mins, 51.9020, -8.6602

44 FOTA WILDLIFE PARK

Fota Arboretum has a dozen 'champion' trees, with winding paths to seek them out. Our favourite is a cryptomeria grove at 51.8937, -8.3017 and a beautiful 30m-tall Bhutan pine about 30m NE from it. The gardens and arboretum cost only the €3 parking charge, there's also a wildlife park (€63.30/family of four) and the grand house itself (€8 guided tour) on offer.

5 mins, 51.8913, -8.3073

38

40

45 BALLINCOLLIG PARK

Explore E along the river into woods for the gunpowder mills that supplied the British army over two centuries – in the Napoleonic era they were the largest in Ireland – spread out across the woods, for safety; steam stove at 51.8931, -8.5994, magazine at 51.8939, -8.5968, and several behind houses on path at 51.8934, -8.5902, an quicker alternative entry point with parking on lane that misses the tangled woods full of birds and bats.

25 mins, 51.8894, -8.6208

46 KILCOLMAN NATURE RESERVE

A rushy limestone fen of flowers, grebes and mute swans in summer, a flooded expanse of whooper swans and ducks in winter. A substantial hide looks on to the pond. Walk up from this to hop over the wire fence and L along the field edge to spy the tilted ruin of Kilcolman Castle, where ferociously anti-Irish poet Edmund Spenser wrote The Faerie Queene; it was burned in 1598 and 1622. Parking near hide, open gate at the road and drive down.

2 mins, 52.2499, -8.6093

47 ARDAROU FOREST (ARD AN RABHAIDH)

Coillte woodland walk with paddling opportunities from a lovely old bridge with picnic table. There's a chance of seeing otters, dippers and kingfishers, or Daubenton's bats over the river after sunset. If the small car park is closed, pull off carefully near the crossroads. The N side above the riverside trees was replanted in 2024.

2 mins, 52.0568, -8.4173

48 THE GEARAGH

An ancient, raised road leads over the River Lee through the stumps of a drowned forest, sticking out of high water, seen rooted in land when levels fall. It was western Europe's last surviving full oak forest, intact since the last Ice Age and with some medieval trees, when the valley was flooded in 1954 to power Carrigadrohid and Inniscarra dams. Now an important Ramsar wetland, noted for otters, rare freshwater pearl mussels, ducks, swans, kingfishers. Medium parking fills up on fine days.

2 mins, 51.8890, -8.9746

CLASSIC PUBS

49 MILLS INN, BALLYVOURNEY

Historic pub dating from 1755, now owned by co-founder of 9 White Deer Brewery, with local brews on the bar and good pub food to go with them, plus a local ice cream shop in the yard. Has rooms, and ruins of a house and tower burned during the War of Independence in the garden. Ballyvourney, P12 FF86, +353 26 45237

51.9457, -9.1706

50 THE DIAMOND BAR

This was Long's Pub, where Irish rebel leader Michael Collins was recognised; the ambush that killed him was possibly planned in the back room here. A very traditional locals bar, where owner Gene keeps his own hours, but generally open from four or five of an evening. Beal na Blath, P14 Y398, +353 21 7336071

51.8217, -8.8555

LOCAL PRODUCE

51 COOLEA FARMHOUSE CHEESE

This Gouda-style farmhouse cheese began as a hobby in 1979, rapidly became an award-winning product and is now a second-generation business. It is an easy product to find locally and even nationally, but if you fail this is where to ask. Coolea, P12 AC64, +353 87 9115757

51.93352, -9.2436

52 THE ENGLISH MARKET

This iconic covered market in the heart of Cork is one of the oldest in Europe and worth a city trip. Head upstairs to have breakfast or lunch on the balcony of the Farmgate Café (the French toast is perfect), drop in for a drink or a meal at the elegant Oyster Tavern, or browse the stalls for everything from seafood, charcuterie, drisheens, and hyper-local Cork Rooftop Farm produce, to olives, spices, and fresh-roasted coffee. Grand Parade/Princes Street. Also worth checking out is Iago's legendary cheese counter nearby (9 Princes Street, T12 A29X).

51.8976, -8.4748

53 TOONS BRIDGE DAIRY *

Great deli plus the shop for their own cheeses made from unpasteurised water buffalo, sheep and local cows' milk; you can also buy these at markets and many local shops, and in the English Market (see entry). On summer weekends you can get stonebaked pizzas at tables scattered through a wild garden. The Old Creamery, Teergay, Toonsbridge, Co. Cork, P12 W864

51.8804, -9.0242

ORGANIC & BISTRO

54 THE TOWN COFFEE COMPANY *

Bright little café serving superb coffee and a small, perfectly honed menu of savouries, sourdough sandwiches and sweet bakes, using local suppliers and striving to be as sustainable as possible. 2 Lower Cork Street, Mitchelstown, P67 R202

52.2688, -8.2700

55 THATCH & THYME, KILDORRERY

A colourful and friendly café serving home-cooked local ingredients with international

influences: vegetarian, vegan, and GF options. Busy, but worth waiting for a table, sunny courtyard out back. Breakfast and lunch Tue–Sat (expanding 2025, possibly changing hours). Main Street, Kildorrery, P67 HX49, +353 87 2823503
52.2462, -8.4256

56 HANNA'S MARKET & CAFÉ FERMOY

Queues for weekend brunch are worth it; ingredients are local and organic as much as possible. 8.30am–4.30pm Mon–Sat, 9.00am–5.00pm Sun, 6.00–11.00pm Fri. 21–25 Patrick Street, Fermoy, P61 Y313, +353 25 51005
52.1379, -8.2742

57 O'MAHONY'S OF WATERGRASSHILL *

Step inside the cheery buttercup-painted door and you'll find a modern rustic interior and a menu that favours produce from local producers with dishes like sea bream with gooseberry and buttermilk; save space for the cheese plate, served with raw local honey. 12.00–3.00pm and 5.30–8.00pm, Thur–Sat. T56 Y9F4,+353 86 8316879
52.0115, -8.34359

58 MIYAZAKI *

Takeshi Miyazaki's legendary little takeaway with a few eat-in stools; you can also take your food over the road to O'sho pub and get a pint to go with it. 1A Evergreen Street, T12 E034, +353 21 4312716. His Michelin-star-winning Ichigo Ichie restaurant is now a more accessible bistro marrying Japanese techniques with local and foraged ingredients. No 5 Sheares Street, T12 RY7Y, +353 21 4279997. Also occasional pop-ups outside the city.
51.8945, -8.4764

RUSTIC RETREATS

59 ANNE'S GROVE MINIATURE CASTLE

Cute little 19th-century Gothic gatelodge, with one double bedroom; adults only, one dog allowed. Castletownroche, P51 X5B6, irishlandmark.com
52.1948, -8.4657

60 THE COURTYARD KILSHANNIG

Lovely 18th-century country house hotel on a stud farm in rolling countryside, a great place for anyone who likes horses to wake up. P61 AW77, +353 87 4648585
52.0608, -8.2796

61 BALLYVOLANE HOUSE

Family-run, luxury country-house hotel, which also has bell tents and 'pig ark' pods. All in beautiful gardens and wooded parklands with winter snowdrops and drifts of late-spring bluebells. Food for the restaurant is as local as possible, some from their own walled garden. This is the home of Bertha's Revenge, a unique whey-based gin. Castlelyons, Fermoy, P61 FP70, +353 25 36349
52.0558, -8.1869

62 THE LOFT, APPLE LODGE & BLOSSOM LODGE

Three separate lets at a country house with magnificent views over The Gearagh (see entry) and friendly hosts on site. P12 V567, on Airbnb and other booking sites
51.8932, -8.9606

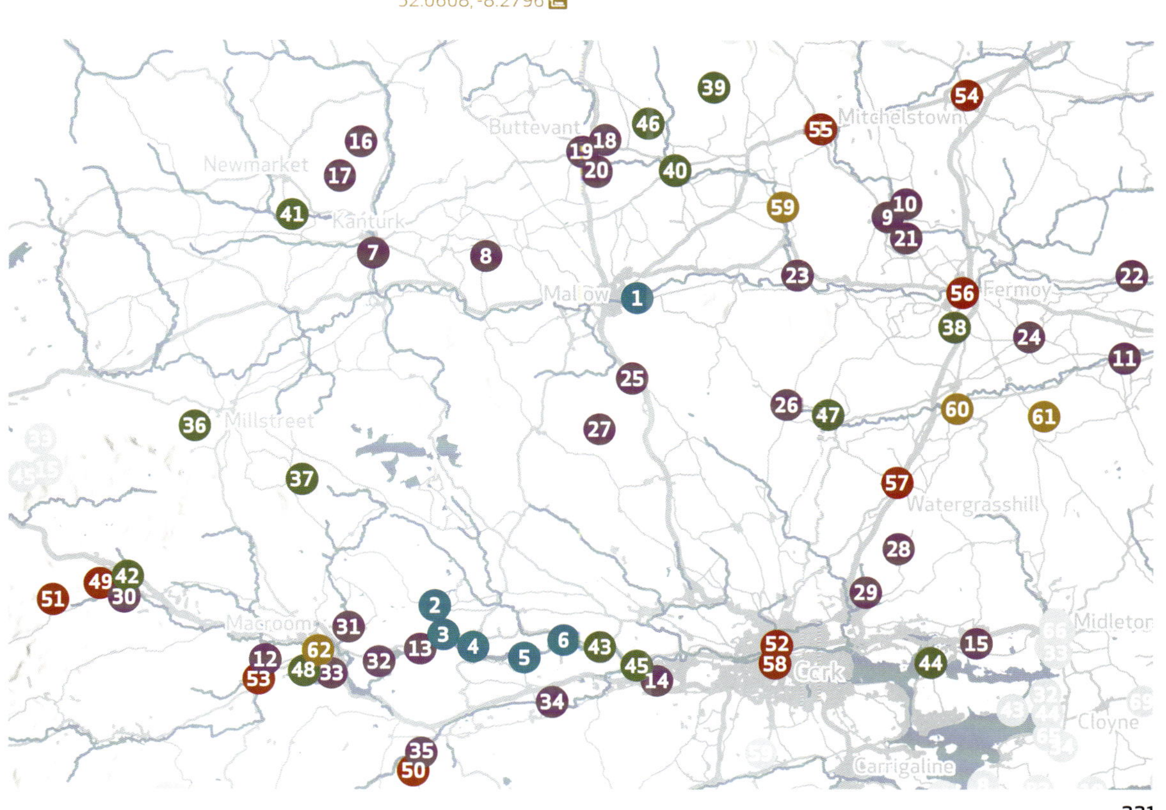

Dromanassig Waterfall, p271

Cloonee Lough, p273

Historical Glossary

Axial circle circle with two portal stones opposite a lower stone, often aligned NE–SW

Boulder burial large boulder raised on smaller stones; none have yielded remains

Bawn the enclosed area around a tower house, or the defensive wall around it

Bullaun stone with a worn smooth bowl or bowls, like quern stones but of unknown function

Currach tarred canvas/hide boat

Cursing stones found at holy wells, turned one way for a blessing and the other for a curse

Fairy fort ringfort associated with particular fairy legends

Famine plot unmarked mass graves from the 1840s Great Famine

Fortified house manor-like Tudor and later homes with gun loops, bartizans etc

Fulacht fia a burning place, an early communal cooking site

Holy Year cross large crosses erected on hilltops across Ireland in 1950

Lazy beds raised beds giving improved drainage in thin, wet soils

Mass rock any suitable flat rock in a safe place that could be used as a secret altar in Penal times

Oratory small one room church like a hermit's cell

Pattern, rounds, or turas a set of prayers and actions on a set path at a holy site

Penal times from the 1690s to 1829, when Penal laws barred Catholics from worship, education, professions, parliament, or owning land or a horse worth more than £5

Piseog a minor curse or blessing invoked by leaving a token at a ritual site

Raggedy tree where ribbons or other tokens are left at a religious sites

Tower house square, lightly fortified homes, late medieval

Wild Guide
West of Ireland
Hidden Places,
Great Adventures and
the Good Life

Words:
Candida Frith-Macdonald
& Daniel Start

Photos:
Daniel Start, Candida
Frith-Macdonald & and
those credited

Editing:
Gina Rathbone, Alex
Davidson, Andrew
Brassleay, Sophie Carran

Design:
Tania Pascoe & Rose Start

Distribution:
Central Books Ltd
50, Freshwater Road
Dagenham, RM8 1RX
020 8525 8800
orders@centralbooks.com

Published by:
Wild Things Publishing Ltd.
Freshford, Bath, BA2 7WG

WILD guide
the award-winning, best-selling adventure travel series, also available as iPhone and Android apps.

hello@wildthingspublishing.com

Photo credits / copyrights

Acknowledgements
Candida: Thanks first and foremost to Richard Frith-Macdonald for uncomplainingly driving me down a seemingly endless array of narrow lanes over the last few years while I recorded notes, to Brendan O'Hanrahan for solid park ranger advice, and to Malcolm Noonan and Petra Ross-Macdonald for a stream of itinerary ideas. I've been inspired and informed by hikers extraordinaire Ellie Berry and Karl Lange of Tough Souls, stone lifter David Keoghan, and found solid historical grounding in the archaeological talks and tours of Tuatha. Daniel: Thanks to those who travelled with us and supported our field research: Binny, Sam, Drummond and Lavina Lascelle, Ciaran Mundy, Cathal O'Flaherty, Andy Thompson, Julian Hodgson, Rosetta Barker & Moira O'Neill.

Health, Safety and Responsibility
The activities and places in this book have risks and can be dangerous. The locations may be on private land and permission may need to be sought. The authors and publishers have gone to great lengths to ensure the accuracy of the information but conditions and circumstances change all the time so the responsibility to assess each place for safety and legality falls to the reader.

Other books from Wild Things Publishing